GOTHIC RAGE UNDONE

A Gothick deluge learning overrun,
But Monks undo what Gothick rage has done.
See Banish'd arts within a Cloyster rise,
Loanesome before, but now a Paradise.

(Dom Augustine Walker, 1749)

Prospectus interior Sacelli Serenissimo Mariæ Magnæ Britanniæ Reginæ Londini ad Sanctum Jacobum

The Chapel Royal, St James's Palace

GOTHIC RAGE UNDONE

English Monks in the Age of Enlightenment

by

Geoffrey Scott
Monk of Douai Abbey

DOWNSIDE ABBEY
BATH, ENGLAND

IN MEMORIAM
RR. D.D. GREGORII FREEMAN O.S.B.
1923 - 1989
Piisimi Patris Doctoris et Ducis

Downside Abbey
Stratton on the Fosse
Bath, England, BA3 4RH

British Library Cataloguing in Publication Data:

Scott, Geoffrey
        Gothic Rage Undone: English Monks in the
        Age of Enlightenment
        I. Title
        271

ISBN   0-9502759-9-9

Cum permissu superiorum

Typeset at Downside Abbey, Bath.
Printed and bound by Hobbs the Printers, Southampton

CONTENTS

FOREWORD

This book is the fruit of over ten years enjoyable labour slotted into odd moments when I found I had a respite from teaching and other work. The popular notion of an English Benedictine monk's life as one of peaceful tranquillity and abstracted contemplation has never been a common one within the monasteries themselves, where the pursuit of one's interests, researches and fads has, of necessity, been developed alongside the demands of the Common Life and the *Opus Dei* and in addition to the regular and relentless work in school or parish. I have found my own study of a little corner of Benedictine history immensely gratifying. It has encouraged me to view the English Benedictine Congregation as a whole, with deeply ingrained traditions common to the larger body of the Congregation, rather than merely the possession of a particular monastery, province or mission. Moreover, I am delighted that the publication of this work comes at a time when England finds herself drawing closer to the continent of Europe, a step which would have won the approval of the great majority of eighteenth-century English Benedictines. In the course of my work I have welcomed the opportunity of becoming intimate with all those eighteenth-century Benedictine monks whose names are now read out daily in the necrologies of the Congregation.

I owe this book to all those who have given me help and encouragement over many years. They have generously admitted me into their circles and freely given of their time and expertise. Although they are too numerous to mention here, I should single out those to whom I owe a special debt: the late Abbot Gregory Freeman, who remained unstinting in his support until his untimely death, and Dr Eamon Duffy, my supervisor, whose patience has been infinite. To these I must add a whole host of monks and nuns, friends, archivists and librarians, who have helped me in countless ways. I acknowledge my gratitude to Her Majesty the Queen for permission to publish material from the Stuart Papers. I am also grateful to David Hatfull for help with the illustrations. Finally, I must record a great debt of gratitude to Abbot Charles Fitzgerald-Lombard and Father Aidan Bellenger and the Community of St Gregory's, Downside, for seeing this work through to publication.

Geoffrey Scott OSB   21st March 1992

INTRODUCTION

This book, largely based on a doctoral thesis presented in 1984, sits on the back of two earier influential works, David Lunn's, *The English Benedictines 1540-1688*, (London 1980) and John Bossy's, *The English Catholic Community 1570-1850* (London 1975). To the first it is a continuation, to the second partly an answer and reassessment. These two works also necessarily help to define the book's readership.

Traditionally, English Benedictine historiography since the Reformation has been focused on the early seventeenth century when the English Benedictine Congregation was revived. The study of monastic roots is, of course, an end in itself, but generations of monastic polemicists have used the seventeenth century in particular as the arsenal for facts and arguments to support what they felt to be the authentic values, principles and forms of English Benedictinism in any epoch. Most often, history has been employed here to support differing interpretations as to whether the English Benedictines were primarily active or contemplative in vocation, conventual or missionary in spirit. That this controversy continues to rage is doubtless an indication that the English Benedictine monk's vocation is something of a mixture of such disparate elements. David Lunn's book has given us the most up-to-date and detailed account of the monks' history in the seventeenth century. His study has a natural termination-point in the Glorious Revolution, and most general studies of English Benedictine history have tended to leap from 1688 to the French Revolution, leaving most of the eighteenth century relatively untouched. The history of the monks in the eighteenth century has, therefore, been much neglected - a period of 'exile and hibernation', according to David Knowles. The present study is an attempt to show for the first time the richness and diversity found throughout the eighteenth-century English Benedictine Congregation and the monks' important place within the English and European history of that time. In beginning the story with James II's reign, this work overlaps Lunn's account, but the more detailed description given here provides a point of comparison with the massive transformation undergone by the Congregation in succeeding decades. Space has not allowed any detailed account to be given of the English Benedictine nuns, especially those at Cambrai, during these years. Their enclosed life was markedly different from that of the monks and deserves separate treatment.

An apology at the outset must be offered for the preponderance of illustrative material and detail, especially in the chapters dealing with the English mission. The life of monks on the mission was of course similar in many respects to that experienced in England by members of the secular clergy and other religious orders, but the Benedictine reader of this study will welcome the opportunity to examine and assess, for the first time, the particular Benedictine contribution to the eighteenth-century English mission. For others interested in the study of eighteenth-century English Catholic history generally, the English Benedictine Congregation is of especial interest because of the wealth of archival material relating to it, which is made full use of in this work. Thanks ironically to the French Revolution's confiscation of ecclesiastical property, we possess a superb collection at Lille of correspondence dating from the early 1750s which once belonged to Augustine Walker, President of the Benedictines from 1777 until 1794. This gives a remarkable insight into the life and preoccupations of the Congregation at all levels, and is part of a collection which has been described by John Bossy as 'the most important body of recusant material remaining in France, especially for the mid and later eighteenth century' (*Recusant History*, ii, 1959, 35).

Besides its immediate Benedictine interest, this book contributes to a debate begun by Bossy in his book mentioned earlier, where he explored the development of the English Catholic community as a 'missionary' body in the eighteenth century, following its failure to constitute itself a 'church' in the seventeenth century. The English Benedictines formed an important part of this community, being the third largest body of clergy after the secular clergy and Jesuits. Taken purely as a missionary order, the monks would appear to fit the role allotted by Bossy to the eighteenth-century English Catholic clergy: that from 1685 and certainly after the 1688 Revolution, the clergy were forced to lay aside their aim of re-establishing the English Church in conformity with the Tridentine model, and found themselves developing a missionary apostolate instead, with all the adjustments required in terms of hierarchical and pastoral structures, civil and political standing, and religious cultural attitudes.

Thus developed, according to Bossy, an English Catholic community which became gradually sectarian. It was served by secular clergy who owed obedience to four Vicars Apostolic, delegates of the Holy See, who lacked Ordinary jurisdiction and capitular privileges, and were similar to other bishops appointed in missionary territories. The

English Catholics' missionary status was further reflected in the prominence of the Jesuits, the missionary religious order *par excellence* and the largest group of regular clergy in England. In contrast, however, the Benedictines tended to identify with the established Catholicism of Europe where their monasteries were found, and on their entry to the English mission, they continued, to a greater extent than any other religious order, to maintain this strong continental attachment. It was from within the context of continental Catholicism that the monks were trained and governed, and to it many of them frequently returned and finally retired. They were, then, as much a part of the European, and especially of the Gallican, Church as they were of the English mission, and it was precisely the introduction by the monks of these attitudes and customs from abroad which helps to qualify the nature of the English Catholic community as predominantly nonconformist, marginalised, and as one which owed its continued existence largely to native influences.

This work seeks to explore the Benedictine contribution to this convergence of continental and English Catholicism chiefly through the illustration of four themes: the degree of English Benedictine assimilation to the structures and character of European monasticism, the relaxed manner in which English monks took their place within continental society, their participation in contemporary patterns of spirituality which affected missionary endeavour on both sides of the Channel, and, finally, the recording of a long-lived tension between monks and the Church's hierarchy represented by eighteenth-century Gallican and German bishops and English Vicars Apostolic.

By the early years of the eighteenth century, all three monasteries within France had been granted the privilege of 'naturalization', and thus shared all the benefits given to French religious houses and orders. By this privilege, English monks could hold benefices, even if they might themselves be on the English mission. The income thus generated from tithes and other dues formed a considerable part of the Congregation's wealth throughout the century. Significantly, the old spectre of a restoration of the monasteries in England, together with the full-scale return of the ex-monastic land to them, appeared most clearly at the precise point when Benedictinism in England came closest to its continental counterpart, that is, during the reign of James II, when at least one monastery was established in England and others planned. It might be argued that this degree of 'naturalization', so well defined and accepted on the continent, and according to circumstances aspired to in England, delayed the Benedictines' participation in the 'death of a church', which Bossy insists was an experience central and critical to the English Catholic community of the later seventeenth and early eighteenth centuries. The example of the English monastery at Lambspring in Lower Saxony approximated even more closely to the conventional picture of an established and privileged Benedictine house; besides the monastery's huge landed estates and a full range of grand conventual buildings, its life-abbot enjoyed a rich assortment of feudal rights and jurisdictions throughout the eighteenth century.

Besides legal status, there were many other bonds which shaped English Benedictines at home and abroad into the likeness of their European brethren. French and German breviaries, for instance, were employed both within the monasteries and on the mission. Many English monks had lived for periods of study within large European abbeys, whilst others went further and sought to experience at first-hand one of the more ascetic forms of the monastic life then coming into vogue in France. There was also a common exposure to the new currents of thought, and an interest in precise historical research and erudition, the particular preserve of certain French Benedictines, which some of the English monks carried onto the mission with them. Even in the latter part of the eighteenth century, when English Benedictines found themselves the victim of a double-edged onslaught from the requirements ordered by the *Commission des Réguliers* on all religious in France, and from the increasing Anglophobia found in French politics, the dogged insistence by Rome on the fulfilment of the *sexennium* requirement, that missioners must return to conventual life within their monasteries at six-yearly intervals, strengthened a perception, held at least in European ecclesiastical and political circles, that the English monasteries on the continent identified more with the national churches under whose jurisdiction they lay, than with the English mission.

If English monks happily identified with the norms governing the religious life on the continent, it was inevitable that there would be a like correspondence between them and the European society in which they found themselves immersed. At the most superficial level of agents, hosts, connoisseurs and tutors, involvement of English Benedictines in continental circles on behalf of their fellow-countrymen was constant and possibly unmatched in its frequency and intensity. Their houses in Paris and Rome put them at the very centre of

4

cosmopolitan eighteenth-century life. In order to appreciate the ease with which monks adapted to life abroad after the 1688/9 Revolution, we need to remember their privileged status at the Court of James II, where some of them stood for moderation and supported early tentative steps towards an understanding with the Established Church. To many Benedictines the Revolution brought primarily a change in circumstances rather than the termination of a way of life; their place within the Stuart Court-in-exile remained assured, and correspondingly their infiltration into the French and Papal Courts grew with their demands for patronage at every level. In this respect, the international character of the English Benedictines in the eighteenth century, with their settled existence in Europe overlapping their apostolate in England, enhances the argument of some recent historians of the period such as Jonathan Clark in his *English Society 1685-1832* (CUP 1985), which seeks to demonstrate the presence of the *ancien régime* in Britain as well as Europe, similar in its framework and ideology.

As far as the English monks were concerned, the key to this European unity was Jacobitism. As in other English Catholic circles, Jacobitism proved eventually to be the watershed dividing those monks more attached to a traditional European society and church, and those willing to accept England's distinct heterodoxy within an increasingly pluralist Europe. It was this choice of radical alternatives, evolving from conflicting attitudes to Jacobitism, which lay behind the most serious Benedictine schism of the century fostered by Laurence Fenwick and his opponent Thomas Southcott. The arch-Jacobite Southcott represented the European Catholicism of the *ancien régime,* hierarchical, institutional and secure, to which the English Catholic body must look for models, inspiration and identity. Laurence Fenwick, on the other hand, lived on the English mission and was apparently more concerned to collaborate both with the Hanoverian regime and the Anglican Church in order to permit the English Catholics a continued safe existence with some degree of independence from Europe and Rome. Fenwick, for all his innovatory tactics, was essentially returning to the Anglo-Gallicanism of some of his seventeenth-century confreres.

Jacobitism could not, of course, last, and even though it might be politically reactionary, it was to be an important influence in introducing legitimist Benedictines to circles in which enlightened ideas were fostered. Foremost among these was the circle around the Chevalier Ramsay which included his monastic acquaintances and helped to

5

expose some monks to novelties in European thought. Not all monks were, of course, as captivated by the Enlightenment as others, but its attraction was sufficiently strong to be carried across from Europe onto the mission by monks like Gregory Gregson. Nor should we underestimate the dependence on contemporary French thought shown by radicals like Cuthbert Wilks, already known to hold so-called dangerous opinions before he adopted his Cisalpine stance in the 1780s. The congregation of French refugees to whom he ministered in Bath seemed to approve of the liberal ideas found in his sermons and doubtless helped him to bridge the gulf between the Gallican Church in which he was formed and an English Catholic missionary community which he encouraged to move towards a degree of independence from Rome and towards a measure of acceptance by the English government. Thus, the English Relief Acts of 1778 and 1791, reducing the risk of persecution descending on the English Catholics, were welcomed by Wilks who continued to support his Anglo-Gallican policies despite the grave damage done to the Church by the French Revolution.

In substance, English Benedictine interest in contemporary modes of spirituality was similar to that found among other English religious orders and circles in the eighteenth century. All these were heavily indebted to continental writers and teachers, translations of whose devotional and spiritual works were prepared increasingly throughout the century as models for a popular audience in England. Although many of these translations suited the needs of the Catholic minority in England and its missionary clergy, there is a growing appreciation among historians that in this period Catholic Europe was itself identified by its church leaders as missionary territory. Thus, these spiritual writings had an increasingly important use at home first. If this is an historically reliable view, then Catholics in countries like France and England shared the same aspirations and were conscious of the same need to reach out to potential converts as well as to defend orthodoxy from the attacks of the secular Englightenment. The English Benedictine development of prayer manuals, catechisms, confraternities and even of new forms of English Catholic apocalyptic literature - possibly a uniquely Benedictine contribution - owed much therefore to the experience of a contemporary Counter-Reformation on the continent.

Throughout the eighteenth century, relations between Benedictine missioners and the English hierarchy, represented in the persons of the four Vicars Apostolic, were strained. Both parties laid claim to a degree of Ordinary jurisdiction which they believed themselves to possess, and which the monks insisted gave them some exemption from episcopal control. As the English Catholic body became more established, so were the monks forced through directives from Rome to concede that the bishops had a superior jurisdiction to theirs over the English mission. Such disputes between the hierarchy and regular clergy, especially the traditional monastic orders, were a common feature on the continent, and monks coming from there onto the English mission found themselves perpetuating a struggle that they had already witnessed in their monasteries. Disputes between monks and bishops over faculties for confession and the administration of other sacraments were as common abroad as in England and not surprisingly, the monks had insisted that their new monastery established in London during James II's reign, was granted the exemption found 'in all Catholic countries'. The interference of the local bishop in the election of the abbot of Lambspring, although right and proper, made the Benedictine superiors of the time identify it with the current demands of the English Vicars Apostolic for more control over Benedictine affairs in England. Tensions at the higher levels of church government in England and abroad encouraged parochial friction; criticisms of the monasteries usurping the pastoral rights of local parish clergy had similarities with the jealousy of some secular missioners in England who treated their neighbouring Benedictine colleagues as rivals. There was resentment too among some of the Anglican clergy who objected to the intrusion of proselytising monks into their own well-established parishes. The demand of the French *Commission des Réguliers* that regular clergy should be subject to diocesan bishops and the later attempt of the Revolutionary government to disband all religious or have them absorbed into a constitutional church partly explains the antipathy of many English monks at the end of the century to the Cisalpine and Gallican tendencies of their confrere, Cuthbert Wilks and to the Catholic Committee of which he was a leading member.

This study is one of the first to give a major emphasis to the pronounced European dimension to be found in the Benedictines who represented one section of the English Catholic body. The attention given here to the English Benedictine involvement in the English mission highlights, furthermore, a dual aspect present in the experience of the monks, which suggests a profound tension present throughout much of the century between the respective lives of a conventual and a missioner, between the pulls which orthodoxy and liberal Enlightenment exercised on the monks, between on the one hand the influences of the wider European stage and on the other the insistent preoccupations with English provincial Catholic life. Finally, there was for much of the century the emotive pull of Jacobitism which prevented an acceptable compromise being fashioned with the Hanoverian government. By the end of the century, however, these tensions had eased, and with the return of the monasteries from exile in Europe back home to England the greatest gulf was closed. Historians of English Catholicism have invariably adopted an historical analysis and scheme which either supported the traditional perspective of the Old Faith surviving through persecution and the catacombs until Emancipation or more recently have favoured arguments like those popularised by Professor Bossy which suggest that Counter-Reformation Catholicism in England possessed many of the forms and attitudes of a growing nonconformist sect. Neither of these approaches does justice to the variety of contemporary European stimuli to which English Catholicism responded and it therefore seems to make sense to demonstrate here the effects of some lateral as well as historical determinants on that body in the eighteenth century.

Sir Thomas Gascoigne and Sir Walter Vavasour, with the Chaplain and Vicar reputedly poaching

CHAPTER I

THE ENGLISH BENEDICTINE CONGREGATION AND THE ENGLISH MISSION 1685-1794.

After the dissolution of the Benedictine monasteries during the Henrician Reformation, Englishmen called to the Benedictine life found it in Europe, where they entered monasteries during the late sixteenth and early seventeenth centuries. Most of these houses were in Italy and Spain.[1] During this period, many of these monasteries were undergoing a spiritual revival and a structural reform based on the principles of the Counter-Reformation and on the policies of some earlier monastic leaders. Thus, in terms of structure, many independent monasteries in these two countries had become more centralised through joining Congregations in order to protect themselves from lay exploitation.

The Counter-Reformation had also encouraged some monasteries to plan missionary enterprises, and by the early seventeenth century, English monks had returned to their homeland from their continental monasteries to begin work on the English mission. The numbers of English monks within such monasteries had been swelled by the entry of a number of English seminarians, discontented with the strong control the Jesuits exercised over English continental seminaries. Only slowly did the moves to found a revived English Benedictine Congregation, independent of the Spanish Valladolid and Italian Cassinese Benedictine Congregations, get under way. A number of English monks envisaged such a Congregation as the successor and heir of English medieval Benedictine monachism. The emergence of such a revived Congregation was the result of much perseverance and protracted discussion. The existence of penal legislation in England would inevitably force a revived English Benedictine Congregation to found its monastic communities within countries which were enemies of England and sometimes at variance with each other. Thus, when such monasteries had been established, they found themselves being exploited on occasion as pawns in a diplomatic war. The delay was also caused by both the Valladolid and Cassinese Congregations being reluctant initially to part with their English subjects. Only a very small number of English monks were willing at the beginning to come together to form a renewed Congregation, and those who did were often to be divided into factions by internal disputes.

Nevertheless, thanks to a combination of perseverance, favourable conditions and influential patrons, the revived English Benedictine Congregation was eventually recognised and ratified by Rome in two bulls, *Ex incumbenti* (1619) and *Plantata* (1633). Both these were promulgated after the foundation of four priories for English Benedictine monks, St. Gregory's, Douai,then in Flanders (1607), St. Laurence's at Dieulouard in Lorraine (1608), St. Benedict's at S. Malo (1611, and which survived as an English monastery until 1669), and, finally, St. Edmund's in Paris (1615). Later, in 1643, the abbey of SS. Adrian and Denis at Lambspring, near Hildesheim, was incorporated into the Congregation.

These monasteries, and the mission to Catholics in England which was their main apostolic work, were governed by a set of Constitutions which became finalised in 1661. These provided for a centralised Congregation ruled by a President General and his Council, known as the Regimen, who were elected every four years by a self-perpetuating General Chapter made up of the various superiors and officials of the Congregation, found in the monasteries and on the mission. The General Chapter remained the supreme executive body within the Congregation. It received nominations, and subsequently elected or appointed the priors of the monasteries, and the two Provincials (of Canterbury, or the South, and of York, or the North), who administered the Benedictine mission in England, and also held their offices for a quadriennium. Other officials also attending the General Chapter included the nine Cathedral Priors, the Censors, the *Magistri* and the Procurator who dealt with business at Rome, and the two missionary Procurators. Lambspring, the only fully-established abbey, had its abbot elected by the whole community, conventuals and missioners, subject to the approval of the General Chapter. General Chapter's business, besides elections and appointments, was that of checking the accounts of monasteries and mission, approving the *acta* of the two Provincial Chapters held in England usually a month before the General Chapter, listening to petitions from the members of the Congregation, and, finally, issuing Definitions which were up-to-date guidelines interpreting the Constitutions.

During the course of the seventeenth century, the Congregation became settled and 'naturalised' in its European base, erecting substantial buildings, practising forms of contemporary spirituality, and building up a role in education through university lecturing, private study, or through teaching in the small schools attached to some of the monasteries. Two convents of English Benedictine nuns were founded in these years, Cambrai (1625) and Paris (1651), which had English monks as chaplains. Most active monks, however, found themselves on the English mission, where their fortunes ebbed and flowed, depending on the government's attitude to papists at any one time. After a year's novitiate, each monk was professed, and took an important additional fourth vow which bound him to go to work on the English mission and return, if so ordered by the President. A monk's ordination generally followed after a six-year course in philosophy and theology, which might be followed by other, more practical courses, on preaching and moral theology to equip him for missionary work. Such an elaborate academic education was not given to the handful of lay-brothers and choir oblates which each monastery contained. These, like the other conventuals, were subject to the prior and his house council. The monasteries had been initially accepted and protected on the continent because of their chief work, the English mission. Here, a Benedictine missioner would perform his priestly duties in a variety of missions and family chaplaincies, leading a life very similar to other English missionary Regulars and secular priests of the period. He would be linked to his provincial by a 'praepositus', a Benedictine missioner who kept his eyes on other missioners within his county or local area. Even so, an individual missioner would be far more independent than the conventuals living within the monastery. He would, for instance, be able to possess his own property and money, his *peculium* to give him some security on the mission.

During the course of the seventeenth century, individual Benedictine missioners were involved in some important controversies, such as the debate over an Oath of Allegiance acceptable to Catholics, and the conflict over rival privileges accorded to Regular superiors and English Vicars Apostolic who, as papal delegates, were the nearest the English Church came to having a recognised episcopate. Such questions would carry on in one form or another throughout the following century. Fortunately, the monks had been able to obtain some patronage at the Stuart Court during the seventeenth century, particularly from the two queens, Henrietta Maria and Catherine of Braganza, and Charles II had been converted on his deathbed by a monk. This 'Court monasticism', as it has been called, meant that the Benedictines on the mission were in a very privileged position at the accession of the Catholic James II in 1685, despite having undergone a momentary persecution after the revelation of the so-called Oates Plot between 1678 and 1680.

The False Dawn 1685-1688.

The years 1685 to 1688 were unique for the English Benedictines because they saw the only serious attempt at Benedictine conventual life in England, leaving aside the short-lived Marian revival, between the medieval period and the nineteenth century. By the 1680s, the English monasteries on the continent had been integrated, as far as they were able, into their local ecclesiastical society,[2] and were ready to receive the increased numbers of novices, many of them Anglican converts, who had turned to Catholicism and the monastic life following the more favourable conditions granted by James II to the Church in England.[3]

The picture given by some historians of English Catholicism under James II is that of a church of contrasts, divided into a 'Court Catholicism' with strong political and continental features, and a 'Country Catholicism' found in the provinces, rather more passive, and attached to that domesticity and discretion which characterised many nonconformist churches of the period.[4] This view does not do full justice to the place within that church of the English Benedictines and other mission clergy trained on the continent. Any of these, coming across to England, might find themselves transferred at a moment's notice from a 'Court' to a 'Country' apostolate, without any apparent anxiety being felt at the change in mentality and conditions. Such clergy might well act as agents in dispensing an aggressive continental Catholicism throughout different levels of English society, and carefully adapting it to the degrees of tolerance and education in the congregations to whom they preached. The similarity between Benedictine involvement at Court and that in some of the urban missions and gentry chapels suggests some affinity between such centres which was largely encouraged by the religious toleration positively encouraged under James II.

During this time, London, which housed the Court, was the centre of much Benedictine activity. Two monks remained at Somerset House in Queen Catherine of Braganza's household, and represented the remnants of what had been a much larger community. Secondly, a cell at Clerkenwell was established during James II's reign by Maurus

Corker, another monk well-known in Court circles, which was derived from an earlier chapel at the Savoy Palace, and had a school attached.[5] Finally, there was a revived Benedictine presence at St. James's Palace, where a community of fourteen priests and two lay-brothers lived under a 'Superior' rather than a prior. General Chapter met here in 1685, and in the king's brief reign it represented the monks' main access to the king and assured the Benedictines of his special protection.[6]

This Benedictine presence in London Court circles not only helped the English Catholic body to relate more easily to European Catholicism, it was also to become, by its positive response to, and active co-operation with, the current policy of toleration offered to Catholics, the model for developments elsewhere on the English mission. 'Court' monasticism's two most important figures were James Maurus Corker and Philip Michael Ellis, who in their writing and preaching vigorously encouraged the English Catholic body to accept the offer of religious freedom from the king as providing the opening for a prosperous future.[7] Both these monks were converts from Anglicanism, and by their portrayal of Catholicism as eminently reasonable, and through their spiritual direction and respect for historical tradition, converted a large number at Court to Catholicism. Corker's most famous convert had been the poet John Dryden.[8]

Like other monks, both of these were daring enough to wear the full habit around London and at the Court,[9] but they nevertheless attempted to act as a restraining influence on the king's determination to force Catholicism on the nation as quickly as possible by the repeal of the penal laws and by insinuating Catholics into Protestant strongholds. In this respect, James was under the control of the Jesuits at Court. In 1686, the king had tried unsuccessfully to force Cambridge University to bestow an M.A. on the Benedictine, Placid Francis, without the latter taking the usual oaths and in March 1688 the king intruded the monk Thomas Augustine Constable into Magdalen College, Oxford, as a fellow.[10] In the face of such moves it is quite certain that monks like Corker and Ellis represented a more moderate policy, and in general, the monks at Court were known to be opposed to the Jesuits.[11] Corker, in particular, had collided with the Jesuits at the Savoy. His chapel lay above that of that of the Jesuits:

> Now as noe one could go up to Fr. Corker's but through an entry by theirs, they struck into ye passage windows like shop-windows in ye

silk-shops, so yt ye noise of their sermons or prayers coming through would invite those to listen yt could not for ye throng get in to see. Ys would so stop up ye passage yt yre was no access to Fa. Corker's Chapel.[12]

The Jesuits encouraged the king, therefore, to order Corker out, and he moved to Clerkenwell. Corker had already by this time written his short work, *Roman-Catholick Principles in reference to God and the King* which became the standard classic of English Gallicanism. It endeavoured both to reduce Protestant fears of popery and to undermine Jesuit ultramontanism.[13]

If the rumour was true that Philip Ellis, Corker's confrere, had been kidnapped as a boy by the Jesuits while a pupil at Westminster School, and brought up at St. Omers, he seems to have had little love for some members of the Society in later years after he had become a Benedictine. At Court, he strove consistently to weaken the influence which Petre the Jesuit had over the king.[14] Ellis, who was to become Vicar Apostolic of the Western District in 1688, appears to have been the most effective Catholic Court preacher of the day, and he used his skills here to eradicate the one major obstacle which stood in the way of the Benedictines becoming acceptable to the upper levels of English society. This was the question over Benedictine claims to the old medieval monastic lands. It was believed, and there may have been some grounds for the conviction, that monks were occupied in the task of accumulating as much of their old estates as possible through employing lay trustees, and hoped that a Catholic king would help this cause further. The monks, especially Ellis, rejected this charge totally[15] but were happy to fan other popular rumours that the Jesuits were planning something similar.[16] The Benedictines' policy of accommodation rather than confrontation was developed further by Henry Joseph Johnston, a monk of the community at St. James's. He tried to increase Catholicism's appeal to the English by literary means. It is almost certain that he collaborated with his brother Nathaniel in a work designed to calm fears over the monastic land question, but he was especially influential as the principal translator of Bossuet's works into English during James II's reign. Bossuet was immediately popular with Anglicans because, although Johnston emphasised that Bossuet's Gallicanism could never be the equivalent of a thinly-veiled Anglicanism, this French prelate had shown Catholicism to be inherently reasonable and to possess a unity which highlighted the factionalism inherent in the Anglicanism of the period.[17] Such attempts by monks to reassure English society and its national Church of the flexibility and tolerance within Catholicism built upon foundations already laid by Benedictines earlier in the century. These earlier objectives could only be realised in the more emancipated atmosphere of James II's reign.[18]

All this feverish activity by monks at Court should not make us forget that most Benedictines in England at the time were dispersed through some twenty five to thirty missions, mostly inherited from the past, but enlarged by half a dozen established in the reign, further evidence of the benefits stemming from toleration.[19] There are, however, few signs to show that the new era produced significant developments in a large number of the rural missions. Here and there, enlarged and more ostentatious chapels appeared, thanks to patrons, many of whom had secured political advancement and took advantage of the new freedom found during the reign. At Coughton Court in Warwickshire, for instance, a new chapel was built by Sir Robert Throckmorton, a recently-appointed Justice of the Peace, to complete the fourth wing of the Court.[20]

It is, however, in the towns that we find the most practical developments on the mission. These stemmed from the advantages granted to Catholics in Court circles. The monastery at St. James's set the lead here, with its uninhibited self-confidence and corporate pride. Its monks passed through St. James's Park in habits, and were escorted by a guard provided by the king. The interior of the monastery's chapel surpassed all others in its magnificence[21]. At York, the blessing of the new Benedictine chapel, which included a bell and was built by the missioner Francis Lawson in 1688, was accompanied by an extravagantly baroque liturgy. The bishop in full vestments was met by a crucifix, holy water, six acolytes, and escorted into the church:

> Father Lawson, the greate preaste, from head to foot in rich white silks bedaubed with gold lace &c., nothing appearing but his bald head; then all the fryers, secularys, Jesiwits, in a greate number, came singing him up with a *Te Deum*, as the Lord knows, for I do not, a greate consorte of musick, organs, violls, and other instrumentes and voices...the altar...richly drest with greate store of lights and incense burning... The sermon was preached by Father Lawson, the monck, in a strange blacke habitt, bald head, with a hood on: his text was 'Blessed be the eyes that see the things we now see'.[22]

York's chapel was independent of a gentry patron, being built with funds acquired by Lawson himself. Similarly at Bath in 1686, the South Benedictine Province inaugurated a new system whereby the Province itself became the trustee for the mission. Bath was to be administered along these lines for the rest of the century.[23] Like Bath was the mission in the small Lancashire town of Fishwick, where property was leased to the monks directly, without a lay patron acting as intermediary. The chapel here which was built during the reign of James II and possessed organ, pulpit and bells, must have been one of the grandest of the new Benedictine chapels in the provinces.[24] Few details, however, remain of the two urban chapels at Bath, or in Newcastle, where there appears to have been a central chapel established between two outlying household chaplaincies at Fenham and Gateshead.[25] The building of chapels in towns was often part of a much more complex plan, for there is evidence that the Benedictines gave serious consideration to backing up their consolidated position here by introducing and developing an educational apostolate. In its short existence, Maurus Corker's cell at Clerkenwell had a successful school attached to it, in spite of its founder insisting that that mission's most essential work was for 'the conversion of souls'. York and Fishwick also seem to have had schools attacked to their missions at this time. These short-lived schools complemented the schools already attached to some of the monasteries on the continent as well as the system of monks travelling on the continent as governors to students.[26]

The Revolution in 1688 proved that monks like Ellis and Corker had been right to advise caution and discretion on the part of the king. Benedictine aspirations were rapidly destroyed in the Revolution's wake. A mob from Alcester pulled down the Coughton chapel, another in London demolished Clerkenwell; the bells and furnishings at Fishwick were quickly hidden away, and a number of monks, including Ellis, were captured and imprisoned.[27] Yet the English Benedictine Congregation survived this disaster, and what follows is the story of how the Congregation adjusted to less favourable conditions, a painful process, particularly in the first decades after 1688, and how it found, after the lapse of a century following the 1688 Revolution, a deeper feeling of acceptance and tolerance in English society. Thus by the 1790s, the Congregation was embarking on another period of expansion similar in some respects to that which it had experienced under James II.

CHAPTER II

THE MONASTERIES 1689-1794.

The three monasteries at Douai, Dieulouard and Lambspring appear to have maintained the numbers of their conventuals at high levels after the 1688/89 Revolution. St Edmund's, Paris, however, experienced a massive drop in numbers. During the last decade of the seventeenth century, the number of conventuals was higher than at any time in the following century. But the flow of newly-professed in all houses almost dried up after 1689, a striking contrast with the 1685-1688 period, when vocations had been abundant.[28] The disturbance caused by the Revolution had forced St. Edmund's to board its younger monks in neighbouring Maurist houses so as to find enough room for monks exiled from the mission, although a surprisingly large number of sudden deaths in this community soon created space.[29] After 1688, the newly-professed in the Congregation came equally from both north and south England, and represented exiled Jacobite families, London mercantile families, or were the sons of northern Catholic gentry.[30] During the first two decades of the new century, only Lambspring showed any sign of expansion in the number of its conventuals; its newly-professed continued to come from all areas of England. In the other houses, professions were much rarer. One feature which became apparent at this time in these houses was the preponderance of newly-professed coming from northern England, and this was especially true at Dieulouard, whither aspirants were directed by missioners originally professed for this monastery. The large number of those professed for a declining St. Edmund's during these years who had been educated in the school at St. Gregory's, Douai, suggests there was a deliberate policy on the part of the Congregation to preserve this house.[31]

By the mid-eighteenth century, professions in all the houses were much more regular, but by this period, the north had clearly asserted itself as the main recruiting ground for Dieulouard, Paris and Lambspring. The novices for St. Gregory's, Douai, still coming from gentry families in southern England, and an education in the school at Douai, were quite a contrast to the large number of those from humble Lancashire origins professed at Dieulouard. This latter house was distinctive also in the early age at which it allowed profession; fifteen years was common, and there were at least two fourteen year-olds professed at this time. In other houses, profession generally took place between sixteen and twenty years. All the houses in France were forced to change their requirements here for profession after the Royal Edict of 1768, which forbade professions before twenty-one years. Professions of those below this age made after the Edict took place outside France, at Mechlin, for instance. Lambspring, being in Germany, was, of course, not affected by this edict. Even before 1768, the English Benedictines had found their houses involved in a contraction which hit all Benedictine monasteries in France.[32] President Fisher, in the face of this, could only recommend 'zeal, and application' by missioners to send recruits to 'thinly stocked' monasteries. He blamed the scarcity on the French edict, and saw Lambspring's similar reduction in professions as due to 'the calamities of the wars'.[33] At Douai, aspirants under twenty one were encouraged to begin their philosophy early as a means of keeping them attached to the community, and more interest was shown in recruiting lay-brothers.[34] Dieulouard always had a high proportion of lay-brothers to work in its brewery, although the community as a whole was never much more than fifteen. In 1778, the prior of Dieulouard admitted that since there were only four priests resident, he was unable to spare anyone for the mission.[35] St. Edmund's, Paris by the 1770s had about the same number resident as Dieulouard, but because it provided lodgings for student monks attending the Sorbonne and was the headquarters of the President, it was acknowledged as the 'principal house and chief centre' of the Congregation in France.[36] Lambspring maintained its lead in terms of numbers. In June 1778, it had twenty choir monks and four lay-brothers, and Abbot Maurus Heatley admitted, somewhat disingenuously, 'quire, regularity and studies are duly observed in peace and harmoney to ye edification of ye whole neighbourhood and credit to ye house'.[37]

This overall picture of slow numerical decline remained largely unchanged in the decade during which the monasteries began feeling the effects of the French Revolution. The President's statement in 1790 to the French authorities spoke of fifty two conventuals divided equally up among the three French monasteries.[38] Shortages at Douai forced the Prior into pushing junior monks through profession, studies and ordination as quickly as possible, and hanging on to would-be apostates as long as he possibly could.[39] However, at Dieulouard between 1781

18

and 1794, there were as many professions as at Douai and Paris together. Doubtless, this was the result of Dieulouard reviving its alumnate in 1779, to which students were directed by the two other houses in France. In this way, Dieulouard became the house in France principally responsible for supplying missioners.[40] Not revealed in any of the profession lists, however, is the disquieting feature of the exodus of an unusually large number of novices between 1781 and 1794, notably at Douai [7] and Lambspring [6]. Such departures from Douai reflect the unease caused by the growing threats to the monastic life in France and at least one novice left, convinced that the monastery constricted his liberal attitudes.[41] Novices leaving Lambspring, especially between 1786 and 1787, left almost certainly because of internal divisions in the community at that time. Even so, Lambspring could still pride itself in 1787 as 'the principal supply to the Mission'.[42]

Northern England was still in these years producing most of the newly-professed, a trend encouraged by new funds established by benefactors over and beyond those established by Benedictine missions and missioners. Thus, one Lambspring monk was sponsored by the Catholic Charitable Society of Preston.[43] While St. Gregory's, Douai still maintained its tradition of novices from gentry families, like the Lawsons of Brough, St. Edmund's, Paris had spread out its net further, and was accepting aspirants from Sedgeley Park school from the 1780s.

During the eighteenth century, the daily life and worship of each of the monasteries were regulated principally by the manuscript Constitutions of 1661, which were to be revised in the first fully-printed set in 1784. Outside these rules, there were adaptations and customaries made by each house to suit local conditions.[44] The best example of daily life in one of the monasteries is the picture given by the monk Benet Weldon of St. Edmund's Paris in 1708.[45] Daily 'Church Duty', he tells us, began with Matins and Lauds at 4:00 a.m., and was followed by half an hour's meditation and Prime. On Sundays and Feasts, High Mass was celebrated together with the Little Hours at 9:30 a.m., but on 'Worky-days', Little Hours and a simple Conventual Mass took place at 11:00 a.m. After a visit to the chapel, following dinner, Vespers was recited at 2:00 p.m. on Sundays and Feasts, and at 5:00 p.m. on ferial days. Then came another meditation period of quarter of an hour, and Compline finished the day at 7:30 p.m., although if this included Exposition it took place earlier.

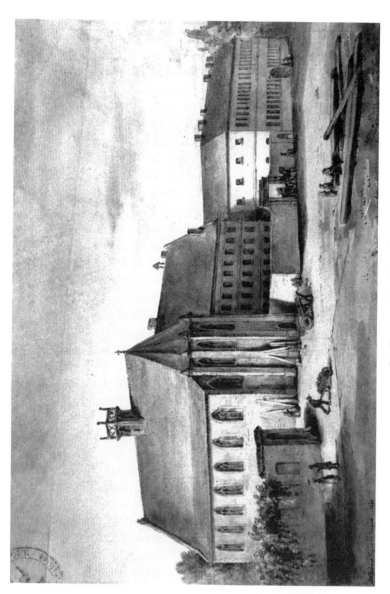

St Gregory's, Douai

Much of the daily horarium at Paris must have resembled that in the other houses. Breakfast was allowed at St. Edmund's only on a small number of feasts. Reading took place at dinner from the Old Testament or a work of patrology or Church History, and after a period of recreation until 1:00 p.m., the community retired to their cells. Supper was taken at 6:00 p.m. and preceded by grace and readings from the Rule and Blosius; reading during the meal was similar to that at dinner. After supper, an hour's recreation or 'collation' had become the custom by Weldon's time. Weldon's censures of some of these customs unwittingly tell us how the community enjoyed various revels. There was, for instance, 'recreation with a Cake-King' on St. Thomas of Canterbury's feast, and another king was elected on Epiphany 'by paper scrawles and the Convent is harmlessly merry'. On these occasions, Weldon felt 'ye balling words LE ROY BOIRE' to be 'a great indecency in ye mouths of Religious Men'. During the three recreation weeks which occurred in September, and before Advent and Lent, breakfast was allowed, more wine and meat were provided, and Compline was brought forward. A fire was allowed at evening recreation from All Saints until the Annunciation, but fires at other times in very cold weather were only granted on the request of the youngest professed, the 'semi-abbot', and the fuel for these was strictly controlled. A celebration took place at Shrovetide: 'we passe ye afternoon in harmless merriment, making ourselves Pancakes, and have a rational plenty of wine, with apples and cheeze and such like things'. Abstinence from meat, even on Christmas day, was observed, as a 'token' to be performed until 'it pleases God to re-establish us in England'. However, thanks to a papal dispensation, the community could take meat generally on three days a week. The Discipline which was to be omitted by the enlightened Constitutions of 1784, was taken daily in the early eighteenth century, 'always rattl'd to at 8 a clock at night'. Finally, 'Conventual Walking into ye Fields' took place once a fortnight, with wine and fruit served on the community's return.[46]

We possess a full picture of the liturgical usage at Paris. Here, French feasts were kept, and French customs, such as processions of relics, were performed. Nevertheless, older Spanish feasts were still observed as a testimony that the Congregation still believed itself to possess all the privileges of the Spanish Benedictines.[47] On major feasts, Exposition took place, with masses said before the monstrance, and these were followed by a rota of 'watching', which led up to Benediction. In other houses, the ceremonial and liturgical customs

21

would have been similar, with all done in conformity to the Congregation's *Compendium Caeremoniale*.[48] The enjoyment of collegiate status and a collegiate church - the monastery formed part of the university college in Douai belonging to the monastery of St Vaast in Arras - brought to St. Gregory's, Douai a reputation for high living but heavy choral obligations. In 1700, Weldon had toyed with the idea of settling at Douai, but he lasted only six weeks, on account of 'ye great burden of Church-Duty yt Convent lyes under by its foundation, together with ye twitches of Conscience upon ye diet which they are in possession of using yre, which thwarts ye Constitutions'. As numbers became fewer during the eighteenth century, these additional offices, ordered by the grant of foundation, became a real burden. Even so, the liturgy of St. Gregory's was splendid enough to impress visiting Maurists.[49] To accompany the choir, all four monastic churches had fine organs, and the music that has survived shows the monks employed the rendering of plainsong then in fashion.[50]

During the course of the eighteenth century, the conventual buildings of each of the houses were either rebuilt or enlarged to suit changed needs, even though, as we have seen, the number of conventuals was not expanding. At St. Gregory's, Douai, the school buildings were enlarged at least twice, in the 1690s, and especially in the 1770s, to house more students.[51] The church at Douai was also altered, according to contemporary fashions. The antiquarian William Cole called at St. Gregory's in 1765, where he found the Prior 'a very large tall black Man...of no striking Address or Behaviour, but rather of a rough and clownish Carriage'. Cole was, however, impressed by the church, 'an elegant Pile...in the modern stile with 2 Ranges of high Pillars to support the Roof'. He noted that the High Altar was being rebuilt in a central position, to imitate St. Peter's in Rome, a 'Taste and Fashion...now very prevalent in France'.[52] At Dieulouard the large collegiate church taken over by the English monks between 1606 and 1608 remained substantially unchanged until its destruction in the French Revolution.[53] Above its sanctuary a library, however, was built after the disastrous fire of 1717 which had gutted the monastery.[54] There was little opportunity for St. Edmund's to expand on its congested site in the centre of Paris. The monastery had been built in 1674 by Charles D'Avilère, a disciple of Mansard. After the deposition of James II, its chapel remained unchanged until the Revolution, although its Stuart connections enticed some English antiquarians into listing its furnishings and effects. Its altar-piece, the Martyrdom of St Edmund, was ascribed to the celebrated artist Charles de la Fosse (1640-1716)[55] Late in the day, in May 1788, President Walker who was something of a connoisseur, produced a set of splendid plans for the entire rebuilding of St. Edmund's on neo-classical lines.[56] The lavishness of the scheme suggests it could only have been implemented with financial help from the Congregation, and indeed, the large, private Presidential suite which Walker envisaged, indicates that Walker aimed to make St. Edmund's the centre of the Congregation in France. These plans show the church opening, through a classical facade, onto a columned nave which led to a grille behind which was a free-standing high altar and retro-choir. A night choir lay behind the apse, in a separate building.

This scheme at St. Edmund's was not realised, presumably because of the outbreak of the Revolution, but like Lutyens' Liverpool Cathedral in the twentieth century, 'the abstraction of its non-completion' made it a supreme symbol of the English monks' aspirations for the future. It can be best compared with the ambitious range of conventual buildings erected at Lambspring in the 1730s by Abbot Joseph Rokeby. These were attached to the magnificent church there, consecrated in 1691.[57] Lambspring's new buildings were largely funded by Benedictine patrons in England whose assistance Rokeby actively sought. Some of them were openly hostile to the palatial grandeur of the scheme and feared the monastery would become bankrupt:

> Your German friends have commenced a vast building 320 (feet) the front, 20 more than Castle Howard. I am glad I did not contribute to so vain and ridiculous an edifice. Friends and foes blame the undertaking.

Although Lambspring's Council forced Rokeby to scale down the building's size, what was built resembled a 'bold and stately Palace', with a great saloon stuccoed and painted, the whole length of the building, and unequalled by any in Germany. It carried the bold inscription, 'Anglia Germanas Josephum mittit ad oras / Hujus ut auspiciis surgeret ista domus MDCCXXXI'.[58] Besides all other features, the scale of the buildings at Lambspring was enough to set it apart from the other houses.

If conventual buildings reflected something of the ethos of eight-eenth-century English Benedictinism, they were, as has been emphasised already, largely projects initiated by superiors eager to realise their own personal aims. By no means all monks were happy to live within such shells, and two opposing forces can be shown gnawing at mainstream conventual life within the houses throughout the century: disturbed missioners returning, and the attraction of the ascetic ideal.

First, it has to be admitted that there was some estrangement between monasteries and mission in the eighteenth century. It was hardly surprising that monks were eager to leave the constraints of the monastery for the freedom and apparently more profitable work of the mission, and many of these were very unhappy at being ordered back later to the houses of their profession. This division can be sensed beneath the surface of the Fenwick Schism of the 1720s which will be dealt with elsewhere.[59] It lay behind the complaints of Wilfrid Helme who in 1729 was ordered to return to St. Edmund's as Prior, after twenty years of a very full and enjoyable missionary career. While admitting to enjoying the entertainments and high life-style which Paris offered, he was still depressed:

> I am now fixed in my troublesome post, and in my black attire, but the black reckonings I meet with make me heartily wish I had kept my secular on, and rather undertaken the hard service in Cumberland rather than this. I will, however, do all I can for the benefit of my poor decaying house, and live in hopes of seeing my Friends again in less than fo(u)r years time'.[60]

Helme was one of a very large number of missioners who were ordered to return to their monasteries and take on the rule of superior; all the abbots of Lambspring in the eighteenth century, for instance, had had missionary experience. Such missioners were chosen as superiors because monks with age and energy in their favour were inevitably found on the mission. Of the other houses, St. Edmund's was the most dependent on the mission for its superiors; of its twenty one priors in these years, fourteen came from the mission, while another four were monks professed at Douai or Dieulouard. Such superiors, imported from the mission, would, it was hoped, tend to be neutral in internal conflicts and would thus help to reduce factions. Finally, their administrative experience in England was seen to be of immense value in contributing to their leadership inside the monasteries.[61] Nevertheless, they often hankered, as we have seen, after the life on the mission and kept as close as possible to it through a frequent correspondence. They willingly assumed the role of continental agents for their English patrons and were often responsible for exporting luxury goods, like wine, to the latter.[62] Meetings of General Chapter in London were a godsend to these superiors, and not a few of them were dilatory in making their way back to the continent after the Chapter.[63] This continuing attraction to England was partly the reason why so many superiors and ex-missioners in the houses were so enthusiastic to have English guests call on them, particularly if these were old patrons. Douai and Paris were fortunately placed on main thoroughfares, and Dieulouard, while more inland, stood next to an important public road.[64] Sometimes the monastery might provide board and lodgings for old patrons in financial distress, as St. Gregory's did for the Greenwoods of Brise Norton.[65] Such monastic hospitality was also extended to English non-Catholic visitors. Prior Welch in Paris had welcomed the antiquarian William Cole, and would show other visitors 'ye curiosities' of the capital.[66] Later, Dr. Johnson, as we shall see, was courteously received at St. Edmund's.

In June 1774 the busy Procurator of the South Province, Bede Bennet, while on a visit to Douai, wrote to Prior Welsh, describing how he had 'transported' himself to the English Benedictine nuns at Cambrai 'for a morning's promenade'. He concluded his letter with the sentiment: 'I am just going to ye grate; ye sooner I get back from it the better'.[67] Words which speak volumes about missioners' attitudes to the nuns' contemplative life. If superiors were reluctant to return to their monasteries, the ordinary missioner would often have also been dismayed, and doubly so if he was being forcibly returned to undergo a form of incarceration following his misdemeanours on the mission. Missioners therefore tended to advance their indispensability to their congregations as an excuse for not returning.[68] This emphasis on activity also reflects changing attitudes to spirituality, dealt with elsewhere, which gave more prominence to missionary endeavour than to the contemplative tradition popular in some English Benedictine circles in the previous century. The revulsion against going back to the monastery seems to have become stronger by the second half of the eighteenth century when conditions on the mission appeared to grow easier and the monasteries were experiencing a variety of hardships.

All the houses, for instance, suffered from a series of internal dissensions and divisions which grew steadily more serious throughout the period. It is clear that in most known cases, ex-missioners were either instigators or perpetrators of this unrest. In the first decade of the century, St. Edmund's, Paris had been rocked by an ex-missioner, Bede Moore, who rebelled against his prior and took a group of impressionable young monks with him. More observant conventuals condemned the irregularity of his observance, his independence and his private means - he refused to hand the proceeds of his benefice over. Yet these were traits that one would have expected to find in many missioners.[69] Moore's case resembled that of Maurus Barrett, another ex-missioner who returned to his monastery at Dieulouard in the early 1770s, 'a fomenter or sower of discord... particularly between the inferior superiors and their subjects'.[70] Evidence suggests that here the prior found it difficult to cope with such dissidents, but it was St. Edmund's, Paris which provided the most obvious example of this problem. The priory in Paris was easily disturbed by ex-missioners whose weaknesses were only given a freer rein by the temptations of the capital. Benedict Catteral had returned to St. Edmund's from the mission in 1784, where he had been known to have a fondness for drink. Prior Cowley was therefore appalled when, after locking up all the drink in the monastery, he found Catterall and another monk coming out of a Paris beer-shop, and determined that Catteral should be given no more of his annuity. This infuriated Catteral so much that he appealed for justice to the ecclesiastical authorities who told him: 'It was lawful to go to a Coffee house or any other place of refreshment, except *Cabarets* and Auberges'. Catteral's attitude throws some light on prevalent monastic attitudes to secular society; he believed that the world of the 1780s was liberal and enlightened enough to permit him to indulge his habit, and he condemned the prior for his reactionary viewpoint:

> an Act of Despotism..To(o) great rigour in monastic discipline, in my opinion, does a great deal of harm in these times especially by causing discontent. Whereas prudent relaxation and condescension would do an infinite deal of good, by making people contented and happy... I must do justice to Mr. Cowley by saying he has been so kind as to let me have a little Brandy wh. has done me good.

Cowley's compromise stopped Catteral from pestering him to be returned to the freedom of the mission.[71] Compliancy in superiors was the lesser of two evils. At Lambspring, for instance, two missioners were terrified of returning to the monastery to face the harshness of Abbot Maurus Heatley who, it was believed, 'never forgives a man for whom he has once conceived an aversion'. After sexual scandals, Basil Kennedy was ordered to return to Lambspring from the mission in 1787 but steadfastly refused, and was therefore sent to St. Edmund's, Paris, whence he apostatised. His fear of Heatley consumed him:

> Another objection (to returning to Lambspring) is the inveterate malice the Abbot bears me. You yourself told me that he threatened to imprison me if ever I had returned. The example of Chaplin terrifies me. Even if I suppose him guilty of attempting to fire the House, I am confident the ill-usage of the abbot must have pushed him to such a desperate step. Besides I have been eye-witness of the ill usage Messrs. Strut, Davis & Hardisty met with. In no Poor House in England would they have led so miserable lives.

Maurus Chaplin had been ordered back to Lambspring in 1788 after scandalous habits on the mission. He interpreted Heatley's severity as a persecution aimed at himself, and reacted accordingly - by taking a cricket bat to the abbot and slashing his portrait. He was therefore imprisoned by Heatley in the monastery for nine years.[72]

If the return of some missioners produced an explosive mixture in the monasteries, these also felt the effects of a second and quite different force which encouraged instability and dissatisfaction. Throughout the century, there were conventuals who demanded either a stricter monastic observance or the possibility of transferring to another Congregation which gave this. It is important to realise that this aspiration appears to have been more idealistic at the beginning of the century than it became towards the end when it was often employed as an excuse to justify an aversion to missionary responsibilities.

The attraction to a better defined conventual life and the preference for this rather than for an isolated existence on the mission had early on been found among the English Benedictines, especially among those who had joined the Cassinese Congregation at the beginning of the seventeenth century.[73] This ideal, together with a pre-eminence given to learning, had attracted Anglican converts, and others desiring the monastic life, to the English Benedictines during the same century. The Benedictine life, for instance, could still attract seminarians as it had in the early years of the seventeenth century. As late as 1703, a young seminarian, Edward Delattre, had petitioned to enter the Benedictines, not feeling himself adequately prepared as a secular priest for the English mission. Foremost among the Anglican converts who became Benedictines was the Paris monk and annalist Benet Weldon, whose literary work will be discussed later. He had been converted by a monk of the monastery of St. James in Whitehall in 1687 and was professed in 1692, but, on account of lameness, never ordained.[74] Weldon was highly-strung and over-sensitive. He found it difficult to settle down at Paris so that throughout the 1690s, he drifted from one Benedictine and Trappist house to another, never finding any real contentment in his own monastery. It appears that his awkwardness did not merely stem from personal unsuitability. Weldon was disturbed by the laxity he found at St. Edmund's, Paris, caused, in his eyes, by the necessity of educating monks to work on the English mission. Thus, as 'a Benedictin Nursery for ye English-Benedictin Mission', St. Edmund's had mitigated customary ascetic practices. Weldon complained of recreation extending 'to(o) far into the night', and condemned feast-day revels. He admitted that abstinence from meat was also not total on account of the monks' missionary status. Against all this apparent laxity Weldon set the stricter and more regular conventual life of the Maurists and La Trappe, where he took refuge more than once, and he demanded that St. Edmund's undergo a rigorous Visitation by the President. Since little redress seemed forthcoming, Weldon cut himself off and became immersed in the history of the past glories of the English Benedictines whose example served to highlight the decline of his own day.[75] Only one English Benedictine in these years went as far as transferring to a stricter monastery; Dunstan Lake was professed at La Trappe in 1698.[76] Later years saw less interest among the English Benedictines in a more ascetical monasticism, for the eighteenth century witnessed an increasing aversion to the monastic life in general which was condemned in certain quarters as unfashionable. Even so, Laurence Barnes of St. Gregory's was attracted to La Trappe in 1781 as a way out of being sent to the mission. His prior was scornful:

> I cannot see how he could expect in such an undertaking. He seems incapable of Austerities, being of a very weak constitution...The

28

Doctor judges fish improper for him even in Lent and would not advise any fasting…The solitude would also I fear be to(o) great for him. He is pious but rather scrupulous and inclined to melancholy.[77]

After a series of fits and starts, Barnes was eventually eased onto the mission in 1792 despite his 'very timorous conscience'.[78] Besides La Trappe, the English Carthusians at Nieuwpoort or a Vannist house were also suggested as alternatives to the English mission by two other Douai monks determined to stay in France, Jerome Digby and Ambrose Allam. Ambrose Allam was attracted to the Carthusians since he hoped he might there be exempt from choir duty because of his melancholic fits.[79] Jerome Digby had returned to Douai from the mission in 1782, but had fomented such trouble in the community and influenced the younger monks so badly that the prior had to admit:

> I dread the prospect of the wintery season, that must frequently bring all the Religious together in the Calefactory, & makes me apprehend too often great disturbance among them unless some scheme can be contrived to prevent it.

Like Barnes and Allam, Digby was later sent to the mission under protest.[80]

Alongside this escapism, one is struck by a revived appreciation of the value of the contemplative life *per se* which occurs in all of the Visitation speeches delivered by President Walker in the 1780s. In the face of attacks by the establishment and intellectuals outside, and of imminent schism and breakdown of observance within, Walker's Visitation speeches in all the monasteries were full of allusions to the value of obedience, seclusion and asceticism of La Trappe, and of impressions of a stylized ideal of past monastic tradition which might encourage a revival of unity and observance. Walker's Romantic sentimentalism was an admission that monasticism had tried but failed to find a secure place in the cool rational world of the eighteenth century.[81]

It was this desperate need for unity both within the houses individually and in the Congregation generally that exercised the powers of most Presidents during the eighteenth century. Time and again the quality of superiors within the houses reflected the nature and strength of the link between a house and the rest of the Congregation. When Bernard Gregson became President in 1697, much of his time was spent healing internal divisions at St. Edmund's, Paris, and finding a solution to the more intractable problem of Lambspring.[82]

Lambspring had traditionally kept its distance from the Congregation. Geographically it was isolated. It had its own customs and enjoyed close relations with the local German civil and ecclesiastical authorities. Finally it was anomalous among the English Benedictine monasteries in that it had a life abbot. Inevitably there would be a conflict of jurisdictions between the English Benedictine President and the Abbot of Lambspring. Within months of being elected abbot in 1690, the ex-missioner, Maurus Corker, had found himself unable to govern the community and had taken an extended leave, delegating his office to another. Early attempts by President Gregson's predecessor to organise a Visitation at Lambspring had been unsuccessful.[83] Corker resigned the abbacy in 1696 and after a hotly-disputed election, Maurus Knightley became abbot, and remained so until his death in 1708.[84] Since the local German bishop had actively interfered in Knightley's election precisely at a time, as we shall see, when the English Benedictines were fighting a fierce battle for their own exemption in England against the Vicars Apostolic, the President and General Chapter of 1697 only grudgingly accepted Knightley as abbot.[85] By 1705 Knightley's self-imposed isolation, and his refusal to send his monks on the mission and to allow a Visitation, forced the Congregation to clarify its control over Lambspring by an appeal to Rome.[86] Knightley's successor, Augustine Tempest, an elderly missioner, came straight to the abbacy from England and with his background might have been expected to be more amenable to recognising Lambspring as an integral part of the Congregation under the immediate jurisdiction of the President. Lingering fears of the abbey's desire for autonomy still remained, however, particularly in regard to election procedures governing a 'perpetual Abbot', which conflicted with the President's authority and involved the local Ordinary. Again, these were clarified by Rome, in the President's favour.[87]

Although Abbot Tempest was quick to disassociate Lambspring from the rebels in the Fenwick Schism which shook the Congregation between 1717 and 1721, he was to be unhappy about the immediate effect of that Schism, which was the plan of the President in 1725 to weld the whole Congregation into a tighter unity. He therefore rejected the proposed union as contrary to the Lambspring Constitutions, and incompatible with his abbatial dignity and his monastery's inherited privileges. The unity scheme was abandoned.[88] In contrast to the other houses, movement of monks at this time from Lambspring to the mission was very slight; very many remained conventuals for life. But the right of all Lambspring professed monks to vote for their superior, not the conventuals only as was the case in the other houses, seems to have balanced missionary and conventual interests at Lambspring to the extent that most of its abbots had had missionary experience before they took office. Tempest's successor, Joseph Rokeby, became abbot in 1730, after a missionary career of some notoriety. Rokeby's ambitious building schemes brought him into collision with his Council and many conventuals. Such a conflict was symptomatic in a community where the superior, elected for life and possessing full abbatial power, lived at some distance from the rest of the community. This gulf also helped to make Lambspring unique.[89] The abbot's aloofness commonly led to the prior becoming responsible for the routine administration, and this was undoubtedly a principal cause of the laxity among individual monks so much condemned in the Visitation *acta* of the time.[90]

This enforced isolation of the abbot both from the Congregation and his own community reached its most extreme form under Rokeby's successor, Maurus Heatley(1762-1802). We have already noticed Heatley's autocratic temperament, and he must be blamed for an unusual feature at Lambspring during the 1780s: the large exodus of novices who had suffered from Heatley's high-handed rule and were condemned to live 'like Dogs' on account of his economic stringency.[91] There were also, however, strong negative pressures increasing the distance between Lambspring and the rest of the Congregation from the beginning of Heatley's abbacy. From the late 1760s, the French government had insisted on interfering in the administration of monasteries on French soil, and the English houses were not excepted from this, being forced, for instance, to centralise their studies and novitiate and to reformulate their Constitutions. Lambspring again dissented from this new unity scheme, continuing to send its theologians to Fulda rather than the French theological faculties, and only grudgingly accepted the new Constitutions as long as they were shorn of all French interpolations. Heatley had taken the customary oaths of loyalty to the Congregation at his installation and had, quite unusually for an abbot of Lambspring, attended General Chapters between 1765 and 1773. From 1777, however, he returned to the use of Chapter deputies, became increasingly suspicious of the French government after the suppression of the Jesuits in 1773, and virtually ceased corresponding with the President.[92] In the face of Visitations insisting on a greater Congregational unity, Heatley warned that such moves would jeopardise Lambspring's position before the Josephist imperial authorities who were jealous 'of Exemptions & all foreign jurisdiction' in their territories. By this time, Heatley who was leader of the largest community among the English monks, was negotiating with Provincials independently of the President in regard to sending Lambspring monks onto the mission, even though these still required Presidential consent.[93] As the French houses went into decline in the two decades before the Revolution, Heatley became confident that not only would Lambspring become 'the principal supply to the Mission', but would be the only monastery to survive. He could afford to be curt with the President:

> ...I cannot say yt I have hitherto had any experience of yr. Inclination to satisfy me in anything. I have been near 30 years Abbot, under great difficulties of all sorts, in ye worst times, but by God's special help, restored all things into good condition & flourishing state. In all appearance, Lambspring will shortly be ye only surviving Monastry of English Benedictine Monks. We suppose a pension allotted each till death rubbs all out.[94]

Without doubt, the French Revolution strengthened Heatley's case enormously. The refusal of the revolutionary government to recognise religious orders gave him an opportunity to delay the 1791 Visitation. The President and other superiors were by now fully aware of Heatley's intended secession; not only were they made suspicious by Heatley's formal requests for professions etc. failing to arrive for the President's approval, but they had inside information about a 'cabal' in Lambspring working for this division. Provincial Warmoll roundly condemned the abbot in 1792:

> His mitre makes him a great man; perhaps his Reverence forgets that he has a superior. His Predecessors were never very plyable, but I think this Gentleman mounts a step higher... I fear union is gone from among us; this evil seems general...Circumspection becomes necessary, or from party spirit we shall be a ruined Body.[95]

Heatley was to cling to his own and Lambspring's independence until his death in 1802.[96]

From what we have already seen of Lambspring, the relationship of each of the monasteries to their local society and local church was a crucial influence on their particular development, as well as a force dividing them more and more from the pattern and rhythm of life in the Provinces on the English Mission. This divergence was a well-defined feature of eighteenth-century English Benedictinism, especially in the light of different European governments renewing their efforts to interfere in ecclesiastical forms and institutions. The houses in France were to find themselves particularly at risk. Up until the mid-eighteenth century, the interference of civil government had been generally benign and it had treated the English Benedictines in France not as foreign exiles but as naturalised subjects, sharing the same rights as French religious. From the 1760s, however, in common with other regulars, the English monks were forced by government pressure to reform themselves, a process which threw up all sorts of attendant difficulties. Pressure came again with the ecclesiastical policies of the Revolutionary government in the 1790s which ultimately left the English monks stranded.

None of the houses was without financial worries during the century, and their economic fragility and dependence increased their vulnerability to control by civil government. This was most obvious in the case of St. Edmund's, Paris, which supported itself on the proceeds from some fourteen French benefices accumulated mainly at the end of the seventeenth century. Since these might be held by missioners, it became a constant problem for this monastery to obtain its portion from the missionary benefice holder. In general, the right of collation remained with some of the greater French Benedictine abbeys like Cluny and Marmoutier, but St. Edmund's was able to provide a stream of graduate monks to fill the titular offices.[97] The priory at La Celle, near Meaux, was fully absorbed into St. Edmund's, Paris, during the seventeenth century. Its 'mensa conventualis' was bestowed on the community, its 'mensa prioralis' on the Society of Foreign Missions in Paris. La Celle usually had four monks from Paris resident. It possessed its own customary, was a centre for pilgrimage, and the local fair and had a confraternity attached.[98] The financial constraints which affected St. Edmund's following the losses sustained in the 1720 crash prompted the house to secure more benefices during the next two decades.[99] The overnight transformation in wealth from a puny mission salary to the large income attached to a grand benefice made an ex-missioner like Wilfrid Helme breathless:

33

Alm. God had already (rewarded me) in this world by a good benefice Fallen to me, wh. will be at least £300 sterling to me; and if the French monks and I can agree about their pensions etc., it will be a good £500 a year, all deductions &c. made; especially if I was to live there for some time, there being vast Royalties, petit Rents, as well as Posts of Judge of life and death, as well as law suits, subjudge, Attorney Notary, Major, all my naming etc. So, My Dear Friend sees I am a great Lord, and what increases the benefit of it is that I can leave it to any Br(other) when I please.[100]

Benefices held by English monks were, unfortunately, subject to all the wearisome litigation accompanying such property. They caused quarrels with the locals, and monastic Procurators found themselves continually travelling around the country to install new titular priors.[101] They were essential, however, to the monastery's budget.[102] The reforms emanating from the *Commission des Réguliers* in the late 1760s were a mixed blessing for St. Edmund's in this respect. On one hand, they promoted streamlining by encouraging communities to have their benefices attached to a house rather than an individual, but, on the other hand, they fostered a general criticism of the benefice system and recommended that monks holding benefices ought to be subject to the local bishop. The English monks were convinced the Commission looked upon them as foreigners, despite any guarantees given. 'Strangers', Gregory Sharrock in Douai had heard his local bishop exclaim, 'could not expect such favours to the prejudice of the natives'. Another bishop was delighted to exploit the rumour of drunkenness among the residents at La Celle, and stories of such scandals were spread about up to the time when the Revolutionary government secularised the property.[103]

Although the monasteries at Douai and Dieulouard had, in the course of the century, been granted the same privileges regarding benefices as Paris, they made little use of them.[104] Nevertheless, a President like Thomas Southcott (1721-41), as a Francophile, had fully supported the system. He successfully petitioned to be chosen as Abbot *in commendam* of Villeneuve, near Avignon, and constantly endeavoured to collect similar favours for his brethren and allies.[105] His action here is another example of the degree of assimilation of the Congregation to the Gallican church in the eighteenth century. Lambspring, with its large landed estate and innumerable feudal rights and jurisdictions, was totally immersed in the economic order of the *ancien régime*. Its manuscript history, listing its wealth and property, had been drawn up by the monk John Townson in 1692 in order to define its patrimony and secure it against future depredation. This work showed the abbey had over 500 acres under its direct cultivation, that it owned some 3500 acres of woodland and possessed extensive fishponds. The monastery employed about one hundred workmen on its own estate, and owned numerous parcels of land scattered over some twenty villages on which tithes and various rents were levied. Lambspring, however, did not escape debt, especially after Abbot Rokeby's ambitious building schemes. His successor, Abbot Heatley, only managed to balance the books by accounting for every penny, which gave him a reputation for miserliness.[106]

On top of landed wealth, all the monasteries relied on the generosity of English friends and benefactors to provide economic security and annuities for conventuals. St. Gregory's was notable for the number of such bequests and was undoubtedly helped by the fame of its school. This house administered some property in England and in the town of Douai, and ran a farm at Esquerchin. The two main sources of its revenue were its landed property and the rents it took from its tenants. In addition, gifts tended to be elicited by the house in hard times; for instance, the community asked for English aid at the beginning of the century whilst suffering 'the pressing calamities because of war in their neighbourhood'.[107] It was largely on the fact of St. Gregory's financial dependence on English support that the community based its appeal for exemption from the Royal Edict of 1768 which sought to reform the religious life. The petition here clearly showed that in comparison with funds coming from England, income from French sources was very small.[108]

For Dieulouard, such help from England appears to have been even more vital than it was for Douai, for Dieulouard was the smallest and least secure of all the houses. It relied heavily on the *spolia* of dead missioners professed for the house and was a constant borrower of money from the St. Malo Fund, the Congregation's central fund, administered by the President from Paris, where St. Edmund's acted as financial agent for a number of English communities' investments in the capital. After the disastrous fire in 1717, the General Chapter had made Dieulouard's restoration a priority and the President transferred quotas of money due to himself to aid the restoration. This monastery's dependence on its large brewery frequently made it susceptible to distress after poor harvests.[109] By the end of the century,

Dieulouard was struggling, its superiors unable to reduce a mountain of debt. This helped to create factions within the community; some realised that the debts could not be blamed on the prior, others condemned his maladministration. The 1789 General Chapter refused to approve Dieulouard's accounts, calling them 'obscure', and determined to change the prior. The plight of the community, enhanced by its interrelated social and economic problems, is well brought out by a veteran missioner who returned to Dieulouard in 1788:

> ...a turbulent 2d superior, disappointed and discountenanced at his being removed from Office, for which he was no ways qualified, is now setting up himself as the head of a Party of unthinking and inexperienced youth, to be a thorn in his superior's side...I found things wonderfully altered at my return: an immense load of debt, and no credit even for a Piece of Beef at the Butcher's, not discharged for almost 2 years, the Bills of other Tradesmen much the same, and Creditors clamouring every day for payment...'.[110]

Dieulouard thus prepared to face the effects of the French Revolution in this desperate state.

Besides these four monasteries of monks, one should not forget the English Benedictine presence in Rome where the *Procurator in Curia,* who administered the Congregation's business with the papal and Jacobite courts, lived in the *Collegium Gregorianum de Urbe* in Trastevere. Originally a house of studies for foreigners, this large residence was let out to tenants during the eighteenth century and accommodated the occasional youth whom the Procurator tutored.[111] The building's maintenance was always a heavy burden for the Congregation and by the end of the century it was very delapidated. The Roman Procurator was paid from the St. Malo Fund also, and he supplemented his annuity by selling in a nearby coffee house the lemons grown in his two large gardens. All attempts by the Procurator to gain financial assistance from Monte Cassino, the building's original owner, failed.[112] Fortunately Placid Waters, Procurator from 1777 until his death in 1808, was continually bailed out by his confidante, the Duchess of Albany, and by other Jacobite benefactors.[113]

As we shall see later, the Roman Procurator was deeply enmeshed in the cosmopolitan society of the city. It was less easy for the communities in France and Germany to forget they were in the last resort foreign exiles there. When the civil power threatened their independence, they tended to affirm publicly their exiled status in order to secure exemption, but generally the advantages of being part of the local church gave them tremendous benefits. We have already observed how in France the civil power had given the English monasteries the full privileges of the French Benedictines, which allowed them to participate, for instance, in the benefice system. In France, the civil power could also be called on to implement a superior's directives, which helps to explain why superiors were so keen to have the disobedient returned to France from the mission. In 1707, soldiers, acting on behalf of the prior, dramatically burst into the refectory at St. Edmund's and carted off two young rebellious monks to the Bastille. The prior had been 'wearied off his legs trying to get the two monks out'. In 1721, the President used letters patent to eject forcibly a prior of Dieulouard who had 'laughed at his censures'.[114] In the early 1770s, a monk of St. Gregory's was detained in a *maison de force* at Armentières after fits and bouts of anger following a consuming infatuation for another monk. In his loathsome confinement he was scandalised by the behaviour of the libertines and debtors and, being freed, took refuge at Lambspring.[115] At the same time, the prior of St. Edmund's had incarcerated the insane Bernard Nechills through a *lettre de cachet*. Nechills' petitions to be freed from the 'nasty stinking pestiferous prison' and be allowed to go on the mission, went unheard by the President. He remained in his misery at St. Venants's: *Sodom est comme dans ce lieu d'abominations*.[116]

Such recognition of the English monks by the civil government encouraged the houses to play their full share in the life of the local church, and this had many aspects which will be dealt with elsewhere. The contrast, certainly at the beginning of the century, between the retired life of the mission and the ebullience of continental Catholicism must have struck any missioner. There were however, points of convergence between the two; English visitors to, and residents in, the monasteries helped to keep conventuals' eyes open to the apostolate on the mission. There was also a degree of fraternisation between the various English religious institutions exiled on the continent.[117] Unlike the three houses in France, Lambspring found itself inside a predominantly non-Catholic area. Its conventuals, then, might have already served a missionary apprenticeship before leaving for England:

> You have it here in your power to preach by your exemplary lives
> to the heterodox people among whom you live, and I doubt not but

37

that many, touched at your Christian and religious behaviour might, God assisting, be brought back to the sheepfold of Christ...But beware of giving bad example; it infallably *(sic)* tends to fortify the minds of protestants in their errors, and to make weak Catholics to abandon their faith'.[118]

Recognition accorded by the authorities to the English houses might, of course, be a mixed blessing. On one hand, the English monks were identified and had cordial relations with others Benedictines. The Maurists and Cluniacs in Paris joined up with St. Edmund's on important liturgical occasions, and the English monks participated in the corporate liturgy of the capital by joining the frequent processions and allowing their chapel to be used as a stational church. Dieulouard was, for its part, friendly with neighbouring Vannists, some of whose students the community welcomed, and we have already noticed the dependence of St.Gregory's, Douai, on the abbey of St. Vedast in Arras.[119] On the other hand, however, the English Benedictines found themselves inevitably held in a web of interlocked and sometimes opposed jurisdictions which caused those long drawn-out disputes over rights and privileges so endemic in the church of the *ancien régime.* In most cases conflict between the English Benedictines and the local clergy arose because the latter objected to the monks usurping their rights over their congregations, particularly those rights of the parochial clergy allowing them to anoint the sick and bury the dead.[120] When the Jacobite Francis Stafford died at St. Edmund's in 1700,

the parish, jealous of this prerogative, took his Body from ye door here and carried it to ye Parish Church where they did duty to it, and yn brought it back hither again, and we buried him in our burying place.

In later years, St. Edmund's took great pains not to offend French susceptibilities in this matter.[121] In 1720, the Bishop of Arras contested the Douai monks' right not only to bury their students and servants but also to hear the confessions of these and to give them the viaticum. The monks' reply to this pointed out their privileges incorporated in such bulls as *Plantata*, and by 1723, they had won their case.[122] This was precisely the precedent used twenty years later at Dieulouard. This house had a history of poor relations with the local priest. There had been a series of early disputes over the Blessed Sacrament procession, and in 1751 relations were bad again, this time over the payment of tithe. Maurus Coupe, a monk of the house, advised the prior on the extent of his jurisdiction and his liability to the payment of tithe. Coupe was:

> much in the spleen about the Curate's behaviour, [for] in these miserable times, when everyone is trying to get what he can from the Regulars, and for the most part succeeds, they must have a double right to maintain what is due to them.

His concluding advice was typical of the discretion monks were forced to exercise by this time:

> According to the sentiment of both of lawyers and of the Maurist monks, you would do well to hush up matters as well as you can with Mr. Simon (the Curate), whom I almost wish at ye D-l.[123]

The general conflict between the monks and the local clergy stretched as far as the question of ordination and enclosure. In 1709, for instance, the Archbishop of Paris had refused to ordain a Lambspring monk studying at Paris because he had received minor orders from the Abbot of Lambspring.[124] In the mid-eighteenth century, the Prior of Dieulouard had had his faculties withdrawn by the local bishop for disobeying the latter's prohibition against introducing women into the monastery. Of all the houses, St. Gregory's at Douai found it almost impossible to wriggle out of the obligations to which it was subject by reason of the terms of foundation. Thus, its early patron, the abbey of St. Vedast in Arras possessed the powers of vetoing the choice of priors-elect, of determining the form of its choral office, and of being ultimately responsible for part of its buildings. As the century progressed and numbers at St. Gregory's declined, the community increased its demand for some mitigation of these duties.[125]

Despite the degree of acculturation to which the monasteries were progressively subject in the eighteenth century and their outward demonstrations of conformity to and co-operation with the demands made on native religious, there always remained some aloofness among the English Benedictines, and an insistence on the unique status of their Congregation. Relations between the monasteries and local society and church are hardly ever touched on in the English monks' extant correspondence with each other. What is constantly mentioned here is merely the details of daily administration like the collection of tithes, the payment of *décimes*, and the bringing of legal suits. If the monasteries themselves had the benefits deriving from 'naturalisation', they sheltered communities which were rarely stable, for the movement to and from England was always present. Missioners' suspicion of politicians and politics in England might easily overflow into the continental setting of the monasteries, despite the guaranteed protection of a supposedly sympathetic government. Thus in France, acceptance of government involvement in the Congregation's affairs was often only grudgingly given because it so often damaged the English mission, especially when the two countries were unfriendly to each other.[126] Since the English Benedictines tended to insist on different treatment by the civil authorities from that accorded to other monastic Congregations, they were consequently less sure than other monks in France about committing themselves to the tightening grip of the government over ecclesiastical affairs in the last decades before the Revolution. Although initially prepared to co-operate with that government, they very quickly found themselves facing, with an increasing sense of foreboding, events over which they had no control.

Prior Henry Parker
(1752–1817)

Dom Charles Smythe
(1727–1780)

CHAPTER III

THE MISSION   1689-1794.

The Management of the Mission.

The *raison d'être* of the monasteries was the English mission, where the apostolic work of Benedictine missioners helped to keep Catholicism alive. Although there were always more monks working on the mission than residing in any one of the monasteries, the mission saw a steady decline in missioners from a peak of nearly eighty at the beginning of the eighteenth century down to between forty and fifty in the early 1790s.[127] A sudden contraction of numbers of missioners after the 1688-1689 Revolution had been reversed by the mid-1690s, when missioners had felt it safe to return to England. These returning exiles, coupled with the large numbers of monks who had been professed in the 1680s and who were moving on to the mission in the next decade, help to explain the high numbers reached in the first decade of the new century. Between 1720 and 1760, however, numbers on the mission went into continuous decline, as missioners aged and went into semi-retirement. Provincial Bolas complained in 1778:

> Many are old and infirm, others long settled in their present residences which they would by no means chuse to quit, nor could they perhaps be so well replaced.[128]

A drift of missioners to the north of England is clearly apparent throughout the century. By the 1790s, there were almost twice as many missions and chaplaincies served by the monks in the north as in the south of England.

The choice of a missioner was primarily a joint decision by the President, a Provincial, and the monk's conventual Superior, although the missioner had also to be acceptable to a patron. A monk arrived on the mission after two years of philosophy, four years of theology, and studies in training in preaching, catechetics and spirituality 'suitable for the mission'. After this, he had two final years debating moral questions and studying scripture. His superiors always ensured that a residence had already been allotted for him.[129] Although the quadriennial General Chapter was the highest executive body of the

41

Congregation, mission strategy was generally decided on in the Provincial Chapters of the North (York) and South (Canterbury) Provinces, meeting separately immediately before the General Chapters. Provincials carried out Visitations of their Provinces every two years, and relied heavily on the *Praepositus*, or local Superior, for information on missioners in each district. From the Provincial would come copies of Chapter minutes, and the Directories which kept isolated missioners in touch with Congregational affairs. He would also be often responsible for the distribution of books, catechisms, and church 'stuff'. For the English Church generally, the 1688 Revolution had put the clock back by dashing all hopes of the establishment of Bishops with full Ordinary jurisdiction. Instead, the English Church returned to the missionary structures it had formed at the beginning of the seventeenth century, with the Regular and secular missioners acting independently of each other, and under different Superiors. The Benedictine Provincials, therefore, remained the key administrators of the Benedictine mission throughout the century. This reversion to earlier forms is clearly seen affecting the monks through the publication of the *Constitutiones Missionis* in 1689, a revision of the 1661 set. These dealt only with the management of the mission.[130] From 1689 also, the Missionary Oath, taken at Profession and obliging a monk to go on the English Mission when asked by the President, appears in the Profession Books for the first time.

The story of the English Benedictine Congregation, and its English Mission, during the eighteenth century is one of a body united only by the thinnest structural thread, for the body was constantly threatened by disintegration at all its different levels. While it remains true that the majority of Benedictine missioners worked harmoniously with their Superiors, the large number of those whose relations, for a wide variety of reasons, were strained, help to throw the eighteenth-century Benedictine mission into relief. Since the President could not call on the civil authorities in England to punish refractory missioners, he could only hope that they might be expelled by their patrons or an excuse might be employed to have them returned to the continent, where he could call on the civil government to punish them. At the lowest level, not all missioners were unduly worried when the lines of commnication were cut between them and their Superiors, provided they continued to be secure in their isolated mission or chaplaincy. Bede Potts, for example, was the acting steward in the 1720s and 1730s for his absent patron, Sir Marmaduke Constable, at Everingham in the East Riding.[131] As Definitor of the Province(1721) and Cathedral Prior of Durham(1733), Potts advised his Provincial regarding choice of missioners for particular patrons. Nevertheless, he strongly objected to giving free board and lodging to transient missioners, and was always extremely reluctant to attend Chapters or to leave Everingham on Congregational business. He used ill-health and the disfavour of his patron as excuses.[132]

This independent spirit of Potts was inherited later by more energetic missioners who, often recently-ordained, came to prefer the freedom of the mission to the more constricted life of a conventual. Reasons for this choice were numerous. They included the desire to avoid the insecurity which threatened the nature of the religious life in France in the late eighteenth century, and the attraction of toleration offered to Catholic clergy and laity in England after the 1778 and 1791 Relief Acts. Finally, there was the encouragement given to young inexperienced monks by Provincials desperate to fill as many lucrative positions as they could in a period when the number of clergy in general was declining steeply. Thomas Welch commented:

> The custom of sending young men into the mission, however necessity may plead for it, is certainly very dangerous. When the passions are most violent, no superiors, no inclosure, no regular and spiritual exercises to retain them, and continual and dangerous objects to foment such passions, it requires a peculiar grace of God and an extraordinary degree of virtue to guard against seductions.[133]

Beyond such practical reasons, lay the support for an individual's freedom and rights which was fostered by contemporary liberalism. Thus, from the 1770s, we have an abundance of material describing attempts by Provincials to cope with ungovernable missioners who adamantly refused to return to their monasteries when ordered to do so. London remained one of the biggest headaches for the Provincial of the South. Here, drifting missioners, 'exotic characters', tended to end up, hoping for a livelihood as chaplain to some wealthy family, and took 'strange liberties' through imbibing 'principles by no means commendable'. The 1785 Chapter of the South Province therefore resolved that London should contain as few missioners as possible,[134] 'for when once fixed (here), it is impossible to remove them, tho' absolutely wanted in a different mission or elsewhere'.[135] Such difficulties for the Provincial ensured ironically that the 1778 Relief

Act was a mixed blessing, because although it gave 'universal toleration', a Provincial could expect no help 'from the Government in favour of their private Laws (i.e. the Constitutions) as they necessarily tend to the taking away the Liberty of the Subject'.[136]

On the one hand, Provincials sought to avoid taking on young missioners who already had a reputation for instability in their monasteries,[137] but, on the other hand, they were eager to lure able conventuals to England:

> D. Harry (Parker) is a regular, well-deserving young man..but I fear he begins to loathe his business and confinement. I am told he wishes much to live in England; probably his asking leave to make an excursion into that country is in a great measure to remain there upon some pretext or other, in which he would be seconded by the Provincials, who would be glad of such an acquisition.[138]

If the Provincials had problems managing awkward missioners, they also had points of conflict with the Presidents, which were usually resolved by each going their separate ways. The Congregation's unity could easily be jeopardised by accident or insensitive policy. Thus, the confusion and lack of direction which crept into the mission following the chaos brought about by the 1688/89 Revolution can be glimpsed in President Bernard Gregson's determination in the 1690s 'to purify the mission'.[139] Gregson had at least experienced life on the mission; some of his successors, notably Thomas Southcott (President 1721-41), found themselves more at home in a continental and conventual setting. Furthermore, a divergence between the interests of the President and those of the mission would doubtlessly have been encouraged by the recommendation of the 1710 General Chapter that the President, if possible, should reside outside England.[140] Such a policy helped to create the Fenwick schism of the 1720s which, in one aspect at least, can be viewed as a contest between conventual and provincial loyalties. However, the greatest degree of harmony between the Provinces and the monasteries was to be achieved later under two Presidents, Placid Howard (1753-66), and Placid Naylor (1766-72), who became Presidents immediately after their term as Provincial. and who continued to monitor the English mission closely. But this harmony was to be destroyed in the following two decades when the President became fully absorbed in efforts to reach a compromise with the

French government over the Congregation's continued presence in France. Inevitably, this forced him to neglect the mission.

This shelving of the affairs of the mission resulted in the Provincials being left to their own devices to deal, as we shall see, with the 1778 and 1791 Relief Acts and the 1780 Gordon Riots. The tilting of the Congregation's balance towards France is vividly demonstrated in the new Constitutions of 1784, produced at the behest of the French government, in which only minimal recognition is given to the mission. Naturally, missioners felt that the provisos, which the French insisted on before the Constitutions were registered, were a 'disagreeable sharp sting'. In all copies dispatched to England, thanks to pressure from missioners, the French Letters Patent and Parlement enregistration were omitted,[141] so as not to worsen further the strained relations between both countries:

> ...and what a figure *Par ordre de Roy* and some other expressions therein contained have made, after we had solemnly engaged ourselves by an Oath of Allegiance to his B(ritannic) Maj(est)y. We make ourselves entirely dependent on the civil Laws of F(rance), and by this, lay ourselves open to every infamous informer.[142]

This letter betrays the new confidence the missioners were beginning to feel in the British government after the 1778 Relief Act. Anti-French feeling was strong enough among missioners at this time to demand that the 1785 General Chapter should meet in London rather than Douai;[143] ultimately, it met in Douai.

The management of the two Provinces necessarily entailed the need for some financial security, and policies regarding income and investment were other ways in which the Provinces differed from the monasteries. Each of the two Provincial Procurators worked under his Provincial, and administered the *Commune Depositum,* the central fund, which accumulated over a period, and belonged wholly to the Province. This Depositum existed over and beyond the funds established for individual missions, and was also independent of some important funds administered by the President and General Chapter for the benefit of the Congregation as a whole. In times of particular distress, General Chapter was prepared to appeal to Propaganda in Rome for financial aid to maintain the work on the mission. The most important of the central funds was the St. Malo Fund, which

Provincials could use, with the President's consent, to pay missioners' salaries or to meet emergencies.[144] The Provincial was himself entitled to a quota from the Congregation, agreed on by General Chapter, which also met his Provincial expenses, although occasionally his salary might be increased by an annuity from funds sunk in the Province.[145] Provincials and their Procurators often also served as Procurators in England for their monasteries, thereby transferring loans, annuities, rents and school fees to the continent. The Day Book of Thomas Bede Bennet, Procurator of the South Province between 1763 and 1800, bears witness to the Procurator's important function as agent to English Catholic families. Bennet provided a service for the procuring of luxury goods, wine, lottery tickets, as well as despatching newspapers and books to English exiles in France. He thus provided a real social bond between the monks and the families who maintained Benedictine chaplains.[146] There is little doubt that the Fenwick disaster of the 1720s forced the Provinces to overhaul their financial arrangements, and this was successfully accomplished by two very able Provincials, Placid Naylor, Northern Provincial 1741-1766, and Placid Howard, South Provincial 1745-1753. Howard and Naylor were to maintain their financial interest in the Provinces after becoming President, in 1753 and 1766 respectively.[147] Two later Provincial Procurators, Oswald Eaves in the North (1773-1793), and Bede Bennet in the South (1761-1800), consolidated their predecessors' work.[148]

Much of the *Commune Depositum* was formed from the *spolia* of deceased missioners, who were required to leave at least £50 to the Province before the residue was taken by their monasteries. Various gifts and rents, besides interest, helped to increase the *Commune Depositum*, which was invested in the Paris 'Town house' or Hôtel de Ville, which issued municipal shares, various English bonds, and on the security of a number of English Catholic Benedictine lay patrons. Money was disbursed from it to pay annuities, salaries, to maintain sick and poor missioners, and for travel expenses. Bede Potts, once Procurator of Lambspring, and steward at Everingham in the 1730s and 1740s, had been Procurator of the North Province in 1717. On occasion, his fear of highwaymen made him travel with a bodyguard when he had the cash of the *Commune Depositum* on his person.[149]

The eighteenth century saw an important development in the use of this *Commune Depositum*, since it became customary for mission funds, established by the laity, to be sunk directly in the Province, rather than be attached to a particular mission, as had been the earlier tradition. Not only did this give the Provincial a greater degree of financial flexibility, but it allowed the Provinces to survive the gradual disappearance of patrons willing to establish specific mission funds. Thus, the North Province in particular, had as a result, enough resources to embark on the great expansion of urban missions towards the end of the century. In this Province, twenty four funds had been sunk in the Province between 1665 and 1740, but between 1741 and 1764, forty four new funds were established under Provincial Naylor, almost double the number in half the time. Whilst the earliest examples of such funds had come from wealthy Catholic county families, the later ones were built up from small sums given by laity much lower down the social scale. Of the thirty sums accepted from Lancashire in 1745, thirteen were lumped together to create a fund of £146.13.4 which, although still small, was thought adequate. This amalgamation was to become the pattern for the rest of the century, with Catholic gentlemen acting as trustees for such funds. When Placid Naylor retired from the office of Provincial in 1766, the Provincial funds stood at £10482.2.5, with mortgages totalling £1839.5.6. In 1721, the same Province had controlled only £1770, and the subsequent improvement in the balance was largely due to Naylor's efforts. One major effect of the Paris financial crash in 1720, where the Province had lost £2120, was a determination to use lay trustees in England more. Thus by 1760, the Swinburnes of Capheaton were trustees for £2000 of the North Province, to which half-yearly interest was paid by the Capheaton chaplain. In this way, not only did the English mission become less dependent on a continental base and more settled in England, but patrons and chaplains moved closer to each other.[150]

In general, chaplaincies worked well if there was harmony between the three parties: the Provincial, the missioner, and his patron. In some missions, not always urban, no independent patron existed, and the Provincial found himself exercising this office. At Follifoot, in the West Riding, for instance, land had been bought by the Province, and a house and chapel built in 1775. Here, the Provincial appointed the incumbent and acted as trustee for the fund. Follifoot's complete dependence on the Province recommended it as a possible site for a Provincial school in 1778.[151]

Bath, however, was the most developed form of this involvement by the Province. With a lodgings for the use of Catholic gentry attached to the mission at the Bell-tree house, the Bath missioner could have great influence. The mission's prestige was enhanced during the eighteenth century when the Provincial and Benedictine bishops, Laurence York, Charles Walmesley and Gregory Sharrock, resided there. Although secured on lay trustees, the Bell-tree property was expensive to run and the Province was compelled to amalgamate and transfer a variety of Provincial funds to maintain this mission.[152] Bath was thus quite unique in that it was run by the Chapter of the South Province who financed it from the *Commune Depositum*, and insisted on inspecting its accounts at every Chapter.[153]

With its well-heeled congregation and its freedom from the constraints of a patron, Bath was the setting for the most violent and lengthy collision, in the eighteenth century, between a missioner and his Provincial. John Placid Naylor, related to two Presidents, was the incumbent at Bath between 1756 and 1776.[154] In that last year, 'Cardinal Nephew', after unsteady relations with his Superiors and some of his congregation, was transferred to Cheam, as chaplain to Lady Stourton. He took with him a sum approaching £1,800, which he had amassed at Bath. Bede Brewer, his successor at Bath, began enlarging the chapel and renovating the buildings, and so applied to the Provincial for Naylor's money which Brewer believed to belong to the Bath mission.[155] Naylor refused, and the dispute forced the Congregation to take sides. Provincial Warmoll lent his support to Brewer, and condemned Naylor as 'a miser in the strictest sense; perverse, obstinate, outrageous and uncontrollable'. Naylor's obstinacy, however, was encouraged by Dieulouard, his monastery of profession, which hoped for a share in his fortune. Warmoll was himself a Douai monk, and Dieulouard took Naylor's side because it was jealous that St. Gregory's, Douai had exercised an indirect influence over the appointments to Bath for too long. Naylor also had the allegiance of notable members of the Bath congregation, and his patron at Cheam, Lady Stourton.[156] This dispute was still boiling when Brewer's enlarged chapel was destroyed in the Gordon Riots of June 1780. Naylor, on hearing of the disaster, 'seemed to exult and shewed not the least marks of compassion. He is indeed a most unaccountable genius'.[157] Although Naylor was forced by General Chapter to return some of the money, he firmly refused to help to pay for a new chapel in 1785.[158] Provincial Superiors remained apprehensive that Naylor might institute a civil case in law against the Province, and the Court might demand to see all the Provincial papers. The air was cleared when Naylor's ill-health forced him to retire to the Benedictine nuns in Paris, but even from there, he continued to fight all moves to deprive him of his money, until his death in 1795.[159] Naylor's quarrel with the Provincial had lasted some thirty years. It revealed, first, the pre-eminence of Bath in the mind of the Province, and, secondly, the strain a Provincial was subject to in attempting to curb the independence of a missioner who, with his own independent means, also had a strong measure of support among his flock and among his own brethren in monastery and mission. Naylor provides a good illustration of the complex nature of mission finances because his case demonstrated the extent to which Provincial and personal financial management were interlocked.

Despite the occasional problems with monks like Naylor, the general picture of the Provinces' economy in the eighteenth century is one of developing efficiency, spurred on by a need to recover quickly from the Fenwick débâcle of the 1720s. There was a move at the same time by the Provinces, possibly unconscious, to slacken their financial dependence on the monasteries, for as the century progressed, far less Provincial money was invested in the monasteries acting as trustees. Secondly, the Provinces also became less dependent on Catholic lay patrons in England, thanks to the latter's natural decline in number, and because the Provinces increasingly favoured the use of their own consolidated funds built up from small benefactions. These latter were a striking feature of the North Province in the last decades of the century when the Catholic population of northern England was increasing enormously. In the South Province, traditional funds established and controlled by the gentry remained the norm. When Rome issued a rescript in 1782 which allowed the Provinces to reduce masses based on lost or inadequate funds, the South Province, with fewer missions and missioners, had no difficulty in reducing its commitment by half. In the North Province, however, where very many masses had been 'accepted at a low rate in different missions, especially in Lancashire where Catholics were numerous' only very few masses were dropped, since the Provincial feared the fury of the multitude of poorer benefactors in Benedictine congregations.[160]

Any controls which the Provincial might exercise over a missioner were balanced in practice by the financial independence the latter might enjoy. Because of the exigencies of the mission, the *Constitutiones Missionis* allowed each missioner to own his *peculium* and the freedom to make his own will.[161] This, and the fact that a missioner might gain permission to make use of some of his *peculium* even after he had retired to his monastery, sharpened the division between 'missioner' and 'conventual'. The *peculium* was paid to the missioner in the form of an annuity from his family's estate, either directly or through an intermediary like the Provincial. Sometimes, a fortune was sunk into the monastery of profession and an annuity from it paid out.[162] Alternatively, some families protected their sons from an insecure missionary future by investing capital in the monasteries on condition their sons received an annuity if they departed for the mission.[163]

Besides this personal money, the *peculium* was enlarged by a monk's salary paid to him by his patron, and sometimes attached to his person rather than to his mission. This salary might have conditions attached: mass obligations ordered by the donor, the necessity of serving various mass centres at specified times, a set amount to be paid out yearly to the poor of the neighbourhood.[164] Up until the mid-eighteenth century, the commonest salary was twenty pounds yearly, although it might drop to ten pounds, if the missioner had a horse and his 'linen mended'.[165] A missioner's income, then, derived from a variety of sources, and the Provincial had to juggle his resources constantly, giving chaplaincies with low salaries attached to incumbents with high annuities, and vice versa. The problem of inflation during the eighteenth century forced patrons in two directions; either to pay larger salaries, or to supplement the salary with perquisites such as board, lodging, a horse and garden; or to agree to share a missioner among a number of chaplaincies which paid low salaries. Certainly, by the 1780s, sixty pounds *per annum* was believed to be the minimum allowable to a missioner for his salary.[166]

A missioner's control over his own pocket was to be of some help in the development of the mission. Money or property could be specifically transferred to a mission during a missioner's life to protect it from going to his monastery on his death. Such money was then used to fund future missioners, to help a building programme along, or to extend a mission's area.[167] The incidence of such investment became more marked with the rapid growth of the mission in the latter half of the eighteenth century. In 1788, Thomas Welch noted in his diary that 'the Rage of building Chappels continues', and he went on to describe how Maurus Chaplin at Lawkland in the West Riding had begun building a chapel there by himself, without the consent of the Provincial, and without adequate security. Chaplin was forced to flee the country, pursued by enraged workmen.[168] To protect themselves from such embarrassment, the Provinces evolved an elaborate system of checks designed to keep a missioner's financial state under constant surveillance. There was always some uneasiness, mingled with

50

jealousy, when individuals managed to amass fortunes.[169] Constitutionally, the Lenten Poverty Bill, the *Memoriale Paupertatis*, which was sent to the Provincial by each missioner, provided a running check on assets, provided it was accurate. Although the Constitutions only allowed the Province to take fifty pounds from a dead missioner's *spolia*, the residue being sent to his monastery, there were many exceptions to this, and from 1777, a missioner was allowed to decide whether to leave his property to his monastery or to the mission.[170] Usually, however, the Provincial Chapters issued Definitions to control the missioners' personal assets. They ordered a tax on all individuals to cover Provincial needs (1697); they prevented individuals alienating money to the monasteries without permission (1741); they forbade missioners depositing their money with layfolk or making loans to them (1781). Finally, in 1794, General Chapter, learning the lesson of bitter experience, forbade missioners from embarking on building without permission.[171]

Throughout the century, the unity of the Congregation was threatened by the practicalities of missionary life, some of which have been outlined here. Above all else, it was the spectre of the Fenwick Schism of the 1720s, when division actually happened, and which involved disputes over policy, structure and finance, which continued to haunt many Provincials for the next half a century.

The Fenwick Schism 1717-1725.

It will be obvious from the preceding section that the Congregation was always in danger of breaking up in the eighteenth century as a result of internal and external pressures on the monasteries and mission on the one hand, and threats to the authority of the President and by the independence of the individual monk on the other. This danger came closest to realisation in the few years after Laurence Fenwick had been elected President in 1717.[172] The origins of the schism associated with his name ultimately lay in the failure of the Congregation as a whole to solve the issues raised in the aftermath of the Revolution of 1688. For a quarter of a century after 1689, there is evidence of much disorder within the monasteries, vocations tailed off, and attachment to the Jacobite cause made life on the mission hazardous. During much of this period also, both monasteries and mission were steeped in financial chaos and deficient in good leadership. Inevitably, factions

51

arose both in the houses and on the mission, some complementing each other in regard to the solutions they believed necessary to apply, others were poles apart, but all of them pointing to a breakdown in authority. In history, it is often said that the losers pay, and in English Benedictine demonology, Laurence Fenwick is uniformly presented as the unprincipled manipulator who planned the demise of the Congregation for his own selfish ends. The received account shows that it was rescued at the eleventh hour by his successor, Thomas Southcott, President between 1721 and 1741, who was forced upon the Congregation by the orthodox party in alliance with Rome. While there is much truth in this story, the reality, on the evidence available, was more complex. The degree, then, of Fenwick's unscrupulousness requires some adjustment after the wider context has been appreciated.

Difficulties experienced on the mission came into the open in 1717 and formed the prelude to Laurence Fenwick's election to the Presidency in the General Chapter of that summer. In the South Province, a head-on collision between the previous President, Francis Watmough, and the South Provincial, Augustine Howard, took place in the 1717 Provincial Chapter over the election of Scrutators. This caused Howard and his two Scrutators to be deprived of Chapter rights.[173] The fact that six missioners in the South Province had appealed to the President against Howard, who was believed to be manipulating elections, is further proof of factions existing in this Province. In the North Province, it was the same story. Here, the 1717 Provincial Chapter had been dissolved in chaos, and the subsequent General Chapter annulled the elections of that Chapter.

At the 1717 General Chapter, held in London, the factions hardened into definite parties. Here the appeals of Howard, and the two Scrutators, Gregory Riddell and William Pestel, were quashed, together with that of the Prior of Paris, Anthony Turbeville, who was accused of maladministration. These four 'appellants' then refused to resign and determined to appeal to Rome. Meanwhile, Laurence Fenwick, the apparent leader of the other party, was elected President in the 1717 Chapter, and proceeded immediately to embark on his plans to safeguard the unity and stability of the Congregation. A series of Definitions were passed which included an order for missioners to obey a validly elected Provincial, secondly, two General Procurators were appointed to sort out money problems, and, finally, an annalist was chosen to collate all Presidential and capitular *acta*.[174] Fenwick then went on to make a Concordat with the appellants. Evidence of

Fenwick's intention to regulate the Province's finances is seen in the appearance in the South Province Account Book which was begun in 1717.[175]

From the evidence available of events after 1721, it appears that the problems of the period were constantly changing, and that Fenwick and his opposition were forced to shift their ground so as to derive maximum benefit from the changes. Thus, it is highly unlikely that Fenwick, even if he had had a master-plan in his head in 1717 for stifling all opposition to his Presidency, could have predicted accurately the long-term effects of the '15 Rebellion and the financial crises in England and France in 1720 and 1721. It is doubtful furthermore whether he had a clear plan of campaign in 1717 from which he never diverged in later years. If Fenwick is to be portrayed in any positive light, some account needs to be taken of the grave problems which the Congregation was facing in 1717, and which he was called upon to solve. The considerable amount of support he had, at least at the beginning of his Presidency, from a wide spectrum of monks in the houses and on the mission cannot be disregarded. Fenwick's main concern was with the internal unity of the Congregation, for which purpose he accommodated himself to a variety of external developments. In contrast, Southcott, his successor, believed from the start that the Congregation's internal unity must be firmly based on clear policies in regard to the external debate on Jacobitism, Jansenism, and to the monks' relations with the British government and the Vicars Apostolic. It is unlikely that Fenwick's attitudes to any of these had hardened to the same extent by 1717. The clarification, however, of his attitudes to these, when he was President, had the effect of alienating groups from him within the Congregation. This process destroyed all hopes of unity, and ended up with a confrontation between his party and an alliance of the opposition groups, which led to his downfall. It was Southcott who managed to retain the support of this opposition and destroy the last elements of Fenwick's party. Conflicting interests were to be seen in the Congregation a decade before Fenwick's election in 1717. At this time, communications between the monasteries, where the President usually lodged, and the mission had become difficult, as religious persecution in England intensified. Internally, there was a growing disharmony between the aspirations of the Congregation's leaders, and the young newly-professed monks within the monasteries. Almost to a man, English Benedictine Superiors of this time were aggressively Jacobite, many of them having experienced conventual life in the short-lived monastery at St. James's, Whitehall during James II's reign. Naturally, then, their minds were closed to the possibility of any compromise with the British government of George I; instead, they supported numerous Jacobite plots seeking to overthrow it. A more flexible attitude could, therefore, only emerge from monks professed after the Revolution, who saw little hope of a Jacobite restoration, and from those missioners feeling the full brunt of the government's wrath, especially after the '15. It is significant that Fenwick's supporters came mainly from these two interests.

Ultimately, Fenwick's attempts to reduce divisions in the Congregation were fruitless. The picture which emerges between 1717 and 1721 is that of the President alienating both monasteries and mission in a desperate attempt to tighten his grip as a means to unity. In aspiring to establish the Benedictine mission on a firmer political and ecclesiastical base in order to consolidate unity, Fenwick merely succeeded in giving different interests within the Congregation a degree of shared hostility to his leadership. Once his powerful Benedictine opponents had translated his objectives into terms which appeared to favour an English form of episcopal Jansenism and conciliarism, whose side-effect would be the heightening of the influence of the British government over the English Catholic body, Fenwick's cause at Rome was doomed. For, as we shall see, Fenwick, in his opponents' eyes, was an ally of the Vicars Apostolic who were suspected of encouraging Jansenist literature, and of belonging to the 'Hanoverian' party of Bishop John Talbot Stonor and the Abbé Thomas Strickland. This party promoted Anglo-Gallican ideas and desired better relations between English Catholics and the British government.

Soon after his election, Fenwick sent a circular letter to the monasteries, in February 1718, which recommended the transfer of house funds to shore up the bad finances of the Congregation in general. This frightened Douai and Paris, whose houses were solidly Jacobite and resistant to any Benedictine overtures being made to the 'usurper', George I. They sensed that the plan to aid Congregational unity was merely an excuse for Fenwick to deprive them of their money for his own purposes, and both houses protested, despite Fenwick having a following among some of the younger monks at St. Edmund's, Paris.[176] These protests were sent as appeals to Rome, coupled with an appeal from the South Province, attacking the President's meddling there also, for Fenwick tried to prove to

Benedictine patrons that his opponents held invalid faculties since these had not been given by him, as President, to them in writing.[177] The charges brought against Fenwick in these were predictable: manoeuvring his own allies into office, acting despotically, attempting to embezzle funds, and refusing to co-operate fully with the four 'appellants' by sending a 'factum' of his contest with them to Rome. Those missioners who formulated the appeal from the South Province knew exactly how to curry Rome's favour, for in the appeal, they demonstrated their acceptance of the Constitution *Unigenitus*.[178] Rome's current campaign against Jansenism was to be a weapon constantly used by Fenwick's opponents in later stages of the conflict. Fenwick's answer to these appeals was conciliatory, and he continued to hope that Rome, where his Procurator, Benet Lawson, pleaded his case, would acknowledge that his determined purpose was to reunite the Congregation and secure the future of the mission.[179]

At this point, Rome, all for peace, recognised Fenwick's good work and confirmed his policy, but it refused to allow him to change the location of the 1721 General Chapter from Douai to London. Rome here was supporting the line of his opponents who now had a spokesman at Rome themselves, in the person of Gregory Riddell. Riddell aimed to weaken Fenwick's apparent hold on the Roman authorities.[180] For Rome, unity was one thing, but for Fenwick to attempt some settlement with the British government through a London Chapter, as his enemies were suggesting, was another. Therefore, on the 22nd of February 1720, Rome decreed that the Chapter must assemble at Douai. It seems that prior to this instruction, Fenwick had published his own 'Defence' in order to further his cause at Rome. This is an important means of measuring the size of his party in the monasteries, and among the Catholic laity and other Regulars on the mission, who registered their support for him in this 'Defence'.[181] Fenwick then moved on to break the alliance his opponents had formed against him. He struck first at the continental Jacobite base, ordering the Pretender's agent, Thomas Southcott, to move out of St. Edmund's, Paris, and blocking the transfer of Jacobite money collected by Southcott in England.[182] Such actions were designed to staunch the running sore of Jacobitism which helped to divide the Congregation and to further Fenwick's own policy of accommodation. In other areas, he was less successful. St. Gregory's, Douai, refused to have his ally, Anselm Crathorne, as Visitor, and the sides were too polarised for him to bring about unity in an extraordinary Chapter he called in August

1720.[183] During the first half of 1721, the divisions became even more marked, as Fenwick still went ahead in his plans for a London General Chapter. Both sides were culpable of smear campaigns. Fenwick's opponents discovered sins of his youth, among them immorality and peculation, while the President and some thirteen of his party launched violent attacks on their opponents.[184] As the time of the Chapter approached, both sides tried desperately to canvass support, although it seems that Fenwick's hold on the mission was beginning to weaken. The two Provincial Chapters in June 1721 were packed with his opponents. In these, he was blamed for the Provinces' bad financial state, after the loss of investments in Paris after the French financial crisis of 1721. At the Canterbury Chapter, another squabble broke out over rival Scrutators.[185] From this opposition, Fenwick could only drag out a dozen partisans prepared to join him in August at a London General Chapter.

This complex internecine conflict tends to blur the influence of outside issues which made the struggle within the Congregation so desperate. Two of these issues were clearly in evidence by early 1721, which suggests they had played a part in the conflict up until this point. The questions of the Congregation's relationship to the English Vicars Apostolic and to the Jacobite cause were sufficiently influential to destablise the constitution of the Congregation, and were themselves interconnected. They were to cause concern to the Congregation well after Fenwick's fall from power in the summer of 1721.

After the failure of the 'Fifteen Rebellion', Dr. Thomas Strickland and Bishop John Talbot Stonor had headed a group of English Catholics determined to secure some toleration for their body from the British government by recognising the legitimacy of George I. Naturally, their objective brought them into conflict with English Catholic Jacobites.[186] During his Presidency, Fenwick seems to have believed some form of alliance with this party could help him to achieve unity and peace in the English Benedictine mission. However, it had an unacceptable face for Fenwick since Stonor, in particular, intended that ultimately the Vicars Apostolic should have full jurisdiction as Ordinaries over the Regulars in their Districts. This policy would be inaugurated once the measure of toleration had come.[187] Stonor's ideal would cut right across the privileges and exemption enjoyed for a century by Benedictine missioners, and was thus totally unacceptable to Fenwick since it would mean the reduction in the authority of the President. It would also disrupt the mission, and show up Fenwick as a weakling, unable to defend traditional Benedictine privileges and unable to grant full faculties to Benedictine missioners. Fenwick's attitude, then, was ambivalent; a champion of Benedictine exemption on one hand, he was, on the other, prepared to join with Strickland and Stonor, and 'to tamper' with the government so as to increase his Presidential power at this moment. He believed that the government could be used to forestall the Douai General Chapter by refusing to allow Chapter fathers on the mission to travel abroad.[188] In the London District, Bishop Bonaventure Giffard feared that Rome's order regarding the Douai Chapter could easily lead to open rebellion among Fenwick's party, and even cause the latter 'to stirre up the secular power' against Giffard himself.[189]

In August, therefore, two Chapters met, one at Douai, and a Robber Chapter at London. Fenwick still had support on the Continent, especially at Dieulouard and Lambspring, and envoys from these attempted to register protests at the Douai Chapter.[190] Predictably, the Definitions passed at Douai vindicated those whom Fenwick was supposed to have oppressed, and connived at the weakening of the Presidential authority, which Fenwick had seen as the main instrument in the restoration of Congregational unity. At this Chapter, Fenwick's party was put under censure until it submitted, and in the person of Thomas Southcott, Fenwick's elected successor, victory was gained by those parties in the Congregation supporting Jacobitism, conventual independence and an English Catholicism heavily dependent on the Continent.[191]

During the years after 1721, Southcott was faced with a schism on the English mission, where Fenwick's party was strongest, still believing that his policies were the most suitable to their circumstances. Southcott only very slowly managed to regain such dissidents. By August 1723, all Fenwick's 'officials' had submitted, and only six of his party remained at large, maintaining themselves on funds acquired by Fenwick.[192] One striking feature of the schism was the number of those who apostatised. The 1720s was one of the worst periods for apostasy among monks during the eighteenth century.[193] In an obvious sense, some of these apostates were surely the sad consequence of Fenwick's policy of seeking a compromise with the civil government, through his alliance with Strickland and Stonor. Laurence Anderton, a Fenwick partisan and professed monk of Dieulouard, contributed financially to Fenwick's campaign out of a large estate in Lancashire he had inherited at this time. The disruption of 1721 undoubtedly made his apostasy easier three years later, when he took the Oath to George I and conformed to Anglicanism in order to secure his estate. Anderton's action should be compared with that of John Savage, a secular priest, who in 1712 also took the Oath of Allegiance in order to inherit an estate and the title of the 5th Earl Rivers. Significantly, Savage was brought to abjure his oath through the persistent pressure put on him by the monk Thomas Southcott, then a young missioner, but who was here already demonstrating his abhorrence of making any compromise with the Hanoverian government.[194]

Anderton's determination to become a baronet in order to gain entry into respectable English society was a more extreme move than that taken by other followers of Fenwick. Among these was Gilbert Knowles, a bookish scholar, whose friendship with some of the greatest English antiquarians and churchmen of the day, is described elsewhere. Knowles, once Fenwick's secretary, became so disillusioned by the controversy and 'the hard usage he hath met with (as he speaks) *a falsis fratribus'*, that he also seriously contemplated apostasy. His vocation and his Catholicism were only saved by his health deteriorating, which forced him back to Douai in 1724. Up until that point, he was actively making a literary career for himself in the upper ranks of English society, and continuing to champion George I even after he had submitted to the 'orthodox' party in the Fenwick Schism. Another apostate, William Denis Hudleston, a Lambspring monk, supported Fenwick more from principle than expediency.[195] His works, published after he had become an Anglican minister, provide us with vital clues which help us to understand the attraction Fenwick had for some monks.[196] Hudleston presents a bizarre spectacle, as an apostate monk turned Anglican minister who, half a dozen years after these events, was still fighting the worsted battles of his past. In these, Fenwick's overtures to the government favourably compare with Hudleston's own clearly-outlined Anglo-Gallicanism and his minimising of papal authority in England.[197] Hudleston's bitter attack on Catholicism was a reply to Rome's manifest injustice to Fenwick, for Rome had reneged on its word, and through bribery and Jacobite pressure, forbidden Fenwick's London Chapter invalidly, so Hudleston would have it. Rome's double-crossing and Fenwick's injured integrity were frequent themes among his party:

A Remonstrance was made to His Holiness upon this (Decree), but numbers of Gold Watches and presents that were sent from London to Rome, made the infallible Chair inflexible. And so the Pope's Bulls, the Plantata of Urban VIII, granted 1633, and the Brief of Paul V, given to the same Body of Men, 1619, were triumphed over by the Congregation of Cardinals.[198]

Hudleston's Anglo-Gallicanism was related to some important theological discusssions of the day, for these were the years in which William Wake, Archbishop of Canterbury and correspondent of Gilbert Knowles, and Gallican theologians in France, such as Dr. Piers de Girardin, were seriously discussing schemes of unity between the Gallican and Anglican Churches, and the mutual recognition of each other's Orders.[199] Inevitably, Fenwick's successor, Thomas Southcott, would be opposed to such dialogue. He continued to be actively engaged in the field of converting Anglicans to Catholicism, believing members of the Church of England would be attracted to Catholicism through his friend the Chevalier Ramsay's *Life of Fénelon*.[200] On Anglo-Gallicanism, he could only be uncompromising: his theological attitude to it was inevitably coloured by his Jacobitism. He was thus easily led into believing that the 'conversations' between the two Churches had been engineered for the political benefit of the Whigs who aimed at isolating English Jacobites and depriving them of French support.[201]

Some English Catholics thought the Gallican de Girardin was pursuing the same calculated political goals as Thomas Strickland[202] and it was certainly the political aspirations of Stonor and Strickland which appealed to Fenwick. Like them, he was prepared to seek more toleration for English Catholics, even if it meant recognising the legitimacy of George I. When Fenwick and Stonor did fall out with each other, it was over the latter's attempts to increase the control of the Vicars Apostolic over the monks on the mission. As his involvement in the disputes of the 1740s was to show, Stonor was never happy with the exemption of Regulars.[203] Southcott, however, was shrewder than Fenwick in realising that if the Benedictines could not persuade Rome of the rightness of their cause through employing traditional arguments for exemption, they might be able to turn Rome's ear by the mention of Jansenism. Southcott was thus determined to exploit the accusation of 'episcopal Jansenism' levelled at the English Vicars Apostolic, who were believed to be sympathetic to Jansenism by disseminating Jansenist books, and interested, it was said, in bringing Gallicanism into alliance with Jansenism. Thus, in the years after 1721, points of conflict in the Fenwick Schism moved away from internal issues towards the broader question of the Benedictines' place within the English Catholic Church, and, indeed, the relationship of that Church to Rome itself. For Fenwick and Southcott were both united in their concern to preserve the privileged status of the monks on the mission, and their allegiance to Rome.[204] They were opposed to each other over the degree of support to be given to Jacobitism or to the English government. Whereas Fenwick floundered in trying to balance internal and external interests, Southcott adopted a simple solution and clear principles from the time he was elected. He sensed that Rome would never weaken the monks' missionary independence and the availability of their direct recourse to Rome in favour of increasing the powers of the Vicars Apostolic if these latter were ever suspected of Jansenism. He therefore took great pains to incriminate the Vicars Apostolic and their clergy by linking Jansenism with Gallicanism, and hinting at the secular clergy's adherence to the usurper George. Evidence that both Stonor and Strickland were Imperial agents, and therefore disloyal to Rome, supported the damning picture Southcott was able to paint.[205] The irony of Southcott's policy here is that, during the Jansenist crisis in the first twenty years of the century, the English secular clergy with Jansenist sympathies had identified Southcott as one of themselves because of his collaboration in translating Quesnel's *Réflexions*, a role Southcott consistently denied. It was essential that Southcott used all this evidence, not only to preserve Benedictine missionary autonomy, but also to project himself to the Benedictine missioners as their champion, rather than Fenwick.[206]

Both these aims would be satisfied, in Southcott's eyes, by having Rome appoint at least one, hopefully two, Benedictine Vicars Apostolic. After 1721, therefore, Southcott used diplomacy to further this goal, while the Vicars Apostolic themselves, desperate to keep their number free of a monk, sought to divide allegiance to Southcott on the mission by actively favouring dissidents belonging to Fenwick's party. A Benedictine Vicar Apostolic, Southcott felt, would prevent the Schism being allowed to continue through such underhand methods.[207] Southcott was himself suggested as a likely candidate, but a vacancy in 1727 was filled by a Dominican, Thomas Dominic Williams, an ally of the monks. It was not until 1741 that a monk, Laurence York, joined the Vicars Apostolic, as coadjutor in the Western District.[208]

To some extent, Williams was a compromise candidate, for the Vicars Apostolic had managed to keep up a strong campaign at Rome against a monk through their agent Laurence Mayes. Nevertheless, Southcott's reputation stood extremely high in continental diplomatic circles. If he had failed in one objective, a Benedictine Bishop, he succeeded in another, that of the preservation of Benedictine autonomy on the mission, which inevitably enhanced his own standing within the Congregation. Compared with Southcott's, Fenwick's reservoirs of influence and his access to circles of political power hardly existed. Southcott was able to place the Fenwick Schism, and its related problems of episcopal appointment and relations with the British government, in the context of European, and more particularly, Jacobite diplomacy. For Southcott, already an accredited Jacobite agent, was not hestitant in appointing himself as the chief spokesman for English Catholic affairs on the Continent.

If an Oath of Allegiance was abhorrent to Southcott as a Jacobite, he nevertheless needed to produce an alternative which would reduce the British government's antipathy to the English Catholic body, and prove his ability as a statesman. This he attempted by indirect means, through diplomatic channels with which he was familiar. He urged England's continental Catholic allies, notably France, to put pressure on George I's government. The best example of this unsuccessful strategy lies in Southcott's attempt to prevent Walpole's government exacting a levy of £100,000 on English papists in 1723. In his frequent correspondence with the papal and Jacobite Courts, Southcott was able to combine his own specific Benedictine requests with a well-informed concern for the general welfare of the English Catholics. He appreciated that these were already hard pressed by double land taxes, forfeiture of estates after the '15, and now, the threat of a huge levy following the discovery of persistent Jacobite activity. Unless this pressure was removed or reduced, Jacobitism, and indeed Catholicism, would wilt in England.[209] By acting as mediator between the French Regent, Cardinals Dubois and Fleury, on one hand, and Catholic nobility, on the other, some of whom were his relatives, Southcott prompted the French to persuade Walpole, the new Prime Minister, not only to substitute a levy in 1723 for a proposed forfeiture of more estates, but also to reduce the amount to be levied.[210] Southcott's diplomatic correspondence was couched deliberately in apocalyptic language, predicting the sad end of English Catholicism, 'the daughter of Zion', unless the Pope encouraged France and other European Catholic powers to embark on a joint crusade to save her. For Southcott knew that their involvement was dependent on his convincing them that it was more of a religious than a political persecution in England. The Bill ordering the levy became law in May 1723, without much oppostion from Catholic Europe, apparently unmoved by Southcott's exaggerated and unrealistic pleas. But Southcott continued his diplomatic efforts 'to obtain some protection from the severity of the Laws that in twenty years time must of course drive us all out of the country'.[211]

Both Fenwick and Southcott survived until the 1740s, the former dying discredited in 1746,[212] the latter following him in 1748, and reckoned to be a saint.[213] There was no doubt that the Congregation was aware of the seriousness of the Fenwick Schism. Over sixty years later, a Provincial was determined to avoid a similar disruption by objecting to a General Chapter meeting in 1784:

> composed of young men, unacquainted with the Congregation business, and perhaps party in influence. The case has happened; the schism in Mr. Fenwick's time should place us on our guard. The Congregation to this day feels the ill Effects of those inconsiderate and unwarrantable proceedings.[214]

If the Schism itself was healed, Southcott cannot be said to have adopted a policy which was progressive enough to have markedly changed the two major problems involved in the controversy. Given his Jacobite stance, no positive overtures to the British government could have come from Southcott to help in establishing a new *modus vivendi* between the government and his missioner monks, or the English Catholic body in general. He contributed to the barrenness of the two decades between 1725 and 1745. Secondly, Southcott succeeded in driving further apart the Vicars Apostolic and the Benedictine missioners. The old conflict ground on through the 1730s,[215] and, despite the success of having Laurence York appointed as Vicar Apostolic in 1741, the monks were reluctant to adjust to changing attitudes on the English mission. They therefore had no new arguments ready for the renewal of the conflict in the late 1740s, and were unable to produce any forceful answer to the Bull *Apostolicum*

Ministerium of 1753, which finally subjected them to the authority of the Vicars Apostolic.

It can be argued, then, that although the conclusion of the Fenwick Schism is usually reckoned to be a victory for the Orthodox party, it was also a triumph for the forces of reaction. Twenty further years under Southcott meant a continued dominance of Jacobitism, which helped to pull the Congregation away from interest in the English mission towards the security of its Continental base. The Congregation in these years began to adapt itself increasingly to habits of French monasticism in particular. As the mission withered - missioners were at their lowest for the entire century in Southcott's time (forty three in 1742) - Southcott made it his deliberate policy to have his monks in France naturalised, and to see they were provided with benefices. He himself became Abbot *in commendam* of Villanova (Villeneuve, near Avignon) in 1729.[216] The dangers here of too close a liaison with the French would become apparent only in the 1760s, when the government intervened to reform the monastic orders in France, the English Benedictines included. It was then time, ironically, for the English Benedictines to begin to emphasise again their primary role as missioners in England, and their status as mere exiles in France.

Monks and Bishops.

The Fenwick controversy brought into the open two contentious issues in which the English Benedictines had long been immersed, and which were to absorb their energy for much of the eighteenth century. These two, Jacobitism and the relationship between monks and the English Bishops, or Vicars Apostolic, underlay the specific points at issue in the Fenwick affair, and partly explain why it achieved such notoriety. Although called 'Bishops', Vicars Apostolic possessed neither a Chapter nor full Ordinary jurisdiction, and were, as delegates, dependent on Rome for their authority.[217] Thus, a missionary church, lacking the full jurisdiction of Bishops-in-Ordinary, could be a battlefield of rival missionary secular and regular clergy, each with their own separate and conflicting jurisdictions. This had been the case in England in the formative years of the early seventeenth century, and when the Vicar Apostolic, Bishop Richard Smith, had claimed full Ordinary powers in 1626 and attempted to subject the regular clergy to his authority, he had forced them to clarify their own missionary status, its exemption and its privileges.[218]

In the face of Smith's pretensions, the Benedictines had produced two statements in their defence, Rudesind Barlow's *Epistolae R.A.P. Praesidis* (Douai 1628), sometimes called the *Mandatum*, and the Bull of Urban VIII, called *Plantata* (1633), which gave total support to the monks' privileges on the mission.[219] Such missionary privileges were based on the monks' claim to have inherited the Chapter rights of the English monastic medieval cathedrals, and, along with these, an Ordinary jurisdiction on the mission. The arguments to back up this extravagant claim were tortuous in the extreme, but from the time of *Plantata*, the monks had gone ahead in appointing Cathedral Priors from among their number to further their claims, especially that of exemption.

This Benedictine exemption was repeatedly contested by the four Vicars Apostolic established in James II's reign. These Vicars were determined to increase their hold on the English Church and to place all regular and secular missioners under their authority. After the Revolution of 1689, the monks translated the old quarrel into new terms, as a contest between the forces of Gallicanism and the defenders of Rome's centralised control and the Stuart cause. Admittedly, the charge of Gallicanism against the Vicars Apostolic and the secular clergy had been used earlier, but the rise of Jacobitism as a potent force dividing the English Church, gave the monks an opportunity to employ it as a handle in their cause at Rome. The conflict was to be prolonged unnecessarily by the vagueness of Rome's rulings on the matter; she continually tried to please both sides. The final word on the affair only came in 1753 with the Bull *Apostolicum Ministerium*, in which Rome came down at last on the side of the Vicars Apostolic, whose jurisdiction the monks were then forced to recognise, sometimes reluctantly. By that time too, Jacobitism was a spent force. In the second half of the eighteenth century, with an increasing Catholic urban population and the transformation of many missions into what were effectively parishes, the monks could hardly ignore the administrative and pastoral role of the Vicars Apostolic. Nevertheless, one can discern at this very time, a curious revival of the old conflict in a different shape. In the 1780s, the monk missioner Cuthbert Wilks became the champion of a new form of Anglo-Gallicanism, later to be called Cisalpinism, which had the support of many leading English Catholics, eager for religious toleration. Wilks's main opponent was

64

the then Vicar Apostolic of the Western District, the Benedictine Charles Walmesley, loyal to Rome and distrustful of any radical compromise, especially in the form of Oaths, being made with the British government as a prelude to toleration. In some respects, then, Wilks was a latter-day Laurence Fenwick. He managed to divide the Benedictine missioners over the question of their political attitudes regarding toleration, but was prepared to go further than Fenwick in the degree of authority within the English Church which he allowed to the Vicars Apostolic. That shift is enough in itself to demonstrate how insuperable the authority of the Vicars Apostolic had become.

A century earlier, in September 1685, the secular priest, John Leyburne, had been appointed Vicar Apostolic, and almost immediately re-opened the conflict by demanding that all regular clergy submit to his authority and seek his approbation to administer the sacraments. Inevitably, the monks retorted with their traditional arguments about exemption and rights. They pointed out that Leyburne was a 'Delegate' rather than an 'Ordinary', and he was forced into accepting their compromise formula that the Benedictine Provincials seek approval from the Vicar Apostolic for all their missioners, rather than the latter approaching the Bishop individually. Leyburne fell into the monks' trap of underwriting the words *salvis Privilegiis nostro Ordini* at the bottom of this agreement, which left the field wide-open for the monks to wring themselves free of episcopal control in the future.[220] Leyburne undoubtedly appreciated the strength of the Benedictine lobby at Court, for the monks had already petitioned their patron King James II that his Royal monastery at St. James's, Whitehall, be exempt from episcopal jurisdiction and directly under the Pope, according to continental practice. They won a brief victory too in the appointment of one of their number, Philip Michael Ellis, a Court favourite, as Vicar Apostolic of the Western District.[221] Stuart support was thus critical for the strength of the monks' case, and it continued to be so after James II's flight into exile in France in December 1688. For he and his successors were to carry on maintaining their prerogative, even as exiles, to approve the appointment of English Vicars Apostolic.[222]

The years immediately following the king's departure were inevitably chaotic after the false dawn of his reign. An attempt was made in 1693 by the Northern Vicar Apostolic to bring some order to bear on the tangle of missionary jurisdictions. He insisted that all Benedictine missioners should present themselves to him for approbation. The Benedictines, for the moment, accepted this decree, but not before they had marshalled the traditional arguments for their privileged exemption and had refused to accept the Vicar Apostolic as an Ordinary.[223]

The degree of interest which the Benedictine annalist, Benet Weldon, showed in the controversy from this point is evidence of the unmistakable threat which he believed the designs of the Vicars Apostolic posed both to the unity of the Congregation and the very survival of the Benedictine mission in England. Much of Weldon's material in this controversy was derived from the lost *Chronology* of Philip Michael Ellis, written sometime after 1681 when he had been a 'private Monk', and which had catalogued Benedictine privileges. Weldon's involvement with the dispute also partly explains why he put such emphasis on the Benedictine contribution to the English Church from the Anglo-Saxon period.[224]

The demand of the Northern Vicar Apostolic that the monks should seek his approbation coincided with the renewal in Rome of the faculties of the four Vicars Apostolic. This was the result of petitions from James II through the person of Bishop Ellis, who had come to Rome and had become the Stuart ambassador at the Papal Court after Cardinal Howard's death.[225] Ellis was not therefore able to sign the concerted, yet vague, demand of the other Vicars Apostolic drawn up in 1694 which insisted that all Regulars must have their approbation to work in their particular Districts. Evidence suggests that the Vicars Apostolic were by this stage gaining the support of James II and Bishop Ellis himself, both at one time allies of the monks. The latter's influence in Rome was also diminished by the premature death of their recently-appointed Procurator, Francis Fenwick, who was to have answered the case put forward for the Vicars Apostolic by the new agent of the secular clergy, George Witham.[226] The secular priest John Betham, preceptor to James, Prince of Wales, wrote to Ellis, demonstrating the weakness of the monks' position:

> You know they (the Benedictines) have always been very unwilling to own the authorities established, of late more than ever... His Majesty answered (their complaint to him) that he was for supporting Hierarchical authority...Although you were once a member of that body, yet I know your love of order and good government, and the high station you hold in the Hierarchy will place you above all those inclinations that education may have left. Were the Benedictines claustered up as in Catholic countries, it were vy. wise they should

66

govern their own people. But when they are pastors...the Bishops must answer, for it is very improper they should be freed from the Ordinary jurisdiction.[227]

In January 1695, the President and two Provincials sought a clarification of the latest decree from the Vicars Apostolic, pointing out the practical difficulties the monks would have in ordering each missioner to apply in person for faculties.[228] Their attempt to bring Bishop Ellis onto their side failed completely. He bluntly told the Benedictine superiors that Rome was currently in favour of enlarging the authority of Vicars Apostolic generally, and he was inclined to support this trend.[229] Thus, the English Benedictines were forced to find a successor to Ellis as their Roman agent in the person of Claude Estiennot, the Maurist *Procurator in Curia*. Estiennot was briefed immediately on the English monks' privileges, encouraged to ally with the Roman agents of other English Regulars, and offered the assistance of some of the more able English Benedictine theologians in order to build up a strong case against the secular agent, George Witham.[230] The monks were convinced that Rome would always prick up its ears at any whiff of Gallicanism:

> ...certainly the government of his (Witham's) Body, and many of his Confreres, lie open to be as much or more justly blamed than any others especially...as appeared in their late general abetting the lawfulness of the Oaths, and too much favouring of Blacklowism, Sergeantisme &c.[231]

Despite the mutual suspicion, however, Ellis, Witham, Estiennot and William Lesley, the Roman agent for the Scottish secular clergy, drew up an agreement in May 1695 which referred the problem to a higher authority, a Congregation of Cardinals. Witham soon had doubts whether submitting the matter to arbitration in this way was sufficient to heal the running sore kept open by the survival of regular privileges on the mission, and the period between July and October 1695, when the Cardinals published their decision, was spent by Witham in a series of interminable and deadlocked debates with the Regulars.[232]

By this time, the monks had begun to formulate a compromise solution. Whilst guarding the ultimate authority of the President over missioners, they suggested the Vicars Apostolic might appoint a Provincial as 'Pro-Vicar', the title given to the Dean of the Chapter of the English secular clergy, who acted in his own sphere as a deputy for the Vicars Apostolic. This, however, was the only novelty in the monks' argument, for the old pretensions based on *Plantata* were again wearily served up to defend the *status quo*. Witham effortlessly felled them by logical argument, appeal to common sense and icy condescension; most, he insisted, were unrealistic, fond hopes, or pure fantasy. By September 1695, the monks were prepared to make the appointment of a Benedictine 'Pro-Vicar' the basis of an 'amicable agreement' with the Vicars Apostolic, but if this was denied them, they would strive to delay the promulgation of any decree. For his part, James II insisted that as little disturbance as possible should be created in the English mission: he would ask Rome to renew the faculties of the Vicars Apostolic, 'Mais sans intention de contribuer ou de souhaiter aucune innovation au préjudice des reguliers'.[233] The Benedictine President, Joseph Shirburne, believed this delay would be helped by an accusation of infidelity directed at the secular clergy; in marked contrast to the Regulars, he hinted that the secular clergy had supported English Catholics who took the Oath of Allegiance.[234] Shirburne also produced a strong practical argument against any change. He maintained that one major reason for the monks' popularity as chaplains was their jealously-guarded privilege of dispensing, through the President, from marriage impediments. Missionary Benedictines were employed frequently in speedily granting a dispensation from the second degree of consanguinity. Thus, to subject them to the Vicars Apostolic would mean the withdrawal of this privilege and , in many cases, the end of a patron's support.[235]

Other Superiors of the Regulars appealed for delay to the Congregation of Cardinals and to James II on account of the dangers of the times.[236] Such appeals came too late to influence the two Decrees of the Cardinals which were published on the 6th of October, 1695 by the Congregation of *Propaganda Fide*. These Decrees took into account the various petitions from Estiennot and Witham.[237] The first Decree abolished all Ordinary Capitular jurisdictions maintained *sede vacante* after Vicars Apostolic had been delegated. The second ordered all regulars to be subject to the Vicars Apostolic in regard to *munia Parochialia*, notwithstanding the privileges granted to the Benedictines in *Plantata*. On account of this triumph for the Vicars Apostolic, Rome tried to console the monks by insisting the Vicars Apostolic proceed cautiously in implementing the Decrees and by praising Benedictine virtues.[238]

The Decrees, in fact, pleased neither side, and showed Rome, once again, sitting on the fence. Both Witham and his Regular opponents now raced each other to modify the Decrees before they were incorporated into a papal Brief. Witham insisted on knowing whether the Vicars Apostolic were to be given the full Ordinary jurisdiction by the Decrees, rather than merely the power to approve faculties already held by Regulars like the Benedictines from their own Superiors. Witham also sought some clarification on which privileges the Regulars would be allowed to retain. Meanwhile, he explained the Decrees, as he interpreted them, to President Shirburne, insisting that they had indeed granted Ordinary powers to the Vicars Apostolic. As for himself, he had sincerely never believed the Regulars were exempt from the Bishops in the first place, and he hoped for amicable relations between the two parties in the future.[239] Witham's complacency made the monks determined to let Rome know that if Benedictine control over faculties given to missioners was indeed to be transferred to the Bishops, the whole missionary pattern and constitution of the Regular missioners would be destroyed. Rome needed to be told that of the six hundred missioners then in England, four hundred of them were Regulars.[240]

President Shirburne was old and sick by this time, and was to die in office in April 1697. He had no wish to prolong the campaign. The publication of the Decrees, however, had unexpectedly activated other Regulars on the mission, who now realised that their battles had been largely fought by the monks alone. These Regulars now recommended the appointing of Regular Pro-Vicars to safeguard Regular missioners, and quoted a Benedictine precedent to heighten their appeal. In Paris, the Archbishop appointed the Prior of the Benedictine Abbey of St. Germain-des-Prés as 'perpetual Vicar General' for the 'vast District' around the Abbey.[241] However, in Rome, Estiennot had his doubts about renewing the offensive. He took Witham's advice that a new process would be long, expensive and ultimately fruitless, and reassured Witham, on Shirburne's orders, that the monks would not seek to disrupt missionary affairs any further by clinging to privileges found in *Plantata*.[242] In England, the Vicars Apostolic worked for peace also. Provided missioners sought their approbation, they need have no fear. But Augustine Constable, Benedictine Provincial in the South Province, was not so easily comforted. He was all for carrying on the battle because the Decrees, as they stood, stripped the Benedic-

69

tine President of all power over his missioners, and led to the Vicars
Apostolic becoming:

> nos maîtres absolus et qu'ils peuvent nous exterminer quand il leur
> plaira.[243]

Constable may well have got wind of reports that the Bishops,
following on the advantage they had gained in the Decrees, were
seeking to secure the same powers of dispensation in marriage cases
which the monks possessed.[244] The Vicars Apostolic had gained this
privilege by September 1696, although Rome took care to ensure the
Regulars still preserved their own privileges as well.[245]

As the balance tilted in favour of the Vicars Apostolic, Innocent XII
issued his Brief *Alias a particulari* on the 5th of October 1696, which,
as expected, embodied and confirmed the two Decrees published a year
earlier.[246] Not surprisingly because of the heat generated in the battle,
the monks tended to drag their heels in obeying its requirements,
particularly that which demanded Regulars appear before the Bishops
for approbation of their faculties; the abolition of Capitular jurisdiction
bothered them less.[247] All was not lost, however, because the Benedictines believed that the appointment of a Benedictine Vicar Apostolic to
succeed Bishop Ellis after his retirement from the Western District in
1705 would strengthen their position. The plan had the support too of
Queen Mary Beatrice and of Ellis himself, who, despite his ambiva-
lence regarding the 1695 Decrees, had cordial relations with the monks
up to the time he became Bishop of Segni in 1708. The secular clergy
attempted to impose their own candidate, Andrew Giffard, into the
office, but he refused in late 1705, and it was not until 1711 that Rome
appointed Matthew Prichard, a Franciscan and compromise candidate,
to the Western District.[248]

The internal conflicts of the second decade of the eighteenth century
shelved the monks' dispute with the Vicars Apostolic, but it emerged
again during the years of the Fenwick Schism. After becoming
President in 1721, Thomas Southcott believed he could solve a number
of his problems by prompting Rome to appoint a Benedictine Vicar
Apostolic. He was quick to take advantage of the secular clergy's low
reputation at Rome, a far cry from the respect they had enjoyed there
during the 1690s. Southcott therefore joined a chorus already struck up
which accused the secular clergy and the Vicars Apostolic of collaboration with the usurper, of Gallicanism, and of Jansenism. A Benedic-

70

tine bishop of unimpeachable orthodoxy, Southcott maintained, would be able to protect Benedictine missioners from ill-treatment by his fellow Vicars Apostolic, would hasten to return the remnant of Fenwick dissenters to the fold, and, finally, be useful in providing approbation for missioners sent into England already carrying faculties granted them by the President.

Southcott determined to bide his time, insisting, after complaints from the Vicars Apostolic about his subjects refusing to recognise their authority, that he had always directed missioners to obey the 1696 Decree, and that it was Fenwick's party who were causing this trouble. He explained to Cardinal Gualterio, the Protector of England, that for thirty years, the monks had followed a compromise , agreed to by the Vicars Apostolic, through which a Benedictine missioner would receive faculties from the President, but, on arrival in England, would accompany his Provincial to the Vicar Apostolic to ask for his approbation by means of a blessing.[249] When an ailing George Witham, Vicar Apostolic of the Northern District, demanded a coadjutor in 1723, Southcott's name was put forward because he had such a high reputation at Rome. To prevent this, the secular clergy hinted that he was guilty of bribery, that he would embezzle funds belonging to the secular clergy,[250] and, ultimately, that the government would refuse to allow him to take on the office:

> ...a fine, good-natured gentleman... he may desire the Coadjutorship for another, but I cannot think he covets it for himself. He is not of the country, nor inured to that labour and climate, nor can he well leave a friend he has in these parts. Besides, he is very obnoxious to the government, and his character printed in the reports of the late conspiracy. I doubt not but his zeal for politics , the good cause ingratiates him with the king, but in what does this affect the Mission?[251]

Rome was very cautious about choosing from any of the three Benedictines Southcott had put forward as candidates, and he was informed that his ally, the Pretender, could only recommend, not nominate episcopal candidates, as he did in Ireland. Bishop Witham died in April 1725, and the monks continued to believe that Rome would look favourably on at least two of their candidates, John Stourton and Southcott himself. Confident that the prize was within their reach, the Chapter Fathers at the 1725 General Chapter ordered that in all future Chapters, Bishops should be invited and take their place immediately after the President. The monks' hopes were, however, dimmed when Rome appointed the Dominican, Dominic Williams, in December 1725 as Witham's successor.[252]

Fortunately, relations between the new bishop and the Benedictines were good. In the past, Williams had supported Southcott's campaign for a Benedictine Vicar Apostolic, although as bishop, he refused to appoint two monks as 'Grand Vicars' in his District. Williams did not press Southcott to alter the traditional pattern of monks bearing faculties from the President, presenting themselves before the bishop for his approbation and blessing. Southcott reciprocated such favours; when the secular clergy attempted to starve Williams out of his District by depriving him of funds, Southcott tried to provide him with a French benefice.[253]

The determination of the monks to have one of their number appointed as Vicar Apostolic, was renewed on the death of Bishop Giffard of the London District in March 1734. By this time, the contest had taken on more political overtones, and it resembled the heated controversy between Southcott and his opponents in the Fenwick Schism a dozen years earlier. As conditions for the Catholic body in England slowly improved, the Vicars Apostolic were determined to develop the Church along more strictly Tridentine lines. They decided to implement the 1696 Brief 'to the strict tenor', and 'to divide the Mission into kind of Parishes', over which they hoped to exercise an Ordinary jurisdiction.[254] The Benedictines, however, clung to their missionary status and vision since the establishment of 'parishes' would inevitably end the full extent of their independence. Against such moves, Southcott continued along familiar lines and tried unsuccessfully to encourage Rome to appoint Benedictine Vicars General in each District. Furthermore, Southcott's own lingering attachment to Jacobitism once again caused him to shy away from any compromise with the civil power in England. Unlike the Vicars Apostolic, Southcott was unable to sense the pulse of change. He condemned the Vicars Apostolic for wishing to exclude 'all Regulars out of the Mission of England, by admitting none but such are agreable to the government', and to 'represent Regulars as turbulent people attached to the service of the Pretender'.[255] With the spectre of Stonor and Strickland before him, Southcott's understanding of the conflict had not changed throughout his time as President.

By the 1740s, the practical success which the Vicars Apostolic had had in bringing the English mission under their control encouraged the monks to maintain their efforts to have a Benedictine Vicar Apostolic appointed. The fulfillment of these hopes came with the appointment of Laurence York as Coadjutor in 1741 to Matthew Prichard, the Franciscan Vicar Apostolic of the Western District. York's appointment shows that Stuart influence at the papal court on behalf of the monks was still present.[256] York's episcopal office gave him something of the status of Provincial, and he was given a place at Chapter.[257] He was supported financially by the Congregation as a whole which was careful to see his successors were also provided for.[258]

Nevertheless, Rome continued to give support to the secular Vicars Apostolic, and in 1745, issued the Bull *Emanavit Nuper*, which, because of the '45, was not officially promulgated until the summer of 1748. The Bull once again emphasised that Regulars must be approved of by the Bishops. It was opposed by the two Regulars, Matthew Prichard and Laurence York, as well as by the Benedictine Provincial, Placid Howard, and other Regular Superiors.[259] The monks were aggrieved at the surreptitious manner in which the Vicars Apostolic had apparently provoked Rome into yet another clarification of this old conflict. All along, they had preferred to let sleeping dogs lie, whilst carefully bolstering their own position by advancing suitable candidates for the episcopate. Their conservative stance in the face of this Bull was shown in a definitive text of *Plantata*, published in 1748,[260] and by the oft-repeated criticism that the Vicars Apostolic were covert Gallicans. At this point, lay support for the monks was crucial in delaying the implementation of *Emanavit Nuper*. Lay patrons, threatened with being deprived of their right to choose their own chaplains, could be utilised by the monks.[261] Rome was prepared to listen to both sides, and the ensuing delay in publishing the verdict encouraged the monks' optimism. With Prichard's death in May 1750, York took over in the Western District, and the monks immediately began another campaign for a Coadjutor to York.[262]

All the Regulars' hopes were dashed with the promulgation of the Bull *Apostolicum Ministerium* on the thirtieth of May 1753, which totally vindicated the claims of the Vicars Apostolic. By this Bull, the latter were given full authority to approve, examine, and grant faculties, limited in time and space, to all Regular missioners within their Districts. The monks believed this degree of control to be 'very strange...in a country where residences are nearly like benefices in

Catholic countries'. The Vicars Apostolic might enforce the removal of missioners from their Districts without being compelled to give reasons. But the most controversial detail was the so-called *sexennium* requirement, which ordered every Regular missioner to return to his convent on the Continent every six years, to live here for three months, and do a fifteen-day retreat.[263] Since the Bull was emphatically genuine, the monks could do no other than abide by its terms. Nevertheless, Placid Howard, elected President in 1753, after being a candidate for the coadjutorship, carried on the fight by protesting to Rome that the *sexennium* was impractical and impossible for English Benedictine missioners.[264]

In Rome, the task of demonstrating the difficulties involved in the *sexennium* was handed to the new English Benedictine Procurator, Charles Walmesley. With the backing of the Pretender behind him, Walmesley was to demonstrate 'the true state of religion with regard to the Catholic Laity and new converts, in hopes that some alleviations at least may be obtained (from the Bull)'. By July 1755, some mitigation had been allowed, for Regulars were absolved from observing the *sexennium* requirement, due to begin in 1759, in the Northern District.[265] Within a year of his appointment, Walmesley himself had become the most suitable candidate for the still-open coadjutorship in the Western District, receiving support from within the Congregation, from the Pretender, and from York himself. That he was successful, despite the strong opposition to him from the secular Vicars Apostolic, says much about the favourable impression he had made in his brief time in Rome. He was succeeded there as Procurator by Augustine Walker, another whose 'firm zeal and steady attachment' to the Jacobite cause were well-known. Walker continued the struggle to have the 'sorry regulations' repealed.[266]

While the Provincial and General Chapters of 1757 formally submitted to the Bull *Apostolicum Ministerium*, a proviso was added that the true state had been misrepresented at Rome by the monks' opponents, and that the Bull had disrupted the structure of the English Church. The Fathers hoped that its provisions might, at a future date, be rescinded. As we have seen in earlier Roman decrees on this question, clarification on how the Bull should be put into effect was soon called for, especially in regard to the forms the Regulars must observe in seeking approbation. The Vicars Apostolic, however, were satisfied with what they had attained, and were prepared to be reasonably flexible regarding the operation of the *sexennium*.[267]

In Rome, Walker was even more determined to preserve Benedictine isolation and independence within the English Church. Divorced from the practicalities of the English Mission, his attitudes inevitably floated in an unreal vacuum. Whilst missioners in England would find it increasingly difficult to disregard completely the Vicars Apostolic in, for instance, the latter's help in withdrawing faculties from awkward missioners,[268] Walker continued to stand out for Benedictine elitism. Reading David Hume's recently-published *History of Great Britain* in 1762, he commented to Andrew Lumisden, assistant secretary to the Pretender, that Hume had been misled in not recognising the leaders of the Anglo-Saxon Church to be Benedictines:

> I think Hume himself totally unprejudiced. I think this opinion gained ground in England from jealousies and disputes which have been for some years past between seculars and the regular clergy in England. Catholic Bishops, though only temporary missioners, fix their hearts on becoming ordinaries... Therefore the Bishops have tried to get Rome to take away Benedictine privileges, to show there was no succession from the pre-Reformation period.

Walker then showed other instances of the secular clergy leading earlier English historians, like Thomas Carte, astray on this point, and he concluded, in the traditional manner, by condemning the English Vicars Apostolic for collaborating with the Protestant government.[269]

Walker's disembodied invective was to be partially shared by his successor, Placid Waters, Procurator from 1777, the year when Walker became President. The Procurators' detached attitude highlights a weakness found throughout the eighteenth century among the English Benedictines: how to achieve a unity of policy between the mission in England and the distant monks and monasteries on the Continent which were surrounded by different influences and whose ambience was quite dissimilar to that of England. Even so, the Procurator in Rome was essential to Benedictine missioners in two practical concerns: the necessity of resolving the *sexennium* question, and that of promoting a Benedictine candidate as Bishop Walmesley's Coadjutor.

As regards the *sexennium* obligation, the monks and other Regulars had been exempted, provided they had their faculties renewed each year by the Vicar Apostolic.[270] After the end of the Seven Years War in 1763 , when travel restrictions were lifted, this compromise had to be reformulated. Thus the Congregation of *Propaganda Fide* had allowed the exemption to continue, provided the Regulars made an annual fifteen-day retreat which they certified by an Oath before their respective Vicars Apostolic. At the same time, their faculties would be renewed for a year. The Provincial of the South, Henry Wyburne, together with Bishop Walmesley, objected to the surreptitious manner in which this agreement had been reached, without the Regulars being consulted. This pressure was strong enough for Bishop Challoner of the London District to have Rome replace the Oath with a simple affirmation.[271] Even by the late 1770s, some monks, coming onto the mission, were still only grudgingly prepared to present themselves before the Vicar Apostolic, his Coadjutor, or 'Grand Vicar' for faculties.[272] The Procurator in Rome had the essential task of using his influence there to renew the papal dispensation from the *sexennium* requirement every six years, and he co-operated here with the other agents of the Regulars. The Benedictines were always ready to seize any opportunity to use Rome to further their own missionary status. Furthermore, there still remained the ingrained habit the monks on the mission had of applying directly to Rome via the Procurator for marriage dispensations, rather than going through the Vicars Apostolic. In London, for instance, in 1777, Dunstan Garstang applied for a dispensation for a mixed marriage in which the parties were related in the third degree:

> Our Bishops here could have dispensed with them, had they been both Catholicks, but have no such faculty when one of the parties related is a Protestant.[273]

The success the Benedictines had in seeing one of their number, Gregory Sharrock, consecrated as Coadjutor to Bishop Walmesley in 1781, was remarkable for two reasons. First, it took place after the Bull of 1753 had begun to modify the influence of monks on the mission. Secondly, after the death of the Old Pretender in 1765, and Rome's subsequent refusal to recognise Charles Edward as king, the monks could no longer easily call on the Stuarts to further their own members as candidates to fill the office of Vicar Apostolic. The monks' victory therefore with Sharrock was largely due to the circles of influence which Walker and Waters, the two Benedictine Procurators in Rome, had there built up. These two had to work alone, with little help from the Stuarts. While Bishop Walmesley was pleased to have the Young Pretender's support for the monk Gregory Cowley as his Coadjutor in 1772, Walker knew the feelings of the Papal Court. He saw that times had changed, and that a developing *rapprochement* between Rome and the British government would inevitably endanger the base on which the claim to a Benedictine episcopal succession supported itself:

> ...the words *sub Dominio Regis Angliae* (in the new form for missionary faculties from Rome) is quite new, by which one may perceive the intelligence there is between this Court and that of England, or at least that those here are courting the friendship of the latter...I don't know how these things are, but I conjecture that the refusal of a coadjutor proceeds from politics, and that no Bishop will be made for the future for England without first consulting that Court.[274]

Walmesley, however, continued to insist that he should have a Coadjutor, and a monk at that. He despatched two names, those of Gregory Cowley and Gregory Sharrock, to the new Procurator in Rome, Placid Waters, whose social graces had brought him the highest respect in Roman society. Waters was therefore able to bring to the support of the Benedictines in this matter the recommendations of Cardinal Corsini, Cardinal Nephew and Protector of England, Stefano Borgia, Secretary of Propaganda, and Pietro Francesco Foggini, the Vatican Librarian, amongst others. Walmesley, Waters hinted, should work on Cardial Rezzonico through Lord Arundell for the same purpose.[275]

As the English Benedictine agent in Rome, Waters knew the whole procedure of petitioning for a Coadjutor like the back of his hand. He felt Rome would be impressed with Walmesley's 'having built a publick chappel at Bath with a house in which the Bishop is to reside'. In late September 1779, Sharrock was eventually appointed as the Coadjutor to Walmesley, and the Roman patrons of the monks were gratefully thanked. Sharrock was at this time Prior of St. Gregory's, Douai, and Walmesley agreed with the recommendation that he should wait until 1781, the end of the quadriennium, before receiving Sharrock, 'to prevent inconveniences and confusion'. In Rome, Borgia wickedly remarked how surprised he had been to find that Bishop Walmesley, weak and growing deaf, had suddenly recovered his health.[276] Waters now turned to his other task, that of putting pressure on the Roman authorities to suppress the *sexennium* requirement by demonstrating 'the *impossibility* and *impropriety*' of it. Here, he was out of luck, despite using the offensive of the French government against the religious orders to bolster his case. Rome was to carry on granting the usual *sexennium* requirement in 1783, 1790 and 1794.[277]

During the time, when exemption from the *sexennium* was sought and gained by the Regulars, the older inherited problem of the nature of the relationship between the Vicars Apostolic and the English Benedictines re-appeared in a new guise. It was to be an integral part of the lengthy confrontation between the Vicars Apostolic, led by Charles Walmesley, and a group of liberal English Catholic gentry and clergy, members of the 'Catholic Committee', and later to be called 'Cisalpines'. This Committee sought a wider degree of toleration for all English Catholics from the British government in return for adopting and promoting a form of radical Anglo-Gallicanism. Most of the facets of this controversy will be dealt with later; here will be discussed only the controversy's impact on the relationship between the Vicars Apostolic and the Benedictines.

At the outset, it is worth noting the similarities which this controversy had to the earlier controversy surrounding the Fenwick Schism, when hopes of toleration and accusations of Gallicanism had also involved the monks. The essential difference for the monks was that by the 1780s, they had the support of a Benedictine Vicar Apostolic with a Benedictine Coadjutor. For Charles Walmesley was to adopt a traditional Benedictine suspicion towards Gallicanism within the English Church, which, by this late period, had the effect of isolating him from most of the other, more accommodating, Vicars Apostolic, and from the leading liberal Catholic laity. The division of loyalties among the Benedictines, between Walmesley and his alliance with Rome on one hand, and the Gallican liberals, on the other, was more definite than had been similar party boundaries in the stirs of the 1720s. This polarisation was produced by the Benedictines being forced either to pin their hopes on Walmesley as the supreme defender of Benedictine rights on the English mission, or to develop further their alliance with leading Catholic families, with whom they had earlier joined forces against *Apostolicum Ministerium* to preserve their freedom. Given this alliance with the laity, it was an easy step for a number of Benedictine missioners, of whom Cuthbert Wilks was to be the most notorious, to slide into a Gallican/Cisalpine mentality, a move also encouraged by the hopes engendered through the 1778 Relief Act, and the liberal attitudes to ecclesiastical authority promoted by the

Enlightenment. Walmesley, decrepit and deaf by the 1780s, spent long periods of convalescence with the Provincial of the South, Bernard Warmoll, at Woollas Hall in Worcestershire. Inevitably they came to think alike about Cisalpinism and Wilks. In sharp contrast to these, the Northern Provincial, Richard Lacon, with a past reputation for avoiding his obligations to the Vicars Apostolic, and living at the time in an isolated chaplaincy under a lay patron, supported Wilks against his opponents. On the continent, between these two interests, sat an indecisive President Walker, already totally distracted with his own difficulties in France. He certainly sympathised with Walmesley, but to condemn Wilks might result in Benedictine chaplains being put at risk. The monks were unable to resolve the problem easily, and elements of it were to continue after Walmesley's death in 1797 and Walker's in 1794.

In April 1797, the Catholic Committee, the group of leading English lay Catholics who sought to put pressure on the government to increase toleration for Catholics by repealing the penal laws, drafted an address which, *inter alia*, begged Rome to appoint Bishops-in-Ordinary. At this stage, Bishop Walmesley, encouraged by Cuthbert Wilks, then the Benedictine incumbent at Bath, supported this motion, although other monks feared it might open up old wounds and threaten Benedictine missionary independence further.Rome however, rejected the request and was able to bring Walmesley and Wilks to agree with its point of view.[278] Wilks, who appears to have been neutral up until this time, was voted onto the Committee in May 1788, and became involved with the other parties over the next two years in protracted discussions about the formula of a new Oath of Allegiance which Catholics might take. This period was critical because during it, Walmesley's opinion hardened against the Committee, and he clashed with Wilks over the question of the Oath. This division between two Benedictines trans-formed the substance of the traditional battle between monks and the Vicars Apostolic. No longer did the parties concentrate so much on opposition to the appointment of a regular Ordinary, rather they now became gradually divided over the larger question of Cisalpinism. Some monks, Wilks included, believed the Congregation must forsake its traditional anti-Gallican stance and support the Committee to ensure that English Catholicism might have a future. There was some similarity between the position of Laurence Fenwick earlier and Cuthbert Wilks here. But the size of Wilks's following and the fact that he was always held in high esteem within the Congregation suggest that he was never isolated in the way Fenwick had been. Almost unnoticed, the centre of the Congregation's gravity was moving away from the continent, where it had been stabilised by President Southcott, towards the English mission. Here, despite the setbacks already alluded to, the mission offered more positive challenges than did monasticism in contemporary France. This helps to explain why Wilks's role in the mission was seen to be so crucial to the monks. In early 1790, he had been recommended by the Committee as candidate to succeed Bishop Talbot in the London District. In the event, he was unsuccessful, and his refusal to withdraw from the Committee spurred on Walmesley and Warmoll to press President Walker to censure him. If he refused, Walmesley threatened to withdraw his faculties in his District.[279]

In his opponents' eyes, Wilks had become the reincarnation of the seventeenth-century English Benedictine, Thomas Preston *alias* Widdrington, an earlier exponent of Anglo-Gallicanism; a fellow-Benedictine compared him to the Abbé Siéyès in the National Assembly.[280] Walmesley went ahead and withdrew Wilks's faculties in February 1791, thus forcing the division among the Benedictines out into the open. The monks had, therefore, to decide whether Wilks was right in asserting that he was only acting in trust as an elected member of the Committee, or whether he was subject, as a missionary, to the authority of his Vicar Apostolic above all else.[281] Such was the unforeseen problem which inevitably grew from the case of a monk on the mission who found himself under the jurisdiction of a Benedictine Vicar Apostolic, but at loggerheads with him. Benedictine interest soon began to focus more on this suspension of Wilks than on its cause, his obstinacy in regard to support of the Oath. Walmesley's reiterated refusal to accept Wilks's submission 'in spiritual matters', merely increased Wilks's support among the monks: 'the Monks favour him and honour him with confidence'. In 1789, he had been elected a Definitor of the Regimen at General Chapter. Provincial Warmoll was pressed to act as a go-between, but after hearing of Wilks's determination 'to perform as usual my ecclesiastical functions, except the care of souls and the administration of the sacraments, notwithstanding the Prohibition of the Apostolical Vic.', Warmoll knew the affair only concerned the Bishop and Wilks. This became Warmoll's rejoinder to those monks who tried to use the dispute to open up old wounds between the Vicars Apostolic and the Regulars. He was determined to prevent other monks becoming involved.[282]

After a temporary truce between Walmesley and Wilks, made in September 1791, had broken down, both Walmesley and Warmoll recommended Wilks be ordered by the President to return to one of the monasteries on the Continent. To fight this, Wilks now tried to translate his personal quarrel into terms which reflected the traditional struggle between Vicars Apostolic and Benedictines. He called upon Provincial Warmoll to defend the privileges of the Congregation as a whole, and demanded his right to a trial if he was ejected from the Province. In a personal letter to Bede Bennet, the Procurator of the South Province, Wilks echoed old themes: Walmesley's attack on him was essentially an attack on all Regular Missioners, and he insisted that the monks should recognise Rome, not the Vicars Apostolic, as the final Court of Appeal in the conflict. His ally, the lay Cisalpine leader, John Courtenay Throckmorton, urged President Walker to support Wilks, so that 'the privileges of your Order should not be sacrificed'. Walmesley, however, had taken care to explain his procedure to the President at every step, and continued to demand Wilks's recall abroad as the only possible solution.[283] In November 1791, Wilks finally left Walmesley's District, with an offer of sanctuary from his fellow monks in the Northern District, who believed he had become a symbol of the fight for Benedictine exemption. The Provincial of the North, Richard Lacon, was joined by his three councillors in condemning Walmesley's violence to a senior member of the Congregation:

> Had the present case happened in this Province, we should have advised you (Lacon) to have maintained Mr. Wilks, notwithstanding the subtraction of his missionary faculties, in the residence, as a subject of our Congregation, & left the Bishop to answer for the consequences. Our Residences & the nomination of them as much belong to our Body as our Convents abroad.[284]

When, in May 1792, Wilks finally returned to France, of his own free will, there was still deadlock in England; Wilks still retained his support here among many missioners, and Walmesley continued to refuse any of the forms of retractation Wilks proposed.[285] While the Cisalpine conflict was to continue in England into the next century, the monks were to find themselves less involved. At the depleted General Chapter of 1794, Wilks was formally exonerated for his part in the controversy. Three years later, in 1797, Bishop Walmesley died. Wilks had become chaplain to the liberal Lord Shrewsbury in 1794, and was to continue to support the Cisalpines when fresh disputes broke out again in 1798.[286]

The Wilks Controversy demonstrates that Benedictine missioners might still, in the last resort, stand out against the authority of the Vicars Apostolic, and there continued to be a strong element of this enmity between both parties well into the nineteenth century. In the Wilks Controversy, as in others, Benedictine Superiors tended to sit on the fence when it came to putting the orders of a Vicar Apostolic into effect against a monk, because it might well result in a Benedictine schism. In practice, however, it gradually became unrealistic for Benedictine missioners to stand up for their exemption, especially as they began to develop their apostolate in large urban congregations by the end of the eighteenth century, and needed the co-operation of the Vicars Apostolic. The Bull of 1753 had forced this co-operation upon them. After this date, claims of Benedictine exemption and privilege only tended to be used as extra fire-power in larger disputes like those relating to Cisalpinism. The Wilks Controversy crippled the key resource which the monks had employed during much of the eighteenth century: an alliance between a Benedictine Vicar Apostolic and the Superiors of the Benedictine Congregation. Faithful to his brethren, as Walmesley had tried to be, he finally had had to assert his episcopal authority over a fellow monk who had questioned the limits of his jurisdiction. It could not have been otherwise, because Walmesley's first duty as Bishop was to the District he governed.

Chaplaincies and Missions 1688-1794.

- Patrons and Congregations.

The foregoing three chapters have sought to show how the English Benedictine Mission was part of a greater whole, the English Benedictine Congregation, which ultimately controlled its development and balanced its interests with other Congregational concerns. We now turn to observe the Mission itself, its shape, life and apostolate. The Benedictine Mission cannot be viewed in isolation from the monasteries, neither can it be ever wholly separated from the English Mission in general, of which it was a part. Thus, parallels between the mission of the monks and that of the secular clergy and other regular missioners are always present. Although the framework of the English

Mission generally given, that of a division into gentry chaplaincies and independent, usually urban, congregations, can be helpful, a closer analysis causes this division to break up. Some rural chaplaincies lay close to, and often supplied priests to nearby urban centres, and, on the other hand, chaplains serving a family in rural isolation, often spent considerable periods in the town houses owned by their patrons. Nor should one forget the considerable number of Benedictine missioners engaged in 'riding missions' or 'circuits'. If, however, one clear single development can be discerned throughout this period, it must be that of the disappearance of distinctive household chaplaincies and their replacement by large urban missions by the century's end. Undoubtedly, the 1688-89 Revolution had been a setback for Benedictine hopes of missionary enterprise. A sudden fall in the number of missioners, caused by those seeking refuge abroad. coincided with a contraction of the Mission, as Benedictine chapels were destroyed.[287] At this time, some chaplaincies moved into further rural isolation, deliberately keeping a low profile until things improved, while some missioners retreated to their own families.[288] From this disruption there eventually emerged the problem of unemployed missioners, suffered not only by the Benedictines. In a number of cases, the monks expressed their thanks to Catholic gentlemen who were prepared to employ more than one monk to ease the burden.[289] What is surprising is the continued presence of some monks in the more disturbed areas, London for instance, and the speed of recovery in the Benedictine English Mission as a whole. In London, monks apparently stayed on, attached to Somerset House, the Savoy, and the Portuguese and Sardinian Embassies. Thomas Brabant, a lay-brother and foreigner, was able to carry on acting as Provincial Procurator in London, untouched by the latest anti-clerical legislation.[290]

The meeting of General Chapters in London in 1697, 1705, 1713 and 1717, even if the time and location of these were kept secret, suggests a lessening of the political tension,[291] although the fleeting life of many of the chaplaincies, whose names only are known to us from this time, points to the shifting nature of the mission. It is likely that a number of these latter were merely stopping-places on monks' circuits, which were then a common feature of the English Mission, and helped to provide work for the eighty or so monks engaged in missionary work, the highest number of missioner monks recorded during the whole eighteenth century.[292] A circuit might easily be launched by a family with a number of residences, like the

Throckmortons of Coughton and Weston Underwood, the Stourtons of Bonham and Stourton, or the Middletons of Myddelton Lodge and Stockeld. Circuits might also range around an urban mission, as in the hinterland around Bath.[293] London alternated with Bath as the head-quarters of the Provincial. It also possessed the largest concentration of monks in England.[294] London's pre-eminence, as we have seen, was sufficient to make it the storm-centre of the Fenwick Schism. The mission at Bath, with its lodging house at the Bell-tree House for visitors to the spa, was unique among English Benedictine missions, and resembled the Jesuit hostelry at Holywell in Flintshire. Extensions to the Bell-tree were made in 1713 to cope with the increasing influx of visitors.[295] Another urban centre, York, provided lodgings for unemployed Benedictine missioners, while at Winchester, there were sufficient numbers of monks living at Hyde House for it to be called a 'monastery'.[296] Finally, there is some evidence for Benedictines being enthusiastic for working in Bristol in the first decade of the eighteenth century, as well as in the coal and tobacco port of Whitehaven, which developed from being merely a staging-post on a Benedictine circuit.[297]

Missioner unemployment was soon to be a thing of the past for between 1720 and 1740, there was a massive drop in the number of monks on the mission. As we have already noticed, this period coincided with the 'continental' policies of President Thomas Southcott. Any increase in the number of missions known at this time suggests they were merely stations on a far-flung circuit, and this is exactly what the evidence for the densest Benedictine missionary territories of Lancashire, the West Riding and Northumberland shows.[298]

Despite circuits ranging from an area of a few square miles to some including several counties,[299] there was nevertheless a strong sense of fraternity present among Benedictine missioners in the same district, and the division of a Province into a network of *Praepositura* clearly encouraged the segregation of the monks within the larger Districts of the Vicars Apostolic, especially in the earlier part of the century. Rural Benedictine chaplaincies tended to form distinct clusters. For instance, Bede Potts at Everingham was on intimate terms with his brethren and their patrons throughout the East Riding. Anselm Mannock's popular spiritual books were designed for a small circle of Warwickshire gentry some of whom had been educated by the Benedictines and maintained monks as chaplains. In Wiltshire, there was a knot of Benedictine chaplaincies all served from the centre of Bath.[300]

Myddelton Lodge, Ilkley

St Joseph's, Brindle

In the 1720s and 1730s, two developments emerged which were to play a decisive role in the Benedictine Mission's future. First, there were the first glimmerings of a withdrawal from the almost complete dependence of a monk on a patron, and in turn the development of 'independent' missions with much larger numbers in the congregation. This move was staggered; for instance, a monk might, as at Beaufront Northumberland, find himself travelling around his patron's tenantry in outlying hamlets. Sometimes, a patron might keep his own chaplain but establish another monk on a separate fund in a nearby town whose inhabitants would almost certainly include tenants of the patron. This was the case at Parlington in the West Riding where the missioner boarded with the grocer in the nearby town of Aberford.[301] The trend can be distinctly seen in the petition of a monk in 1721:

> I hope you will help me to get money off the Esquire because I have long wished to need not to be confined to a residence, but to go about to help the poor Catholics that are far from any residence, and to help them, rather than to be a burthen.[302]

The second major development in these early years of the eighteenth century was the opening up of mission registers. The earliest surviving Benedictine examples date from this time: Everingham (1719), Brindle (1722), Hengrave (1734), and Ormskirk (1736).[303] Neither Brindle nor Ormskirk was by this time dependent on the support of one particular patron. Both were situated in areas heavily populated by Catholics, a feature which would have aided the establishment of an independent congregation. At Brindle, baptisms, which stood at twenty one in 1722, had risen in 1740 to thirty one. By 1725, the Benedictine incumbent had built a house and chapel from his own *peculium* and later transferred the property to the Province.[304] Such early registers throw some light on how the monks viewed their apostolate, for these registers were evidently personal documents rather than the property of a particular mission or chaplaincy. Thus the Brindle register incorporates extraneous Benedictine material, such as obituaries of monks from throughout the North Province, and its incumbent appears to have seen himself as a type of Dean, with some responsibility for other Benedictine missions in the area, whose statistics he also included in the Brindle register. The small Everingham register was incorporated into the chaplain's personal account book. The personal nature of these early records is even more striking in the case of John

Hardcastle's register. He was a chaplain at the Portuguese Embassy,[305] and entered baptisms which he performed between 1720 and 1741 which are also found in the official register, but presumably also provided proof of the missionary faculties he held, which could be thus certified when he moved on. Later registers also continue to demonstrate their value as a missioner's personal property. The Sefton register is tucked between leaves from Richard Challoner's *The Touchstone of the New Religion* (1741) and other tracts, whilst that of Parlington, begun in 1759, forms an appendix, like the Everingham register, to the missioner's personal accounts.[306] It is more than likely that such monks saw their missions as a series of loose congregations rather than as neatly-defined, self-contained parochial units. From the 1730s an increasing number of registers survive, compiled mainly in traditional household chaplaincies. Provincial Chapters from 1733 had insisted that registers be kept for inspection by the Provincial 'so that difficulties in these matters can be checked'. The increase in registers is therefore an indication of the Congregation's determination to overhaul its procedures, following the chaos during the Fenwick Schism. Furthermore, these early registers suggest that the monks were also participating in a rapid consolidation of the English mission occurring throughout the country which can be seen in the growth in number of registers in many other, non-Benedictine, missions.[307]

By the mid-eighteenth century, northern England had overtaken the south in terms of the number of Benedictine missions it possessed. Most of these still remained household chaplaincies. But monks were aware that their posts as chaplains in these were unstable, for the chaplaincy could disappear overnight with the decease of a patron, which caused the estate to be sold or to fall to a non-Catholic, or which resulted in the remaining family preferring to employ a secular clergyman or another Regular rather than a monk.[308] It was this total dependence on the patron, who would apply to the Praepositus or Provincial for his chaplain, which caused much resentment among missioners who added their voices to the campaign for more missions independent of patrons.[309] The expansion of missions in the mid-eighteenth century was, however, mostly an overlap from already existing missionary work, that is, an extension of area, a wider circuit or perhaps a supply to the second residence of the patron.[310] What however was becoming more common by this time was the transformation of a household chaplaincy into a bigger enterprise through smaller supplementary funds being added by members of a congregation to the original endowment of the patron, especially when this had become insufficient to maintain a missioner. In this way, wealthy Catholics in commerce, poorer members of a congregation, and even missioners themselves, might directly ensure the continuity of a chaplain's work but change its character towards a wider field of activity.[311] The registers of this time reveal the degree of this increased missionary labour and the mission's size. Brindle and Sefton were Lancashire missions covering approximately the same extent of territory; the first was an independent mission and had some thirty baptisms a year; the second, with an average of only ten baptisms, which included members of the patron's family, was only just beginning to outgrow its chaplaincy status. From this time also, the Benedictines felt confident enough to open public chapels in some missions. Bath, with its enlightened and wealthy congregation, was an obvious choice, and Laurence York was the ideal man for incumbent here. In 1740, even before he became a Coadjutor, York's facility was recognised:

> (He) has at present one of the chief posts amongst us, living in our house at Bath where he is exceedingly agreeable to all the chief of both Protestant and Catholick nobility that frequent that place...He preaches in a publick chappel we have there and is a man fit to appear in the best company.[312]

Although the number of monks on the mission from 1750 did not vary much between forty and fifty, they tended to be older and therefore not too well-equipped to meet the large increases in the Catholic population, particularly in the urban centres, which appear at this time.[313] Comments on this problem were frequently made to superiors. Provincial Naylor in 1766 asked for help to be sent to an old blind chaplain, admitting 'we have a great many old and invalids here', a sentiment echoed by a successor of his in 1778. It was the same in the South Province also:

> I hope you have ordered some supplys for our parts, as there are several wanting. Nobody as yet at Flixton, which congregation owing to Mr. Westbrook's deafness & late disposition, is almost entirely lost, & I am afraid it will be very difficult to bring them to their duty after so long a want of a proper person.[314]

88

The difficulty that Benedictine superiors had refused to face in their determination not to be ruled by the Vicars Apostolic was that of monks casting themselves adrift of all authority while on the mission. This became acute in the second half of the century. In London, Bede Bennet stated that in his experience,

> I am not surprised that we don't succeed better; our people, particularly at ye first coming over, are so wise that they will take no advice from anybody.

He had just witnessed a patron, Lord Stourton, of Witham Place, replace a monk with an ex-Jesuit because his Benedictine chaplain, 'that whimsical unaccountable genius', the 'cracked' John Barnes, had tried to dictate his own terms to Stourton.[315] At a distance there was little the Provincial could do if the missioner disliked his post. Coming to Strangeways in Lancashire in 1773, the new missioner found his predecessor still in residence, living with his niece and taking up all the room. Despite entreaties, the new appointment refused to stay in a fit of pique, or perhaps 'he was frightened at the sight of the labours attending a Lancashire Congr(egation)'.[316] In Cornwall, in 1780, Lord Arundell asked the Provincial to remove his chaplain, Boniface Hall, because of his 'too much familiarity with the sex'. Hall went, but to no place determined by the Provincial, rather to Plymouth where he 'kept a shop' with Arundell's maid. Surprisingly, this prodigal son ended his days in his monastery.[317] A Definition at the 1773 General Chapter was to forbid unsuitable candidates being sent on the mission if they lacked 'knowledge, piety and zeal of winning souls'. The very next year, the President was asked to order the return of three difficult missioners to their monasteries: 'Melancholy doings to burden the Houses with useless members'.[318] As the Benedictines found themselves increasingly responsible for congregations in large towns, so did the temptations grow more insistent. John Placid Bennet was known to be weak-willed, and hence the Provincial would not countenance him at Whitehaven:

> In my opinion, there cannot be in the whole world a more improper place, a sea port and full of bad women, as such places too generally are, and fifty long miles from any Br(other) and no one to be a check on his conduct.[319]

At this same time, Benedictine superiors had the problem of John Placid Naylor and his squabble over the Bath mission on their hands. This has been dealt with in detail elsewhere, but it represents the longest and most violent struggle between superiors and a monk who had ploughed a lone furrow in his mission, made a personal fortune, and isolated himself from the Congregation. Even after his removal to Paris, Naylor still had a 'strong party' who attacked his successor at Bath and the Provincial against the 'hard usage to (their) saint'. Naylor's party was made up from 'among the lower class, such as Barbers, Taylors, Blacksmiths etc.'.[320]

The two missioners who apostatised in the 1770s, however, were not lured away by the attractions found in a town mission; they left from household chaplaincies. Michael Lewis 'very absent and rather giddy', apostatised in 1776 and married the niece of the housekeeper of his patron. He was enlightened enough to continue attending mass which infuriated and embarrassed monks in the neighbourhood of his new home.[321] The other apostate, John Augustine Hawkins, took leave of the Congregation in 1780, having served as chaplain to the Bodenham family. He soon married 'Miss Berney, a dancing master's daughter in Worcester', the niece, in fact, of Dr. Burney.[322]

By the 1770s, the weaknesses inherent in the traditional household chaplaincy were becoming quite obvious, and more missioners were beginning to feel they might be reduced by transferring to an independent, generally urban, mission. There were some important exceptions: the poet Cowper's friend, Gregory Gregson, for instance, was happy to use rural isolation in the 1780s to walk forth 'to meditate at eventide' and Dunstan Sharrock at Danby still preferred to live with the family once his chapel was finished in 1792. Without any doubt, however, there was a general contraction in the traditional chaplaincy. At Holme in the East Riding, for instance, John Fisher carried on in the 1770s as chaplain to an absentee patron, but was very aware of the depressed nature of his flock, and its disintegration as the young moved off to find work elsewhere. Reduction in the number of available missioners prompted some gentry households to begin to share a chaplain. At Sefton, Lancs., the Provincial was forced in 1785 to keep a missioner on in his old chaplaincy since his flock refused to join up with neighbouring congregations:

> Where must we apply for help? Ince, the nearest place we have to go to, three miles off for many of us & farther for some. They pray at

90

nine o'clock in the morning, and in winter their clock is an hour too fast, so that they pray as soon as it is light upon Sundays & Holydays, and sometimes by candle...It will be almost impossible to have our children instructed in their duty, considering the length & badness of the road in the winter time wheresoever we go.[323]

The end of at least three chaplaincies was caused by the insufficiency of the mission fund or the patron's bankruptcy. By the 1780s, a number of chaplains were dispensed with when the patron and family paid a long visit to the continent, stopping off in Benedictine monasteries.[324] A recurring disaster from the 1770s was to be the apostasy of the patron who as a Catholic felt cramped and alienated from mainstream English society. Two leading Benedictine patrons took this path at this time: Viscount Molyneux of Sefton (1768), still a minor when he inherited, and Sir Thomas Gascoigne of Parlington (1780) The leave-taking was gracious and accommodating, for special provision was made for their loyal Benedictine chaplains who were thus able to to establish the independent missions of Netherton and Aberford respectively. As far as Gascoigne was concerned, his apostasy was hardly total, for he continued to remain sympathetic to Catholicism.[325]

Such pensioning-off brought some benefit to the missioners involved since it gave them freedom from a patron's immediate control. It was this inescapable grip of the patron which had been responsible for making such work unpalatable to many monks. It did have some compensations. A patron might be attached to a particular monk, rather than to the Congregation in general, and provide a fund for his chaplain's own use and a home for his retirement.[326] At Brandsby in the North Riding, the patron made 'strict friendship' between himself and his chaplain the excuse for refusing to release the latter on the Provincial's orders for work in a new urban mission.[327] It had been to safeguard this privilege of free choice which had brought such patrons into an alliance with the Regulars in the latter's dispute with the Vicars Apostolic in the 1740s and 1750s. Twenty years later, it was still a jealously guarded right. Patrons were accustomed to inform the Provincial whom they wanted, and, fearing the loss of the chaplaincy, superiors deferred:

I must tell you that Sir Edward Swinburne was greatly discomposed at not having Mr Shaw and made me rather apprehensive that family which we have had the honour of supplying I imagine time immemorial might have been lost during my administration, which would have given me much chagrene.[328]

Even so, superiors recognised the danger of pushing unsuitable monks into chaplaincies, especially as the numbers on the mission continued to decline. In Lancashire, for instance, Maurus Bulmer advised the President not to send Benedict Macdonald to the Towneleys at Standish because he 'has to much of the North-Britton'. Macdonald was a rugged individualist, as his later career in Liverpool was to bear out, and something of an embarrassment for English gentry of this time because of his Romantic Scottish Jacobitism. 'We are blameable', Bulmer maintained, 'in sending, promiscuously, subjects, when nothing would make us shine better than properly adapting Persons to Places'.[329]

Although it was the President's right according to the Constitutions to appoint a missioner, problems of distance often required that this function devolved onto the Provincial, who was forced to act as an agent for the patrons, speedily putting their wishes into effect and being prepared at their behest to transfer chaplains in conflict with their patrons. Patrons preferred experienced missioners:

> Pray when is it that we are to expect your smirking face? Should Bradshaw die, how would you like to succeed him? Her Ladyship hopes in that case that we shall not send her a sucking monk.

Patrons were also more discriminating in their choice if the missioner was forced to lodge with them; in that case, he would need 'politeness and good temper'. Although no monk was in fact sent in 1790 to be chaplain to an incapacitated octogenarian because the post was an obvious sinecure and monks were needed in more important posts, the qualities he would have needed were carefully laid down:

> ...his spiritual functions will give him no trouble; his whole congregation when I was last there consisting only of two persons. He must be able to bear solitude, and be master of himself, to overlook any forward expressions from his Patron as the natural effects on an unhappy temper rendered worse by living alone, old age and infirmity.

A 'propensity to drink' made a missioner unacceptable to patrons, and if missioners had not developed this bad habit while in their monasteries, there was always some anxiety it would grow when they were placed in lonely missions, like Lawkland on the moors of the West Riding. Mutual support and the presence of brethren close by were important considerations for a Provincial to bear in mind when trying to place a missioner. The Riddells of Northumberland were particularly fastidious in their choice. Mrs. Riddell preferred 'a respectable character & not very young' who would not be a bad influence on the children, while her husband saw regularity as the greatest virtue of a chaplain:

> (The Provincial) knows the great Regularity which is kept up in it (the Riddell household), and how much Mr. R. admires good sense, particularly sobriety. The Family is accustomed to have Prayers at the half hour past eight o'clock on common days for most of the days in the week.

Some monks were exasperated by such fussiness:

> I do not recollect having assigned a reason for his (Riddell's) appearing to have an objection to a fat unwieldly man. As he and some of his family may not infrequently go for a few days to Swinburne Castle, he apprehends it might be unpleasant to have a person of that description to accompany him, tho' to another man agreable and even amusing.[330]

A recurring feature of many household chaplaincies was the relationship of the lady of the house to the chaplain, which in some cases was one reason why such work became too constricting for some missioners. The dowager Lady Stourton at Cheam had hung onto her chaplain Richard Harris from 1772. He was a source of 'great uneasiness to the President and the Provincial', and was believed to be 'wrong in his head', with the makings of a 'scabbed sheep'. But while he enjoyed his patroness's favour, he could not easily be moved. Later, she became dependent on another monk, John Placid Naylor, whom superiors again found difficult to uproot:

> Her Ladyship continues steady in not parting with Mr. Naylor on any account unless you absolutely insist on it. As she goes every summer to Cheame, she looks on Mr. Naylor as her domestick chaplain, and

at her term of life, she does not like to see new faces. She hopes you will drop all thoughts of removing him.[331]

By 1775, the Benedictines' banker, Wright of Kelvedon, Essex, had had a handful of unsatisfactory monks as chaplains, and Mr. and Mrs. Wright therefore asked to have Thomas Welch, then in France, who was a great favourite with the gentry. Bede Bennet in London filled Welch in: Mr. Wright was 'good and cheerful', Kelvedon had a small and trouble-free congregation and was in a good neighbourhood, but 'the lady, I believe, not altogether so good humoured, but with a little address may be easily managed'. Welch was unwilling to risk living with a shrew and declined, even though it would means losing a valuable chaplaincy to the secular clergy, for Mr. Wright would not hear of employing either a Lambspring monk, or a Benedictine who had never been in England or had not 'lived in a family'.[332] Likewise, at Lawkland in the West Riding 'the squire and his sister flew out most furiously and declared absolutely' they would not admit the Provincial's choice of chaplain. In the 1780s, there appears to have been at least nine ageing Benedictine chaplains who served old ladies. But female patronage reached its most influential level in the case of Edmund Hadley who was left a huge fortune by his patroness in 1784. His superior attempted to prevent him inheriting it since it would likely make him less dependent on his authority. In the end, however, he was allowed to inherit a portion of it and to remain in London, 'the Age is too critical to try experiments'.[333]

The reverse of a matriarchal chaplaincy was the famous example of Gilling in the North Riding where the weak-minded heiress Anne Fairfax was dominated by her chaplain Anselm Bolton. By 1774, Bolton had antagonised his patroness's relations by gaining a favourable verdict on a Chancery case to have the estate transferred after Miss Fairfax's death to a trust. Bolton was by this time acting both as chaplain and steward of the estate. Building up his material empire seems to have made him negligent of his religious responsibilites, and stories of his indiscretions began to filter through to his superiors:

> ...his behaviour is as haughty as ever, impetuous in his temper, his language sometimes quite profane, that he does not frequent ye duty of Confession,...that he declares if I persist to tease him, he will renounce all...There are also given out some other very scandalous reports of a very unbecoming intimacy.

94

Benedictine superiors were at a loss to know what to do because they believed many of these accusations were trumped up by 'peevish and meddling' neighbours who were constantly putting pressure on the Provincial to remove Bolton. Miss Fairfax firmly refused to part with her chaplain, so the monks, always anxious to please patrons, turned for help to the local Vicar Apostolic, 'who will withdraw his Faculties, and Bolton will extinguish like a vapour'. This suggests that at the last resort, Benedictine missioners were not averse to solliciting the authority of the Vicar Apostolic when faced with problematic missioners like Bolton who had 'the character and temper of (John) Wilks, a Firebrand, a Rebel'. Attempts to shift Bolton all failed, and he even refused to become a London-based chaplain for Miss Fairfax. It was at this point that the Provincial decided to wait and see whether the legal proceedings taken by Miss Fairfax's relatives against Bolton would manage to extract him from his Gilling fastness. Provincial Lacon, chaplain to Mr. Cholmeley at Brandsby, lived only a few miles down the road from Bolton. Cholmeley, a sworn enemy of Bolton, was responsible for some of the wicked rumours against him. Lacon preferred to see Bolton's negligence as the result of tension between duty to his patron on one hand and service to the local congregation on the other:

> I am witness to a total neglect of duty with regard to his people, but in that respect, perhaps he may alledge that he is the domestic chaplain to the Lady & will not concern himself with that care. However the people are almost lost.

By 1786, Bolton had got into even deeper water, for in that year, he was committed to York Castle for supposedly converting the daughter of an aggrieved tenant to Catholicism. Fortunately the perjury of a witness ended the trial and he was acquitted, achieving some notoriety on his release. When Miss Fairfax died in 1793, Bolton moved to Ampleforth Lodge, to a property she had made over to him.[334]

If Gilling represented the older pattern of intimate relationship between patron and chaplain, many chaplains, especially from the 1770s, found such a role not only constricting but an embarrassing luxury when their chaplaincies were near to increasing harvests of souls in urban settlements. The unease is quite definite in a statement of President John Fisher in 1777, himself a traditional household chaplain:

As to myself, I have no great ambition to engage in families, unless it be such as have for generations been our Supporters and friends, which I think Duty, honour and gratitude oblige us to serve. Such as only apply to us as a last shift, and preferably to ye Clergy, because they can have a great command over us and more easily dismiss us, tho' well-behaving, I am very indifferent about them. A County Town or circuit in Lancashire or elsewhere, manned by a laborious, zealous and diligent Incumbent, is in my opinion preferable to half a dozen families, as in such places, recruits are to be gained and reputation, in a way of life more suitable to our Instruction and education. Its inconceivable how the Cath. people are upon the increase in almost all the trading towns of Lancashire and elsewhere, and with what tranquillity the practice of religion is tolerated. The Clergy are conscious of it and will use all their endeavours to prevent us from getting footing in any of those belonging to the late Society (Jesuits). The want of subjects or Policy has occasioned us to miss many opportunities never likely to happen again in Lancashire. It's lucky we are in possession of Warrington and Ormskirk.[335]

Here, the reasons for the decline of chaplaincies and their replacement by more independent urban missions is highlighted. Inevitably, chaplaincies were soon to be despised as sinecures. Holme Lacy in Herefordshire, for instance, was looked down on as 'of no consequence in the world to us'; it was better that its chaplain be transferred to the new urban mission of Morpeth. In contrast to what had been a common habit earlier in the century, superiors now frowned upon monks returning to their families to serve as chaplains of leisure, a wasteful retreat. Abbot Maurus Heatley of Lambspring spoke disdainfully of his nephew Jerome Heatley becoming chaplain to his father in Preston:

> ...with his Father, it would have been quite an idle life, without any real good to him or ye body & his talents buried.[336]

Even in chaplaincies there developed a deliberate distancing from the patron, as chaplains left their apartments in the large house and moved to separate accommodation. Sometimes circumstances forced them to seek independence. Thus at Beaufront in Northumberland the 'chief', John Errington went mad in 1787, and his capriciousness made it hard for his chaplain who only managed to survive by voluntarily keeping out of his patron's way.[337] At Birtley in Durham, disorderly heirs pushed the chaplain into 'thoughts of purchasing a small spot and building himself a place to pray in', although he was prepared to build the new chapel onto the house of another family he went to lodge with, so that they 'will not be under a sort of necessity of keeping the person that serves it'.[338] Most of these new departures occurred in the North Province and were occasionally promoted by patrons eager to help a missioner's apostolic work. At Morpeth, for instance, the mission's end came with the suppression of the Jesuits, but it was soon re-established by a local patron, Thomas Riddell of Swinburne Castle, who was determined that the town should have a Benedictine, and used a fund, which he administered, for that purpose. At first, the monks did not like the strings attached:

> if (the fund was)settled properly on the Province, (the offer) was not to be rejected, but if he (Riddell) keeps the power and direction of it in his own hands, it may be with the Incumbent as with his own domestic Chap(lai)n: *Turn out at an hours warning*, and consequently not worth accepting.

Finally, however, it was accepted once assurances were given.[339] The end of a chaplaincy, through, for instance, the patron's death, might direct the chaplain towards an already-formed congregation on his doorstep, as was the case at Warwick Bridge in Cumberland in 1774. Or a chaplaincy might become the mother of an urban daughter mission; Woolston's chaplain established the Warrington mission in 1771. In rural chaplaincies the decline in the number of missioners might increase the area for which a missioner was responsible. At Haggerston, Northumberland, and at Aberford, an absentee landlord and an apostate patron respectively encouraged the missioner to concentrate on 'pretty numerous' congregations.[340] At Standish, Lancashire, 'Fisher ye Monk' remained a family chaplain while supplying 'now and then' at the much neglected but enormous congregation of Catholics at Wigan.[341] Follifoot in the West Riding was the northern Benedictine equivalent to Bath, not only because its house and chapel were directly run by the Province, but also because it served the expanding spa of Harrogate:

its vicinity to Harrowgate will not admit of that place being unsupplied, more especially in the summer season.

By 1788 the missioner at Follifoot had also become chaplain to two families in the area, and thus established a wide riding mission.[342] The evidence for the drift to the towns on account of the urgent need to supply numerous congregations is provided by the wealth of statistics available from the 1760s. The House of Lords' Returns of Papists for 1767 and 1780 give reliable figures for a number of Benedictine congregations.[343] These can be compared with the statistics available in the larger number of extant registers from Benedictine missions, for, from the 1760s, there was a greater emphasis given to the need to compile such records, one of the side-effects, perhaps, stemming from the Bull *Apostolicum Ministerium* of 1753.[344] Baptismal entries reflect the three types of congregation. Gentry chaplaincies generally had very few baptisms; Acton Burnell, for instance, averaged two a year for the 1760-1780 period. Those chaplaincies which served a populous urban congregation as well had more; Sefton, Lancashire, had twelve per year over the same period. Brindle in north Lancashire, town and environs, had a record of forty one baptisms per year during this time. The sudden leap in the Birtley (Durham) register from three baptisms in 1766 to ten in 1777, a level which was afterwards sustained, points to a great expansion of population in this mining district. Even with these growing numbers, a chaplaincy's area continued to be far-flung. Acton Burnell reached as far as Welshpool, some eighteen miles distant, and urban Lancashire missions, where Catholics were very thick on the ground, were also responsible for wide tracts of territory; Sefton stretched for over thirteen miles. Contraction in the number of missioners might be responsible for this. Between 1763 and 1768, the Coughton chaplain also supplied at the private chapel at Abbots Salford, seven miles to the south, whilst the chaplain was absent. Not surprisingly, the crisis of manpower precipitated a further reduction in wasteful household chaplaincies. Warrington might now look after its parent chaplaincy at Woolston:

> The mission at Woolston embraces I believe a very small number of Communicants; it's near Warrington where we have a very sensible and well-behaved missionary.

98

When Whitehaven lost its missioner, the Provincial, Anselm Bolas, living over fifty miles away, was forced to supply there occasionally. He was at the same time already looking after two gentry chaplaincies in northern Cumberland, and Whitehaven was also responsible for the Isle of Man.[345] The most numerous congregations cared for by the monks lay in Lancashire. The Ormskirk missioner looked after 500 Catholics in 1773, compared with 271 in 1767. The 371 given in the 1767 Returns for Brindle is probably an underestimate; in 1770 the missioner spoke confidently of 600:

> From Palm Sunday to Low Sunday, I had 560 Communicants and 22 since. I suppose with ye outlyes, ye Congreg. is as near 600 as possible.[346]

The decade before the French Revolution, which transformed the monastic face of the English Benedictines, saw further attempts by the Congregation to suit the Benedictine mission to changed times. In the household chaplaincies which still remained after 1780, the determination of the chaplain to increase his independence became stronger. At Craike in the North Riding, the retired chaplain purchased his own property and garden, and in Lancashire, at Sefton and Hindley, chaplains built separate houses. At Hindley, however, deference was still paid to the patron who, since he was the principal benefactor, was assigned the front pew in the new chapel. At Sefton, the apostasy of the patron, Lord Molyneux, had caused the chaplain to transfer to the nearby village of Netherton . Similarly the apostasy of the Duke of Norfolk, and subsequent sale of his estate at Deepdene in Surrey, made the chaplain move to Dorking where he developed 'a small garden, a comfortable neat house and a bijoux of a chapel'. At Broughton in the West Riding, the chaplain was given the choice of living in the household or in a separate dwelling, while at Danby in the North Riding, the patron hoped to attract a good chaplain by offering him his own house, half a mile distant from the patron's. Cuthbert Simpson at Coughton in Warwickshire was fortunate in that the Throckmortons rarely lived for long at the Court.[347] At Etal in Northumberland, Jerome Digby was frustrated by the 'family hours':

> in Summer, we never dine till three, not even on fast days, & in Winter not till four.

He preferred the compromise of the Swinburnes, at little further south at Capheaton, 'where the priest... lives out of the family & has his own hours'. Capheaton provides an excellent illustration of the patron rather than the chaplain encouraging a missioner's independence. By 1782, Sir Edward Swinburne had given his Benedictine chaplain a salary and a house in the village; 'he was to have no concern at the Hall but to say prayers only when he was invited'. The chaplain soon became discontented with village life and was particularly distressed because he was constantly distracted from saying his breviary 'on acct. of ye noise of children playing about etc'. In fact, he wanted the freedom of 'some Embassador's Chapel', or 'an independent place either in the North or South Province'. The chaplain believed that he had been cleared out of Capheaton Hall in the first place because the family had already become lukewarm in the practice of their religion. In early 1786, Sir John Swinburne finally apostatised and so was able to enter the ranks of local society and national politics. His liberal Catholic uncle, the traveller Henry Swinburne, a great friend of the monks, did not object:

> I have half-persuaded the Curate that the masses he has said on the altar of which you laid the first stone are not worth a farthing since you made le saut périlleux.

After a short respite, the missioner at Capheaton was discharged completely, 'because it seems inconsistent with his (Sir John's) principles of Religion & politics', and, without a substantial congregation or funds to count on, the Benedictine presence here melted away.[348]

The growth of missions independent of household chaplaincies brought particular problems in its wake. The comparative freedom which missioners were beginning to experience made the mission rather attractive to those monks uneasy in their monasteries, and caused old and erring missioners to fight off any moves to make them return to the continent. Superiors tried to prevent missioners on the move ending up in London:

> where they imbibe principles by no means commendable and declare them to others. I am now endeavouring to remove them from that State of Liberty, and see if the country aire and dependancy will bring them to their senses.[349]

100

Such missioners 'doted on this residence' because of the excitements it offered. In London, monks were already chaplains at the Portuguese Embassy, and to the distiller Thomas Langdale. The Provincial was determined to contain drifters by directing them to the new Spanish Embassy Chapel:

> (Digby)…will do well (at this Chapel), as his ambition was to settle in Town, tho' for my part, I think none but such are absolutely necessary should be permitted to reside there, for when once fixed it is impossisble to remove them, tho' absolutely wanted in a different mission or elsewhere.[350]

Jerome Digby had been a problem both in monastery and mission. Despite his trying to seek refuge on the continent with the Carthusians, the Trappists, Maurists or Vannists, he had been pushed out on to the mission in 1783, with 'a prodigious repugnance to undertake the care of souls'. At Liverpool he had refused to hear confessions, and at Bath, where he succeeded in expelling Bishop Walmesley from the mission house, he had had similar problems:

> His rudeness and severe temper disgusts them (many of the Bath congregation), and many will not put confidence in him at the Trib(una)l.

After this, he continued to be shunted from one mission to another. The Provincial blamed his misbehaviour on a strain of mental illness in his family which had gone unnoticed by Benedictine selection procedures.[351] At Hindley the errant missioner tried to prevent his superiors moving him by getting his congregation to draw up a petition 'armed with the formidable names of several children and even Methodists'. Another, Dunstan Garstang, attained a record of forty six years as chaplain at the Portuguese Embassy, largely however because he refused to move, and 'pen'd down a long list of our fallen Brethren in country missions, in vindication of those in London…and lashed the houses abroad'.[352] There was the case of Robert Goolde who refused to leave London for 'a Country Family', and emphasised his good work in the capital as a confessor and chaplain to the Duke of Norfolk. He was shrewd enough to play his Benedictine superiors off against the Vicars Apostolic, and hence got his way:

The poor little ignorant man seems to set certain limits to the power of Superiors and that in some case, which he imagines essential, he may, with safe conscience, refuse submission. These notions from the liberty of the times gain ground... It will be extreamly dangerous to apply to have his Faculties annulled. For in case the B(isho)p refused, all our Authority in the mission must drop.[353]

Finally, London housed monks like Basil Kennedy who fled there after he had been sent to St. Edmund's, Paris, to mend his ways following spells of alcoholism and after fathering a child in Aberford in 1787. In London, he lodged with his sister, endeavouring to squeeze money out of his mission superiors for 'the Education & Maintenance of my Child'. He had no success for they continued to think him 'literally an apostate', and refused to recognise him as a member of the Congregation, despite his assertions to the contrary.[354]

Both Digby and Kennedy had supplied at Liverpool, and it was in the north, especially in Lancashire, where most of the Congregation's interest was concentrated with the explosion of missions here. In 1788, Thomas Welch had noted 'the Rage of building Chappels continues'[355] and we know of some ten new or enlarged chapels being built in the north at this period. Three missions, Bath, and in the north, Liverpool and Ormskirk, were now given two missioners each to care for expanding congregations. By 1780 the Benedictines were running some forty missions in the north compared with just over twenty in the south. As for missioners, in 1781 there had been twenty missioners in the south compared with twenty five in the north, and, despite falling numbers generally, these had become by 1794 eighteen and thirty respectively. Both Provinces found that, after the suppression of the Jesuits in 1773, they were constantly asked to provide more chaplains, but most new missioners tended inevitably to be channelled to the expanding missions of the North Province where the Provincial could even speak of a surplus in 1787, 'my number is increased beyond my ability to supply them with places'. The Provincial of the South, discerning the trend, blamed the President for favouring the north.[356] Whilst many registers of rural chaplaincies show a drop in the number of baptisms from 1780, the baptisms in urban missions continued to increase; Brindle, for instance, was now averaging fifty baptisms a year. Statistics for 1783 show Brindle had six hundred in a congregation, whose good observance has drawn the conclusion that here was 'a community of almost complete adherence'. In 1783 too, Ormskirk had two hundred in its congregation, and served Lydiate; Brownedge had five hundred, Woolton, eighty, Warrington, two hundred and fifty, Woolston, one hundred, Standish, two hundred, and Sefton, three hundred. Such numbers allowed the Provincial of the North increased bargaining power with the President, and further enhanced the prestige which the mission was enjoying within the Congregation which was faced with monasteries abroad close to disintegration. The Provincial of the North could object from a position of strength to the suggestion that the 1785 General Chapter meet in France rather than England, even though he went unheard:

> ...in consideration of the inconveniences attending our long absence from our respective Congregations if held abroad. Some of these Congregations are very numerous: Walton (Brindle), Warrington, Sefton; and my own (Warwick Bridge), tho' not numerous, very extensive, perhaps few so.[357]

The most important urban Benedictine enterprise in the north after 1780 was undoubtedly the mission in Edmund Street, Liverpool, handed over to the monks in 1783 by the bishop after a series of disputes between the two ex-Jesuit missioners there, and their parties. Liverpool was one of a number of Jesuit missions which were taken over by the Benedictines after the suppression of the Society of Jesus in 1773. At Liverpool the two Benedictine incumbents, in their turn, also quarrelled with each other, and in 1788, the senior, Archibald Benedict Macdonald, went off to found another Benedictine mission in Seel Street. Liverpool is the best-known early example of a mission in which congregational control had reached significant proportions, though by 1787 the new chapel in Bath also had a committee of the congregation meeting to decide on pew rents and how to maintain the building.[358] Macdonald had found on his coming to Edmund Street, a congregation of some six hundred divided into factions, and headed by a board of trustees who controlled the incumbent's income through bench rents. Being of an independent frame of mind, Macdonald was determined to break this control;he had never been happy with the curbs imposed in a domestic chaplaincy. He aimed to seize control of the bench rents by ousting those who had not paid up, and was prepared to use violence. On the 5th of September 1783,

...just as Macdonald was coming out to begin prayers, Messrs. Laurence, Kaye, Billinge & an Attorney rushed into the vestry & stopped him by force, asked where the Benches were etc. (Macdonald had deliberately removed them). & ye Attorney asked him if he knew a certain statute of Queen Elis. & how he dared to appear in that dress. In the interim, Billinge stepped to the Altar & proclaimed yt there shd. be no prayers there that day. The Congregation hearing this, cried out: "Put them out, Put them out". Whereupon they were seized & dragged out, but no farther harm done to them, except to the Attorney whom an Irish sailor followed down ye street & knocked him down & tore his cloaths.[359]

The quarrel continued, with Macdonald's lay opponents submitting the dispute to the arbitration of members of the Catholic Committee, until the Vicar Apostolic, Bishop Matthew Gibson, announced that Rome had granted him full control of the property after the suppression of the Jesuits, and that he wished to leave the Benedictines in possession. From then on, until it was finally solved in 1788, the dispute continued between the bishop and lay trustees, the monks trying to keep at a distance. In the autumn of 1788, the ex-Jesuits finally handed over the trusteeship of the mission to the monks who declared they were prepared to co-operate with the bishop.[360]

Besides providing an excellent illustration of how powerful lay involvement might be in the running of an urban mission, Liverpool was also a very clear indication of the way in which the old conflict between Vicars Apostolic and Benedictines was beginning to resolve itself. Provincial Lacon had in the past tended to assert traditional Benedictine mission rights, but here, in Liverpool and later elsewhere, he was prepared to work with the bishop. For Benedictine superiors, another headache at Liverpool was Macdonald himself who continually quarrelled with any Benedictine assistants given him, but who was difficult to remove from Liverpool until the bigger conflict was settled. Liverpool throws light on the new difficulties individual missioners were faced with when trying to work as a team in an urban mission after long years alone in isolated chaplaincies, for at Liverpool they are shown falling out over salaries, over the distribution of tasks and being hampered by mutual incompatibility. Assistants for Macdonald were, in any case, not easily found:

I have tried several. Some are told by their Doctors they cannot undergo the Labours, some have neither voice nor breath to make

104

themselves heard to half the congregation. Others I fear wd. not be moved from their old congregations unless in virtue of obedience, and some are really unfit for the place, wch. I am sorry to say is the case of Mr. McDonald, he either cannot or will not preach & he reads equally bad...Besides I am told yt he has lost the confidence of his congregation.[361]

Considering Macdonald was a prolific writer of popular commentaries and catechisms, this charge against him, of failure to communicate, is puzzling. Macdonald however relied on famous visiting preachers at his new chapel in Seel Street to instruct his congregation. An educated Presbyterian was astonished by the brilliant eloquence of Joseph Berington who preached at Seel Street in November 1790, although the visitor admitted that 'few of the congregation' might have fully comprehended the sermon. It is likely that Macdonald's removal to, and establishment of, a new chapel at Seel Street in 1788 was caused by his refusal to work with any assistant given him. It may also have been the case that the ex-Jesuits may have insisted on his removal before they handed over the trusteeship of Edmund Street chapel. Seel Street was Macdonald's own project, and from the outset he ensured there would be no congregational control. At first he tried to do without any Benedictine assistant, employing instead an Irish priest to teach catechism at 'a cheap rate'. However the Provincial persuaded the bishop to refuse him faculties, and Macdonald was forced to take a monk.[362] He remained at Seel Street until his death in 1814.

In conclusion, it is useful to compare Liverpool with Bath. Both were large, urban, and needed two missioners. At Bath, Benet Pembridge was, like Macdonald, responsible for publishing popular spiritual works for his congregation. Bath's congregation was also growing, Pembridge called it 'this bustling city, the seat, centre and sink of vanity and luxury'. By the 1790s, it had reached 400, and a new layer of noble families, the French émigrés, were adding to the numbers of Catholic gentry frequenting the spa. Like Liverpool, Bath had considerable congregational control in the running of the mission. Its earliest trustees had been lay. In the 1770s, the congregation had taken sides for or against the incumbent Placid Naylor in his financial disputes with the Province, and factions were to appear again in support of either Cuthbert Wilks or Bishop Walmesley in the Cisalpine stirs of the 1780s.[363] The wealthy Bath congregation had helped build the chapel destroyed in the 1780 Gordon Riots and was active in a re-building scheme which, with the help of compensation from the authorities, produced a new chapel, opened in 1786.[364] Bath also had its share of awkward incumbents, the most extreme of whom was Jerome Digby spoken of already. He was responsible for throwing Bishop Walmesley out of the mission house, but was fortunately replaced by Cuthbert Wilks in 1786, a highly intelligent and articulate socialite who was to be the ideal missioner for Bath. Wilks 'was much in vogue with his fashionable audience,...pleasing in his discourses and...sociable in his visits'. The dark days of his involvement with the Catholic Committee were some way off in the future. In Bath, he was accepted immediately:

> Mr. Wilks has gained the goodwill of all ranks of people at Bath, and as much respected by Protess. as Caths., and people of all denominations esteem him a man of litterature, good breeding an aimiable endowments.

This description of Wilks puts us in mind of his predecessor at Bath, Laurence York, and Wilks possessed the latter's eloquence in preaching which, as we have already seen in Liverpool's case, was essential for a city missioner:

> The Chap. is crowded on Sundays with all ranks of people, and clergy of every denomination, and they in general speak well of his discourses as containing good Language, good reasoning and good instruction.

In 1788, Wilks preached an elegant sermon to his Bath congregation on the subject of the king's madness, which extolled the virtues of social utility and emphasized that life might be seen as a 'feast'.[365] Wilks was undoubtedly continuing here the sort of life and intercourse he had known as a monk in Paris. There he had moved in fashionable circles, and in Bath it was he who witnessed the marriage of the Comte de Calonne in 1788. Other monks, like Gregory Cowley for instance, looked across from a Paris on the point of revolution to a healthy retirement in 'the easy sinecure' at Bath, with its 'many beautiful prospects...in the neighbourhood of the hot wells'.[366] When Wilks fled 'abruptly' from Bath after his suspension by Walmesley in 1791, factions reappeared in his congregation. Pembridge, Wilks's successor, found he had the approval of 'the middling class', but, predictably, 'The Rich pay to Mr Wilks their Money, to Mr Pembridge, cold

Civility, perhaps occasionally a Bow, or a how-do-you-do, seldom an invitation'. Pembridge eventually disappeared in favour of a far more suitable candidate, Ralph Ainsworth, a bright if immature thirty year old who fitted the Wilks's mould:

> Tho' Mr Ainsworth is young, he is of such character that must render him amiable in the eyes of good people. Time will ware that diffidence which is at present objected to him. Not is it material to preach memoriter. There are few that persue that method, nor are there many blessed with such memory to preach off Book on every occasion, nor is it practised to my knowledge. But on particular occasions, when intitled to a select audience, Mr Ainsworth will undoubtedly be intitled to the same privilege as his Predecessors who all made use of reading their discourse. I may perhaps example Mr Bradshaw, but his performances were ill-connected, too often the case when depending on memory.[367]

Ainsworth died in Bath in 1814. By that time two of the monasteries, after escaping from France, were attempting to establish themselves in England, and the Benedictine mission was about to embark on a new phase in its history in which distance between monastery and mission would no longer be such a problem.

- *The Apostolic Life.*

By this stage it should be realised how complex a task the Provincial had in providing the most suitable monk for a particular congregation. Not only was there a continuous transformation in the types of mission during the eighteenth century, but at any time, monks were to be found supplying a great variety of missions. At one level, there were the cosmopolitan and shifting flocks in Bath and Liverpool, balancing the scattered and largely independent rural congregations, and, at the other, there survived the outcrops of Catholics encircling a household chaplaincy. We have already noted how these last two kinds of mission tended to merge together as the century progressed and produced missions like Ormskirk, where wealthy Lancashire gentry worshipped with a wide social spectrum which included prosperous tradesmen and farmers.[368] Life in a household chaplaincy continued, however, to require a more sedentary missioner, able to find his own level in regard to his flock and local society. Thus the monk at Lanherne was

107

'by no means calculated to live in the great world..not very communi-
cative.. (and) not the most civilised..but will please people of the
moderate class'. And at Woollas Hall, Worcestershire, the old chaplain
was relieved to be sheltered from election fever which had hit his
locality: 'as the Parlt. is dissolved, we expect nothing but confusion...However, we are exempt.. and a civil answer is soon
given'.[369]

Whatever the type of chaplaincy, or the degree of involvement with
society, a missioner's first concerns were spiritual. His personal
spirituality thus spilled over into the direction he gave to the souls
committed to him, for whom he provided catechisms, employed
scriptural commentaries and encouraged membership of Confraternities. Very many funds established for Benedictine missioners insisted
that these took on a special responsibility for the poor of their
neighbourhood. A number of missioners were able to see the rewards
of their direction in aspirants whom they sent to Benedictine houses on
the continent.[370] The daily duties of a missioner, however, centred on
the rhythmn of the Church's feasts and fasts. At Everingham, Bede
Potts condemned those who had not made their Easter duty as 'rotten
members' and, as we have seen, the number of Easter communicants
was used by a missioner to ascertain the size of his cure. Potts was a
stickler for the observance of the Lenten fast, but because of his
health, a neighbouring patron and his Franciscan chaplain worried
about him:

> I call it a disobedient Lent because I am sure Mr. Bulmer (the
> Definitor of the North Province) would have you eat meat.

Potts reluctantly gave in.[371] Some patrons demanded a daily mass for
the household, and in some urban chapels by the century's end there
would have been a daily public mass. Generally, however, a public
mass in a household chapel was celebrated only on Sunday and
perhaps, as at Everingham, on a First Friday also.[372]

A household chapel provided a centre for the celebration of the
sacraments of baptism and marriage. *Confirmandi* from Benedictine
chaplaincies tended to be sent to a neighbouring mission which the
bishop was due to visit to administer the sacrament, once every six to
twelve years. Not surprisingly, monks were heavily involved in
arranging and witnessing marriages, perhaps even more so than other
missioners because of the privileges of dispensation which they held.

Monks whose careers was spent in various chaplaincies found themselves acting as marriage agents who recommended Catholic partners living far apart from each other, and their function was to disclose tactfully the amount required for the dowry.[373] At Fawley in Berkshire, Sir Richard Moore was involved in a prolonged altercation with his estranged wife, but had the full support of his Benedictine chaplain against meddling Vicars Apostolic who had taken his wife's side.[374] Most marriage registers belonging to household chaplaincies indicate the degree to which the patron insisted on employing Catholics on his estate. Separate Catholic marriage registers were obviated by the 1753 Marriage Act which ordered all Catholic marriages to be legalised in the parish church. Thus, the Holme register ceased to contain marriages from 1754, but recommenced doing so ten years later following an order from the Vicar Apostolic, and at the insistence of General Chapter. Only one surviving Benedictine register, Cheam, gives details of a non-Catholic partner, so the proportion of mixed marriages is difficult to gauge in other missions. In general, however, the proportion of such marriages in a household chaplaincy is thought to have been one in three or four. Cheam's Benedictine missioner made no attempt, as we shall see, to accommodate himself to the local Anglican incumbent. Only one of eight Cheam marriages recorded was mixed and here the non-Catholic bride was made to swear explicitly that she would educate her children as Catholics.[375]

Mixed marriages aroused the same anti-Catholic feelings as zealous proselytism. In 1762 Placid Jefferson had to flee back to Paris from Cumberland when, after he had performed a marriage, one of the parties accused him of being a Catholic priest. His superiors kept him out of the mission for eight years, until 'the reputation of his indiscretion' was forgotten.[376] Likewise, in 1764, John Charlton rushed back to Douai after arousing local hostility in marrying a couple in the West Riding.[377] The incidence of these examples might suggest some ill-feeling against clandestine marriages performed after the passing of the 1753 Act, but there was doubtless an element of fear also against the expansion of popery. On the eve of the Gordon Riots, John Courtenay Throckmorton, a Benedictine patron, could write to President Walker:

A Protestant Lady ye other day said she believed that all ye young women would be Catholics, for she heard of nothing but matches for them and none amongst ye Protestants.[378]

Monks were never slow in putting the blame for domestic disputes onto the scandal of a mixed marriage. Benedict Macdonald's niece, for instance, had unfortunately married a Protestant,

> a Brute of a fellow, who besides using her otherwise very ill, would not permit her to come to prayers. His barbarous treatment they say occasioned her death...(her) two children who were both christened at church..have now no chance of being better instructed.

Benet Cawser's superiors were extremely uneasy, knowing his unstable character, at the suggestion that he leave Paris to go and live with his family at Ormskirk, since 'his father is an Innkeeper in that town and unfortunately a Protestant. We cannot think it becomes his Character to live with his father thus circumstanced'.[379]

The intimacy of a household chaplaincy and its relatively light load of spiritual duties inevitably encouraged patrons to employ their chaplains in other areas. A missioner's role as physician and his indispensability as tutor and as the link-man in obtaining places for the children in continental Benedictine schools will be treated elsewhere. Such a missioner often acted as steward and house-keeper when the family was absent. This was the case with Cuthbert Farnworth at Capheaton and Bede Potts at Everingham in the 1730s, both of whom provided a model for Anselm Bolton's full involvement in the Gilling estate at the end of the century. At Capheaton, a succession of chaplains were given the responsibility of stocking and farming the stew pond.[380]

The missioners' own views about their congregations and local society are of particular value. Such comments that survive also underline the differences between north and south, between the gentry chaplaincy and the independent mission which have already been discussed. As a spa, Bath attracted the wealthiest English Catholics as well as monks in the south, eager to convalesce there. In the north, sick missioners frequented the spa at Harrogate or bathed at Scarborough.[381] Experience of these places made the monks very aware of the vices inherent in such fashionable retreats. With gambling, the chiefest entertainment at Bath, they were rather tolerant:

> Mr. Walmesley at Bath is on ye morale severe. He has forbid, or at least desired that nobody of what rank soever to play a game of cards on Sunday evenings which causes a great talk among Cath. every-

where. Whether ye other Vicars will follow his example, it is not said, but I should think not. I should think his proceedings very singular indeed.

Even before he became incumbent at Bath in 1781, Benedict Pembridge had pointed out the 'Fifth Duty of Parents' to be

> to avoid gaming, alehouses, to avoid obscenity, and to watch against the baneful practice of naked bathing in company with others...where they (children) often learn abominable vices.[382]

Although the monks had provided a large complex of buildings for the Bath mission, which included lodging house, chapel, library and perhaps school room, visiting gentry with plenty of time on their hands to niggle, treated the mission as though they had substantial proprietary control over it. Certainly, lay trustees had helped to get it established at the beginning of the century:

> I am apprehensive that some people will pretend the (Bell-tree) house too good and large for the purpose, especially some of the quality who hold the Priesthood rather in a contemptible light and would treat everyone of that state in the same manner they generally do their chaplains.

Bath, in other words, was viewed, much to the monks' dismay, as a gentry chaplaincy, and it is not surprising that it was an early centre for Cisalpinism:

> Some of the Gentry who are glad of any pretext in this age of Luxury and dissipation to hinder their subscribing, except against the house which they look on as too grand, and indeed, there may be such an objection in the idea of those who do everything, as is to common among the Cathol. Gentry to depress the Priesthood.[383]

Back in their houses, the Catholic gentry found they could continue the delights they had experienced in Bath. Mrs. Anna Maria Throckmorton of Weston Underwood, Bucks., the mother of the Cisalpine, John Courtenay Throckmorton, was devoted to her old chaplain Benedict Simpson, and kept him informed on all matters regarding his old congregation. These glimpses provide a vivid picture of a Benedictine household chaplaincy in the 1770s. Mrs.

Throckmorton spoke of her visits to Bath and Cheltenham to take the waters, of the large numbers of Catholic marriage alliances she had heard of, of the family attending race-meetings, and of new families in the district: 'They are Cats (Catholics), & I hear Card Players'. Other Catholics in a new house nearby would, she believed 'find it far & dirty to come to Prayers'. Simpson would be interested in the details of births and deaths in the congregation of which his correspondent informed him, and would have been intrigued to hear of the variability of Lenten observance: 'We have a strict Lent in all Places, except the North'. The lady sent Simpson medicines devised by her new Benedictine chaplain, Gregory Gregson, the friend of the poet Cowper. For his part, Simpson encouraged his patroness to come over to France for Louis XVI's coronation in 1774, and join her sons whose education Simpson kept an eye on at St. Gregory's Douai.[384]

In Lancashire, where John Fisher found in 1775 'Trade & Religion in a very flourishing condition in all our settlements', the picture was rather less genteel and more rustic. Placid Naylor had been at Brindle from 1722 until 1769, and had developed that mission through the use of his own *peculium*. He was perhaps the nearest a Catholic missioner could be to a squarson. Naylor continued to be informed of his old mission by his successor at Brindle, Joseph Hadley. The latter sent precise details of deaths, with news of Naylor's friends, and described problems of suicide and alcoholic addiction in the congregation. Since Naylor would be concerned about the state of his old property, Hadley drew up lists of creditors for him. and discussed in great detail the livestock he kept, seeking all the time Naylor's advice.[385] Such incidental interests should not divert us from appreciating the centrality of the missioners' spiritual responsibility. Nowhere is this more clearly defined than by Bede Brewer at Woolton, just outside Liverpool in 1782:

> My first and principal care should be directed towards my Congrega-
> tion..Tho' my Congregation be not very considerable in number, it
> is very much scattered for 5 or 6 miles around me and composed of
> many very illiterate ignorant people, who require great instruction,
> and of many that are very remiss in their duty (many more than ever
> I imagined when I came first into these parts) who must be frequent-
> ly admonished and visited. The stray sheep must be sought by every
> Pastor...I am very well convinced that a person in my situation who
> will make it a rule to preach to his people every Sunday or holiday

momenter, instruct the poor now and then in the week, be careful to perform his own Devotions every morning & look after his flock, will have full employment & time little enough for his own private & necessary studies.[386]

Such devotion justly resulted in the loyalty of a missioner's congregation, and there were many such missioners and missions in Lancashire. At Ormskirk, eighty-year old Maurus Bulmer struggled to keep up his daily mass despite bouts of gout and 'violent looseness'. Close by at Hindley, the congregation of two hundred refused to allow the President to move their missioner, Edmund Duckett, and threatened to cut off all funds. They played their trump card by suggesting that a similar catastrophe to the war of factions at Liverpool would result if the President continued obdurate. Duckett remained.[387]

The eighteenth century was an age of tolerance and that tolerance was granted to English Benedictine missioners, as well as others, provided they ministered only to their own congregations and did not attempt to convert others to Catholicism. It was the determination to proselytise above all else which stirred up the last remnants of local anti-popery. In general, relations between non-Catholics and missioners were good, despite the continuing operation of the penal laws. At Brindle, friendly Protestants had purchased the mission property on behalf of the missioner in 1726 in order to establish a chapel, and acted as its trustees for some years. At Everingham, Bede Potts was happy enough to drink a bottle of beer with the parson's son, and the latter's father took care to omit Potts's name from his 1733 Papist Returns. In Archbishop Herring of York's Returns of 1743, parsons made no mention of the well-known Benedictine missions at Everingham and Holme. At least two monks were commemorated in the north and south of the country by tablets in Anglican churches. Finally, among a multitude of similar examples, we might choose that of the Throckmorton chaplain, Benedict Simpson, who had a warm friendship with the antiquarian and clergyman, William Cole, who relied on Simpson to provide him with monastic hospitality while touring the continent.[388] Nevertheless, monks still remained enthusiastic about making converts. Their methods were not uniform but depended on time, audience and place. If anything, they became cruder as the eighteenth century progressed. The task of conversion in Court and aristocratic circles had fallen in the 1670s and 1680s to the monk Maurus Corker, reputed to have brought a thousand souls to

Catholicism, including the poet Dryden. Corker had been imprisoned during the Popish Plot. He was himself a convert, the son of an Anglican clergman, and published a justification of his own conversion in about 1700, *A Rational Account given by a Young Gentleman...of the Motives and Reason why he became a Roman-Catholick.* This work elicited an Anglican reply in William Wake's *The Church of Rome No Guide in Matters of Faith,* (London 1700). It was followed by his *Queries to Dr. Sacheverell*(c1710), which combined an account of his conversion with an attack on Anglicanism. Corker, like so many seventeenth-century converts, many of whom became Benedictines, saw his conversion as the result of a passive acceptance of the light of faith rather than as the fruit of intellectual argument, and his hope was that his book might stimulate readers into following the same path. In a sense, Corker was one of the last surviving Benedictines whose education had been centred on the Benedictine mystical traditions of the seventeenth century.[389]

One convert of Corker's who became a monk was Obed Alban Dawney, who was active in Wiltshire in the second half of the eighteenth century, where he explained that he was enthusiastic about bringing 'many to the truth'. Gentry patrons were often unhappy about their chaplains proselytising because of the disturbance it might cause in the locality, but Dawney felt compelled to make 'good Christians' in the area around Fonthill in Wiltshire where his patron lived, even if some 'uneasiness' resulted. Significantly, it was with the ladies of the household and his female correspondents that he tended to discuss the question.[390] In 1721, he became Procurator in Rome and there set about a correspondence with the Non-Juring antiquarian Richard Rawlinson. At this level, Dawney moved away from the methods he had used to convert ordinary English countryfolk, mainly, it appears, social pressure put upon his patron's tenants, and employed instead those intellectual arguments for the validity of Catholicism which had appealed to his master, Maurus Corker: passive acceptance of the authority of the Roman Church and the rejection of the Protestant belief in *scriptura sola.*[391] At the time Dawney was debating with Rawlinson, another monk, Thomas Southcott, was promoting among sophisticated Anglicans *The Life of Fénelon* by his friend, the Chevalier Andrew Michael Ramsay. This biography also tried to show the proximity of Catholicism to Anglicanism through a common mystical tradition:

Christianity adds nothing to your pure Deism but the sacrifice of the understanding; and the Catholick Faith does but compleat this Sacrifice. Pure Love and humble Faith are the whole of the Catholick Religion.[392]

As the eighteenth century wore on, however, this Benedictine sensitivity to the Anglican position appears to have become less obvious. What angered the Anglican authorities about eighteenth-century Benedictine missioners, 'busy Zealots of the Romish Church', was their enthusiasm for making as many converts as possible, which upset the peace of well-established local communities, especially when the converts came from outside a patron's tenantry. In the early 1720s, the Benedictine Joseph Rokeby was such a zealot at Everingham, and he was a danger to his own superiors because, as a member of Laurence Fenwick's schismatic party, they feared he might continue to aggravate the Anglican authorities whilst refusing to recognise either the authority of the local Vicar Apostolic or the Benedictine President. Despite submitting ultimately to his Vicar Apostolic, Rokeby continued his work for converts as before and was consequently presented to Archbishop Blackburn of York, together with his new patron, Lord Fairfax of Gilling, who, presuming to help his chaplain, provides an exception to the opinion that patrons were generally hostile to proselytism:

> Mr Rooksby was greatly complained of by several neighbouring clergy for having been very assiduous in gaining proselytes.

The result was that the monks were forced to transfer Rokeby discreetly back to his monastery at Lambspring, where he was soon elected abbot. Rokeby's activities caused Archbishop Blackburn to send out summonses to all Catholics in his archdiocese in 1733, with a view to enforcing the penal laws against priests. In 1735, his clergy sent in detailed returns of papists which appear to indicate that Rokeby's success at conversion had been more limited than the Anglican clergy had imagined.[393]

There were to be many later examples of Anglicans becoming alarmed by missioners' tactics in seeking conversions. At Capheaton in Northumberland in 1751:

> Mr Ellison of Whelpington has taken a peak against Mr Eastham (the Benedictine chaplain to the Swinburnes) abt. christening a Child of

Thomas Daniel's and that at the last Visitation at this town, made a Complaint to the Bishop, but cannot ascertain it forthwith, tho' it's talked round the Neighbourhood. Things are all aflame in that Neighbourhood at this time, but I hope they'll subside in a little time.

Within two years Eastham had been paid off as chaplain.[394] At a village near Bath, another Anglican rector complained of a Benedictine missioner's 'zealous efforts to gain proselytes' in the late 1770s, and it may have been the same monk who was pelted in the street and hanged in effigy.[395] At Cheam, Maurus Heatley, who was later to become Abbot of Lambspring, began his *Liber Ab Haeresi Conversorum* in December 1755 and from then until 1760, he listed forty eight converts, with important details attached. This is a staggering figure when one realises that Heatley was essentially a household chaplain caring for a small congregation. Again, his work angered the local Anglican clergyman, who forced Heatley to go into hiding in 1760:

> Hoc anno mota est persecutio per Jacobum King, ministrum Protestantem de Cheame aliosque adversus pastorem gregemque Catholicam hujus districtus, qui vexati sunt per tres menses continue per litteras citatorias vulgo *summons*; non tamen ante tribunal comparente, tandem sedata est persecutio.

Heatley was to be back on the job the next year, making another five converts, one of them a fifteen-year old Welshman. Once again, King renewed his offensive. In 1763 and 1765, he refused to allow the burial of a Catholic infant in the parish churchyard, weakly justifying his refusal by stating he had not been informed of the child's name. He defiantly asserted to the child's mother that death was still the penalty for any Roman priest caught baptising or converting.[396] In household chaplaincies, as have seen already at Gilling, the patron might well co-operate with the missioner's proselytism. Another later example of a similar case is found at Coughton in Warwickshire, whence the patron was absent for long periods. Here, this co-operation devolved onto the shoulders of the patron's steward, John Wilks, and his family. John Wilks was the father of the famous Cisalpine Benedictine, Joseph Cuthbert Wilks. From the 1750s, this family was present in the chapel at Coughton to witness abjurations from heresy.[397] If such conversions were aided by the encouragement of a patron, this function was to be replaced usually in a large independent congregation like Brindle by the influence of Catholic members of the convert's family. As can be seen frequently at Brindle where the missioner made one hundred and twenty converts between 1740 and 1760, the majority from the labouring class who now formed the bulk of his congregation.[398]

Unfortunately the methods employed by monks in making conversions are more rarely recorded than are the statistics. At Gilling, we have the evidence of how Anselm Bolton was supposed to have introduced a serving girl to Catholicism, and for his labours, was committed to York Castle in 1786. The evidence produced described how after he had told the girl that she would be able to retain her job if she became a Catholic, Bolton went on:

> (She would) be taken up to London with the Family in the season if she should refrain from going to Church, and read proper Books; that he sent her by his Maid a small book before she went, a catechism Book. In London, he said, bring the Book which he sent her by his Maid. She went up to his Chamber to be instructed from this Book every day or week.[399]

The Bolton Case, although so late, indicates that isolated rural communities were still apprehensive about the threat of popery as a disruptive force, and while it is admitted that the quotation above was used as evidence against Bolton and might not have been strictly true, it is probably largely correct in describing the general method of procedure. More revealing still was the monk John Barnes's plan to convert the gentleman Marlow Sidney. Sidney had given his wife a guitar sometime around 1771, and a professor friend of the couple had recommended that it was best tuned by a priest he knew. This was enough to deter the Sidneys, as conventional Anglicans, from wanting to meet Barnes, despite Marlow's fascination with 'Romish doctrine'. While however the couple were dining with the 'liberal-minded' professor, an extraordinary coincidence happened:

> I wish, Mrs. Sidney', said the friend, 'you would consent to see Mr. Barnes, the musical gentleman I named to you... Mr. Barnes is so agreeable and clever, quite a man of society, and evidently accustomed to the best. Besides, I am by no means sure that he is a Popish Priest, though I conclude he is a Papist, as he has been much abroad...Why, I declare, *there* is Mr. Barnes just passing on his way back to town. Do let me ask him in.

117

Barnes was admitted, the guitar tuned, 'troubadour ditties, then so much in vogue', sung, and Barnes admitted he was 'a proscribed Popish Priest'. At first, he hesitated to discuss theology:

> I regret much, Mr. Sidney, that I cannot give you the explanation you desire, for in fact I am under a promise to my patron, Lord Stourton, to enter on no controversial matter with any one while I reside with him...The position of a Catholic nobleman is one demanding great caution, as you must be aware, with the existing penal code in full force, and sometimes even acted upon...

However, Barnes did lend Sidney books dealing with Catholic belief in the Real Presence, and Sidney was eventually converted to Catholicism, with his wife following him later. Even when allowance is made for the sentimental overlay of these later reminiscences, Barnes's charm, talents and discretion emerge as the deciding factors in this story of conversion.[400]

In the eighteenth century, despite the continued existence of the penal laws, active persecution of Catholics was sporadic. Those periods of persecution which were most violent and had a national effect, were generally aroused by traditional fears of Catholicism as synonymous with tyranny and Jacobitism, and they often took place during periods of political and sometimes economic tension. We might cite as examples of such agitations, the anti-Jacobite campaigns of the 1690s, the attacks on Catholics in the wake of the failure of the '15, and the Gordon Riots of 1780; Benedictine missioners were involved in all these. By way of contrast, there was a larger number of smaller, localised persecutions of Benedictine missioners, some of whose causes are ill-defined. In the case of others, local jealousy and suspicions of the insidious spread of Catholic influence led some neighbours of Catholics to see a conspiracy against the Anglican establishment. Jealously appears, for instance, to have lain behind the charge against Charles Cottington for harbouring a Benedictine missioner in Wiltshire in 1696, but we are less well informed of the reasons behind Denis Bishop's arrest in 1721, for we are only told he had 'rendered himself obnoxious to the penal Laws' while a missioner in London.[401] In the East Riding, an Anglican rector complained earier in the century of lay Catholics proselytising through putting destitute children in Catholic families, and he was forced to found his own charity school to counter monk missioners distributing catechisms and providing some rudimentary schooling. Sometimes the missioner was able to refuse to quit the country after being charged with being a priest.Gregory Watkinson was so charged in 1770, and ordered out of Myddelton in the West Riding by the son-in-law of the local clergyman, but he stayed in his mission until his death there in 1792.[402] Persecution could affect the mental health of a missioner. In Norfolk in 1771, old Maurus Westbrooke, presented as a recusant as far back as 1745, suffered delusions in old age:

> Mr. Fountain…made him a visit & to his surprise found him in ye greatest hurry & confusion of mind & a degree of insanity, and incapable of any duty, even looking into a book etc. He appears in constant terror & fear of being apprehended & carried to prison, & having his house & goods seized, which has taken such possession of his mind yt he can scarce be prevailed upon to quit his room. While Mr. Fountain was with him, he seemed in a continual anxiety & was constantly pressing him to quit ye house least he should be involved in his fate. In short, his head seems quite disordered.

Watkinson was sent back to his monastery at Lambspring.[403]

There is little doubt that local persecution was stirred up time and again by the local Anglican clergyman. Sometimes, like King at Cheam, he might be deliberately obstructionist, at other times, he would demand that the civil authorities act to suppress the further spread of popery. This antipathy continued throughout most of the century. Alban Dawney in its second decade, was afraid 'the Minister' would persecute his 'new converts' in Wiltshire, and twenty years later, the development of Benedictine missions in north Lancashire made local justices determined to prosecute any Catholic priest working in their district.[404] Anti-Catholic feeling seems to have been particularly strong in the 1770s in areas not apparently associated in any way with the Gordon Riots of 1780. In the summer of 1777, the Benedictine Provincial was forced to replace 'Mr. Bolas at Hesleyside (in Northumberland) driven from there by a persecution raised against him by ye Parson'. Catholicism seems to have been already in decline at Hesleyside by this time.[405] In Lancashire, where the Catholic minority was very numerous, the Anglican clergy inevitably felt threatened, and therefore applied the normal indirect and direct sanctions to halt Catholicism's progress. At a Catholic funeral in Brindle in 1770:

Ye Parson ordered ye cross to be taken off before the entrance of church yard. He has likewise by a letter forbidden Betty Tootell to teach.[406]

Much more serious, in the same year was a tardy campaign which attempted to shut many Catholic chapels in south Lancashire:

> Now I here send you Melancholy Nuse, *Peter Wearing* and Blakey, you know them both very well, are turned Renogadoes and informers. *Wearing* has informed against Davison and Jones who are fled, against Mr. Mansell of Litham who prays privately, against Mr. Jones and Cuerdon or another whose name I know not...*Wearing* and *Blakey* herd much with one Buck, the Curate of Kirkham, a firebrand, and is supposed to have sent for the *paire* to come into Lancashire. Mr. Mansel has sent strict orders to Mr. Norton of Wigan to admit no strangers. Wearing keeps still saying M(ass) and his son assists... Nobody goes near *Wearing* but two old women, unable to go anywhere else...What I have writ is all over the country.

It appears that the two informers were renegade priests, familiar with the patterns of local Catholic life. No Benedictine mission was informed on, even though Maurus Bulmer had refused in the past to be responsible for seeing Wearing's son was educated in a Catholic school. When the monk John Fisher visited Lancashire five years later, he found the Catholics contented and 'all quiet again relating to Wareing and Blakey'.[407] Such sudden alarms must have been a common experience among local Catholic communities.

Despite all these momentary setbacks, time was on the side of the English Catholics. The first Relief Act, which would eradicate spying on Catholics, was passed in 1778. With the slow repeal of other penal laws following on from this Act, persecution lost its teeth once its judicial support was removed, and could only be sustained as a force built upon embittered emotion.

The Architectural and Liturgical Setting of the Benedictine Mission.

The reign of James II had seen some important advances among the Benedictines on the mission in the development of an elaborate liturgy in splendid surroundings. The decade after the Revolution, however, shows little evidence of this continuing; rather there was something of a withdrawal towards a more hidden liturgical celebration within Catholic households. An example of what presumably happened elsewhere at this time to Benedictine chapels was the destruction of the chapel at Fishwick in Lancashire. Here the bells were buried and chapel furnishings hidden to await better days.[408]

It was presumably the private chapels in patrons' houses which mostly survived the Revolution, but it is only from the 1730s that we can gain some impression of them. A number were being rebuilt during these years and were, significantly, opened to the public. Gilling in the North Riding had a chapel refitted in a room of the front wing of the castle in 1730, where the Blessed Sacrament was reserved and an outside staircase allowed access to the public. The use of incense here suggests some solemnity in the liturgy. Gilling's chapel would have been very similar to that of neighbouring Brandsby which the local congregation entered from a courtyard by a narrow staircase.[409] In 1740, when Capheaton in Northumberland was the residence of the Provincial, its chapel, above the main doorway of the Hall, was opened up:

> I have presumed to make an alteration in the Chapel. I have taken away the ptition. or plasterwork that went under the Ribb before the windows. In place of which we have placed 5 pillars with Base and Capitals, ye Ribb cased and a handsome Cornich. By this the windows spread their light all over the Chappele which before was confined to ye places opposite to ye windows. The Great Window is well done and a great addition both to ye front and Chapel.[410]

Further south, in Yorkshire, increased agricultural wealth allowed Benedictine patrons to employ well-known architects to rebuild and enlarge their chapels. John Carr rebuilt Everingham between 1756 and 1764, and James Paine, the chapel in his new Stockeld Park between 1758 and 1763. Everingham had already had an elaborate chapel liturgy. From at least the 1740s, its chapel had been found on the house's first floor, and its sacred vessels had included a 'Remonstrance'.[411] In his Palladian villa at Stockeld, Paine devoted the left pavilion to building a large elaborate chapel taking up two floors, and including a tribune on the first floor for the family, the Middletons. The priest lived in the basement of the house.[412] In 1766, ten years after rebuilding Everingham, Carr designed the house chapel at Holme in the East Riding for the Langdales. This was, and is, a substantial building, forty six feet long, in the Palladian style, with fitments and pictures brought from Italy. Like elsewhere, a gallery was provided for the family.[413]

Further afield, in Lancashire, a 1755 inventory of the Standish family's chapel at Standish Hall suggests similar fitments to those in Yorkshire chapels. At Standish, there were fifteen sets of vestments, two tabernacles and steps, but no thurible.[414] Some household chapels were however never 'improved'; at Swinburne Castle, the home of the Riddells, the domestic chapel remained above the brewhouse until the mid-19th century and was reached from outside by a flight of stairs.[415] Although monks were concentrating on building their own separate missions chapels from the 1760s, a few patrons continued to develop their own domestic chapels in conformity with the latest fashions. Gothic was favoured by the 11th Duke of Norfolk at Deepdene, Surrey, as early as 1768 and by John Errington at Beaufront, Northumberland in 1777. As regards Beaufront's design, Errington sought the advice of Augustine Walker, the Benedictine Procurator in Rome, a connoisseur and collector, who had already executed commissions for works of art in Rome on behalf of Errington. His new chapel would have been, like others already mentioned, open to the public:

'...procure me a plan of a chapel to hold a large congregation. I would have it neat, light, of the Gothick construction, the less ornamented, the better, with a place for a Bell if required. Where I would have it fen'd is at the west end of the inclosed plan (the stable crossed to be removed); the chamber floor below is eight feet high, the chapel above ten feet six inches, and the House four feet six inches higher than the Chapel roof; this chapel which I built not long ago, I think of converting into a Tribune to the new one by removing the fire-place. The tribune must be part of the plan, as well as the altar etc.[416]

The independent mission chapels which were to become so common, especially in the north in the latter part of the century, had had earlier models. The house, chapel and land at Brindle which the missioner Placid Naylor handed over to the Province in the 1720s, was typical of a number.[417] Independent urban missions in contrast to some household chapels, were generally simple in style and close to nonconformist chapels. Whitehaven's (1786) was tucked down a lane;

Warrington's (1779) formed part of an ordinary terrace, and was built of brick; it replaced an upstairs room used as a sack warehouse. The chapel at Gillmoss, established after Viscount Molyneux's apostasy in 1768, was in the attic of a farm. Netherton, built as late as 1793, had a fine interior, but was built at the back of a house. Ormskirk's chapel of the early 1760s was on the first floor of the 'presbytery' built by the Benedictine incumbent. The Brownedge chapel of 1780 was in a house adjoining the presbytery.[418] The Hindley chapel took over two years to build, was raised by public subscription and was a large but simple brick building, with cellar and vestry. It was opened in 1791 with the performance of an Oratorio which involved forty participants.[419] In 1786, the Brindle chapel was rebuilt, and became a large plain structure, without decoration. It is an example of many constructed in 'the rage of chapel building' engulfing the north-west. Brindle's elaborate gilded mahogany altar furnishings, added a few years later, were the work of the well-known furniture maker, Richard Gillow, who had convalesced at the Brindle presbytery. The gilding of the 'remonstance' and altar crucifix had to be executed in Gillow's London workshop since there was no one, Gillow apologized, skilled in such work in Lancashire. Among Benedictine missions, only Brindle and Stockeld Park seem to have employed Gillow, suggesting that the bulk of decoration in Benedictine churches was the rustic work of local craftsmen unless it was provided by *objets d'art* imported from the Continent.[420] Benedict Macdonald's new chapel at Seel Street, Liverpool (1788) was similar to other Benedictine town chapels in Lancashire, but was smaller than the other chapel in Edmund Street.[421] Seel Street's chapel was a fashionable resort and its ceremonial elaborate. In 1790, a non-Catholic was moved by the beauty of 'High Mass' celebrated there:

> I seated myself in an empty pew, & composed my thoughts to the solemnity of the Occasion. Though I have often been in Catholic churches, yet I was attracted by the splendour & ceremonial of the worship which led me, at times, into involuntary musings, on the advantages which result from making the senses auxiliaries in our devotion...[422]

This description comes from the late eighteenth century , when the outward forms of Catholic worship were more readily tolerated. Even so, the monks had been familiar with a full liturgical life in the

123

Portuguese Embassy chapel and in their own chapel at Bath. A new embassy chapel had been opened in 1740, and was supplied by a handful of monks throughout the century. A fine singing voice was one of the qualities looked for in those taking up the office of chaplain.[423] Bath's chapel continued to grow bigger and more elaborate as the century progressed.[424] A new chapel was built by Bede Brewer between 1777 and 1780 in St James' Parade with 'no kind of opposition, tho' the spot we are building on is in a very conspicuous part of the town'. 'The Grand Building' would accommodate a third more than the old Bell-tree chapel, but Brewer, witnessing the rapid increase of his congregation, forecast it would be too small within twenty years.[425]

This chapel was the work of a master mason, a convert of Brewer's, and the contemporary description of it is perhaps the most detailed we possess of any Catholic chapel of this date. Its galleries stood on twelve-foot pillars, and had their own ten-foot columns supporting an arched roof:

Our new building in nearly covered in. I examined it very minutely and found no deficiency either as to Foundations or a lightness of the walling. The Chapl. and House are well situated and every way convenient. The House is single which makes it appear larger than it really is; the Front is elegant and neat, corresponding to the opposite buildings, according to the rule at Bath, and therefore necessary, and extends near 40 feet in front and 16 deep in the clear. The Chapl. is 61 feet long and 35 broad in the clear entirely hid from the Parade by the Chaps. and another House. The Nobility and Genty. who are indisposed may be carried thro' the Chapl., or have the conveniency of hearing prayers in two small rooms in the House by flinging up a sash looking upon the Alter. There is a Gallery in Front the whole Breadth of the Chapl., 13 feet wide; the side Galls. extend within 10 feet of ye Alter, 9 Feet wide. These and side roofs are supported by 6 stone pillars with carved capitals. From the Floor to the Gal. is 10 feet, and from the Gal. to the roof is 12 feet. The middle roof is coved, and from the pavement is 26 feet high. The wall behind the altar is arched, by which means the Chapl. may be enlarged at small expense in case it ever becomes necessary. At present it will with ease contain 600 persons, and many more if necessary. On the side next, a spacious street where coaches with all conveniency may drive up and turn. The Chapel is hid by three Houses, adjoining to these Houses is the Entery for all classes of People. Before you enter the Chapl. on the right hand is a good staircase which leads to the Galls. and another corresponding, from the Chap's. house. Neither of these are seen in the Chapl. The Magistrates and leading people at Bath are pleased and promise protection. There will still be wanting at least £700 to finish it; subscriptions come in but slow, (at) which I am rather surprised, considering Bath a place of such resort from all parts. However, am in hopes that the next season will prove successful.[426]

Just before Brewer was to move into this chapel, it was tragically burned by the mob in the Gordon Riots of May 1780. The authorities paid compensation, but the next chapel was built away from the public eye in the hope that the 'deal of bitterness against Catholics' would soon disappear. The decision 'to buy a house in some retired spot...when the purse will allow', led to the erecting of a new chapel in the congested area of Corn Street in 1786.[427]

It was natural that chapels like that at Bath or Seel Street should develop a more elaborate liturgy, such as was also developing in some Anglican churches in the 1770s and 1780s. But, rather surprisingly, conservative lay and monastic opinion did not always readily adapt to these changes in style. From April 1778 there were a series of lampoons in the Bath and Bristol press against Bede Brewer's attempt to introduce singing into the Bath chapel. Brewer's critic blamed the 1778 Relief Act for this novelty, and had no patience with clergy who welcomed the Act and vaunted their newly-found freedom by indulging in vulgar liturgical ceremonial. Provincial Warmoll, and by inference, Bishop Walmesley, who were both experienced missioners, also condemned singing as an inappropriate and 'unnecessary devotion'.[428] Walmesley had nevertheless consecrated Lord Arundell's splendid household chapel at Wardour in 1776. Although there were exceptions, as we have already seen, the liturgy in the majority of Benedictine missions was subdued and domestic, and missioners, accustomed to such, could not easily change their preference for almost Jansenist simplicity. The Benedictine apostate, Denis Hudleston, whose Protestant sympathies and Gallicanism are discussed elsewhere, had once been a missioner. Becoming an Anglican in the late 1720s, he had condemned Catholicism for deceit caused by pomp:

This Church is not begotten of Christ...it has brought forth ... a Worship full of Pageantry, rich Dresses, gaudy Shows, antick Postures, Heathen Habits, for the most part Female (which) fills Christian Chancels, blinds the eyes of the vulgar, and takes from them the Thought that God is to be worshipped, not in Things, but in spirit and Truth'.[429]

A change in attitude between simplicity and ceremony, between the old type of Benedictine missioner and the new breed, can be pinpointed accurately in the 1780s, that is, between the Relief Acts of 1778 and 1791. The 1785 General Chapter forbade missioners from introducing singing or music into their chapels without permission, and insisted that only the type of singing which increased piety be allowed. Singing must not be used by missioners as a substitute for instructing their congregations. Two years later, Thomas Welch, the archetypal domestic chaplain, summarised the feelings of all missioners attached to the old order:

> The zeal of our missioners is greatly abated since they begin to vie with each other in building elegant Chapels, in singing high Mass and in setting up organs in their Chappels. The young people of both sexes, instead of being instructed in their religion and in their moral duties, are taught musick and singing, and strolling companies of singers go from Chappel to Chappel to perform their parts for hire or drink. This disorder prevails chiefly in Lancashire, which formerly was respected for the religion and piety of its Catholic inhabitants, and for being the nursery of ecclesiastics and nuns.[430]

In Lancashire, the oratorio at Hindley was performed four years after this condemnation, and by then the dignity of High Mass at Seel Street had an appreciative congregation. In London, Bede Bennet was helping Lord Arundell to enhance the ceremonial in his magnificent chapel by sending him supplies of incense and other church effects. The most positive attitude to change and to the future came from an enclosed Benedictine nun at Cambrai. Dame Margaret Burgess told President Walker in 1784 how delighted she was in the development of the Second Spring in Lancashire: 'We have lately had the satisfaction of hearing that Religion begins to flourish in England, especially in Lancashire, where a few miles from Preston at a place called Fernyhall, Our Lady's Chapel, High Mass with Music, Vespers and Litanies were sung upon all the great feasts at Christmas, and since. People came twenty, some thirty miles to be present, and thought the trouble of their journey well bestowed; the singers were preparing a year beforehand'.[431]

126

CHAPTER IV

THE SPIRITUALITY OF THE
ENGLISH BENEDICTINES 1685-1794

During the course of the seventeenth century, the English Benedictine monks and nuns had been responsible for a revival of contemplative prayer, largely based on a return to the English late medieval
mystical writers. In this renaissance, Augustine Baker (1575-1624) had
been a leading spirit. He was a convert who, in his later life as a
monk, was to foster this form of spirituality, particularly among the
English Benedictine nuns at Cambrai. Bakerism was clearly a major
force in encouraging a return to affective prayer during this time, but
its strength in general is difficult to gauge, despite the large number of
manuscripts of Baker's teachings which his disciples left to posterity.
It was, most likely, one of a number of rather similar spiritual
traditions which monks used during this century.[432]

By the early eighteenth century, however, Bakerism was in decline.
From the mid-seventeenth century, Baker's disciples among the monks
had tended to be educated and mature Anglican converts, attracted to
Catholicism through respect for its historical continuity and emphasis
on contemplative prayer; both of these they discovered in
Benedictinism.[433] After 1689, this flow of converts well-nigh dried up,
and by the first years of the eighteenth century, novices tended to be
largely cradle-Catholics, professed at a very early age, and perhaps
less receptive to the higher flights of mystical prayer practised by some
of their forbears.

Moreover, the living tradition of English Benedictine spirituality
seems to have become narrowed down by the 1680s to a few specific
pockets in the monks's houses, and in the enclosed monasteries of
Benedictine nuns.[434] We know that nuns at Cambrai and Paris
continued to copy out Baker's teachings, and to follow them. Dame
Justina Gascoigne, for example, was still experiencing the 'bitter
Desolations', described by Baker, up until two years before her death
in 1690.[435] Weldon likened her to St. Catherine of Bologna on account
of 'these times of obscurity and dereliction'. Her spiritual directors,
Maurus Corker and the Dominican Alexander Pliny, believed her to be
a saint. The convents preferred chaplains well-versed in such forms of

prayer, whose Baker manuscripts still survive.[436] As regards the monks, surviving evidence points to Lambspring as the house most involved in the perpetuation of Baker. Here, Baker's disciple Maurus Corker was abbot between 1690 and 1697. Corker had encouraged the establishment of educational burses containing instructions that beneficiaries should be schooled in Baker's principles. Students at Lambspring who became monks there were, furthermore, directed by at least one novice master familiar with Baker.[437] On the mission, interest in contemplative spirituality had grown in the recent past among aristocratic converts, especially among those who had been counselled by monks of the monastery of St James in London during James II's reign. Maurus Corker had been well-known for such work, having reputedly made over a thousand converts. He remained the quintessential Stuart Benedictine, quite at ease in aristocratic English circles.[438] Much of this work had, however, been brought to an abrupt end by the Glorious Revolution, when Court Monasticism faded away, at least in England.

On the Continent, however, we find its survival in monks like Thomas Southcott who, like his predecessors, was to build up a circle of wealthy converts, centred on the Stuart court in exile. As the English Benedictine President (1721-41), living in Paris, Southcott was engaged in 'showing the truth' to wealthy ladies discontented with their Protestantism, and he deliberately dressed in secular clothes for such meetings to prevent alarm.[439] Southcott acted also as spiritual director to nuns, counselling a full resignation to God's will in order to 'taste by anticipation those joys that exceed all sense and never will have end'.[440] There is no evidence, however, to show Southcott used or was directly influenced by Baker; if his exterior world resembled Corker's, his spiritual world was more identified with the teachings of Fénelon than Augustine Baker. The condemnation of Quietism in 1687 has been taken as a major reason for the decline of Bakerism among the English Benedictines,[441] but the similarities between Bakerism and French Semiquietism prompt one to discern a sensitive modulation of the former into the latter. Southcott was a great friend of the scholar and enthusiast, the Chevalier Andrew Michael Ramsay, and an active patron of the latter's influential spiritual life of Fénelon.[442] For Southcott, Fénelon's teaching regarding 'disinterested love' had the same practical effect as Baker's writing earlier; both were vehicles for attracting Anglicans, interested in mysticism and contemplative prayer, to the Catholic Church. He believed:

128

il y a parmi les Protestans une infinité de personnes qui ne se tiennent éloigner de l'Eglise catholique que par une fausse persuasion que Rome a rejette la parfaite charité…qui gouttent nos livres de dévotion, surtout les contemplatifs canonisés, et qui se réuniroient a l'Eglise s'il voyoint la doctrine de la parfaite charité authorisée par Rome.[443]

Southcott had observed, while on the English mission, growing Anglican interest in Catholic spirituality, and he firmly believed Fénelon might act as a bridge. For the Bishop of Cambrai, in Ramsay's hagiographical work, was shown directing a group of recently-converted women, but was opposed at the same time, to all use of force in the work of conversion. Non-Catholics, Ramsay suggested, would be impressed by Fénelon suffering for his principles, and by his willingness to distinguish the essential elements of Catholicism from its trappings.[444] There is evidence that, by the beginning of the eighteenth century, Fénelon's teaching was infiltrating into strongholds of Bakerism like Cambrai. The chaplain there between 1702 and 1705, Denis Bishop, a Lambspring monk, culled texts from the Fathers and St. Francis de Sales to define 'the law of love', and after a caveat against too frequent a reception of Communion, as leading to mere habit and vanity, Bishop concluded in terms close to those Fénelon would have used himself:

> You chaste spouses know this (that love is not of thoughts or words, but is the language of a loving wife), more by practice that by speculation; Our Lady of Comfort (the community's patron) has had these disinterested lovers in the past, and I hope also in the future.[445]

Fénelon was to emerge during the eighteenth century as an early hero of the philosophers,[446] and Ramsay, his biographer and a converted Deist, had one foot in the older world of 'Pure Love and humble Faith', and another in the newer world of the early scientific Enlightenment. By the second decade of the century, the English Benedictines were also being forced to bring their spirituality into conformity with the new philosophical outlook, which required a sloughing off of inherited spiritual traditions. The higher spiritual concerns which had characterised the mystical tradition of the previous century had little place in the enlightened spirituality of the eighteenth-century English Benedictines. In this, there is less concern to employ a system and language to describe refined mystical or psychological states. Eighteenth-century English Benedictine spirituality was rather more practical and closer to the patterns of daily life, even, perhaps, more superficial. The manuscript compilation of mystical treatises appears to have ended among the monks by the 1720s. Those still in the possession of monks who were on the mission in later years were presumably treated more as heirlooms rather than as effective manuals for prayer.[447] Furthermore, at Lambspring, the Cotton Fund's obligation to have scholars schooled in the principles of Father Baker fell into desuetude after 1728.[448]

It is not surprising that emphasis on contemplative prayer within the monasteries at the end of the seventeenth century encouraged ascetic practices which complemented some of the rigorism already contained in the Congregation's early Constitutional settlement. Again, the eighteenth century was to see a major transformation of this aspect of spirituality. Ascetic practices which had not fallen into disuse by mid-century, were to be deliberately omitted as anachronisms from the new Constitutions of 1784, which aimed at modernising aspects of the regular life. The Congregation's *Caeremoniale* was the shell protecting the practice of asceticism within the monasteries, and was itself supplemented by house customaries. We have already described the daily routine at St. Edmund's, Paris, at the turn of the century. But fashions changed during the course of the eighteenth century to complement more 'enlightened' attitudes and to meet the needs of expediency.[449] In the 1680s, old Maurus Nelson at St. Edmund's, Paris, had impressed younger monks like Weldon by his insistence on taking 'the Discipline, though it rattled on his plaisters'. A century later, President John Fisher hoped the use of the Discipline might be omitted altogether from the new Constitutions, together with the traditional abstinence on the three great Solemnities, 'an absurd practice'.[450] Shortage of numbers and the burden of work were practical reasons given for the reduction of the Choir Office at St. Gregory's, Douai, whose lengthened Office resulted from a stipulation in the original charter of foundation.[451]

Changing attitudes to the value of asceticism were also reflected, as we have already seen, in the Congregation's relations with the stricter monastic orders. Until the end of the seventeenth century, the eremitical life had flourished at St Edmund's conventual priory of La Celle, and at the same period, La Trappe had lured away three English monks, one for good. Despite offering 'a place of greater security', La Trappe was too severe for most English Benedictine aspirants. Benet

Weldon had dreamed its abbot, de Rancé, had ordered him back from La Trappe to St Edmund's, Paris, forbidding him from settling there. Nevertheless, La Trappe came closest to Weldon's picture of an ideal monastery, an institution he saw portrayed in St Bernard's third sermon on the Dedication of a Church.[452] Despite the preference of Laurence Barnes for La Trappe in 1779, which we have already noted, and which was condemned as escapism, Barnes can still perhaps be seen as clinging to older fashions in spirituality even at this late date. We hear he had 'a great repugnance to Philosophical and Theological Studies', but that 'his Reading has generally been applied to spiritual Writers, particularly the Saints Lives, & his Reflections drawn from thence are pertinent enough, & edifying'. Clear evidence of what forms of spirituality attracted Barnes is lacking, but his own admission that he could not understand theology suggests he had a simple faith.[453]

There is no evidence that, despite the practice of regular asceticism at the end of the seventeenth century, the monks within the monasteries or on the mission were tainted with theological Jansenism, even though earlier, in 1661, they had been invited to celebrate mass at Port Royal. An interest in the Oratorian spirituality of Pierre, Cardinal de Bérulle (1575-1629), considered a formative influence on the Jansenist movement, was the closest some monks came to the spirit of Jansenism. Benet Weldon's historical annals, for instance, which contain a wealth of autobiographical detail, and reveal his psychological state, show also his attraction to the Oratorian spiritual teacher, Charles de Condren. Weldon approved of Condren's teaching on confession for he was convinced that it was necessary to appear before God alone and even to exaggerate faults, for 'it is better to condemn than to approve outselves'. Condren had also opposed the forms of meditation associated with Ignatian spirituality in favour of the inculcation of an attitude which manifested a total dependence on God.[454] As regards frequency of reception of communion, which was another source of Jansenist conflict, the monks seem to have been quite orthodox, and encouraged the non-ordained to communicate on Sundays and Feasts.[455] Jansenism seems only to have reared its head among the English Benedictines as a political brickbat, used by rebellious monks against their superiors, and by the enemies of the Congregation. Jansenism was evident in this loose sense when most of the Congregation's houses were surrounded by institutions and individuals suspected of Jansenist leanings. Dieulouard, for instance, was surrounded by Vannist Benedictine houses who were known to favour Jansenism. Bede Moore at Paris, during his long battle with his Prior, Joseph Johnston, over religious obedience, condemned the latter in 1706 as a Jansenist and a 'Presbyterian'. Moore went on to insist that the community at St. Edmund's, Paris, took the Formulary against the Jansenists. Moore's protest was an attempt to prevent his arrest by the civil authorities, by diverting their attention to the Prior, and President Gregson spotted the worthlessness of the accusation immediately:

> As to the objection of Jansenism, I look upon it as a very wild fancy, or as a sham pretence to elude the precept. He might as well for anything I know, object Mahometisme.[456]

The same use of 'Jansenist' as a gibe was found during the 1720s in the battle between the Benedictine President Thomas Southcott and the English Vicars Apostolic over the vexed question of privileges on the English mission. Southcott went out of his way to rebut any charge that he was a Jansenist, insinuating, perhaps with some justification, that the English secular clergy and even the Vicars Apostolic were more prone to heterodoxy than himself.[457] Even so, the accusation that he had helped in the translation of part of the notorious Jansenist Quesnel's *Réflexions* came from so many different quarters that there might have been a grain of truth in it. In any case, this English translation appeared before the promulgation of *Unigenitus* in 1715. Behind Southcott's *cri de coeur* lay his determination to bring Rome down on the side of the monks in the conflict. Therefore Southcott acknowledged his loyalty to the papacy, and to the Thomism he had studied at Douai, and recommended Fénelon as a model of obedience to Jansenists.[458] 'Jansenism' as a term of reproach continued to be used by monks and secular clergy against each other throughout the century,[459] but in this conflict, it had little spiritual meaning. It is not after all surprising that English monks, living as favoured guests in France, needing to take the anti-Jansenist oath to be presented to benefices, and constantly seeking to establish the authenticity of their missionary status through recourse to Rome, would not have dared to be found guilty of Jansenism. Co-operation against Jansenism was evident both on the part of the authorities and that of the monks.[460]

Possession of Jansenist books, furthermore, offers little proof that some monks were heterodox since the evidence is ambivalent; there was, for instance, alongside many French works believed to show Jansenist tendencies, an increasing number of anti-Jansenist works in monastery libraries as the century progressed. The mission presents a similar picture. Here provincial censors were clearly involved in first isolating, then banning Jansenist works.[461] Indeed, one of the lasting effects of the Jansenist controversy was the tightening up of censorship against the reading of forbidden books, at first Jansenist, later 'philosophical', in the monasteries during the eighteenth century. Censorship was however not always tight enough; one Lambspring monk apostatised in 1737 after reading heterodox books on the eucharist and after persuasion from a Protestant prince.[462]

The seventeenth century's intense involvement in spirituality was responsible for two bequests to the eighteenth-century English Benedictines, the Rosary devotion and the compilation of hagiography. Both had been rooted in the monasteries during the seventeenth century, and their transference and popularity in the English mission from the 1680s represents a successful adaptation of traditional spirituality to altered times and circumstances.

The Confraternity of the Rosary had flourished in London with an aristocractic membership from the mid-seventeenth century under Benedictine direction. There, it had boasted a chapel and devotional literature, compiled and published by monks. During James II's reign, the Confraternity's base was Maurus Corker's new chapel at Clerkenwell, which was destroyed at the Revolution.[463] Other Confraternities attached to the monasteries and not specifically based on devotion to the Rosary, were, however, unaffected, and carried on, using their own manuscript manuals, and enrolling members from the communities and monastic schools. At St. Laurence's, Dieulouard, local townspeople began to be enrolled from 1689, perhaps providing the inspiration for missioners in England to develop later the Confraternity among their own laity.[464] On the mission, the extra-liturgical devotion of the Rosary was popularised by monks who were allowed to admit new members into the extensive Dominican Confraternity of the Rosary, and who secured Diplomas *pro Rosario* for their patrons' chapels. Such missioners made use of the Dominican John Clarkson's *Introduction...to the Holy Rosary* (London 1737) to spread the devotion.[465] Besides its most obvious virtue of increasing the devotion of the laity — a large number of those enrolled were women — the Confraternity in general was a valuable method by which the regular clergy could compete with a rival group like the secular clergy in attracting souls into their cure. Thus, the printed *Constitutiones Missionis* (Douai 1689), whose publication marks the coming of age of the English Benedictine mission, contains the form for admitting seculars, especially patrons, into the Confraternity of St. Benedict, with attached privileges.[466] If the Rosary was a pioneering method by which monks introduced a wide cross-section of their congregations to private prayer, it was to be superseded, if not replaced, by other devotions as the century progressed, like those found in the manuals compiled by Archibald Benedict Macdonald discussed later. These were to be more in harmony with the worship of large urban congregations to which the monks were ministering by the century's end.

Like the Rosary, the Benedictine interest in hagiography also spilled over into the changed world of post-Revolution England. Seventeenth-century Benedictine involvement with the saints had quite definite aims, over and beyond fashionable antiquarianism. It sought to provide models of an heroic age, usually the Anglo-Saxon, easily identifiable with the seventeenth century. Secondly, it unashamedly tried to prove that the English Congregation as a whole was in direct line of succession from the founding fathers of English Christianity, Augustine and his Anglo-Saxon descendants. The latter point was hammered out in debates over the existence of a medieval Benedictine Congregation, and in the early controversies with Bishop Richard Smith who claimed the full powers of an Ordinary in the 1620s. The defence of English Benedictine antecedents and pre-eminence had been ably disseminated in Clement Reyner's *Apostolatus Benedictinorum in Anglia* (Douai 1626) largely the work of Augustine Baker, and in Hugh Serenus Cressy's *The Church History of Brittany* (Rouen 1668).[467] Hagiographical writings by English Benedictines during the same period also contributed to this defence.[468]

An identical revival of the past occurred after 1688, and was the inspiration for much of Benet Weldon's writing, which is steeped in the moral lessons of history. Devotion to the saints, within the English monasteries on the continent, was, of course, taken as part of the ordinary daily round of liturgical life, with the communities participating in events like annual processions of relics of local saints.[469] At Lambspring, however, Abbot Maurus Corker subtly enhanced the traditional reverence for saints inside a wealthy established monastery with devotion to the relics of English saints in particular, a move by which he hoped to demonstrate continuity with the past and the inevitability of suffering as the lot of Catholics in England after the

Revolution. There were thus brought into the new church at Lambspring, consecrated in 1691, the head of St. Thomas of Hereford and the body of Oliver Plunkett, martyred in 1681 during the Popish Plot scare. Later, there were moves to transfer St. Cuthbert, the Anglo-Saxon saint especially associated with the Benedictines at Durham, from his secret resting-place in Durham to Lambspring.[470]

This medieval revivalism at Lambspring had no place, of course, in the disturbed world of Catholicism in England after the Revolution where, in default of martyrs, the heroism of missioners became idealised, and types were found among the Anglo-Saxon monastic missionaries. Such models were used time and again to assert Benedictine continuity and pre-eminence on the mission during the conflict with the Vicars Apostolic. The only work of English Benedictine hagiography published after 1688, was an edition of the monk Jerome Porter's *The Life of St. Edward, King and Confessor* (1710). This was extracted from his larger general work of 1632, and incorporated enough changes in the text for it to be viewed as a Jacobite work. In it, the Confessor is seen to embody all the strengths and none of the weaknesses of the Stuarts.[471]

The Stuarts, like the Confessor, had served as patrons of English Benedictinism, and with James II's flight, and the resulting confusion in the English Church, Catholicism was here reduced to the status of a missionary force, persecuted from without, and weakened from within by little leadership, differing strategies, and conflicting jurisdictions. The English Benedictines did not shift their position in all this, and merely rehearsed earlier arguments to preserve their separate identity, and their exemption from the Vicars Apostolic. Providence and Rome were cautiously on the side of the latter, but at each bout of the contest, there were bursts of interest by the monks in their own clutch of saints, now hailed as spokesmen for the maintenance of the unique Benedictine presence within the fabric of the English Church. Thus, the various attempts to define that presence by means of a distinct English Calendar, coincided with periods when battle between monks and Vicars Apostolic was at its hottest.[472] Anselm Mannock's *Annus Sacer Britannica* (1747-50, with additions), came soon after its published Secular counterpart, Richard Challoner's *Britannia Sancta* (London 1745) and in the middle of the most serious conflict with the Vicars Apostolic. That dispute was mostly resolved, as we have seen, by the bull *Apostolicum Ministerium* of 1753, in favour of the Vicars Apostolic, but it did not prevent the Benedictines publishing their own Calendar in 1755, based on Mannock's researches.[473] This was the first formal Calendar for monks working on the mission; it deliberately segregated them from their counterparts among the seculars and other regulars who had their own Calendars. Mannock's work is a digest of earlier (named) authors' work on early English monastic saints, and the correct liturgical rank given to each saint in the work suggests its primary use was in the monastic Office.. Even so, it was in some sense a devotional work, for the author appended personal meditations after each entry, some taken from Fénelon, which were apparently designed for individual monks.

Two external factors helped to reduce partially such Benedictine isolationism. First, the Relief Act passed in 1778, which regularised the Catholic Church's position in the country and made the missionary clergy a more united body behind recognisable leaders in the persons of the Vicars Apostolic. There were secondly, the liturgical reforms of the Catholic Enlightenment initiated by Pius VI (1775-99), which had the practical effect of tidying up Calendars, closely scrutinising them for bogus saints, and removing their dead wood. It was the suppression of feasts by means of such reforms that helped ultimately to integrate further English Catholics into society generally.

For the monks, also, this enforced liturgical conformity, by which a common Calendar was generally followed, reduced their isolation from the rest of the clergy on the mission, and this was welcomed by Bishops Walmesley and Sharrock who represented both the monks and the bishops.[474] A similar move towards integration can be glimpsed in the changing attitude to the Benedictine 'secret' regarding the where-abouts of the body of St. Cuthbert in Durham Cathedral. Despite the existence of other conflicting 'secrets', notably that traditionally handed down by the secular clergy, the monks had used theirs in the past to validate further their claims to the cathedral priory of Durham and their inherited rights over its Chapter.[475] Only when the monks were restored to Durham would the secret be disclosed. By 1791, however, the reasons given for not allowing Thomas Weld to carry off the relics for enshrining in his new chapel at Lulworth Castle in Dorset, were based more on the fear of arousing the wrath of local Catholics and their bishop, than on the necessity of maintaining the 'secret' in Benedictine hands.[476] This growing sensitivity to other parallel missionary interests laid the foundations for the monks' co-operation with diocesan bishops and clergy in the next century.

It would be wrong however to understand Benedictine separatism merely as a negative force designed to preserve missionary independence. In very many ways, Benedictine missioners were identical to all the other missioners, secular and regular. They followed the same daily routine, mixed in the same social circles and it seems certain that on the mission, in contrast to inside the monasteries, the monks prayed the Roman, not monastic, breviary.[477] As Benedictine missioners, their spiritual life was regulated by the *Constitutiones Missionis* of 1689 which emphasized traditional Benedictine practices such as the litany at Vespers, the half-hour period of meditation, fasting thrice weekly, and wearing the habit, if convenient, when preaching. All these were designed to make missioners realise the importance of the monastic vows amidst the distractions of the mission.[478] Monk missioners were perhaps more involved than others in the transfer of continental spiritual works to England, thanks to their close links with the continental monasteries. Benedictine missions therefore often became the home for Gallican liturgical texts and commentaries. The works of authors like Bossuet, Bourdaloue, and Mabillon's *Traité des Études Monastiques* all made their way to England in missioners' pockets. Even if Benedictine missioners could be maddening to others through the assertion of their privileges, their contemporaries were impressed by their preaching skills which had been taught in the monasteries. Sermons which survive combine traditional Benedictine themes of submission to God's will with more practical advice regarding spiritual duties. The secular missioner Simon Bordley admitted in 1789:

> The Monks and Ex-Jesuits in these parts are excellent preachers, at least the people think them so; our priests are backward in discharging themselves in this duty.[479]

The most popular Catholic spiritual writers in England during the century were the secular priests John Gother and Richard Challoner whose spirituality was essentially activist. They used earlier continental models to educate a popular readership in the spiritual life. Their works were found on most Benedictine missioners' shelves and no doubt helped to replace any elements of the seventeenth-century Benedictine contemplative tradition which had survived among monks on the mission.[480] Both Gother and Challoner gave a solid spiritual base to the work of reconstructing the English Mission after the Revolution. In their own way, the monks shared in this reconstruction and revival. Frequent instructions of General and Provincial Chapters tried to tighten up discipline on the mission; mental prayer was regularly recommended, missioners were to see they were adequately instructed in preaching and catechising, and were, finally, to avoid hunting, gaming, and incriminating circumstances and places.[481] The monasteries were encouraged to take the spiritual formation of future missioners seriously, and for this purpose, the English monks produced a number of spiritual and practical works which would help to implement the Tridentine reforms through their emphasis on missionary endeavour, popular catechesis, and the central role of the priest. The Lambspring monk, John Townson, was teaching in Hildesheim when he produced his two Latin works on the Mass and the Sacrament of Penance. The former, *Brevis Expositio Missae* (Hildesheim 1703) even if written initially for a German audience, did inevitably find its way into English Benedictine mission libraries. The book made full use of post-Tridentine writers to teach priests to understand the Mass themselves so that they, in turn, could instruct their people. Townson emphasised the value of allegorical and tropological explanation. However, the book's almost Neo-platonic use of symbolism gave it a static quality, making it appear outdated when put, for instance, alongside Gother's more direct approach, which became the norm in the eighteenth century. Townson's other book, *Enchiridion Confessariorum* (Hildesheim 1705) was a methodical instruction manual for confessors, and like other similar earlier eighteenth century works dealing with moral theology, it condemned probabilism.[482]

Any missioner needed an understanding of the catechism and of scripture, and therefore we find at the beginning of the eighteenth-century, a series of works written specifically for the use of Benedictine missioners themselves, which formed the basis for later published books. It was in the eighteenth century above all that a large readership demanding popular catechetical works grew up in England. The manuscript, 'Brevis Symboli Apostolorum', written by a Lambspring monk, used a scheme based on the Apostles' Creed in the same way as Bernard Wythie's *The Creed Expounded* (1735). Wythie's book seems to have been the first English Benedictine published work approximating to a catechism; 'cooking the same meats' as the Council of Trent's catechism, 'after a different way to give them a better relish', *The Creed Expounded* was funded by the Congregation itself. Its classical and patristic references, together with its finely-worked 'soliloquies', suggest it was a work designed for monk missioners and their wealthy patrons, and hence it belonged to the classical period of the household chaplaincy.[483] Wythie's book successfully bridged the gap between the serious spiritual concerns of the seventeenth century and the more popular devotional attitude of the eighteenth. Thus it was able to progress quite naturally from describing the 'movement of Affections ..and Infused Knowledge' and the use of apophatic theology towards encouraging contemporary devotion to the Name of Jesus. The same genre was followed in the monk Paul Gilmore's *A Pious Monitor of the Divine Presence*, published in 1746. Earlier attempts at catechisms, like Gregory Greenwood's, had been largely derived from continental models, or were digests of English catechisms already published.[484] Similarly, manuscript scriptural commentaries by English monks written in the early eighteenth century, employed continental and English spiritual authors, many of whose books were already on the shelves of rural missions.[485]

The writing and disseminating of popular catechetical works by English Benedictines for a wide audience would only come when such authors began to publish their work from the 1750s. The older tradition of missioners compiling their own manuscript editions to be used as the framework for sermons and instruction certainly survived until that time. The shift from old to new is vividly illustrated in the three manuscript discourses on Witches and Witchcraft by Gregory Greenwood, missioner at Coughton in Warwickshire, which were written apparently just before his death in 1744.[486] They were addressed to 'Christian Auditors', and made much use of graphic reports of witch trials in France in the late sixteenth and early seventeenth centuries. Witchcraft was in steep decline in England by the end of the seventeenth century, but Greenwood, judging by the questions he supplied and answered here, still believed it was a living force of the Devil.[487] Even so, his side-swipe at 'Socinians, Free-Thinkers and Latitudinarians' indicates his awareness of contemporary rationalism.

When published Benedictine catechisms in paraphrase-form did appear for a popular readership, they were grafted onto two forms already in existence. First, they used traditional English works already in print, such as the Manual, Primer and Douay Catechism,[488] and secondly, they were the descendants of earlier Benedictine manuscript compilations. Both these influences are convincingly illustrated in the labours of John Anselm Mannock, a prolific Benedictine spiritual writer, on the mission from 1709 until his death in 1764.[489] By the

1740s, Mannock had in his possession a collection of manuscript sermons and commentaries written by monks earlier in the century.[490] Mannock's first published work, on the Mass, was published by his wealthy gentry patrons in 1726, and was in the tradition of Townson's *Brevis Explicatio*. This had had a limited circulation, but his *The Poor Man's Catechism* (first ed. 1752) was instantly popular, being bought by monks on the mission, and becoming recommended reading for young monks in the houses training to be future missioners.[491] The book combined the structure of the secular Turbeville and Douay Abstract catechisms with a series of spiritual 'exhortations' similar to those found in earlier Benedictine catechetical works like Wythie's.[492] Mannock's catechism was popular because of its practical directions. It listed the manual works forbidden on a Sunday, reprimanded sins against the seventh commandment, such as racking of tenants and 'forcibly with-holding Servants Wages', and devoted much space to a clear exposition of the 'Impedimenta' involved in marriage cases. Its simple summary form, giving clear practical guidelines, and its handy size, suggest that it served a need precisely at the time when many expanding congregations were moving away from a household chaplaincy and patrons' control.

A line of similar Benedictine catechisms was to follow through the rest of the century, and these were to become increasingly important as the need to educate the growing congregations was realised. Towards the end of the century, it is not then surprising to find monks in charge of the very large congregations in Bath and Liverpool trying their hand at such writing. Like Mannock, Michael Benedict Pembridge, at Bath between 1781 and 1786, had begun his interest in catechism-writing within a household chaplaincy. While here, he had published his *The Whole Duty of a Christian* in 1775, which aimed to direct 'Parents in the Christian Education of their Children', a necessity he believed might grow as the numbers of active missioners decreased. Pembridge's *The Family Manual of Morning and Evening Prayers* (1777) was taken directly from a manuscript copy of prayers which he had used with a particular family for eighteen years. Pembridge went on to attempt a prayer book suitable 'for Young Children and the lower class of people', but he was forced to revise this, following the Benedictine censors' advice to him to remove 'indelicacies'.[493] Much of this work was later incorporated presumably into his *A Manual of Daily Prayers and Duties of a Christian, with Historical Lessons from the Old and New Testaments, very useful for*

Children (1785). In the north, at Liverpool, the Benedictine incumbent, Archibald Benedict Macdonald, used much of his energy in the 1790s publishing small booklets of devotion to enhance the liturgy, large numbers of which had been published in Lancashire from the 1760s, and were popular with Benedictine missioners. Macdonald worked from the principle of the importance of congregational prayer for 'the laborious part which compose the bulk of the faithful'. He had felt constricted in not being allowed by the Congregation's censors to edit the unintelligible sections of the psalms, but he remained in the mainstream of popular English Catholic devotional writing through his acknowledgement of his debt to Gother and Challoner.[494]

Anselm Mannock's *The Poor Man's Controversy*, which was published posthumously in 1769,is less straightforward than these works of Pembridge and Macdonald. Although written 'in the plainest and lowest style to be understood by the meanest capacities', the book tried to reconcile Protestantism to English Catholicism by explaining controversial Catholic doctrines, adopting a minimalist view of the Papacy, and admitting Catholic excesses:'I know of none well-instructed Catholics that carry their devotion to Mary too high'. For its authorities, the book made liberal use of Anglican divines. The Congregation again backed this book by making itself responsible for its publication and distribution.[495] *The Poor Man's Controversy* can be interpreted as either a work designed to allay non-Catholic fears at a time of increasing toleration for Catholics, or as a book reflecting the liberal attitudes of what has been called the Catholic Enlightenment. If it is the latter which is more likely, the book shows the development of Mannock's thought during this period, and presumably that of other monks. It is quite certain that the Enlightenment had some effect on the spirituality of monks on the mission, especially regarding their pastoral concerns, even if it came late in the day. An example of this is the prayer-book called *Devout Miscellany* which Gregory Gregson, the Benedictine chaplain to John Throckmorton, a leading English Catholic liberal, tried to publish in 1791. It was condemned by the conservative Bishop Walmesley for its liberal use of Protestant versions of Scripture, for 'Englishing' parts of the Ritual, and trying to bring up-to-date the language of Challoner and other authors of devotional literature whom Gregson had used. Despite Walmesley's criticisms, the book passed the Benedictine censors and the first edition was quickly sold out.[496]

Gregson's liberalism gives the vital clue to an understanding of the spirituality among the English Benedictines during much of the eighteenth century, and explains the peculiar void which seems to exist, especially in the monasteries, after the previous century's feverish interest in the spiritual life. If we wish to discover the monks' spiritual concerns during the eighteenth century, they will not be found in some arcane spiritual tradition or highly complex mystical school. English Benedictine spirituality was built on prevailing contemporary religious attitudes, and the eighteenth century was the age of reason, which frowned on religious fervour. It was believed religious feeling should be related to the ordinary rhythms of life, as far as they touched the individual and society. This century's involvement with science, as the key to understanding and progress, made religious men embark on a scientific quest themselves, in order to understand creation through natural as well as scriptural revelation. Thus a more positive and mechanistic attitude to the created world helped to cast away all earlier dualistic theories of spiritual states in favour of a more general, and perhaps more superficial, nature mysticism and Deism. Christianity, which found itself embedded within this process of transformation, sought to meet the challenge by clearing away all unreasonable anachronism, by expanding its influence into the new secular areas of scientific interest, and by insisting on the orderliness of religion. The danger of diluting the Christian message into forms such as Deism and Latitudinarianism, was balanced by a missionary enterprise which was prepared to accept what was of value in different cultures and sects, and by an attempt to rest revelation and the history of the Church on sound historical scholarship.

Therefore, if we wish to understand the spirituality of many eighteenth-century monks, we must look first at the effects on them of that complex liberal movement called the Enlightenment. This will reveal that it is not possible to categorise English Benedictine spirituality into the more restricted traditions of the previous century; eighteenth-century spirituality was heavily impregnated by eighteenth-century material experience. Except for examples like Gregson's prayer book, it is almost impossible to notice any strong philosophical currents affecting the spiritual attitudes of Benedictine missioners during the course of the eighteenth century. On account of its history, the English Mission was inevitably conservative and dragged behind most continental religious movements. If there was any conflict involved, it was that waged against the national Church, rather than against philosophers. The eighteenth-century English Catholic community has thus tended to be depicted as demoralised, depressed and hardly propitious for the development of innovatory religious literature.[497]

The theories, however, of a recent historian, Michel Vovelle, deduced from an analysis of religious behaviour in eighteenth-century Provence, can be helpful in making this received picture of English Catholics more positive. Vovelle has suggested that France experienced a great diversity of religious attitudes during this century. He described the seventeenth-century mystical movement as an *invasion mystique*, which became an *invasion dévote* between 1680 and 1740, when popular devotions multiplied but had their roots in the great mystical teachings of the previous century, which they, in turn, simplified.[498] It is this industrious spirit of the Counter-Reformation which we can discern in the English Catholic community throughout most of the eighteenth century, and which was still continuing when the so-called 'deChristiansiation' hit France some thirty years before the French Revolution. The English Benedictine Mission was part of this expansion. Those monks in France, however, found themselves being rapidly carried along in a ferment of new ideas which constantly questioned received ideas about Christian teachings and spirituality. Traditional spiritual classics may well have continued to lie on the shelves of the monastic libraries,[499] but whether they were read frequently is uncertain. What is certain is that from the evidence of monks tainted by liberal and philosophical attitudes, described in the chapters on Learning and the French Revolution, the critical spirit attached to 'deChristianisation' was present in the monasteries, especially in St. Edmund's, Paris.

To end, however, on this negative note would be to neglect morepositive features which showed the English Benedictines in France were capable of adapting their spirituality to combat fashionable attacks on Christianity. In the first place, it seems that a missionary counter-offensive against the enemies of the Church was still in full flood in 1789, and had some success through its enormously successful parish missions, its thundering evangelical preachers, and its popular devotional books of 'exercises'.[500] Thomas Welch, chaplain at Cambrai supported this latest crusade wholeheartedly. He appreciated the fiery sermons in Cambrai cathedral of the famous ex-Jesuit preacher, Jean-Nicholas Beauregard, Voltaire's 'monster' and scourge of the Jansenists, who had in 1775 predicted in apocalyptic terms the fall of

143

the throne and the rise of the cult of reason. Welch also counted the Abbé Guénée, the hammer of the philosophers, as one of his friends, and was an ardent reader of a large number of apologetic books then being published.[501]

It was Welch also who highlighted the second influence on English Benedictine spirituality in the last years of the *ancien régime*. The scale of the Lisbon earthquake in 1755 had shattered the supercilious stability of Enlightenment Europe, and introduced throughout society, a note of depression and unease which had been articulated by Voltaire. Later earthquakes in Italy in the early 1780s also had a sobering effect and made Welch pause for reflection: 'The dreadful disasters...make more impression in my mind than all the sermons on the last judgement I have ever read'.[502]

The uneasiness stemming from such uncontrollable disasters resulted in a return to the writing of apocalyptic works by Christian and non-Christian authors, which cut across any confidence in progress and made men mightily aware of the frailty of human institutions. The Benedictine Charles Walmesley's famous commentary on the Apocalypse, "Signor Pastorini's" *General History* (1770)is the most important English example, though written from a continental standpoint, of this genre, and is discussed elsewhere.[503] It was as the prophet of this age of uncertainty and the embodiment of that complete indifference by which men must approach it that Benedict Joseph Labre, the tramp of the Colosseum, achieved instant canonisation on his death in April 1783. Walmesley was fascinated by this holy beggar who showed up the folly of the world, and the saint's biography by Joseph Marconi (London 1785) was popular among Benedictine missioners.[504] Labre was a late type of the wandering ascetic of the early Church, but his literal carrying out of the gospel precepts was too extreme for most English Benedictines. He was better admired than imitated. By the time Labre became famous, the English Benedictines were already adopting a Romantic, but moderate, form of Rousseauism to serve as the future model of the monastic life. A sermon by one of them in 1771 described the monk as a Christian 'philosopher' rather than an 'epicure', who would best reach happiness through a retirement to solitude, religion and books.[505] The Gothic Romanticism of the nineteenth century was on the horizon.

CHAPTER V

MONKS AND LEARNING 1685-1794.

The English Benedictines were subject to an extraordinary variety of academic and intellectual influences throughout the eighteenth century. In a century of massive change and adjustment, the natural ability of some monks combined with good fortune of time and place to produce an enthusiasm for learning which was continually adapting itself to new modes.

Primarily, learning was focused on theological studies, the means to equip monks training to become competent missioners. Thus, the monasteries continued to maintain the traditional two-year philosophy courses for their students for most of this period, despatching them later to the universities to complete their theology. The universities of Douai, Trier and the Sorbonne in Paris were all used in this way, with the more able monks carrying off doctorates in divinity. As the century progressed, however, the Sorbonne became the undisputed centre for higher English Benedictine studies, especially as St. Gregory's involvement in the theology faculty at Douai went into decline.[506] Monks from the different houses, attending the Sorbonne, lived at St. Edmund's, and not only benefitted from all that Parisian society had to offer, but were tutored by some of the foremost theologians of the day. This latter apprenticeship was to change profoundly the monks' theological standpoint over these years. Doctoral theses of monks in the early eighteenth century, for instance, especially those accepted at Douai, were traditionally Thomist. But by mid-century, theses were incorporating the latest theological ideas of the Enlightenment in regard to nature and revelation, thanks to supervision by Sorbonne professors of the calibre of L. J. Hooke.[507]

Beyond the compulsory theology, the most pronounced academic interest of the monks in the late seventeenth century appears to have lain in monastic history. This was inspired by two movements to which the English monks found themselves directly linked. First, the *érudit* tradition of historiography fostered by the Maurists, and exemplified at this time in the works of Jean Mabillon; secondly, and perhaps of more importance, some monk-scholars were attracted to English Non-juring antiquarianism.

The exile of many monks in the monasteries after the Glorious Revolution had caused overcrowding and the boarding of junior monks in Maurist houses, where at least one 'notably profited of the Noble Library he there found'. St. Edmund's had traditionally sent its aspirants to Maurist colleges to study the Humanities.[508] Among these was Benet Weldon, the Congregation's greatest annalist, who took to heart Mabillon's belief in the marriage of the monastic life and study. Weldon made use of Maurist opinions and attitudes in his own works,[509] and between 1707 and 1713, he produced four historical works.[510] The most important of these, the *Memorials*, was written in the form of annals, with an appendix of extremely important original documents. As Weldon approached his own time, autobiographical material in his works increased. During the production of the *Memorials*, Weldon lived as a recluse in his monastery, insisting he was persecuted by his community who called him 'a mad-man and cracked-brained'. It was to serve as a distraction from this phobia, and to prevent Weldon fleeing to a Maurist house, that President Gregson had set him to work at writing up the Congregation's annals, promising to transmit to him any useful documents he might find on his travels. Mabillon was himself already engaged on his *Annales O.S.B.* at this time. Like his *James II*, which was a work of Jacobite sentiment and largely derivative, Weldon's *Memorials* and its distillation, the *Chronological Notes*, had a sharp polemical edge which provided the impetus behind a great deal of antiquarian study in the seventeenth century. For Weldon's works sought to preserve the unity of the English Benedictine Congregation against enemies within and without by tracing its historical pedigree in order to show its present privileged status.

If, as a convert, Weldon was attracted to the life of a Maurist scholar, he nevertheless always remained an English Non-juror at heart, for he had found in Catholicism a guaranteed respect for his legitimate monarch. In the late seventeenth and early eighteenth centuries, it was Anglican Non-jurors who were primarily responsible for awakening historical research in the Anglo-Saxon and English medieval periods so as to establish the veracity of Anglicanism's historical continuity and its independence of Rome. The massing of evidence to argue this case, which also benefitted the Stuart cause of *de jure* monarchy, was spurred on by a great deal of antiquarian interest, which expanded after the Glorious Revolution. Benedictinism provided an acceptable alternative to a number of Anglicans, dismayed

146

by the political changes of that Revolution for, in some respects, there was much common ground between English Benedictines and Non-jurors. Both supported the Stuarts as *de jure* monarchs, both looked on the king as the protector either of the Church or of monasticism, and used history to validate their respective claims and status. Benet Weldon and Henry Joseph Johnston were the two foremost historians amongst a substantial number of Anglican converts who became English Benedictines in the last couple of decades of the seventeenth century, thus proving an exception to the contemporary claim, 'a little skill in Antiquity inclines a man to Popery; but depth in that study brings him about again to our religion'.[511]

The tradition of Benedictine antiquarianism had been established earlier in the seventeenth century by other Anglican converts, notably David Augustine Baker and Hugh Serenus Cressy. These had tried to trace a Benedictine line of continuity in English history,[512] but Benedictine historical research after 1688 was broadened to incorporate the Non-juring and Jacobite positions. Weldon, for instance, liberally acknowledged his debt to Anglo-Saxon and medieval historians, and to seventeenth-century Anglican antiquarians like Camden and Selden, while at the same time demonstrating the monarchy's constant protection of the monastic order.[513] Henry Joseph Johnston, a patron of Weldon's and of the same community, was professed in 1675, after a career in the office of the great Anglican antiquary, Willam Dugdale, who had employed him in etching and drawing. Johnston had toured Yorkshire in the early 1670s, collecting items of historical interest with his brother, the antiquarian Nathaniel Johnston. Dugdale had been unhappy with Henry's carelessness, his poor writing, and weak Latin, but was sufficiently shocked when he had heard of his pupil's entry into the monastic life, to reverse his earlier verdict. He was sorry he had:

> buried himself alive, considering how well he might have lived in the world and been a comfort to his friends by his honest labours, so dextrous was he at etching and drawing'.[514]

As a monk, Johnston was to be a translator and commentator of Bossuet, some of whose works were an answer to the Anglican position outlined by William Wake, later Archbishop of Canterbury, who was to help at least one monk to convert to Anglicanism.[515] As one might expect, Johnston was particularly impressed by arguments

147

built upon Catholicism's historical continuity: 'Our Plea is good, *olim possidio prior possidio*. If you will dispute the Title, you must show your positive Records of a more Antient Date'.[516] On the other hand, Johnston also tried to demonstrate the common ground between Catholicism and Anglicanism, 'the Reform'd Religion', by underplaying divisive elements and establishing central beliefs.[517] In 1687, Johnston helped his brother to compile *The Assurance of Abby and other Church-Lands in England to the Possessors*, spoken of already, which made much use of Dugdale's researches as well as Johnston's own extensive knowledge of Yorkshire.[518]

Although the Non-juring antiquarian tradition is thought to have declined by 1730 and was succeeded by the first phase of the Enlightenment, with its confidence in science and its preference for philosophic history rather than painstaking erudition, antiquarianism continued to be a very influential force right up until this point. Its survival was largely due to the keen interest shown by a dedicated group of wealthy and able laymen in the study of history.[519] Their expertise in scientific and artistic specialisation produced a degree of cross-fertilisation which aided academic unity and presaged the enthusiasm of the later academies of the Enlightenment. The English Benedictines' involvement in this expanded antiquarian endeavour reveals their continued scholarly alliance with Non-juring and Jacobite circles.

English Benedictine involvement with the celebrated Oxford antiquary and gossip, Thomas Hearne, stemmed as much perhaps from sympathy at the persecution he underwent for his Non-juring opinions, as from interest in his erudition. Hearne knew that Nathaniel Johnston's brother was a monk from the Yorkshire antiquary Ralph Thoresby, who suggested that Johnston, the monk, might help Hearne to decipher the script of Nathaniel Johnston in his antiquarian collections, which Thoresby believed to be no better than 'ancient Runic'.[520] Hearne counted many Benedictine patrons as his friends, among them a fellow antiquary, Charles Eyston of East Hendred, Berks., whose son, another Charles, was also acquainted with Hearne, and ensured that the English Benedictine monasteries were not deprived of the antiquarian's works.[521] Direct involvement between the monks and Hearne came, however, in 1719, when the Benedictine, Gilbert Knowles was introduced to Hearne by Dr. Richard Mead, scientist, bibliophile, and antiquarian. Knowles showed Hearne the three manuscript volumes of his work *Materia Medica Botanica*, a herbal which included Latin verse and two volumes of drawings of plants:

> This all done by himself, he being a Poet and a Botanist, and indeed a learned Man. He is a papist and hath liv'd much in Yorkshire. He thinks of printing this work.[522]

Knowles was grateful for Hearne's patronage, which doubtless helped to increase the long list of subscribers in the later published work:

> I wish it may meet with ye success of your Accurate Edition of Gulielmus Neoburgensis, which makes a glittering show in every Learned Man's Library, and a brighter when dipped into,

for he could not:

> be so vain to think my undertaking is anyways so serviceable to ye learned commonwealth as yr. most curious and elaborate pieces... but I believe nobody has attempted the like before.[523]

The publication of Knowles's work was delayed after he had lost money through 'a vilainous pretended friend', and after he was sent to the backwoods to be chaplain to the Gascoignes at Parlington in the West Riding. Nevertheless, he continued to correspond with Mead from here, asking for Hearne's advice on some scarce books by Greek poets he had sent to Mead in repayment for some eye-treatment. In return, Mead sent Knowles copies of his own medical works. There is little doubt that Knowles missed the academic life he had known in London and Oxford; he was always eager to learn from Hearne 'what piece of Antiquity you are now going to oblige ye learned world with', and wrote abhorring the philistinism of his northern abode:

> I live in a country more renown'd for fox hunting than ye *belles Letres*, but I shall do my best endeavours to get you wt. subscribers I can.

What local Catholics thought of Knowles's literary pretensions, can be gauged from a note of Cuthbert Constable appended to a letter from Knowles to Constable, asking him to subscribe to another botanical work:

This poor monk went mad either with racking his brains with Poetry or drink, or both, and was sent to his monastery where he lived some time.[524]

Knowles's *Materia Medica Botanica* was published in 1723, an attempt to launch a second herbal having failed. The work's theme, a description of four hundred herbs, strung together in nearly four thousand Latin hexameters, was an unusual subject for a monk. The book appears to have been the first non-religious work produced by an English Benedictine, an illustration of the ease with which monks moved in high English literary circles at this time, and proved the excellence of Knowles's own classical education. It was dedicated to Mead, and listed Anglican bishops, members of the aristocracy, and thirty Benedictines among its subscribers. Knowles was corresponding with Archbishop Wake at this time, when Wake himself was engaged in discussions with Gallican theologians regarding Anglican Orders. Wake was a loyal patron of Knowles and encouraged other Anglican bishops to subscribe to his herbal. In return, Knowles sent Wake samples of his Latin epitaphs and verses. Another of his subscribers, the Bishop of Oxford, suspected him of being 'in orders of the Church of Rome', but this had not prevented Knowles, so the bishop related, desiring the post of librarian to the 'Duke of Chandos'. Knowles, the bishop felt, was on the point of becoming an Anglican if he could be provided for or be allotted a position in Oxford, such was Knowles's attraction to English literary circles. Fortunately, perhaps, an illness intervened, and Knowles was sent back to Douai, but even here, he continued to put himself at Wake's service by combing the libraries of neighbouring monasteries for books sought by the collector-archbishop.[525]

Knowles's taste in books suggests that he had his own important library or at least access to valuable collections. Knowles wrote to Sir Hans Sloane in 1724 suggesting he translate Sloane's Catalogue of plants in Jamaica into 'elegant Latin', and complained bitterly that he had been forced to sell his 'little library' which was the fruit of thirty years' collecting and which contained scarce books on botany and poetry. Most missioners' libraries, however, were not specialist collections, but catered for the practical pastoral concerns of the missioner.[526] Occasionally these libraries incorporated 'old' liturgical manuscripts, and it seems probable that these found their way eventually to the libraries in the monasteries.[527] The catalogues of these latter reveal holdings of medieval manuscripts collected over a period of time,[528] and indicate the libraries' size. The detailed catalogue of St. Edmund's, Paris, compiled in 1702 was, significantly, the work of Benet Weldon; it listed some 7000 works. Laymen contributed to these libraries, as well as monks; Lucan's *Pharsalia* (London 1718), for instance, was a gift to St. Edmund's, Paris, from its publisher, Jacob Tonson, 'the gentleman-usher to the Muses'.[529] Superiors took great care to prevent the dispersal of books, especially to the mission, but fire was a constant danger, and that which broke out at Dieulouard in 1717 destroyed a great deal of the library and some original manuscripts relating to Mary Queen of Scots.[530]

Inevitably, English Benedictine studies were affected by changing fashions. While seventeenth century scholarship and antiquarianism had lingered into the first three decades of the eighteenth century, it was soon to give way to more contemporary pursuits. It is very difficult to pinpoint the developments which gave the years of the early Enlightenment their shape, but one can trace the outline, as far as the monks themselves are concerned, in a tendency to diverge from the study of strict theology as such, into other disciplines.

The late seventeenth century saw a number of autodidacts, shaken out of the somewhat constricting world of the cloister, taking advantage of the wide variety of fields of study which living in Paris offered them. Those we know of were nearly all eccentric, at least according to the not unbiased pen of Weldon, who was alternately threatened or amused by their originality. He gives us the vignettes of the 'excellent Humanist', Martin Stone, a '*verus Israelita*', and a gifted linguist, 'but a strange piece to look at', and that of the convert Charles Dominic Green:

> a very little creature, but very skillful in Musick, bred up from a child to it in the Royal Chapel at Windsor.

Green was accustomed to sit at the back of the convent of Val-de-Grace next door to St. Edmund's, and to scribble down surreptitiously the nuns' music, of which they were very possessive. He was also fascinated by shorthand:

> in hopes to invent such a way of writing that he could carry into England what he lifted without the Custom-officers or Tyde-waiters

151

being able to comprehend anything of his papers anymore than Arabick,

but he stored so much in his memory that 'his writings became unintelligible to himself'.[531] More unacceptable, but closer to intellectual currents outside, was the cosmological system of the strange genius John Columban Phillips, which was known to his bemused brethren as the 'Systema Philippicum'. After profession in 1632, Phillips had left for the mission, married, fathered a child, become a soldier, and fought against the Moors in Tangier, before returning repentant to his monastery, where he lived as an isolated cantankerous figure until his death in 1699. Phillips cut his scientific research free from theological constraints, and attempted to construct an alternative system to those of Ptolemy, Copernicus and Tycho Brahe, in which the sun and earth were found almost in the same orbit, and were themselves encircled by the planets' orbits. The philosophical principles, based on a world soul, which lay behind Phillips's System, were sufficiently novel for the System to be formally condemned in 1685, after Phillips had been accused of Socinianism by the monastic censors. Phillips admitted his dependence on the early seventeenth-century Carmelite, Paul Antony Foscarini, whose works were already on the Index, but who had tried to demonstrate the compatibility of Scripture and Copernicanism.[532]

The extent to which some monks in the generation after Phillips were able to cultivate secular studies without becoming isolated within the Congregation is a clear indication of the force of the early Enlightenment. A central figure here was Thomas Southcott, a theologian and Jacobite, and President of the Congregation between 1721 and 1741, an unusually long time. Although Southcott remained committed to the Thomism of his early student days, by 1731 he had advanced views about the content of the traditional seminary course, in which he believed,

a great deal of Pedantry mingles with the schools both of Piety and Divinity.

He preferred that ordinands should see 'a great deal of the world, and be of an age not to be a companion to boys'.[533] The monks were provided with an entry into this secular world by possessing two distinct advantages. First, they had a monastery in Paris, where they could continually avail themselves of the rapid developments in intellectual life, and meet a wide spectrum of people.[534] Secondly, the English Benedictines were generally committed Jacobites, and Jacobitism, if a dying cause in England, was of overwhelming importance in providing a 'diaspora' for the fruitful commerce of ideas through Jacobite aristocratic and literary circles in most European courts.[535] Jacobitism thus provided the thread linking the Non-juring antiquarian tradition to the expansive world of the European Enlightenment.

In England, the most important Benedictine contact with the early Enlightenment was that made between Thomas Southcott and the poet Alexander Pope, after the monk had helped the poet during an illness. They both shared a common Catholic faith and Jacobitism which prompted Southcott to defend Pope's *Essay on Criticism* from the attacks of the Protestant Williamite author Dennis. Pope knew Hearne and Mead well, and was also a subscriber to Knowles's herbal, but the new mood had led him away from following Hearne in his devotion to 'rare monkish manuscripts' towards a self-confident humanism. He had thus decried the 'second Deluge' brought over learning by 'the Monks (who) finish'd what the Goths began', and was therefore criticised by Southcott:

> The only difference between us in relation to the monks is, that he (Southcott) thinks most sorts of learning *flourished* among 'em, and I am of opinion that only some sort of learning was barely *kept alive* by 'em. He believes the most natural & obvious sense of that line ('A second deluge *learning* over-run'), will be thought meant of learning in general, and I fancy it will be understood only, as 'tis meant, of polite learning, criticism, poetry etc. wh. is the only learning concerned in the subject of the Essay.

Ultimately, however, Southcott approved of the *Essay*, despite its being criticised by other monks. It was Pope who, after Southcott had become President in 1721, was party to a concerted Jacobite plan to obtain for Southcott a wealthy benefice in the papal enclave of Avignon. Pope asked Sir Robert Walpole to put pressure on Cardinal Fleury to see Southcott obtained the benefice. Whatever might have been Southcott's inclination towards the new culture and learning, it is as well to remember how aspects of his belief still remained fixed in a traditional mould. As late as the 1730s, he was sponsoring the cause of King James II's canonisation, following his cure some years earlier at the king's mausoleum in Paris.[536]

Southcott's introduction to the world of the salons follows closely that of his great friend, the Jacobite Andrew Michael Ramsay, another formative influence in the early Enlightenment. Ramsay's interest in Fénelon's spirituality had developed later into the recognisable eighteenth-century study of science, non-Christian cultures, education, history, philosophy, literature and, above all, Freemasonry. Ramsay's *Les Voyages de Cyrus* (Paris 1727) was modelled on Fénelon's *Aventures de Télémaque* (1699), a very popular work in England and praised in the 1720s by another monk as 'one of ye finest systems of Morality I ever saw, couched under an elegant poetical History'.[537] The book's themes were discussed by the author and his 'mutual friends', Southcott and Thomas Carte. Both Southcott and Ramsay found themselves embarking on a common intellectual course at a time when science and religion were still complementary, for from the middle of the eighteenth century, science was to be used increasingly to attack Christianity. During the 1720s, Southcott had been joined at St. Edmund's, Paris, by Ramsay who lodged there 'in his solitude', and corresponded with the political philosopher, the Abbé de Saint Pierre, over the Abbé Houtteville's work of historical apologetic, *Religion Chrétienne prouvée par les faits* (Paris 1722), a famous orthodox apologetic work.[538] By the 1730s, Ramsay, acclaimed in Britain and France for his scholarship, had become notorious for his interest in Masonry. This movement was not to be condemned by Rome until 1738. Until then, and even afterwards, Jacobitism was heavily involved in it, and was largely responsible for the preservation of Masonry's higher form, the so-called 'Scottish Rite'.[539] Masonry was in a sense the secular equivalent of the Jacobite Church, and if Southcott cannot be, for want of evidence, seen to be directly implicated in Masonry, it is certain that he must have fallen under its influence. Masonic internationalism, its underground network, its secrecy, and its loyalty, its pseudo-nobility and subterranean anarchism would all have appealed to Southcott, who was quite at home in European circles, and who demanded 'blue ribbons' from the Pretender for his political allies. In his work in Jacobite espionage, Southcott used elaborate ciphers and cant, and was, above all, closely allied with Ramsay, the 'Chevalier', the most influential Masonic author of the day.

Coming very quickly after the deaths of Southcott (1748) and Ramsay (1743), was the foundation of an English Benedictine

154

Academy, 'The Society of St. Edmund', founded in Paris in 1749 at the monastery of the same name, and ostensibly modelled on Abraham Cowley's plan for a philosophical College. This 'Society' benefitted from the respect which religion and science still had for each other, though many of the new scientific societies of the eighteenth century followed the lead of the Royal Society in London and forbade discussion of religious and political topics. The Society is clear proof of the English monks' zeal for the Enlightenment at this time.[540] It may be that in the establishment of this academy, the English monks were imitating similar models found amoung the Maurist and Vannist Benedictines. Membership was open to the laity and monastic community, but the guiding spirits, from the Society's inception on the 17th of June 1749, were the Rector, the distinguished mathematician, Charles Walmesley, and a band of enthusiastic younger monks. Contrary to fashionable prejudice outside, the inaugural speech gave pride of place to the medieval monasteries as the successors of the classical academies, and identified the Society'a role as:

> urging us on to study (for) we are all destined for the Mission, where we are to preach the gospel, and to engage in polemical combats with perhaps the most learned and formidable Adversaries in the whole world.

The weapons recommended to combat unbelief in England were study of 'sacred and profane History' and 'mathematicks and …all Natural History'.

Between June and December 1749, the *philosophes* of the Society delivered fourteen wide-ranging papers, demonstrating their range of interests. Walmesley's, on the propagation of light and the rise of vapours, were soundly Newtonian, and made use of the contemporary astronomer, James Bradley. Walmesley was an obvious influence behind Augustine Walker's contributions. Walker's poem, celebrating the inauguration of the Society, vaunted 'Great Newton' and 'Immortal Pope', and begged a place for monasticism in the Enlightenment, by rejecting the contemporary identification of monasticism with Gothic barbarism: 'Monks undo what Gothick rage has done'. Walker enthused about deduction and experiment as methods of proof and condemned 'many Cartesian hypotheses,..based on metaphysicks, with no regard to nature or experience'. His conclusions mixed religious and scientific principles with ease and, although he criticised the Abbé

Pluche's theories in the latter's *Spectacle de la Nature*, Walker found himself agreeing with Pluche in his purpose of showing 'the narrowness of our understanding' and admiring 'the wisdom of the Creator...the works of nature show the existence of a supreme all-wise and intelligent being'.[541] A young monk, John Barnes, frequently alluded to Pluche's natural theology in his paper delivered in 1750 on 'fire considered as a fluid invironing ye earth in the way of an atmosphere', which was approved by Walmesley and Walker.

It is significant that a number of these contributions passed the bounds of strict orthodoxy and tackled some of the day's controversial questions. Barnes, for instance, in his opinion that other planets were inhabited, combined *bienfaisance* with utilitarianism:

> What was the chief thing which made me think up this system, and is an opinion which pleases several people (Walker was one) and myself, is that the rest of the planets are inhabitable, and are really inhabited, as our earth is. I am delighted to find other globes are not created for mere show, but for real use and service.[542]

A number of contributors to the Society worked on the vexed question of chronology in relation to the Bible.[543] Thomas Welch, inspired by Walmesley, based his findings on the astronomical calculations of Newton, and was forced to admit the inaccuracy of Christian commentators. Welch also showed his interest in chronology in a paper he delivered on the Druids.[544] In the debate over natural and revealed religion, Deists and philosophers alike had seen in the Druids a fine example of pure patriarchal religion, even a form of Masonry. Christian authors furthermore, had preferred to find evidence for an essential Christian basis in Druidic religion which awaited a future maturity. Using Theophilus Gale's *The Court of the Gentiles*, which tried to prove the Hebrews had possessed the original patriarchal religion, Welch traced the Druids' origins from the Jews by way of Phoenician merchants. He remained, however, impressed by their degree of civilisation, attained in their 'natural' state. For the Druids were interested in 'phisiology, mathematicks, Astrology and Poetry (and).. associated in Colleges together, according to Pythagoras' precepts, and searched into occult and sublime mysteries'. Welch finally admitted that the Gospel had dispelled the 'darkness of ignorance', of the Druids which he set alongside the free thinkers of his own day who, like the Druids, despised Christianity as 'unworthy of the gravity and profound judgement of a philosopher'.

Questions of origins and chronology were closely tied to current debates on the meaning of scriptural revelation, and Bernard Catteral, in his contribution to the Society on the sense of scripture, followed the liberal attitudes then predominant at the Sorbonne.[545] He argued for the traditional Catholic view that scripture contained both a literal/historical, and a spiritual/mystical sense, but recognised the need to understand the mind of the scriptural authors and Hebrew and Greek idioms. Ultimately, he felt that the fullest sense of scripture must be preferred to the allegorical sense alone, a sentiment which would have pleased the liberal Jesuit scripture scholar Isaac Berruyer. Catterall was followed by Charles Walmesley who sought some solution to the current *âme des bêtes* controversy.[546] In this debate, there was a surprising degree of affinity between orthodox Catholics and sentimentalist philosophers over the word *âme* being applied to humans. For both these, it was used in the sense of 'soul', but for their rivals, the sensationalist thinkers, it merely meant 'personality'. In regard to animals' souls, Walmesley represented the middle ground. Like the sensationalist Locke before him, he rejected Descartes' view that animals were 'mere Automates'; 'what sallies of gladness', he observed, 'when a hunting dog is led to its game'. Walmesley went on to admit that animals had an intelligence, or an *âme* in the sensationalist sense only, and not in the full Christian sense:

> to allow immortality to Brutes as well as man, would not be consonant with religion.

Other papers of the Society dealt with less controversial but equally topical subjects. Welch's review of William Guthrie's *History of England* (1744-51) strove to demonstrate the author's anti-Catholicism, and to reply to his suggestion that monks had introduced papal despotism into England.[547] Jacobite interests were evident in Augustine Walker's panegyric in honour of the Young Pretender, and Placid Naylor's paper on English kings *de jure and de facto*.[548]

Between 1751 and 1756, the Society began to break up as its members were sent to Rome or the mission field in England. The volumes for 1754 to 1756 mostly contain the personal anthology of the Secretary, John Barnes,[549] mainly *pièces d'occasion* in a classical style, with a dash of vulgarity. Charles Walmesley, who had become English

157

Benedictine Procurator in Rome from 1753, regretted the imminent death of the Society. In 1750, with his reputation growing, he had contributed half a dozen papers on Newtonian astronomy which show him using the theories of some of the foremost astronomers of the day, men like Jacques Cassini(1677-1756) and John Machin(ob.1751). It was in Rome that Walmesley became the good friend of the mathematician and Newtonian, François Jacquier. Earlier, as Prior of Paris (1749-53), Walmesley had been criticised for spending too long on his mathematics and neglecting his community.[550] The specialist knowledge found in Walmesley's contributions must surely have made a clear exposition of them heavy-going to other more amateur members in the Society. Walmesley, indeed, appears to have envisaged the minutes of the Society as a vehicle for the dissemination of his own theories, in much the same way as he used the current *Philosophical Transactions*. Walmesley, as a corresponding member in Rome, introduced the Society to the ideas of contemporary Newtonians like James Stirling(1692-1770) and Colin Maclaurin(1698-1746). In 1756, Walmesley moved to England, as coadjutor bishop, and his correspondence in this area forthwith ceased.

This incidence of corresponding members of the Society throws some light on how the Enlightenment was affecting the mission, for, as we have seen, unlike the seething intellectual atmosphere of Paris, the English mission was quiet, and its monks more involved with spiritual and pastoral, rather than academic, interests. Yet the new learning was also infiltrating into some missions; at least one missioner had purchased the *Spectacle de la Nature* by 1737,[551] and Augustine Walker, who moved from the salons of Paris to the mission of Tanfield in Durham in 1750, took his scientific and cultural enthusiasms with him. For in his chaplaincy, he became a corresponding member of the Society, transmitting reports and diagrams, for instance, on the latest developments in machinery used in the coal industry. He condemned the local coal king, George Bowes' new Gothic Banqueting Hall at Gibside, near Tanfield, as 'a costly heap of Rubbish...with barbarous sculpture'. Walker, who always prided himself on his architectural taste, however, spoke approvingly of Gibside's formal garden where 'art and nature rule with equal sway' and of its chapel, by James Paine, then under construction.[552] The only known lay member of the monks' academy, Philip Howard Esq. of Corby, Cumberland, sent reports back from Turin, whither he was accompanied by his tutor, the priest scientist Joseph Turbeville Needham. These described the peculiarities of the Savoyards, and geological features of the country. Later, back in his family home at Corby, where his friend the monk Thomas Welch was chaplain, Howard put his scientific interests to good use in agricultural improvement.[553]

In no sense did every missioner join the *illuminati* or *curiosi* as the century progressed. The nature of his apostolate ensured that the traditional learning which folk-religion accredited to the priest survived the massive offensive against religion. One striking example of this was the lasting belief in monk missioners' medical craft, a talent which had great potential on the mission.[554] There is evidence for a great deal of interest in herbal medicine among monks in the early part of the eighteenth century, which is seen most clearly in Gilbert Knowles's learned *Materia Medica Botanica* (London 1723), and by 1750, medical prescriptions or 'receipts' compiled by monks were being enthusiastically copied by interested lay-folk. Roger Joseph Whittell, for instance, took advantage of his time at Bath spa to dispense his own and other monks' patent medicines.[555] Later in the century, there was a lively correspondence over new preventatives like inoculation, but traditional medical lore, often derived from standard medical works lining the shelves of mission libraries, continued to survive.[556] The happy juxtaposition of zeal for the new learning on the one hand, and reliance on older, less scientific remedies, on the other, is glimpsed in the interests of Gregory Gregson, the liberal chaplain to the Cisalpine leader John Throckmorton of Weston Underwood, Bucks. Gregson was a great friend of a neighbour, the poet William Cowper, and because of his skill in medicine and diagnosis, acted as a sort of general practitioner in the district. In 1786, dining with Gregson, whom he always called 'the Doctor', and Throckmorton, Cowper teased the monk about his dual office of priest and physician:

> I happened to say, that in all professions and trades, mankind affected an air of mystery. Physicians, I observed in particular, were objects of that remark, who persist in prescribing Latin, many times no doubt to the hazard of a patient's life, through the ignorance of an Apothecary. Mr. Throckmorton assented to what I said, and turning to his Chaplain, to my infinite surprize, observed to him: '*That is just as absurd as our praying in Latin*'. I could have hugged him for his liberality and freedom from bigotry, but thought it rather more decent to let the matter pass.

Three years later, however, Cowper was to recognise Gregson's medical skills without any qualification. What these were can be seen in Gregson's elaborate and traditional cure for 'hickup', for which he recommended a series of juleps, followed by 'a gentle Cathartic of one gros of pulverised Rhubarb...This will strengthen the stomach & viscera by dislodging the peccant faeces'. He had no time for the new-fangled remedies of the French physicians, who 'attribute the hickup to ye Rheumaticism, which cannot possibly be sealed so near ye primum mobile without snapping all ye thread of Life'.[557]

Gregson's conservatism in medicine had survived his attraction to liberal attitudes in religious practice. The truce however between Christianity and the philosophic and scientific forces of the Enlightenment began to break up in the 1750s; at a time when the Society of St. Edmund was holding regular meetings. An analysis of the works added to the library of St. Edmund's, Paris, between 1740 and 1756, when John Barnes was apparently librarian[558] gives clues to this developing conflict. It is significant that only three of the library's twenty sections were developed during these years, *Controversiae*, *Historici Prophani*, and, above all, *Libri Heretici et Heterodoxi*. This weighting in favour of controversial works, with dangerous texts shelved alongside their orthodox refutations, explains why superiors exercised such a strict control over junior monks' access to the library. In addition to numerous accessions of contemporary anti-Jansenist authors like H. Tournely, Bernard d'Arras and C. Le Pelletier, and the scientific works of Walmesley, Needham and Trabaud, there were substantial numbers of English controversial works added, presumably because of their value to future missioners, and because English government censorship over publishing was less restrictive. Here, as elsewhere, latitudinarian and Deist authors like Tillotson, Middleton, Bolingbroke, Sykes and Anthony Collins, were answered by their non-Catholic rivals, West, Sherlock, Leland and Bishop Butler. The middle ground, that is, those liberal authors seeking a *modus vivendi* between religion and contemporary philosophic and scientific scepticism, was represented by works such as L. J. Hooke's *Religionis naturalis* (Paris 1752) and I. J. Berruyer's *Histoire du Peuple de Dieu* (Paris 1742).[559] A supplement to the catalogue, 'Books in Hell', was drawn up *c.* 1750, and included Locke's *Human Understanding*.

The divergence between Religion and Enlightenment after 1750 caused the English Benedictines to move in two directions. First, there were those who continued to try to effect some compromise with the

160

new learning, as Hooke and Berruyer had attempted to do. Naturally, there were degrees of commitment to this task, as there were also positive and negative results. Secondly, another party among the monks became increasingly disaffected with much that was championed by the Enlightenment, and, unable to stem the growing tide of scepticism and irreligion, adopted a mood of deep pessimism. This estrangement was felt especially keenly by those early pioneers like Charles Walmesley and Augustine Walker, who had accepted the Enlightenment in their youth, and still, up to a point, had some sympathy for aspects of it.

For those monks who were always enthusiastic about the continuous advances in learning, but kept their heads and vocations, the world was ever-expanding. At the same time as academic restraints were overcome, so did civil liberties increase. William Cowper and the monk Gregory Gregson were 'like two great Inkle-eaters', a latter-day Pope and Southcott, in their joint work in translating Homer. Cowper always teased 'Griggy' on his keeping the Lenten fast, but felt certain that the monk had no ulterior motive of conversion in the friendship.[560] The antiquarian William Cole, who was also introduced to the monks by the Throckmortons, visited the monasteries at Douai and Paris in 1765, and as his antiquarian forbears would have done sixty years earlier, Cole made copious notes on architecture and examples of epigraphy at both houses. At Paris, the Prior told him he had just returned from the mission after thirteen years' absence, and 'found the French People much altered in both their Religion & Morals'. Cole's attraction to monasticism demonstrates the influence of the new cult of sensibility on him. He had 'a Secret Inclination in favour of this House, & Religious Order, formerly so flourishing in England', and would have liked

a Lodging at their Convent...as I never had any other Views in Life, than to live retiredly & quietly, & pretty much to myself, after the Monkish Manner: which I yet, tho' more in the World, in paying & receiving Visits, than many of my Condition, I can't help, privately & in secret, to prefer to such Dissipation.[561]

Ten years later, Doctor Johnson visited the monks in Paris, dined with them, and joined a sight-seeing party. Despite his strong views on the social utility of 'convents' as being 'only retreats for persons unable to serve the public', he enjoyed his visit, being allowed inside the

161

enclosure, spending a 'meager day' there on an insipid diet, but made the most of the library. For Johnson, the monastery resembled a salon. He was entertained by two monks of liberal opinions, one of whom, James Compton, later apostatised after reading the *Rambler*, and received help from Johnson in London. To the other, the gifted Joseph Cuthbert Wilks, Johnson gave an introduction to the Master of Pembroke College, Oxford:

> The Gentleman who brings this is a learned Benedictine, in whose monastery I was treated at Paris with all the civilities which the Society has means or opportunity of shewing. I dined in their refectory, and studied in their library, and had the favour of their company to other places, as curiosity led me.[562]

Johnson did not take up the offer of a cell in the monastery. His distaste for the confinements of the monastic life, an opinion once fashionable, but by the 1770s being replaced by a Pre-Romantic appreciation of solitude, was only alleviated by his meeting monks of liberal attitudes similar to his own.

The easiest attitude for monks to adopt in the face of attacks on Christianity was to co-operate with the assailants, as far as orthodoxy would permit, in a common search for Truth, and to recognise, with many leaders of the liberal Catholic Enlightenment, that the Church did need to modernise and to peel off the dead bark of superstition. One result of this reformation of manners was that many monks tended to avoid straight theological conflict, preferring instead to be accepted by the intelligentsia through a common enthusiasm for art and literature. Taste and aesthetics thus replaced apologetics as some monks cultivated the role of connoisseurs, and sought to set themselves up in Paris and Rome as collectors and even cicerones.

The Benedictine Procurator in Rome by the 1770s found himself at the centre of a circle of men of culture and learning attracted by a line of scholarly popes and by a renewed interest in Roman and Italian art. From the time he became Procurator in 1777, Placid Waters had been a great friend of Stefano Borgia, the Secretary to Propaganda, and a formidable scholar, historian and collector. Borgia was delighted by the gift of the *Apostolatus in Anglia* (1626) from Waters because it contained rare medieval texts, and Waters promised him more English books in the future. In a gesture which throws light on the priorities of the clergyman connoisseur, Borgia 'insisted on procuring me

(Waters) a licence for life to read all sorts of books…If ever I returned to England, it would be most useful to me.[563] This introduction into the sophisticated world of the Roman dilettanti was really the work of Waters's predecessor, Augustine Walker, Procurator from 1757 until 1777. Walker had made friends in Rome with the distinguished Scottish architect, Robert Mylne, for whom he published verses after Mylne had won the first prize for architecture in Rome's Academy of San Luca, as well as the artist and cicerone, Colin Morrison, and the Irish sculptor, Christopher Hewetson. He was also acquainted with the Czarina Catherine II's 'first architect', Charles-Louis Clérisseau. But his warmest friend was James Byres, 'the pope's antiquary in Rome', who continued to call on Walker in Paris after the latter had become Benedictine President.[564] To Rome and Walker came also important Benedictine patrons and connoisseurs like John Errington, 'the chief of Beaufront', whose art agent Walker became, and Sir Thomas Gascoigne of Parlington. Unfortunately, Walker had left by the time his old pupil Henry Swinburne had arrived in Rome, with his family, in the early summer of 1778. Swinburne was sorry to have missed 'his old friend and master'. He was engaged in writing up his *Travels in the Two Sicilies*.[565] After Walker's departure, Waters continued to maintain this artistic circle, although he was reluctant to frequent the English coffee house in Rome to the extent that his predecessor had done.[566]

Benedictine familiarity with some of the influential English visitors and artists to Rome, many of whom figure in the contemporary portraits of Pompeo Batoni, complemented already existing bonds, for the Roman circle of artists known to Walker represented a last phase of the cultural Jacobite diaspora. Walker was himself close to Andrew Lumisden, secretary to the Pretender, and brother-in-law of Robert Strange, the engraver. These Irish and Scottish artists found them- selves, almost to a man, in a Roman exile on account of political loyalties,[567] and Waters was himself to be the counsellor and personal friend of Cardinal York and the Duchess of Albany. This did not prevent Waters developing a warm friendship with Sir William and Lady Hamilton. Moreover, the relationship between Jacobitism and Masonry was a traditionally close one, and Mylne, Errington and Swinburne were either freemasons or were known to have masonic sympathies. Walker's own attitudes to the Enlightenment appear to have developed whilst at Rome. Here, he gave less time to his earlier enthusiasm for science and mechanics, and began to appreciate the

Romantic in nature more. Thus, while still admitting he was interested in 'everything new, architectural and Mechanical', and while he could help to plan classical additions to the monasteries at Douai and Paris, he became an avid collector of Piranesi's prints which extolled the sublime in nature and fed the Romantic imagination.[568] The picturesque is also a recurring theme in Swinburne's *Travels*, and there can be little doubt that Walker also shared his pupil's liberal criticisms of Mediterranean Catholic superstition. Waters, his successor, however, was to live to see the repression of liberal sentiments in Rome as panic spread in the wake of the French Revolution:

> Our Friend Hewetson was a few days ago called coram vobis for unguarded expressions in the coffee house, which had been exaggerated to the Secretary of State. However, he came off with flying colours, which notwithstanding, will put him on his guard. Was I in his place, I never would put my foot in the English Coffee house. I have long ago set him the example.[569]

Walker was to die in 1794, but the force of Romanticism was assured of a place among the Benedictines through the poems of Ossian, published at the beginning of the nineteenth century by Benedict Macdonald, himself a Scotsman and Jacobite.[570]

As in literature and the arts, so in theological studies does it seem that a number of the monks made efforts to come to terms with the new philosophy by giving it a theological underpinning. During the 1760s, the need to produce a convincing reply to scepticism became more insistent as evidence based on arguments from social utility were marshalled against both Christianity and the religious life. The expulsion of the Jesuits from France in 1762, a triumph of the unlikely alliance between Jansenists and *philosophes*, further weakened attempts to produce satisfactory apologetics. For above all other theologians, the Jesuits had tried to formulate a theological justification for Christianity based on contemporary philosophy, a natural development in keeping with their earlier liberal attitudes over Probabilism. Slowly, such broad natural theology, however, whittled away unpalatable definitions of sin, revelation and the nature of the supernatural. It is striking that the very large number of anti-Jansenist books introduced into St. Edmund's library, Paris, from the 1740s, belonged precisely to this form of Jesuit humanist theology. Amongst such works, those of Collet and Berruyer, for instance, demolished the doctrine of hereditary sin and replaced it with a belief in the natural moral goodness of man. If there be any doubt as to whether such books as these affected monks, it is easily dispelled by appreciating the very intimate relations the English Benedictines had with the Abbé Luke Joseph Hooke, influential Sorbonne theologian and brother of an abbess of Cambrai. Hooke had applied empiricist criteria to theology. He explained, for instance, in his *Religionis Naturalis et Moralis Philosophia Principia* (Paris 1752-54) that intuition was a kind of taste, and the understanding of right, merely a perception. For Hooke, all men were possessed of a general benevolence. His *bienfaisance* implicated him, somewhat unjustly, in the case of the Abbé de Prades's unorthodoxy. He was dismissed from his post, but recalled in 1753, although from 1762, students were forbidden to attend his lectures.[571] English monks, however, still remained in the faculty he continued to supervise. Foremost among them was John Bede Brewer, who finished his doctorate under Hooke, and went on to edit the second edition of the latter's *Religionis Naturalis* (Paris 1774) which included a preface by Hooke, thanking his wisest and dearest friend.[572] The monks at Paris were largely responsible for this book's distribution to English Catholic booksellers. Brewer, who read other books of a liberal tendency in Paris, like the dissenter Hugh Farmer's *On Miracles* (London 1771) also became a long-standing colleague of Joseph Cuthbert Wilks, the Paris monk and later famous English Catholic liberal. Wilks's own thesis on Daniel was supervised by the Hebraicist, J-R. Asseline, himself suspected of unorthodoxy, and was published in 1770. It made much use of the contemporary defence of revelation by attempting to prove, through a strongly literal interpretation of the text, that it was an historical fact.[573]

Wilks had not proceeded to a doctorate, having refused to take the oath affirming his belief in the doctrine of the Immaculate Conception. In 1779, Thomas Welch, then at Cambrai, ordered Placid Waters, in Rome, to send Muratori's controversial *De Superstitione Vitanda*(1740) and elude the Roman censors by tracking it down in Florence or Modena. This work tried to distinguish between essential Christian beliefs and those which were secondary, and to explain Muratori's hostility to the doctrine of the Immaculate Conception also.[574] In Rome, English Benedictines in Rome were already in touch with the main currents of the Enlightenment . Augustine Walker had discussed David Hume's *History of Great Britain* there in 1764, with his friend

165

and fellow enthusiast, Andrew Lumisden, assistant secretary to the Pretender. Walker had commended, rather surprisingly, considering Hume's reputation among Christians, Hume's historical veracity and lack of prejudice.[575]

Understandably, there were casualties resulting from too great a sympathy for the Enlightenment. These emerged from the very troubled timess of the 1770s and after, when superiors constantly bemoaned the disobedience and irresponsibility of their subjects. These problems were gravest on the mission, where monks could indulge their freedom. The South Provincial, Bernard Warmoll, harked back to a less complex missioner:

> For my part, I prefer Mr. Simpson, with a moderate genius, to our refined Gentlemen too conversant in the Philosophy of the time, and the Belles Lettres, as now in vogue; as little is to be depended on from these worthies.[576]

Like Bishop Walmesley, he blamed the cultivation of the 'new Philosophy' in the monasteries.[577]

At least two monks apostatised largely as a result of the influence of such learning, James Compton and John Augustine Hawkins. Compton's friendship with Dr.Johnson and his apostasy as a result of reading the *Rambler* has already been outlined. He had been ordained as a Jesuit, and become a monk after the Society's suppression. An academic and a reputedly able teacher, he was known to have 'wild and strange notions'.[578] Thomas Welch commenting on Compton's apostasy in 1782, dismissed him as a man without principle:

> His view was an independent life, which could only be had in England... I am very well assured he has the art of accommodating his tenets and system to his feelings and bent of his passions. If this be the case, he may figure away in Robin Hood's congregation, or as a Methodist preacher.[579]

Compton ended up as a married Anglican minister, with a fashionable following in London churches.[580]

The career of John Augustine Hawkins demonstrates even more forcibly the attractions possessed by the 'liberal spirit'. At Douai, he had been well-read in the most recent philosophical writings, and on the mission in the late 1770s, he had produced a book of *Morning and Night Prayers*, which was condemned for making a 'strange Jumble of the Trinity'. By 1780, after a spell as a 'governor' to his patron's son in Turin, he had returned to England and written three heterodox pamphlets which attacked transubstantiation, suffrages for the dead, prayers to the saints, and the religious life; a battery he rounded off with an attack on the Trinity itself. All these were the stock-in-trade of anti-Christian philosophers, and Hawkins insisted that he was merely echoing the fashionable ideas on the continent. Further, he replied to Gregory Cowley, the Prior of Paris's criticisms of his works by insisting 'that he intended nothing against faith, but that Theologians were so divided among themselves, and so hard to please, that they were not to be dealt with'. Hawkins apostatised in 1780, married, and, like Compton, entered the Anglican ministry, where he soon established a reputation as an authority on Catholicism. Monks who read his tract on celibacy, published in 1782, dismissed it as a justification of his own conduct, but Bishop Walmesley recommended it ought not, as a 'dangerous book',to be read in the monasteries. Hawkins achieved some notoriety because of his pamphlet war with his old acquaintance, Joseph Berington, the English Catholic liberal. Berington's *Reflections addressed to the Rev. John Hawkins* (1785) was the most influential Cisalpine defence of the Catholic position in this period.[581]

If we have tried to establish the variety of positions taken up by English monks *vis-à-vis* the eighteenth century Enlightenment, it is also necessary to balance this picture with an alternative one which demonstrates the slow growth of suspicion of that movement, culminating in a revulsion to all that it represented.

The most obvious early example of the Congregation putting itself on guard against dangerous new ideas was the stricter regulation of the studies of its student monks, the group most vulnerable to the new philosophies. The 'Method of Studies for the Professed', dating from the early 1760s, and most probably drawn up by Bishop Charles Walmesley,[582] had an impact throughout the monasteries. By this time, Walmesley had already published a work on Newtonian Physics, was a fellow of the Royal Society, and was on friendly terms with its secretary, Thomas Birch. The 'Method' was designed to give some shape to the formation of future missioners by controlling their reading as students. It balanced standard theological texts with the work of contemporary philosophers like Hooke, and included some Newton and Hume: 'It is not meant that the whole doctrine contained in them (the Authors) is to be approved. Particular passages may occur deserving

167

censure.' Such a balanced judgement would necessarily harden in favour of stricter censorship as attacks on the Church increased. It was a losing battle:

> Our Divines here are very nice about reading any books that have any mixture of erroneous or suspected Doctrine. Mr. Naylor (a former President), to prevent any scruple, permitted the reading of books of History and other subjects not directly concerning Religion. I suppose we may continue...Who is to allow this to the Scholars of our College?[583]

The short-lived Education Scheme of the Congregation, discussed 1779, implemented 1781, and dead by 1786, was designed partly to safeguard the philosophical and theological formation of the young monks by monitoring their progress through selected masters, and through reading and examinations.[584] In introducing the scheme in 1781, President Walker condemned liberal philosophy since 'bad subjects..were first corrupted by reading such books and frequenting such company'. Commenting on the troubles which Prior Cowley in Paris had as a result of these temptations, Provincial Warmoll frowned:

> The world is ripe in every kind of iniquity. Men observe no bounds, and are neither ashamed nor afraid to speak their own Tenets, poisoned with the writings and opinions of the Philosophers of this and former Ages. But what is still to be more dreaded, is the great profligacy of sentiments and manners which I am told have taken root in most r(eligious) Communities, to the overthrow allmost of good Government and Subordination.

In a later letter, he hoped that 'the new Philosophy, the Bels. L. and other books equally pernicious to young minds' might be less encouraged in the monasteries.[585] The Scheme's failure in 1786, because of internal dissension, after an auspicious start, merely increased the risk of young monks, deprived of a well-defined course, and sent back to ailing monasteries, falling prey to the prevailing mood.[586]

The failure of nerve which characterised the Church's general attitude to the Enlightenment in the last two decades before the French Revolution, was also shared by many monks. The earlier harmony betwen Religion and Philosophy had been succeeded by a conflict between the two, with the latter usually seen to be winning. Two clear

168

trends among the Benedictines in the face of this war can be discerned. In the first place, as we have seen, there was a closing of the ranks by a reaffirmation of traditional monastic virtues through an appeal to an earlier heroic age. Secondly, there emerged what must always be the final response to insurmountable problems in society, a belief in the fulfillment of apocalyptic prophecy.

Augustine Walker became President in 1777. In his youth, the vitality of the early Enlightenment had appealed to him, especially the field of scientific exploration, and even after 1777, he could still use the analogy of a watch to explain the workings of the human mind, and continue his interest in book-collecting and in his circle of scientific friends.[587] Nevertheless, his Visitation addresses became increasingly pessimistic. In 1779, for instance, he made the same point at Dieulouard and Douai:

> (The Enemy's) emissaries, under the appearance of friendship and humanity, of reason and Philosophy...have long endeavoured to corrupt the hearts of every class of Christians. Their insinuations, sarcasms against every duty of Religion, have long been current and received applause in every conversation. And their writings spread like a deluge... the press groans everywhere under an infamous load of books, fit for all the different stages of seduction'.[588]

In 1781, he condemned those who encouraged monks to mix more with the secular world, rather than remain in their cloisters, which bred, the seducers believed, 'illiberal sentiments and want of good breeding'. For Walker had seen, presumably at Paris, that those monasteries 'where there is the greatest commerce with the world' had 'the least good breeding and the greatest dissentions'. He hoped to stem the tide by eloquently praising primitive monastic obedience, solitude and asceticism, and by conjuring up before his audience the Anglo-Saxon period as the heroic age of the English Benedictines. He was thus able to draw out parallels between England and Europe then, and their present sad state.[589] In 1788, he was still blasting the insidiousness of enlightened liberalism, which 'under the appearance of friendship, a tenderness for humanity, of reason and philsophy', managed to seduce monks through 'lascivious books'.[590] Walker found the most satisfactory defence of the monastic life in a contemporary French work, *De l'état religieux* (Paris 1784), by the Abbé François Lambert Bonnefoy de Bonyon and the Abbé Bernard de Brindelles. It was warmly received by other monks, including Charles Walmesley, as not only a good 'illustration' of the Rule, but as a valuable defence of the monasteries in terms of their social utility. Despite the philosophers' criticism of the monasteries' worthlessness, this book:

> shews that Religious men are still the chief people that cultivate Sciences and instruct all the ranks of mankind.[591]

Walker's pessimism made him an enthusiastic supporter of Charles Walmesley's swan-song, *The General History of the Christian Church* by 'Signor Pastorini' (1771), a commentary on the Book of Revelation, with strong apocalyptic overtones related to contemporary problems. It had an extraordinary degree of popularity and was to be the monks' final answer to the irreligion of the Enlightenment. This work is the most obvious English Benedictine expression of the *Inquiétude des Lumières* which had troubled so many philosophers since the middle of the century and which led to to a renewed interest in apocalyptic prophecy.[592] Like Walker, Walmesley, who looked at Europe from Bath, had championed academic interests in the early period of the Enlightenment, only to find that the movement twisted away from orthodoxy in its later stages. In Walmesley's eyes, therefore, the Enlightenment not only became distasteful but positively diabolic. The *General History* was written while Walmesley maintained his interest in earlier ideas, now increasingly outmoded on the Continent. He read Hugh Hamilton on Natural Philosophy, and sent copies of *The General History* to his friend, the celebrated Italian Newtonian mathematician and physician, Paolo Frisi in 1781, and even with the gloom of the French Revolution and Cisalpine stirs encircling him, Walmesley still retained a youthful interest in astronomy. He was eager, for instance, to view Sir William Herschel's telescope at Windsor in 1790.[593] But as the key Benedictine figure in the early Enlightenment who witnessed it turning sour, Walmesley lived to see the outbreak of the French Revolution, the fulfilment of all he had predicted in regard to the disastrous course of the Enlightenment. The destruction of the monasteries which soon followed seemed also to suggest Walmesley's prophecies had been correct.

CHAPTER VI

MONKS AND EDUCATION 1685-1794

Within the monasteries, an educational apostolate, seen especially in schools, was the main external work.[594] There were also periodic attempts to establish schools in England, and a continuous supply of monks was always to be found in a tutorial role in chaplaincies or acting as governors to one or more wandering scholars. Unfortunately, the monastic schools have usually been treated in isolation, as the particular concern of each house alone, rather than as an integral part of the structure of the Congregation whose General Chapters constantly referred to these places of education in their discussions, and whose Presidents were essential in the selection of masters as they were also of governors. This Congregational involvement is also glimpsed in the responsibility which Provincials and Provincial Procurators had in transferring students to the schools on the continent. On the other hand, there is also evidence for supporting the belief that some missioners preferred to channel students to the house of their profession in particular.[595]

The primary object of the Congregation in maintaining such schools was that of providing recruits for the monasteries, and thus they were often called 'Seminaries'. Lay pensioners whose presence admittedly encouraged close links between the monks and English Catholic families, were thus essentially supernumeraries. Thus, St. Gregory's at Douai, which had the most important school in the Congregation, was re-established as a seminary after 1693, and by 1701, this school, and that attached to Lambspring were described as training schools for future missioners.[596] Significantly, a substantial number of students from Lambspring, on completing four years of humanities there, went on to study for the secular priesthood at the English College in Rome.[597] The schools which the Congregation planned or established in England during the early years of the eighteenth century were part of this monastic scheme, their main function being to train students up to the standard required by the Benedictine schools on the Continent. Similarly, students seem to have been sent to the Benedictine continental schools from the small Franciscan school at Osmotherley in North Yorkshire. It is not then surprising that such missionary schools were

171

proposed when the senior schools abroad were suffering from a decline of monastic recruits in, for instance, the 1720s and 1770s. At one such time, in 1725, two Provincial schools were projected, of which only one, at Redmarley in Worcestershire, was eventually established.[598]

The relationship between recruiting patterns and the schools is seen most clearly in the variety of bursaries established to maintain pupils in the schools. Up until the mid-eighteenth century, benefactors tended to invest capital to provide a bursary for a student from their family, or chosen by the family, whom, it was hoped, would later become a monk.[599] This assured the monasteries of a steady supply of capital, and during a period of financial hardship like the 1720s and 1730s, they rushed to accept such covenants, and, at the same time, demanded financial help from Propaganda 'to be able to furnish...missionaries'.[600] However, by the mid-eighteenth century, bursaries given by laymen to maintain Benedictine aspirants disappear, although monks on the mission still used their own money to provide bursaries when necessary.[601] This gradual disappearance of funds established by lay patrons coincided with a reduction in students entering the communities from the Benedictine schools.

Until the 1770s, our picture of the monastic schools and of those established in England is fragmentary. Attempts to set up small Benedictine schools in England during James II's reign to feed those on the continent came to grief in the Revolution.[602] After the Revolution, St. Gregory's at Douai expanded its school so that it could accommodate up to eighty students by the 1730s, although it had only reached sixteen 'pensioners' in 1733, twenty three in 1735, and was to drop down to eighteen by mid-century.[603] With only a handful of 'pensioners' until the late 1770s, St Laurence's at Dieulouard could hardly be said to possess a school. In 1756, only a library and eight rooms were given over to its alumnate. Many of its students were then already tending to come from Lancashire, sent over by Placid Naylor at Brindle.[604] Lambspring came close to St Gregory's in the style and size of its school. Here, the large numbers of the seventeenth century had levelled out by the beginning of the next century to about twenty students, with an erratic yearly intake of between one and six. On becoming abbot in 1730, Joseph Rokeby stated he found nineteen students resident.[605] St. Edmund's, Paris concentrated most of its educational work at its priory of La Celle, just east of Paris, in the earlier part of the century. La Celle was a sanatorium for sick monks, and housed a small alumnate of four or five students.[606] Aspirants

172

waiting to enter St. Edmund's, Paris were either educated here or sent to local Maurist houses.[607]

The closest we are able to get to a Benedictine philosophy of educatiom at this period is found in a series of notes by Augustine Walker which date from the latter half of the century. Presumably Walker had read *Emile*:

> each system of education should be changed to suit the disposition of the individual;

education is thought of too late - it should begin 'with the first dawning of reason in the infant, who is, rather barbarously sent ot he nursery to vegetate, but where most of the vices of the later man develop'. Walker recognised some of the weaknesses found in children sent to 'colleges' abroad, whence they return 'ignorant, rude or loaded with vices and fopperies of these countries'. Parents, he felt, should not hand their children over to 'ignorant and vicious' nurses, but should actively encourage them to question, to treat reading, writing and drawing as a diversion rather than a study. Only those games should be preferred which exercise the 'whole muscular frame', those causing the body to stoop or incline should be avoided. Earlier the reminiscences of Gilbert Langley, a lay pensioner at St Gregory's, Douai, between 1721 and 1726, give us the clearest picture of life within one of these schools at the beginning of the century.[608] Born of a Catholic father, with gentry and commercial connections, and a Protestant mother, Langley appears to have been brought up a Protestant. He transferred to Douai from Charterhouse, where he insisted the teaching was rushed and standards poor. John Stourton, a monk on business in London, was responsible for bringing the eleven-year old Langley to Douai, where the pension stood at £25 p.a. for an elder brother, £20 p.a. for a younger, being much the same in the other schools. In his autobiography, written in prison in 1740 before transportation, having been found guilty of petty crime, Langley described the cassock, which was the school uniform, the examination system, the obligation to speak Latin in conversation, the lay-out of the buildings and the prefectorial system at Douai. He went on to speak of the diet, the horarium, and the games, which included the election of a Christmas king and his court. Finally, Langley narrated some of his exploits; the smuggling of drink into the school from the town, and the stealing of food from the kitchen, which led the boys to take revenge

173

on the scullion who told on the culprits. From La Celle, pieces of verse survive which show life within its alumnate. These are mostly the work of the monk John Barnes, who taught humanities there in 1754. They dwell on the natural beauty of the setting, the cordial relations between monks and boys, and the sports played. Barnes wrote an elegy to mark his departure to Paris from this paradise.[609]

In the latter part of the eighteenth century, two developments caused the Congregation to modify this traditional role in education. First, the relentless attacks on the Church in France which built up after the 1760s, and, secondly, the first Catholic Relief Act of 1778. The effect of both these was to encourage more interest in developing Benedictine education in England. Up until this time, this had taken two forms: individual chaplains acting as tutors in families, and, as has already been mentioned, the maintenance of 'feeder' schools.

A monk's role as tutor had evolved naturally from his position as catechist to the household.[610] Such instruction could lead on to him giving a more secular education. In the 1770s, Edward Hussey was acting as 'preceptor to the son' of the Hyde family at Marlborough, much to the annoyance of the local Anglican rector. It was a short step from such personal tuition to the setting-up of a small school by a missioner. In 1790, Gregory Cowley, a successor of Hussey at Marlborough, educated ten of Mr. Hyde's children there, before becoming President in 1794, and establishing a private school at his house at Vernon Hall in Lancashire. In a similar way, Anselm Bromley, who had taught for many years at Dieulouard, expanded his tutorial work into a small school at Woolton near Liverpool.[611]

Immediately after the passing of the 1778 Relief Act, which allowed Catholics to run schools, various schemes were put on foot to develop the small missionary ventures already existing. These new schools, nevertheless, were largely to maintain the traditional role of 'feeder' schools, preparing students for the Continental schools, at a time when these latter had falling rolls. Myddelton Lodge, on the moors of the West Riding was one early suggested location: 'a retired place, and at no great distance from Lancashire, the County that in all appearance will contribute most towards furnishing Recruits to ye Seminaries abroad of every denomination'. Unfortunately, the owner of the property objected, and another site further east, at Follifoot, where the North Province already owned a house and land, was judged too near to Harrogate and Knaresborough, 'where provisions for Life are rather dear'. The 'cheap and retired Countries of north Lancashire or

Westmoreland' were therefore preferred. In these new schools, the monks were at first reluctant to employ any lay-masters because the students' parents could hardly afford to pay the pensions out of which salaries would have had to come.[612] The picture gained of these projected schools in the north is that of a fairly large establishments, educating a lower class of student than that entering the Continental schools earlier in the century. There was still some hesitation shown to the founding of a large town school; after all, the Gordon Riots would break out within two years of most of these schemes being tabled. Even so, the Northern Provincial, Anselm Bolas, who had one eye on the future, realised that the French bar on young aspirants being professed in religious orders in France, together with increasing freedom for Catholicism in England, would force the Congregation to think seriously of founding a school in England. As a pilot-scheme, he recommended a school for a dozen boys at Brindle or Woolton, two Benedictine missions in Lancashire, which would serve as a model for a larger 'school of note', and be funded in the first instance by the North Province.[613]

By late 1778 a project based at Brindle, catering for thirty students, was put under the care of the Provincial Procurator, Oswald Eaves. Northern missioners, therefore, did not take too kindly to the Congregation's Education Scheme of 1779 which would by-pass the Brindle project in favour of developing a full-scale minor seminary at Dieulouard. Such a move, the missioners felt, took no account of contemporary realities. Those unhappy with the Brindle scheme, on the other hand, argued that Lancashire's new industrial wealth might be transient, and in a recession, the Province might be left with a school on its hands which it was unable to fill.[614] After some delay, the General Chapter of 1781 deputed Bede Brewer, just recovering from the attack on his person in the Gordon Riots at Bath, to start an English Benedictine school at Woolton, near Liverpool. This was to be a reversion to the earlier formula of educating boys in their early teens, before transferring them to a monastery school, which in this case, was to be at Dieulouard. Lack of space, an anti-Catholic neighbour, and paucity of funds made Brewer proceed cautiously. He insisted he would only begin with three pupils of the same age because he still believed his 'principal care' was his congregation rather than a school. He envisaged however, building the school up to twelve pupils, all under twelve years old, employing a lay usher if necessary 'to be constantly with the Boys to see they keep to their studies, and

175

prepared their lessons for me to hear, and two governesses'. Brewer believed his school, at fifteen guineas a year, would compare favourably with the neighbouring school for Liverpool 'tradesmen's' children (£20), and the £17 charged 'in the Cath. School lately set up beyond Preston'. Brewer above all else, insisted on professionalism, and objected strongly to the ramshackle mission school which Placid Naylor had run at Brindle in the 1760s as a feeder school for Dieulouard:

> As for Mr Naylor, he frequently sent over (to the Continent) boys without ever having them at his house, and I believe those he had with him, he seldom taught anything than their accident (accidence?). And I have been told that as to the learning they got there, it was of very little service when they came abroad. His occupations were so various that he could not properly attend to such an undertaking. It is in vain to expect that Boys will make any progress worth speaking of unless they be kept and taught in a regular manner.[615]

Brewer had his way; his house was extended in 1786 to supply the needs of his school. James Bastwell's educational fund, set up this year, was to be administered by the Provincial Procurator, and was designed to help poor boys in five Lancashire Benedictine missions, with the residue being used to help boys already at Lambspring and Dieulouard. St Edmund's was prepared to help finance the school at Woolton, provided it might send boys there who in later years might become novices for St Edmund's. By April 1792, there were thirty five pupils at Woolton.[616] The success of Woolton encouraged other Benedictine schools in the vicinity. Brewer recommended that Laurence Hadley at Brindle turn his small day-school into a boarding establishment under the Abbot of Lambspring's patronage. The Provincial of the North also believed a new Benedictine school in the recently-acquired mission of Liverpool would prevent families from deserting the continental Benedictine schools. The French Revolution stopped any further progress here, although Brewer's school at Woolton was taken over by the refugee Cambrai nuns in 1795, and the refugees from Dieulouard eventually joined Gregory Cowley's new school at Vernon Hall in Lancashire.[617] This merger, marking the establishment of monasteries and their schools in England, ended the long history of feeder schools here, whose main purpose had been to supply recruits to the schools abroad.

The Provincial of the South, Bernard Warmoll, devised a parallel scheme in the 1780s, presumably more suited to conditions in the south. Warmoll's more radical scheme of a large college, along the lines of the monastic schools abroad, resulted from his belief that, after the 1778 Act, the French would no longer be gullible enough to view the English monasteries as full of persecuted English refugees, and, given the tense relations between both countries, would expel the communities. Warmoll therefore saw no future for the schools in France, believing only Lambspring would survive. He therefore aimed 'to procure a large wholesome situated house in England' which would 'open a larger field to our advantage, if by our example and regularity, we draw upon ourselves the favour and good will of our Patrons and neighbours'. Warmoll felt the plan for a new northern 'feeder school' to be too 'narrow':

> There are a number of such kind of little schools in England. Both the Clergy and Fryars are before us in this sort. We must aim at something better and to have it carried in a better stile, in imitation of the best schools in the kingdom, but under a better government and regularity.

Warmoll's intention appears to have been the creation of a large lay establishment, rather than a seminary. At first, he hoped it might be established at Bath once the chaplain had vacated the Bell-tree House, but later he favoured a property close to London, or another in Gloucestershire, near good communications and with plenty of ground. His advisers were more pessimistic, insisting he would have neither scholars, funds, nor masters to undertake such a large scheme, and they counselled delay, hoping for a further Relief Act, since 'an undertaking of this kind so soon may give umbrage to enemies, at least to such who are sanguine against us'. Warmoll saw the ex-Jesuit college at Liège as the monks' main competitor which threatened Benedictine schools in England and abroad. Warmoll's plan, was, however, delayed for in the 1780s, the Congregation's main preoccupation lay with the Education Scheme on the Continent, with which Warmoll was himself unhappy. Even so, Warmoll's idea was revived after 1789 and after the Catholic Committee's declared intention of founding a school for tradespeople:

At present, the prevailing notion of home education renders some such plan very necessary, if we wish to retain our existence as a Body... Undoubtedly, a school for the sons of gentlemen should be in the South Province..Unless he (Warmoll) plans a school, I fear the loss of some gentlemen's sons of an age to go to school, & these I flatter myself we could procure for him. Master Cholmeley is gone to London for education & I fear the loss of others in case we do not proceed to action.[618]

The flight of the communities to England three years later ensured the implementation of such a policy.

Save for Lambspring, the monasteries were all heavily involved in the 1779 Education Scheme, which aimed to unite the houses more closely together through the merging of their educational works. Benedictine schools throughout France were, from the mid eighteenth century, undergoing a massive transformation, partly because of financial and social pressures, partly through the Enlightenment's emphasis on utility. The Education Scheme endeavoured to halt the decline in numbers of monks and pupils, and to consolidate staffing and resources. To a large extent, it was forced on the Congregation by the demands of Commission of the Regulars in the 1760s which encouraged centralisation and utilitarianism. Indirectly, the Scheme was one result of the English 1778 Relief Act. The constant danger present to the Congregation throughout the eighteenth century was that of fragmentation, as the different elements found themselves being progressively absorbed into their local societies, and hence distancing themselves from the Congregation in general. This explains the constant appeals for unity sent out by Presidents and General Chapters. There had been earlier education schemes with the same motive of unity behind them, but, like the one after the 1689 Revolution, they had never been fully implemented. The General Chapter of 1769, meeting the year after the French edict insisting on the amalgamation of separate novitiates and houses of study, was faced with a Memorial from England demanding moves 'to cement a close and firm bond of the whole Body'. This recommended that only St. Gregory's remain a college giving a 'Classical education', with six masters, two professors, and funds for fifteen boys.[619] The Scheme of 1779 which was, however, to be adopted, differed considerably from this first suggested plan.

Before attempting to examine in detail the debate on, and the result of, the 1779 Scheme, the pressures which the schools were facing up until this time need some examination. St. Gregory's described itself as a *collège conventuel* in the 1760s, hoping thereby to remove any threat of suppression by proving its value to the Commission of the Regulars. It had at this time about thirty students in the school, described as coming from 'families of distinction', but by this period very few postulants were entering St. Gregory's from its school.[620] The plan to rebuild the school at St. Gregory's agreed on in 1768 had been presumably as much the result of panic caused by the French edict of 1768, forbidding professions under twenty one years old and the clothing of foreigners, as the result of the need to repair a building in a poor state. This rebuilding policy envisaged a central accommodation block for pensioners, which still survives, and was funded by wealthy English benefactors. The foundation stone was laid in April, 1770.[621] The operation was directed by Prior Augustine Moore (in office 1755-75). Moore had repeatedly attempted to make St. Gregory's more independent of the rest of the Congregation, and, in a way, the large school he erected with money sometimes collected by him personally, was the expression of his determination. The closing of the English Jesuit college in Bruges in 1773 and the transfer of boys to Moore's new building would, it was hoped, give further support to his policies. He died, however, in June 1775, in the midst of tension and discontent within his own community and school, and was succeeded by Gregory Sharrock as Prior, ' a good religious, cleaver at business and a good scholar, which are necessary qualities for one to be at the head of a community and a college to make it flourish'. Sharrock immediately turned down the offer to take over the old English college at St. Omer, which had been under the English secular clergy since 1772, for fear of offending the latter, and because 'we are so far advanced in the building of our new house, few in number, solidly settled in peaceful possession'.[622]

It is clear that Prior Sharrock was faced with problems in the school at St. Gregory's which he believed only a Congregational Education Scheme could solve. Riots were frequent in the school during these years, and the general education of the boys apparently neglected.[623] This had the effect of reducing numbers even further, as parents began to transfer their sons to the English College, Douai, or to the college of the ex-Jesuits at Liège. This led to the school being filled up from the 1770s with French and other foreign pupils. One cause of this

179

disruption may have been the disappearance of pupils who came to the school at St. Gregory's as aspirants to the monastic life. It was also increasingly difficult to secure monks from the mission as masters at Douai. There were strong pressures to make the school more secular at this time, by, for instance, abolishing the cassock or *toga talaris*, traditionally worn by the students.[624] The monks seemed unable to cope with an increasingly lay establishment, which probably provoked Sharrock into formulating a plan for a future division between clerical and lay students:

> Not only few of our Boarders incline of late to the Monastic state, but we are very unsuccessful with such as are admitted gratis. Want of capacity in some, of good will in others, has forced us to send back several. If we could bring up the young People destined for the Religious Profession separately, and join the candidates of the three houses, training them immediately to more severe discipline and to a plan of study calculated for the particular ends of our Institute, two Colleges might be of service. My ideas begin to multiply...[625]

The school at Lambspring was also subject to the general decline in numbers at this time; sometimes there were years when no new students entered, and in the 1780s, there seems to have been only ten pupils in the school. Lambspring had accepted at least one pupil from Bruges after the suppression of the Jesuits in 1773.[626] A clear picture of Lambspring's school can be obtained from the 'Rules...or The Method of educating youth at Lambspring, dating from 1767.[627] Spiritual concerns are predominant in these; daily Mass, the Confraternity of the Rosary, and the teaching of the Catechism (Anselm Mannock's *The Poor Man's Catechism* all find a place). The Rules insist on silent meals, forbid going to ale-houses, and making contact with the locals. They encourage all manner of deportment and make special mention of training in parsing, with a need to avoid 'ye filthy & disagreeable custom of speaking and reading through their nose'. But the reality was rather different. Missioners, for instance, were constantly pestered by parents anxious about their sons' welfare at Lambspring, following reports that it was no better than a prison, with its students forcibly cut off from communication with their families in England and badly treated. Evidence of such complaints makes moves at this time to found a Benedictine school in England easier to understand.[628]

Lambspring, being outside France, was not included in the 1779 Education Scheme of the Congregation, through which the latter hoped to halt the decline in numbers in monasteries and schools. This Scheme was part of a single development in the latter half of the century to consolidate the unity of the Congregation, and cannot be easily isolated from this total policy. Here, however, only that aspect of the Scheme relating to the schools will be discussed. By late 1778, the Priors of Douai and Paris, Gregory Sharrock and Gregory Cowley, had agreed in principle that student aspirants should be sent to Dieulouard, and that Douai should be a novitiate and house of studies for philosophy. The school at Douai was to be continued, although the emphasis in the community's work would switch to the common novitiate. It was felt 'absolutely necessary to separate the Boys who are for the world from those who are for Religion. Not all parties were enamoured of the Scheme. Dieulouard objected to the insufficiency of the pension agreed on; secondly, it saw its community being drained of younger members sent to Douai for their philosophy, and, thirdly, an increased school at St. Laurence's would require three full-time Professors who would be forced to be frequently absent from choir duties.[629] Another dissentient voice was Bernard Warmoll, Provincial of the South, who was unhappy about the precedent which might be set by the new Dieulouard school. He condemned the enforced segregation of clerical students there as a retrograde step, and one which blasted his own hopes of a liberal English Benedictine education being offered in England:

> Your establishing a school solely for the benefit of our body has the appearance of a kind of banishment for the youth and monopolisation in respect to ourselves...It will be looked upon as a Decoy, where methods may be used to sollicit these youths to enter among us, their tender minds may be kept in ignorance that a choice of life ought to be free. All schools ought to be for the general Benefit of mankind. I believe this is the first attempt of the kind ever to be thought on; even that political Body, the Jesuits, were never bold enough publickly to adopt such a plan.

Warmoll condemned the manner in which the new school might unduly influence the minds of young children towards becoming monks, 'such a kind of education to me don't carry with it that generous disinterested principle wh. ought to conduct all good men'. He preferred that the mixture of monastic aspirants and lay pensioners, found in the school at St. Gregory's, Douai, was more likely to flourish than a seminary school:

> Those of a different class who are prudent and well-behaved will have this advantage of being educated under the same roof with their betters and establishing a lasting and advantageous connection with them...Boys who are not inclined to a Religious Life will unavoidable (sic) be ridiculing and impertinently witty on the others. Besides such vocations as can't stand the attack of a Joke are in my opinion very slippery.[630]

Towards the end of 1779, the Scheme was put into operation, with twelve students sent to Dieulouard from Douai and Paris. The latter backed the Scheme wholeheartedly from the start, but Prior Sharrock at Douai had some early problems; parents and sons often differed as to whether the latter should be transferred to Dieulouard, and Sharrock was unhappy about siphoning off some of his best students for Dieulouard. There was also the perennial problem of the monasteries finding enough income to pay the fees of their students at Dieulouard. Finally, Dieulouard itself had difficulty in finding the right staff from the community there at such short notice.[631] Despite all these irritations, Prior Sharrock at Douai was convinced that segregation was the only answer in attempting to maintain the number and interest of monastic aspirants. Experiments nearby assured him of this:

> (Douay College), being essentially a seminary, they will hurt it by introducing Modish plans. This again confirms me that our school at Dieulouard was a useful and perhaps necessary expedient for preserving our houses'.[632]

Despite having the backing of the 1781 General Chapter and the three Priors of the houses in France, the Scheme had disintegrated within four years, 'because of difficulties of times, places and persons', and the 1785 General Chapter was forced to acknowledge the failure of it. The common novitiate had proved unworkable, although the division of the schools does not appear to have cause insuperable difficulties. Nevertheless, Dieulouard had been unhappy about sending its philosophy students to Douai, and supported a return to the older system of clothing pensioners immediately after their schooling. These would be called 'candidates', and clothing them would avoid any danger of losing them before their canonical novitiate could be started.[633] Even after the breakdown of the Scheme, Paris continued to send its aspirants for their early education to Dieulouard, which began to take on French pensioners to keep numbers up. This introduction of French pupils had already commenced at St. Gregory's to compensate for the loss of clerical students to Dieulouard. It seems probable also that Douai was finding it increasingly difficult to attract sufficient lay pensioners from England, especially after the 1778 Act. By 1782, the school at Douai had only twenty students, many of whom were Irish or French. In 1786, Prior Jerome Sharrock neatly summed up the problem:

> We must either give up education entirely, which ought by no means to be thought of, if possible to avoid it, or we must send our young people to the public schools, which many are averse to. Or foreigners must be taken into the house for this purpose & ample salaries allotted to them, which the circumstances of St. Gregory's cannot admit of, or Masters must be afforded from other houses, which their low situation will not permit, or two or three Missioners, able & willing to teach, must be brought over to perform this task, who it would be impossible to find, or I must lay down my charge & undertake it myself, which I would most willingly do.[634]

St. Gregory's school survived through to the Revolution firstly, by sending out some of its students to the 'publick schools', secondly by promoting an energetic advertising campaign in England, and finally, by taking in more French pupils and staff to teach them.[635] The Prior hoped that the work of educating French boys would be an excuse for preserving the community from the anti-clerical legislation of the Revolution, which became more intimidating after 1790. An offer of sanctuary from the magistrates at Courtrai, over the border, was therefore turned down. Ultimately, petitions for exemption were to no avail, and the school was suppressed with the community in 1793, at the same time as the other English Benedictine houses.[636]

Always existing in parallel to the established monastic schools, and to a large extent complementing them, was a highly-organised tutorial system, by which one or more students moved about Europe accompanied by a monk-tutor who directed his pupils' education. As such, this system was the natural outcome of a lone chaplain's educational role in the family he served, but because the Benedictines were ideally placed for English travellers, through their possessing houses in France, Germany and Italy, this domestic tutorial role was easily

183

extended abroad. This developed system was of enormous benefit to the English mission since it allowed the monks to maintain their position as chaplains in particular families over a long period of time, because generations of sons were to be escorted across the continent by fellow monks. The popularity of the Grand Tour in the eighteenth century was to allow a larger number of monks to become involved as governors of young Catholic travellers. Like the schools, this tutorial system was a fully integrated part of the Congregation's apostolate, for generally, a Benedictine patron would apply to the President, often through the Provincial, for a tutor for his son.[637]

The tutor system survived the Revolution of 1688-89, despite the hardships met by tutors and pupils trying to travel around Europe.[638] The number of unemployed priests at this period allowed employers to choose tutors from a well-qualified body, eager for the job. President Bernard Gregson in 1699, for instance, could recommend three able monks to a patron; the first was 'ingenious and careful', the second, 'a very good schollar... (and) has a particular art (wch. is naturall to him), he gaines youth', and, finally, the third, was a Sorbonne doctor and 'a man more dignified'.[639] The dangers of the system which took boys away from their families for long periods of travel and which deprived them of communication with their families, are vividly illustrated in the story of the 'lost heir of Capheaton'. John Swinburne was taken by his monk tutor, Cuthbert Farnworth, from Capheaton in Northumberland, to the Continent, following the family's implication in the '15. Swinburne was educated for some of the time in a college in Belgium, perhaps St. Gregory's, Douai, as *un enfant trouvé*, his real identity hidden until, half a dozen years later, he was discovered through his looks and breeding to be a Swinburne. He was returned to Capheaton where he recognised his old toys. Farnworth, his tutor, later became his chaplain at Capheaton.[640] From this period of the early eighteenth century comes the monk William Champney's summary of what a tutor might hope to teach and show to his pupil on their travels: 'How to pass time Abroad', lists of 'Opinions of Learned Men', 'The Decadency of the Lattin Language', surveys of the French, Florentine, Lotharingian, English and Papal Courts, catalogues of antiquities and ecclesiastical art, lists of academies, and, finally, the need to keep a full diary of travels.[641]

The monasteries acted as convenient stopping-places to these students and governors. This was especially the case of St Edmund's, whose central position in Paris made it a convenient lodging house, although St. Gregory's, Douai, was close to Calais, and St. Laurence's, Dieulouard, close to main trans-continental thoroughfares. At St. Edmund's, pupils would 'treat' their Benedictine hosts, who, in return, would conduct them around Paris and Versailles.[642] The later connoisseur, Charles Towneley, as a young student, stopped off at La Celle in 1759, with his tutor, the famous scientist John Turbeville Needham. La Celle was also responsible for the early education of the well-known traveller and writer, Henry Swinburne, who was there in the 1750s.[643] However, as the Grand Tour became more elaborate and expensive, a number of Catholic families came near to bankruptcy in finding money to fund it. The Benedictine houses increasingly played the role of hosts to a floating population of students with their governors or preceptors, who often stayed a few months before moving on to Paris or other capitals. In Paris itself, English Catholic youth would be put under the direction of monk tutors or guardians to finish off their education before returning home. In 1774, for instance, Philip Howard of Corby, Cumberland, transferred his son Henry, the future writer, from St. Gregory's, Douai, to the care of his old chaplain Thomas Welch, then at St. Edmund's, who was already supervising the education of a Walmesley of Wigan. The young Howard's continuing under Benedictine tutelage was an enormous relief to the monks who at this time believed themselves to be losing out to the more fashionable ex-Jesuit academy at Liège:

> I am afraid we are going to lose young Harry Howard at Douay, and that he is going to Liège, to ye Academy ye Ex bon Peres have established there. Several here putt it up greatly as the finest scheme that was invented and that nobody is capable of teaching but ye Bon Peres. It may do for ye present, but I cant think that it will be permanent. Novelties gain at ye beginning, but they will soon grow tired with them.[644]

Welch was to provide the polish 'by rubbing off the rust of College (St. Gregory's), by taking care of Henry's deportment, his manners and his dancing lessons. He would also take Henry 'to see the King's Cabinet, Palais Royal and other curiosities of Paris', but his main task was to keep the boy's father fully informed, by reporting on 'a thorough knowledge of his disposition in every respect: Religion, morals, manners, inclinations, capacity', so that Henry might be well-fitted for the military career his father planned for him.[645] The

185

monks in Paris were trusted by parents because of their considerable expertise in finishing off their sons' education, and by the 1780s, a pattern had established itself: boarding school at Liège or St. Gregory's, two years in Paris under a monk's supervision, concluding with the Grand Tour, again often under another monk. The Prior of St. Edmund's, Paris, would recommend the best colleges there for English students, pointing out the value of the discipline of a college rather than 'the dissipation..inevitable in a private pension'. Occasionally, through lack of funds or innate academic ability, the period spent in Paris under the monks was planned as the conclusion of a youth's education, and was not followed by the Grand Tour. The eighteen year old son of Squire Salvin of Croxdale, Durham, came to Paris in 1787, 'rather wild and giddy', with no academic interests. His father understood the boy's character well and could only hope that he be given the advantage 'to acquire French and the Graces which we hear he is totally unacquainted with at present'. The boy very quickly fell out with the tutor allotted to him by the monks' President, Augustine Walker, and was packed off home.[646]

After the spell in Paris, many students either moved off on the Tour with a monk companion to provide various courses of instruction en route, or they journeyed to Rome, to lodge with the English Benedictine Procurator at his house in Trastevere. Occasionally, Turin was preferred to Rome, and Thomas Welch, after supervising Henry Howard in Paris, had accompanied young John Smythe of Acton Burnell on his Tour to Turin in 1775, putting him under the charge of Sir William Lynch there. Welch spent two years in Turin, sending back critical reports of the Turin Academy to other prospective travellers.[647] When he had returned to Paris, Sir John Webb applied to the President to have Welch as governor to his son in Paris for two years. By this time, Welch was heartily tired of such work, but accepted this invitation out of a sense of loyalty:

> It is an employment I am not at all fond of, but he has one of the very best estates of any R. Catholick in England (15000 ll. p. ann), that this boy is an only son, and that he might be of very great service to Religion. I sacrifice every private inclination to this end.

After providing the best masters in Paris, and Antoine Guénée, the scourge of the philosophers, as director of young Webb's studies, Welch and his charge eventually set out for Switzerland to consult doctors about the boy who had 'a Rheumatick gout'. They were away for nearly a year, returning to Paris only after Webb had attended to the last ball in Spa. Welch admitted he had seen all the weaknesses of the governor-system during this tour; the young Webb had retained his 'many childish and awkward tricks', his *mauvaise honte*, and his 'extreme indolence and unsteady disposition'. Welch's plea that the boy be 'put into some place of public education' went unheard, and it was not until the summer of 1780, that he was mercifully released of his charge.[648] Webb's rooms at St. Edmund's were then immediately given over to two Swinburne brothers who, under a French tutor, were studying with the Eudists in Paris. The Prior hoped that their pensions would help to balance the cost of sending monastic aspirants from St. Edmund's to Dieulouard.[649]

Like St. Edmund's, the Procurator's lodgings in Rome provided acceptable accommodation for students, who were usually from families traditionally connected with the monks. In earlier days, the monks had merely recommended English visitors to contacts they already had in the city, but as the English interest in things Italian developed during the century, the Procurator took on a more identifiable role as host to English visitors and governor to English students.[650] As Procurator in the early 1770s, Augustine Walker had successfully supervised the two Throckmorton brothers from Coughton, and was given a handsome annuity from Sir Robert for his pains. His successor, James Placid Waters *alias* Duviviers, was already on a European tour with a young Mr Greenwood, a charge of Sir Robert Throckmorton's , when he was appointed Procurator. Greenwood accompanied Waters to Rome, where he learned to dance and fence, but gave Waters 'a great deal of trouble'because of his propensity for low company', and by the end of 1779, he was dispatched to France by Waters who now determined 'never more to expose myself to such plagues with anybody'. Greenwood had been orphaned at an early age, and it seems that Sir Robert had put him under Waters' care to avoid his responsibility for the boy.[651] Despite Waters' resolution to stay clear of future educational entanglement, he was asked by President Walker in the spring of 1783 to take on the governorship of two Riddell brothers from Northumberland, then finishing their education in Paris. Waters had learned from his earlier mistakes:

I think Rome is a most dangerous place for youth who have not employment for at least a considerable part of the time,..and if the younger has no relish for improvement or study, he must be amused to prevent bad consequences.

Waters took on the task with the consent of the President and Regimen, but these insisted that his main work remained that on behalf of the Congregation at the Papal Court.[652] Nevertheless, during 1784, Waters accompanied his two charges around tours of the Roman antiquities, armed with Nathaniel Hooke's *Roman History*, and the boys drew some of the monuments.They continued their English lessons and met up with other young English students on the Tour. Waters was impressed by the elder's enthusiasm, but the younger, Edward, proved an embarrassment, cutting 'but a sorry figure', having 'come late to school':

It's hard still to get him up in the morning, but one way or another, he is hawled out of bed & ready for the first master. He is improved in his writing English & most of his Bodily exercises. That's all I can say of him. I have now a soldier to make him walk upright & teach him the exercise.

In the autumn, Waters took the boys to Naples, where he deliberately avoided the Court because of the expense and the danger of the younger Riddell making a fool of himself, but he did introduce them to the Cardinal Archbishop.[653] The next move was a circular journey to conclude the Grand Tour, through Austria and Holland, where the party would meet English envoys and ambassadors. As a preliminary, Waters ensured that he had his Superiors' consent to be out of Rome; this was easily granted because they saw the benefits likely to accrue from the trip, i.e. the continued patronage of the Riddell family, and the widening of Waters' and the Congregation's reputation abroad. At Venice, Waters reported how delighted he was with the advancement of the elder Riddell who had been cultivated by the famous cicerone, James Byres, in Rome:

(He) is become an excellent Cicerone & a great Virtuoso. Nothing I think has been so beneficial to him in that way, as the grand tour he made with Mr. Byres who took a great deal of pains with him on the occasion.

By the late summer of 1785, Waters had escorted his two pupils back to England, although he had to wait some time for Squire Riddell to pay the bill. In his eagerness to give his sons the best fashionable education, the father had almost bankrupted himself.[654]

As in other areas of the Congregation's work, the French Revolution was to destroy this fruitful intercourse. Thanks to the Revolution, Waters' supply of pupils dried up overnight. The loss of salary from France made him unwilling to accept the modest fee which Lady Blount offered in 1790 for her son's education, for he was quite uncertain what the future might hold.[655] As for the schools, the Revolution forced the communities at Douai and Dieulouard to return to England after 1793, and with the attraction of the continent gone for the moment, it was in England that the Congregation began to revive its educational work.

Abbot Maurus Heatley
(1722–1802)

Prior Augustine Moore
(1722–1775)

189

CHAPTER VII

MONKS AND JACOBITES 1689-1794.

The identification of the English Benedictines with the Court of James II not unnaturally committed the Congregation to the Jacobite cause after 1688. At this time, the majority of the Congregation's superiors had come from families loyal to the Stuarts, and a number had experienced conventual life in England in the short-lived monastery at St. James's. Some monks believed that James II's exile would be brief, and this conviction helps to explain the thorough commitment to Jacobite plots by some monks in the decade after the Revolution, and beyond. Attachment to the king's cause was not however merely a sentiment springing from his grant of toleration to the English Catholic community, something which it was felt the usurper William III would almost certainly withdraw. For Benedictine loyalty to the Stuarts was heightened by two other factors which made the length and degree of this connection unique.[656] First, the destinies of 'Crown and Cowl' were seen to be unmistakably intertwined in history, and great play was made of the alliance in past English history. Throughout the 1690s, this appreciation of the long historical pedigree of royal Benedictine patronage was merged with contemporary doctrines of anointed kingship and non-resistance, both held tenaciously by Anglican Nonjurors, to form a synthesis and literary expression in the work of the Congregation's annalist, Benet Weldon, himself an Anglican convert.[657] Secondly, in the same way in which the Stuart Court went into continental exile after the Revolution, so too, thanks to that catastrophe, did the English monks from the 1690s tend to enhance the importance of their continental monasteries within the Congregation as a whole, and to run their two English Provinces from a secure continental base and more obviously as a missionary endeavour. Thus, until Jacobitism died a natural death in the last decades of the eighteenth century, English Benedictines found themselves not only caught up in the various political alliances which used Jacobitism as a weapon in European diplomacy, but their monasteries became key centres within the Jacobite diaspora by helping to ease the entry of Jacobite exiles into the ranks of continental society.

If one is correct in dividing English Catholicism in the reign of James II into a 'Court' and 'Country' tradition, a similar separation can perhaps be maintained among the Benedictines after the Revolution of 1688. For 'Court Monasticism' was to survive in a continental exile and to maintain a heady Jacobitism among individual monks through much of the following century. On the mission, Jacobite sentiment was generally more passive, related to local grievances and inherited tradition rather than to more abstract questions like non-resistance. From the start, the royal presence was far more immediate to the monasteries than to the mission. King James visited St. Edmund's, Paris, where he knew some of the community personally, on at least two occasions, one being for his Lenten retreat in 1694. He demanded that the Congregation should honour his monk chaplains and that missioners should continue to further his cause in England. General Chapter accepted these requests and ordered prayers for the royal family.[658] Significantly, the early Jacobite literary tradition among the monks projected James II and Louis XIV as protectors of English Catholicism, for English monks in France seem to have been determined supporters of Louis's revocation of the Edict of Nantes in 1685. They were in a similar manner to condemn James II's declaration of toleration to Anglicans in 1692,[659] an illustration of how far conventuals were removed from the English scene.

It was the emergence of this militant Jacobitism on the continent which was to be responsible for helping to polarise opinions of Catholics in England, and by loosing a continuous stream of Jacobite plots, to force the government of William and Mary towards persecution.[660] Without this active campaign, it is more than likely that Benedictine missioners would have gone to earth until the disturbance caused by the king's flight had abated. Certainly some Benedictine patrons were prepared to try and accommodate themselves to the new regime rather than suffer continuous harassment.[661] The so-called Lancashire Plot of 1693, in which Benedictine patrons were involved and monks implicated, sprang initially from such harassment and the threat to Catholic gentlemen's estates by the revelations of government spies.[662] This 'plot' was more the result of a shocked response by papists suddenly made vulnerable to the penal laws than a stand taken for their *de jure* monarch. The Lancashire Plot must then have been representative of the pattern which much provincial Jacobitism adopted on the mission. This plot and its form of Jacobitism should be compared with the more elaborate conspiracy and doctrinaire

Jacobitism which produced the famous Assassination Plot of 1696. Henry Joseph Johnston, the monk heavily involved in this, had earlier encouraged the rebels in Lancashire. He was to be the archetypal Benedictine Jacobite of the period. From a rigid Nonjuring background, and a member of the Benedictine monastery at St. James's, he became a leading Jacobite spy after the Revolution. He had fled after the 1696 Plot's failure, hotly pursued into France by Williamite agents. In 1697, he became prior of St. Edmund's, Paris, and was a forceful patron behind the annalist Benet Weldon's work. One of his fellow conspirators in the 1696 Plot was Christopher Knightley, a brother of Maurus Knightley, the future abbot of Lambspring.[663]

In England, the degree of Jacobite involvement among the monks appears to have subsided during the decade leading up to the '15 Rebellion, although at least one monk, William Joseph Kennedy, a chaplain at the Florentine Embassy, was in prison in 1710 as a suspected Jacobite agent. Attention on the mission appears to have turned to a maintenance of Jacobitism through literary channels. The curious new edition of the seventeenth-century Benedictine Jerome Porter's *Life of St. Edward, King and Confessor* in 1710 was suitably emended, as we have seen, to portray the Confessor as a royal type now reflected in the person of 'James III'.[664] The Jacobite Rebellion of 1715, which affected much of northern England, directly involved a number of Benedictine patrons, especially in Northumberland and Cumberland, but it was essentially a manifestation of 'Country' Jacobitism, and the couple of monk missioners known to have been involved suffered because they were chaplains to conspirators rather than because they were Jacobites.[665] Government policy in dealing with the aftermath of this rebellion followed a pattern developed during the plots of the 1690s: commissions were set up to enquire into lay trustees holding land for Catholic religious orders, and such estates were then subject to confiscation or sequestration. The failure of the '15 thus saw the sequestration of rebels' estates and the registration by the Commissioners of the estates of Catholics, Nonjurors and others who persisted in refusing to take the Oath of Allegiance to George I. The uncovering of Benedictine land held in trust, the closing of some missions, allegations that the Benedictines were the accomplices of the Pretender, and, finally, evidence revealed of annuities being paid to monks, all contributed to the instability of the English Benedictine mission in the years following in the wake of the '15.[666]

Such setbacks, however, did not deter the strengthening of Jacobitism in the monasteries during this time. Recruits from Jacobite families continued to enter as novices.[667] After James II had been laid to rest in 1701 in St. Edmund's, Paris, that monastery rapidly became a mausoleum for the Stuart court. Jacobite exiles were buried in the crypt, the royal family became important benefactors of the monastery and, in return, the monks offered prayers for the success of the various Jacobite expeditions and for a future Stuart restoration. This Court monasticism, now transferred to the France, reached its apogee in the monastery in Paris leading the process which advanced James II's cause towards beatification, a labour which lasted some thirty years.[668] Jacobitism survived among the Benedictines on the continent not, however, on account of sentiment alone. It had a sharper edge, for the conspiratorial mantle of monks like Henry Joseph Johnston fell on the shoulders of another monk, Thomas Southcott, after the failure of the 1715 Rebellion. Southcott was undoubtedly the main reason why the monks were so committed to Jacobitism up until the mid-eighteenth century, because, as an active Jacobite, he held the office of Benedictine President between 1721 and 1741. From a wealthy Jacobite family, Southcott had entered St. Gregory's, Douai, and was professed there in 1688. By 1700, he had been chaplain at a number of Jacobite households in England, and became, as we have seen elsewhere, the friend of the Jacobite and poet, Alexander Pope.[669] At the outbreak of the '15, Southcott, as an accredited Jacobite agent acting under a variety of pseudonyms, was already a wanted man. Since he was familiar with many English Catholic noble and gentry families, he was able to build up successfully a circuit of benefactors among these. He was involved by August 1716 in preparations for the so-called Swedish Plot, but his indiscreet zeal caused him to be edged out of the network and replaced as principal agent by the Nonjuror Bishop Atterbury.[670]

Southcott's emergence as the leader of the 'orthodox' party in the Fenwick Schism, which has been described elsewhere, suggests that that affair had a strong Jacobite colouring. Once he had become President in 1721, Southcott was able to turn from his Jacobite mission in England to become a key figure in Jacobite Court circles on the continent. Here he saw himself as a diplomat carefully arranging alliances and using his influence to introduce exiled Jacobites into circles of the French nobility. At the same time, he was able to provide vital information for the Old Pretender through his many contacts, some Benedictine, in England. He therefore saw his mission from the 1720s as an ambassador for the Jacobite diaspora. In making any judgement about his role or any analysis of his massive correspondence, we need to bear in mind the dangers of loss of perspective, of exaggeration and distortion which hamper any historian dealing with Jacobite material from this period. Southcott's letters, supposedly revealing the powerful influence Jacobites had in European political circles and the desperation of Jacobites in England suffering under a persecuting government, need to be placed in a broader historical perspective to be measured accurately. His excessive zeal, recognised even by his Jacobite allies, prompted him to unbalance the facts in favour of his cause.

As President, Southcott began to correspond immediately with the Pretender. It was the time when the Layer Plot was being hatched, and Southcott channelled back information about the weakness of the British government and the degree of popular support for the Pretender in London, where Benedictine agents were numerous and kept in touch with Jacobite prisoners in the city's gaols. Not surprisingly, Southcott overestimated the problems facing British politicians and the ease which he maintained Spain could mount an invasion of England.[671] The Layer Plot fizzled out by early June 1722, although something of it remained in the fantastic schemes of Christopher Layer to assassinate George I. Its effects were, however, damaging for Southcott because the British government used its failure to clap his ally, Bishop Atterbury, in prison, and to attempt to divide English Catholics by forcing a land tax or a large fine on them. The strength of Walpole, who had just come to power, showed up the untrustworthiness of Southcott's intelligence. At a distance, he was only able to deride Walpole for making political capital out of Layer and for trying to engineer a new Popish Plot.[672]

Since Southcott as President generally resided in Paris, he became a leading figure in French Jacobitism. It was he who induced the Pretender to take his friend the Chevalier Ramsay as tutor for the young Prince Charles Edward, and who tried to persuade the Stuart Court to return permanently to Avignon. Southcott was determined to use every possible diplomatic channel to prevent France and England entering an anti-Jacobite alliance. He had no success in this last objective; another indication of the weak leverage Jacobitism possessed by this time in European affairs. Faced with an alliance between Walpole and Fleury, Southcott was forced to turn to Spain, then engaged in naval combat with Britain. Behind the scenes, he attempted

194

to influence the delegates representing the Catholic powers at the various peace congresses in the 1720s towards encouraging them to insist that England lighten the burden of taxation crushing the English Catholic nobility. He knew any success here would have increased his and Jacobitism's standing among these nobility. It was essential, he felt, for the future of English Catholicism and for the Benedictine mission, to nip in the bud any overtures being made by leading Catholics towards a truce with the Hanoverian government. Thus his policy had not essentially changed from the lines it had taken ten years earlier during the Fenwick Schism, and his tenacity received some reward when France and Spain allied in the early 1730s in the first of the Family Compacts.[673]

Southcott's use of diplomacy at the highest levels to ensure leading English Catholics remained Jacobite, was only one facet of his involvement in that extraordinary web of noble intrigue which constituted the Jacobite Court, a fraternal brotherhood with strong quasi-masonic undertones through its secrecy, mutual aid and cosmopolitan influence. This brotherhood seems to have expanded particularly in the late 1720s when English Catholic gentry, fearing increased taxation, left for France for a lengthy period or even exile for life.[674] Southcott's personal correspondence with John Hay, the Pretender's Secretary of State in Rome, was on a familiar level, and full of wit and jocularity. It shows the ease which he felt in mixing socially at this level. The asides might have emerged from any Court circle of the time: the prodigality of James 'III' in granting knighthoods of the Garter, the debate over the provision of benefices, a contempt for the dilatoriness of the Papal Court. All these mingled with recommendations for persons thought worthy to serve the Pretender and for tutors for the royal children. There was much salon talk about academic matters and, on top of all such domestic affairs, the relaying of imformation about foreign, especially English policies.[675]

Southcott appeared here in the grand style, as a typical eighteenth-century prelate of independent means, carefully cultivating the channels of patronage and enjoying the cut-and-thrust of politics. His most important office, the Presidency of the Benedictines, only occasionally peeped through this density of Jacobite concerns. He insisted, for instance, that the traditional prayers by the Congregation for the royal family continued to be said. In common with his predecessors and successors, he found the Pretender's privilege of nominating clergy for vacant Vicariates in England useful for advancing Benedictine candidates. He was always enthusiastic that the Benedictine Procurator in Rome should avail himself of the offer of support from the Stuart Court, even though the latter was not too successful in winkling money out of the Pope for the English Benedictines. Southcott's pleas were persuasively couched in terms which would make the Pretender listen. He insisted, for instance, that Jacobitism was only maintained in England because of the continued existence of the English Benedictine mission there. It was monks, he maintainted, above all others, who refused to join with other English laity and clergy and make a pact with the Hanoverians.[676]

Southcott kept his Jacobitism after his retirement as President in 1741, continuing to drink loyal toasts until his death in 1748.[677] He had ensured that the Congregation in the future would move along the lines he had marked out by manouevring sympathetic monks into key posts in the 1740s. Thus his successor as President, Cuthbert Farnworth, took over his office after being chaplain at Capheaton to the Northumbrian Jacobite family of Swinburne. Farnworth began his term of office with a profession of loyalty to the Pretender.[678] In Rome too, the delicate position of Procurator was given up to a string of Jacobite supporters following Southcott's death. This office required supreme diplomatic skill in administering the Congregation's business at the Papal Court while acting as the other side of a triangle which bound the Jacobite and Papal Courts together. In the very years when Jacobitism withered in England after the 1745 Rebellion, it remained a living reality in Rome for the succession of Benedictine Procurators there: Bernard Wythie (1737-43), Charles Walmesley (1754-57), Augustine Walker (1757-77), and Placid Waters, *alias* Duviviers (1777-1808).[679] Southcott had achieved one of his greatest victories for his brethren just before his retirement when he had successfully forwarded in 1741 the nomination of Laurence York to be coadjutor to the Jacobite Vicar Apostolic of the Western District, Matthew Prichard. York would be, in turn, succeeded as coadjutor by Charles Walmesley, thus ensuring a Jacobite and Benedictine presence in the Western Vicariate for some years in the future.[680]

The failure of the '45 Rebellion delivered some sharp knocks to the plans so carefully articulated by Southcott. Ultimately, that rebellion was to force Benedictine missionary superiors to adopt a more realistic picture of the value of holding onto Jacobite loyalties in England. Bishop York, as a well-known Jacobite, had been forced to flee during the rebellion, and at least one Benedictine mission was ransacked.[681]

196

After its failure, some Benedictine patrons remained staunchly Jacobite and stuck to their guns, like Sir John Swinburne of Capheaton, for instance, who contributed to the upkeep of Jacobite prisoners in Carlisle Castle. Some, like Sir Marmaduke Constable of Everingham, fled to the continent.[682] All the Pretender was able to do was to express his sorrow to the President that 'any of them (the monks) should be brought into trouble in the present conjuncture'.[683] Significantly, there were far fewer vocations from Jacobite families in the aftermath of the '45 than there had been following the Revolution of 1688/89 or the '15 Rebellion.[684] In the years after this Jacobite catastrophe, Placid Howard had become President (1753-66), and replaced Cuthbert Farnworth. Howard came from a Cumbrian Jacobite family and went through the usual profession of loyalty to the Stuarts at his elevation, which protocol demanded. He believed that the influence of the family was still of use in Rome to the monks and was prepared to continue in the tradition of President Southcott by raising money for the Pretender. What money he collected on his travels around England was sent to Charles Edward via St. Edmund's, Paris. But this fund-raising was brought to an abrupt halt when Howard discovered that nearly every Catholic family he visited was in heavy debt:

> most pleaded inability of doing what they wished in their power from the heavy load of taxes the nation groans under, and other distresses R(oman) Catholicks are subject to.

Furthermore, Howard had received information in 1762 that he was being watched by government spies, and therefore he hastily suspended his fund-raising activities.[685]

Because of the heavy pressures to which it was subject, it was inevitable that Jacobitism should wane on the mission before it did in the monasteries, where many conventuals continued to reflect Southcott's earlier dedication to the cause. Thus Augustine Walker could declaim his classical panegyric, *'On His Royal Highness Charles, Prince of Wales'* in 1750 to a literary audience at St. Edmund's, Paris. The work had been written to celebrate the prince's arrival in Paris on his way to organise the '45. The poem depicted the Pretender as a Christian king who neglected his own fate in order to heal his people's wounds. However, there were some cracks beginning to appear after the '45 even among conventuals who had maintained the wall of Jacobite support up until this point. A paper which had taken 'its rise in the late rebellion against King Charles' was delivered by the monk Placid Naylor in 1750 to the same audience which had enjoyed Walker's eulogy. Naylor discussed the question of English kings *de jure* and *de facto*, and reached an inconclusive answer, but demonstrated, to the chagrin of the Jacobites, how often kings *de facto* were ultimately accepted by their people.[686]

The European base of Jacobitism itself narrowed in the years after after the '45, becoming focused on Italy which contained the Stuart households in Florence and Rome. Benedictine Jacobitism was similarly narrowed as it slowly receded from being a central interest of the Congregation as a whole. This shift can be clearly seen by comparing the voluminous Jacobite correspondence of Gregory Cowley, Prior of St. Edmund's, Paris (1773-89) with Thomas Southcott's correspondence earlier. Cowley acted from 1775 as agent in Paris for the Pretender's substantial financial interests in France, presumably taking over this role from Thomas Welch, Prior of St Edmund's until 1773.[687] His letters were written purely in the line of duty and, dealing strictly with business, they lack all the marks of personal affection and interest in matters of mutual concern found earlier in Southcott's correspondence. Occasionally, this regular pattern was broken. Cowley, for instance, gave Charles Edward news of his illegitimate daughter, Charlotte, then living in Paris. He also described in detail the Gordon Riots, and amply supplied the Pretender with details of the American War. Cowley always remained deferential to Charles Edward and encouraged him to believe that the fortunes of the family were always about to improve. Whether he himself actually believed this to be so is doubtful. Not all monks were happy that Cowley should be so bound up with Jacobite concerns. One missioner was 'not very pleased with Mr. Cowley' for not writing to him:

> I laugh and excuse him, saying he is a man of very great importance, and perhaps too many Avocations from Court and Acquaintance to talk or write to us little Folks.[688]

Rome was to remain the last bastion of Benedictine sentiment for the Stuarts. The city became not merely the setting for the remnants of an exiled court in the last decades of the century, but, as we have also seen, the centre for a lively academy of the arts which benefitted from Stuart and papal patronage and attracted to itself an appreciable number of artists and connoisseurs with Jacobite sympathies. The Benedictine

198

procurators in Rome participated fully in this cultural explosion and owed their appointments at least partially to their Jacobite loyalty. Augustine Walker, the author of the Jacobite panegyric of 1750, was procurator between 1757 and 1777, and built up a wide circle of artists and connoisseurs as friends. He ranked Andrew Lumisden, Assistant Secretary to the Pretender, as his chief friend, and wrote an account of James 'III's' end in January 1766. Walker went on to act as agent for the French affairs of the new 'king', Charles Edward.[689] In 1767 he castigated the new Benedictine President, Placid Naylor, for not having given Charles Edward his correct titles. Naylor's letter, Walker admitted, would have been quite acceptable if it had come from England, but as it was written in Paris 'more is expected'. In later letters, Naylor used of the correct form.[690]

Walker himself was fortunate to maintain his contact with the Roman Jacobite circle after he had become President in 1777, and was delighted that Placid Waters *alias* Duviviers, a man with his own sympathies, was chosen to replace him as Procurator. Waters found himself at home immediately in the Jacobite literary and artistic ambience of Rome. He was fortunate too that he was adopted as the spiritual director and close friend of Charles Edward's daughter, Charlotte, Duchess of Albany, once father and daughter had come to live in Rome in 1786. Here, Waters became Major-Domo in the household of the Duchess. Waters was to be the last and perhaps most perfect representative of the Court Benedictine, a type which had emerged a century earlier when monks had been at home in the Stuart Court in England. Now Stuart patronage was of little consequence either in England or abroad for the interests of the English Benedictine Congregation, and Waters frequently apologised for allowing his Jacobite activities to distract him from his official Benedictine business:

> She (the Duchess) goes on well, but gives me a deal of trouble... I am so much tied to her apron that I must be with her every day.

Nevertheless, he believed it important to keep his contacts with the Stuart court and acted as a British ambassador by introducing English visitors to the royal father and daughter. He sollicited the Duchess's support for Irish episcopal candidates and for allotting benefices to Benedictines.[691]

When Charles Edward died in January 1788, the Congregation held memorial 'dirges', and Waters increased his influence over the

Duchess of Albany. He was given, after the Pretender's death, the task for which he was to make his name outside religious circles: he became officially responsible for the collecting and sorting of the vast corpus of Stuart papers in Florence and Rome, an activity he had been dabbling in since 1786.[692] The Duchess herself died on the 17th of November 1789, and Waters soon found that Cardinal York began in turn to rely heavily on his ministrations.[693] It was the Cardinal whom President Walker approached, through Waters, over the question of finding an Italian refuge for the Congregation once the Revolution had broken out in France where the Congregation was already seeking help from the Fitzjames family, the Cardinal's close relatives. The effects of the Revolution, however, were already being felt by Cardinal York and Waters, both of whom had lost their French pensions and were very apprehensive of the future.[694] The advance of the Napoleonic armies into the papal states in 1796 and the proclamation of the Roman Republic in February 1798 forced the Cardinal to flee to Naples. His departure also marked the end of the Jacobite enclave in Rome. Waters, however, stayed behind until his death in Rome in 1808. He acted as custodian of the Stuart papers until 1805 when he sold them to the British government in return for a pension.[695]

Lambspring Abbey: The Choir

CHAPTER VIII

FROM REVOLUTION TO EMANCIPATION.

Through hindsight it is possible to see fortune turning to favour the English Benedictine mission rather than the continental monasteries as early as the 1760s. Because this shift was operating some twenty years before the Revolution finally suppressed the monasteries, the Revolution itself fitted into a pattern and, affixing the seal to a long chain of related events, formed their climax. The improvement in conditions for Catholics in England, balancing the enfeeblement of the Church in France, was admittedly rather slow and not without spasms which reflected disapproval and opposition. These obstacles to emancipation were treated seriously. Together with the legal, ecclesiastical and economic security the Congregation had gone out of its way to seek in France, they prevented the emergence of a radical policy among the superiors in France which would have encouraged the Congregation to ditch its French base and return to England. Inertia and tradition favoured the maintenance of the *status quo*. A prolonged hibernation had two major effects. First, it lulled the President and priors into believing at least initially they could ride out the storm in France through adopting delaying tactics and resorting to constant petitions for exemption from damaging legislation. Secondly, as far as the mission was concerned, failure on the part of the Congregation's superiors to move towards new options caused English Benedictine responses to toleration for English Catholics to be guarded. Thus some Benedictine officials on the mission were reluctant to adopt wholeheartedly the adventurous compromise with the English government which the monk Cuthbert Wilks and his allies in the Catholic Committee were seeking. Throughout these years then, the Congregation's leadership was seen at one time and another as ambivalent, vacillating and ineffectual: weaknesses which did much to foster internal disunity.

In England, the nation's qualified approval of Catholics was acknowledged in the Relief Acts of 1778 and 1791. Both were permissive in their terms and in their scope. That of 1778 removed restrictions on land-ownership, abolished penalties against the Catholic clergy and allowed schools to be run by clergymen, provided an Oath of Allegiance had been taken.[696] The Benedictines, with their peculiar position straddling England and the continent, gave only a moderate approval to this Act. Benedictine missionary superiors stressed the need for caution and were in their own sphere apprehensive that toleration would merely increase insubordination among Benedictine missioners. They shrewdly pointed out the harm the Act might cause the conventuals in France by removing their strongest argument: that they deserved special treatment because of their status as exiles persecuted for their religion. At the outset, a paradox needs to be borne in mind when the history of the three decades before the French Revolution are traced: that the monks generally found their position in England much more satisfactory, despite the continued existence of hostility and penal legislation, than it was in Catholic France during the same period.[697] The build-up of anti-popery fever in 1779 by the Protestant Associations seemed to confirm Benedictine fears of reprisals against the 1778 Act. The new Benedictine chapel at Bath was one of the prime targets of the rioters. It was burned to the ground in the Gordon Riots which flared up in the summer of 1780, the papers of Bishop Walmesley were destroyed and the Benedictine missioner forced to flee for his life. This catastrophe came as a great shock to Benedictine opinion on the continent, unable at a distance to appreciate the force of an English anti-Catholicism inflamed by England being at war with its Catholic neighbours. At the time of the riot, the Bath congregation was divided over support for the missioner, Bede Brewer, and it is possible that some of his opponents connived at the chapel's destruction. Brewer was quickly replaced. Whatever be the case, the event paradoxically vindicated the English establishment's commitment to further Emancipation. The Bath municipality, eager to court Catholic favour in the city, had paid £4,000 compensation for damages within the year, at the behest of

> The Lord Chancellor who is now in Bath for his health, (and) has not scrupled to say in public that the Town must indemnify our losses.[698]

Despite the damage they caused, the Gordon Riots were no more than a momentary setback to the galloping toleration being shown towards Catholics. The success of the 1778 Act made some Catholics bolder in pushing on towards another Act and these revived the Catholic Committee in June 1782 for this purpose. Significantly, a high proportion of the Committee's lay members had been educated abroad by the English Benedictines, and the Committee very soon had a number of sympathisers among ordinary Benedictine missioners who held liberal views.[699] The behaviour of some of the latter seemed to justify fully the fears of missionary superiors that toleration would breed insubordination and unchecked liberty.[700] In France, disobedience and frequent insidious attacks by the civil authorities were causing some alarm. This built up a reaction against liberal values, especially among superiors who were being led to discover that the grant of too much freedom to subjects threatened to destabilise the monastic life.[701] However, as far as England was concerned, it was too late for monasteries to regret their encouragement of liberal attitudes. If liberalism was now suspect in monastic circles on the continent, its inculcation in progressive English Catholic circles, where a Benedictine presence was strong, was to help these to make an important contribution to the advancement of toleration in England.

The Benedictine Cuthbert Wilks as incumbent at Bath was persuaded to join the liberal Catholic Committee in 1788 to work for further toleration. He already had, as has been seen elsewhere, a reputation for liberal ideas dating back to his early years as a monk in Paris and this was to reveal itself on the mission in, for instance, his advocacy of radical liturgical change, which found support among the Committee and some monk missioners:

> He (Wilks) indeed wishes as I believe most judicious men do, that the Church would equally authorise the service to be performed in a language suited to the people, as it seems very unnatural that a Congregation can't join with their Pastor, and know not a word he says. This change would certainly have a good effect, and more so in countries who are not in communion with R(ome). For my part, I could never conceive any solid reason for the above practice. However I am thoroughly persuaded that every missioner conforms to the rules prescribed by the Church in the above particular, tho' in general read the Gosp. or Ep. in English with an explanation before prayers, but the M(ass) as usual.[702]

Wilks's long controversy with the Benedictine Vicar Apostolic Charles Walmesley over the question of the establishment of papal and Ordinary episcopal jurisdiction in England is dealt with elsewhere. Here it is only necessary to trace Benedictine reactions to Wilks's determination and that of his fellow Committee members to find a *modus vivendi* between Catholics and the English government which would form a prelude to a new Relief Act and Oath.[703]

The few stray comments dropped by monks at the beginning of this controversy suggest that most monks opposed the Committee's liberal and 'Cisalpine' policies. Missioners tended to side with Bishop Walmesley, living with the South Provincial Bernard Warmoll during the 1780s and undoubtedly influencing him. They therefore joined with 'the sober part of the R. Catholics' in condemning the Committee's 'Protestation' and the 'new-fangled Oath'. Abroad, the Roman Procurator, Placid Waters, persuaded his superiors into believing Rome would have no truck with such liberal advances.[704] As one might expect, it was among particular missioners that Wilks received most sympathy, especially those whose patrons stood most to gain from another Relief Act. In the north, Provincial Lacon held to the middle ground, hoping a compromise might gradually emerge between Walmesley and his party, and the Committee and its supporters:

> all will be settled & then we shall go on quietly, if our worthy Bps. be so happy as to conciliate the minds of our Committee by framing such an Oath as may prove acceptable to the government. For we still entertain hopes of a mitigation of the penal laws.[705]

Similar opinions began to be expressed by some individual monks on the continent. Prior Henry Parker in Paris, appreciating the degree of accommodation the Committee was prepared to make for the sake of its opponents, insisted that schism, such as had broken out by 1791 in France over the Civil Constitution of the Clergy, be avoided at all costs in England.[706]

After long and involved Parliamentary debate, however, a formula acceptable to the Vicars Apostolic was reached, and the Bill became law in June 1791. The Act allowed worship in registered churches whose incumbents had taken a new Oath; Catholic schools were permitted and various offices and professions were now thrown open to Catholics. Immediately before and after the passing of the bill, Benedictine interest had been concentrated on the dispute over jurisdiction between Bishop Walmesley and Cuthbert Wilks after the latter's suspension by the bishop. In general, however, monk missioners seem to have accepted the terms of the new Act and to have proceeded to register their chapels.[707]

A comparison between England and France was inevitably made by the Benedictines during the debate surrounding the 1791 Act. Parallels between the two countries, especially in the sphere of lay and secular control of ecclesiastical institutions, were pointed out. The recent policies of the Revolutionary government had highlighted the danger posed by such interference.[708] In the past, the Congregation had usually accepted that degree of state intervention to which the whole of the Gallican church was subject, because the French government had never seriously impeded the development of the English Benedictines in France nor the mission in England. Indeed, it had often furthered the cause of the Congregation. However, the work of the *Commission des Réguliers*, which sat between 1766 and 1780 posed the first serious threat to the continued existence of the Congregation in France, and was to set in motion the train of events which ultimately forced the Congregation to return to England.

The Commission's one task was to reform and renew the religious life in France by subjecting its forms to close scientific scrutiny and formulating various recommendations based on utility and efficiency. While this aim was appreciated by many who saw a genuine need for reform, the Commission, given the tenor of the times, could easily become a weapon employed by the enemies of the Church and the religious orders. The appointment of Loménie de Brienne, Archbishop of Toulouse but a notorious free-thinker, as *rapporteur* of the Commission, confirmed the fears of religious.[709] By an edict, based on the Committee's suggestions and passed in March 1768, all male religious were to have reached the age of twenty one years before they might be professed, the Constitutions of religious orders were to be revised, and each monastery was to house no less than nine choir religious if it belonged to a Congregation, and sixteen if it was independent. The edict forbade the entry of foreigners into novitiates and insisted that no more than one monastery of a particular order be allowed in any one town, Paris being excepted.

Such reforms showed the way enlightened theorists recommended bringing the religious life up-to-date, and they were a pattern to be followed by later schemes of reform elsewhere, like those of the Habsburgs in Germany and Italy in the 1780s. In Rome, Placid Waters was to perceive another parallel; he was to identify the innovations of the liberal Synod of Pistoia in Italy in 1786 with the objectives of the Catholic Committee in England.[710] The 1768 French edict brought immediate protests from religious in France who were supported by the

Papacy and in some cases by the Parlements also. These had little effect and the government went ahead, closing or amalgamating monasteries (the Benedictines lost 122 of their 410 houses in this way), and those which survived were to be seriously affected by the ruling on the age of profession. Clearly the work of the Commission was a prelude to the ecclesiastical legislation of the Revolutionary period.

This edict had the worrying effect of highlighting the total ambiguity of the English Benedictine presence in France.[711] The inventories of all three English monasteries were sent up to the Commission and were approved in October 1766, and in June and November 1768. The English monks came down heavily on the argument from utility, hoping this would secure them exemption from the edict. The English Congregation, they insisted, was pre-eminently a missionary foundation, and being poor, was very dependent on financial support from French benefices to support the work on the English mission. Its school at Douai had been of use to France, having educated many army officers and university professors.[712]

The Congregation felt hardest hit by the injunction about the age for profession. This was particularly serious because, as we have seen, there had already been a sharp reduction in professions from 1760. Against this unpalatable decree, the Benedictines appealed, demanding exemption on a variety of fronts: the new law, they said, did not apply to Flanders where Douai was situated, and the long delay between finishing school at fifteen years and being professed at twenty-one would cause indolence and indiscipline among postulants. Since English law allowed sons to inherit property at fourteen years, a youth might be discouraged from entering the religious state if he had to wait. On the other hand, if he had no portion, the monastery, with limited funds available, would be forced to maintain him. President Naylor was particularly worried that the edict spelled the death of St. Gregory's school in Douai, and from this anxiety stemmed the Congregation's decision to safeguard its future by building up an alumnate at Dieulouard to feed a central novitiate at Douai, which was the main feature of the 1779 Education Scheme discussed elsewhere.[713] No exemption was, however, granted, and the monks remained apprehensive. By 1777, a working compromise had been engineered by President Fisher which would help to solve the profession problem. Postulants were to be clothed at sixteen years and treated as novices until they reached twenty one years when they would be professed.[714] From 1785, this scheme was formally adopted. A 'candidate' who had lived as a novice for some years would begin a 'strict novitiate' and be clothed again at twenty years before profession the following year.[715] In comparison with other Benedictines, the English Benedictine houses were apparently much less responsive to the recommendations of the Commission. They reluctantly did what it ordered them to do, and there was little of that enthusiasm for reform among individual monks which we find in the monasteries of French Benedictines. The English monks believed that, as foreigners with a different monastic tradition which was essentially missionary, many of the recommendations of the Commission did not apply to them.[716]

The Congregation dragged its heels in fulfilling the next major hurdle presented to it by the Commission: the requirement to revise and submit new Constitutions. The 1773 General Chapter appointed two deputies to begin this revision. Their aim was to extract all antiquated sections which did not agree with contemporary enlightened thought about the monastic life.[717] All the Congregation's superiors had, however, to be consulted by these deputies, and Prior Augustine Moore of St. Gregory's, Douai, who had been awkward over the profession issue, brought up a vast number of objections to draft clauses produced for the new Constitutions. Some believed this was the result of Moore's well-known 'peevishness', and his obstinacy was another example of how difficult it was by this time for the President to keep the Congregation united on key issues. Moore however believed his suggestions would help to protect the English monasteries from being tampered with by the French government.[718] Fortunately for all, perhaps, Moore died in June 1775, and was succeeded as prior by Gregory Sharrock who was eager to expedite the work on the Constitutions and preserve the unity of the Congregation intact. The wearisome business of pruning and refining the series of drafts continued for some years. In 1779, for instance, the Commission rejected the latest draft of 1777, alarmed at the use of *juro* in the *Formularium*: 'they will not admit oaths..they will admit nothing but a simple promise'.[719] Further delays convinced one of the deputies, Thomas Welch 'that the Court are not inclined to give us a legal establishment, but would be glad to turn us out of their dominions', sentiments reinforced by the outbreak of war between France and England, and the passing of the 1778 Relief Act in England:

> we shall be looked upon with a more jealous eye if any concessions are made to the R. Catholicks in England.

207

The approval of the Constitutions was still in abeyance when the Commission itself ended in July 1780. All the President could then do was to have the latest draft approved at the 1781 General Chapter. This set of Constitutions was then registered in the Parlement of Paris in July 1784 and published in the winter of that year.[720]

This new set was clearer and more systematic than its predecessor of 1661. In the substitution of promises for oaths and the omission of flagellation and frequent abstinence, these new Constitutions revealed the influence of the Enlightenment, or perhaps the need to make politic concessions to the Enlightenment. The centralising policy of the *Commission des Réguliers* was reflected in the emphasis given to the roles of the President and the General Chapter. Although it was not forgotten at the time that these Constitutions had been forced on the Congregation by the French government, superiors in France were nevertheless prepared to see them in a positive light, as a means of preserving an already fragile Congregational unity.[721] They hoped however in vain, for these 'Gallican' Constitutions had the effect of driving a wedge between the monasteries and the mission. Missioners had all along feared the monastic preconceptions entertained by the Commission would whittle away Benedictine missionary status in England, especially in regard to financial independence, and portray missioners in England as French agents and perjurers in regard to the new Oath of Allegiance found in the 1778 Relief Act. Such opposition was strong enough to remove the French royal Letters Patent from those sets of Constitutions sent to Lambspring and to the mission for distribution. Missioners' suspicions were further increased by the conditions attached to the registration of the Constitutions in the Paris Parlement: the Congregation was in future to insist that the Gallican Articles of 1682 were to be taught in all theology courses in the monasteries, and that the monasteries were to be subject to French laws governing property. This 'disagreeable sharp sting' made Provincial Warmoll determined to petition that the 1785 General Chapter should meet in London so as to avoid French influence.[722] His object in attempting at the same time to have the 1784 Constitutions approved at Rome was partly to defy the ruling on the teaching of the Gallican Articles, partly to provide a device to prevent wayward missioners repudiating the 1784 set as merely an unwelcome burden forced on the Congregation by France. But solid advice from his colleagues in Rome counselled him against making such a move because it would lead to further complications and Rome itself would be edgy about ratifying a document with strong Gallican tendencies.[723] In the end, the Constitutions were left unconfirmed, but the long struggle behind their formulation points to the dangerously fragile position of the Congregation in France by the early 1780s.

If the President and superiors of the three houses in France felt unsteady in the two decades before the Revolution, there was little alternative for them to adopt except that of appeasing the French civil and ecclesiastical authorities, while trying at the same time to reduce the internal troubles within the monasteries. Evidence suggests that the French authorities were less and less tolerant of their English guests. The Congregation had had its privileges reaffirmed by 1774 and had agreed to overhaul its benefice system, in the light of the proposals of the *Commission des Réguliers*, by attempting to ensure benefices were in future attached to the monastery rather than to individual monks.[724] As this streamlining was put into effect, however, hostility to the regular clergy by some of the French bishops began to surface, and the English monks were a prime target. Such bishops saw in the transference of benefices the first step to reducing all regulars to ordinary diocesan jurisdiction, as well as an opportunity to acquire a number of benefices for more useful projects of their own, like the endowing of seminaries. Designs like these undoubtedly lay behind episcopal claims on English Benedictine benefices at this time,[725] and help to explain the anxiety surrounding La Celle. This benefice, fully absorbed into St.Edmund's, Paris, served as a *refugium peccatorum* for recalcitrant monks, and its superiors were especially sensitive to scandalous rumours being broadcast:

> The Bishop of Meaux complained to me of ye Religious of Laselle as being drunken, idle, scandalous people, who far from living up to their rule, neglected shamefully all regular duties; Matins sometimes said in the afternoon, no mass said on week-days, excepting now and then by D(om) Joseph.

It was an easy step to move from such complaints to an outright condemnation of unpatriotic behaviour, especially when it was admitted La Celle was held by courtesy of the French:

> ...complaints were made at the Police of Paris of (Benet Cawser of La Celle's) talking indiscreetly against the French...(which) will reflect upon the whole body and bring bad consequences.

209

When it was surrounded by spies eager to report all false steps to the authorities, La Celle already had the bishop's ultimatum hanging over it, which ordered the monks out if they could not perform the Office adequately.[726]

Inevitably, the growing problems the monasteries faced outside had repercussions within. The restlessness among conventuals took some extraordinary turns. It led to an uncontrollable wildness which reached its apogee in the embarrassing self-inflicted castration in Paris of the newly-professed John Cromblehome, a 'refractory spirit', in early 1789.[727] Contraction in numbers, disaffection among conventuals, and antipathy from neighbours made the labours of the priors impossibly heavy, and a large number elected to the office of prior refused to shoulder it in the last decades before the Revolution.[728] The accumulation of all this distress was responsible for the feeling of despondency which had attached itself to superiors by early 1789. Belief in the ineluctable destruction of the Congregation spread, once all attempts at appeasement had brought no reward. By 1789, President Walker's speeches were lacking the confidence and force which had been found in those delivered ten years earlier. He now took solace in the apocalyptic guarantees of Pastorini's *General History*, the work of his contemporary, Charles Walmesley.[729] Seeking to retire, he could hardly become a strong presence once the Revolution broke out. Both Walker and Walmesley had been monks of St. Edmund's, Paris, which was, of all three monasteries in France, the house where pressures were felt most and which came closest to annihilation in the years immediately before 1789. Here, the new prior, Henry Parker, blamed the coincidence of internal and external burdens, and was prepared to support moves to have the monastery suppressed and to transfer its members and revenues to help build up other houses:

> Our situation internal and external is acutely exposed to greater difficulties than it has ever been hitherto. The external circumstances which threaten our existence tend to undermine it by the spirit of independence which grows universally... It has often occured to me that it would perhaps be better to have no community at all.

From 1789 the monastery's slide towards anarchy merely confirmed Parker's feelings.[730]

Amidst all the decay Henry Parker, however, foresaw one slight glimmer of hope:

One consideration ought to predominate...the general interest of the English mission ought as much as possible to be drawn from the wreck of our little body, and as much as possible of the little we enjoyed secured.[731]

The presence of the two Benedictine Provinces in England was to be ultimately responsible for the Congregation's survival. The English mission had always encouraged the monks in France to remember that they were foreigners and therefore needed special treatment. Patriotism was never far from these exiles' hearts. By the time of the American War of Independence, when France allied with the colonists, the English monks had come to speak of the English forces as 'our ships' and 'our forces'.[732] England was to provide in the end a refuge for the remnants of the monasteries during and after 1793, and in the course of the Revolution itself, it was the awareness of the work being done on the English mission which helped the English monasteries to avoid the same fate as the French Benedictines. Although conventuals were to be classified as foreigners by the Revolutionary authorities, their distinctness can also be seen in other ways. By the 1780s, there was already some contempt present for the Maurists, 'our unfortunate confreres', who had collaborated fully with philosophers and politicians and prostituted themselves.[733] In comparison with other monasteries, the number of English monks who were secularised once permission to do so had been granted by the government was tiny.[734] A civilian career in France was apparently neither acceptable nor attractive to most. The English monks' persistent interest in the mission needs, then, to be remembered during the sad narration of the Revolution; it was an essential bond between all the communities in the midst of a hostile environment, and it opened up the possibility of a toleration denied them in France.

Not unnaturally, the English monks had an interest in the principal events affecting Church and State in the few years leading up to 1789. Thomas Welch at Cambrai had become nervous in 1786 after he had heard of the ambushing of the Archbishop of Cambrai, and was sceptical of the success of monastic demands for more representation in the Assembly of the French Clergy: 'such pretensions are highly unseasonable..when Religious Houses are on so precarious a footing'. In the wake of the meeting of the Assembly of Notables in 1787, the exile of the Paris Parlement to Troyes and the appointment of Lomenie de Brienne as *principal ministre*, superiors were made aware of

France's apparent bankruptcy and feared the imposition of new taxes on the English monks.[735] The elections to the States General in which the English monks were involved because of their holding of benefices, raised the fond hope that 'this country will rise up, fresh, young and vigorous like the Phoenix'. But the number and seriousness of local disturbances brought doubts about the possible success of a peaceful constitutional transformation. One monk watched hungry women, 'Amazons', attack convents in Cambrai; another was shaken by the attack on the Archbishop of Paris in June 1789 and believed insubordination among the troops was an ominous sign. The fall of the Bastille was commemorated by a dirge for the dead at St. Edmund's; only after the event did some of the community visit the scene to view the devastation.[736] By August 1789, superiors were finding themselves inextricably bound up in the turmoil. Travel between England and France was becoming more difficult, the abolition of tithes on August 4th filled many with foreboding, and by October, St. Edmund's was under guard, and its prior ordered the following month to bless 'the colours of our Milice bourgeoise' next door in the church of Val-de-Grace. In Paris, monks were by now convinced that the powder-keg would explode very soon and 'raise a conflagration' if the king used his veto on the Declaration of Rights. Meanwhile the Congregation attempted to secure support from favourable deputies in the National Assembly.[737]

The 'fatal decision' which brought the President and Regimen towards seriously considering the possibility of evacuation from France was the decree of the 2nd of November 1789, which put church property 'at the disposal of the nation'. President Walker suggested Bardsey Island off North Wales, safe by its remoteness, or Rome where, with financial help from the Duchess of Albany, the Procurator's residence might be enlarged. Both were judged unsatisfactory. The former because 'the (English) government here will certainly admit of no corporate body'. The latter because the Duchess had no money. One after another, possible refuges were suggested and then found wanting: Savoy, Spain, Portugal, Germany, Flanders, or the Scottish abbeys at Ratisbon and Würzburg. Sadly, most states seemed to be going the same way as France, 'to diminish all Ecclesiasticks whatever'. Tension was already high within the monasteries. Since the provisional decree to suspend the taking of religious vows had been passed in late October 1789, no profession ceremonies had taken place at Douai. It was beginning to be doubted whether Douai and

212

Dieulouard would survive despite their usefulness 'as places of public education', since they were already close to existing schools, and the study of English seemed to be out of fashion.[738] The handing over of church property to the nation weakened the monks' financial credit in France. Dieulouard's situation in particular was desperate; it had debts of "24,929 *livres Lorraine*", brewing had been forbidden and its creditors were demanding immediate reimbursement. Provincial feeling was, however, strong around Nancy, and the prior hoped that his house might be protected by the Provincial Assembly from offensives launched at Paris. The break-down of Congregational unity, fought against for so long, was becoming a reality in the early months of 1790. Some monks were prepared to sell monastic property and make off with the money, and the priors were being forced increasingly to fight their own battles as the President's authority over conventuals crumbled.[739] At the beginning of 1790, agreement had been reached about the necessity of saving St. Gregory's, Douai, as a first priority, even to the extent of subjecting it to the jurisdiction of the local bishop as a way of preserving it. In the meantime, the case for the continued existence of all three houses was still to be put before the National Assembly.[740]

In February 1790, a decree ordered the closure and merger of religious houses, with the exception of educational and charitable establishments. By other decrees, monks were granted pensions, and solemn professions were forbidden. As foreigners, the English Benedictines were forced to petition the National Assembly directly for exemption. During this time, the detailed inventories of property and numbers of conventuals were drawn up. Each monastery sought a solution in its own way. Douai remained solidly loyal to the President and the Congregation, and volunteered to be sent to any 'retreat' the President might order. At Dieulouard, Prior Marsh was prepared to have his community remain in their home, dressed in secular attire. They would thus be able to keep their pensions, rent the buildings, and conform outwardly 'but our consciences would always dictate to us the same duty and Obedience'. Paris was now insignificant in terms of its wealth and numbers and the government were prepared to merge it with a French Benedictine monastery in Paris, although it might still be of service, the prior believed, as a *maison d'éducation* and seminary.[741]

The comprehensive Civil Constitution of the Clergy, voted by the Assembly in June 1790, 'nationalised' the French Church and ultimately helped cause civil war. As foreigners, the English monks were exempt from its conditions, and during the months that followed, the monasteries tried to buttress their extremely vulnerable position. All were determined to procure pensions once ex-ecclesiastical property had been sold off, and each monastery drew up a list of those wishing to remain monks; these would be eligible for pensions. Dieulouard attempted to improve its standing with the new Provincial Assembly by supplying a monk to teach in Metz. Although the community here was allowed to resume brewing, the house still laboured under heavy debts. Paris, which had been supported largely by benefices, looked forward to its pensions; only two of the seven conventuals listed had taken advantage of the freedom given by the new legislation and had abandoned the community. At Douai, Prior Sharrock still had it in mind to move his community and college out of France. He demanded guidelines from the President as to how his community should act towards the new legislation.[742] With the decrees exempting foreign religious from oaths to the Civil Constitution which were passed on the 6th and 28th of October 1790, the English Benedictines were for the moment safe, provided they conformed to the legislation already passed regarding profession. However, a major headache was the necessity of finding enough conventuals to constitute a resident community of twenty before a house might be legally recognised. Various solutions were put forward like that of including missioners professed by the house, or emphasising the houses as integral parts of a centralised Congregation. Douai solved the profession problem by sending its young monks abroad for profession. Since the property at Douai was on land belonging to the now 'nationalised ' abbey of St. Vaast, Arras, the Prior continued his search for a refuge in Flanders, in case his buildings were nationalised also. Prior Parker in Paris, in no doubt as to the failings of his subjects, some of whom were already in secular dress, feared that with ties of religious obedience being broken and pensions obtained, the conventuals would opt to sell the property and divide the spoils. To safeguard against this and to assure the authorities that he had the full complement of conventuals, Parker made use of the argument that the priory belonged totally to the Congregation. It therefore could not be sold by its members nor could its monks be transferred to other houses without the President's consent. Parker agreed with Prior Sharrock that if summoning an extraordinary General Chapter was out of the question at this stage, then a smaller *ad hoc* meeting must be called to determine the way ahead. This was to take place at Bruges in May 1791. Parker already had a strong premonition that if the Pope refused to agree to the Civil Constitution, schism would break out in France.[743]

In the early half of 1791, while the monks tried to speed up the procedures which would result in their pensions, they were unable to ignore the divisions developing among the French clergy. The condemnation of the Civil Constitution by the Pope in May 1791 produced the schism between jurors and non-jurors which Parker had foreseen. Douai and Dieulouard were determined to ignore their new constitutional bishops as far as they were able, and to refuse to receive any faculties from them. Douai avoided direct confrontation by sending its monks over the border to Bruges for ordination and by declining offers to participate in joint liturgical services. Dieulouard was able to maintain a similar resistance and was helped by the degree of local antipathy to the Civil Constitution. By the time of the Flight to Varennes in June 1791, whose failure was to produce a new surge of clerical persecution, the *ad hoc* meeting of superiors at Bruges had adopted Prior Parker's policy of nominal secularisation as a way of cutting the Congregation's losses, even though Parker's 'wild schemes' and 'Romantick ideas' had been opposed by Prior Sharrock. Waters, the Procurator in Rome, went ahead to secure the necessary faculties for the President to dispense in certain cases on account of the persecution suffered by the English monks. These allowed the Congregation, through the President, to accept solemn professions in the church, in a simple ceremony privately before the community, with doors locked and with no secular witnesses present. Secondly, the President might allow secular dress to be worn rather than the habit in order to prevent monks suffering abuse.[744] As anger rose against non-juring clergy towards the end of 1791, foreign ecclesiastics became identified in the popular mind with these non-jurors. Attacks on Parisian clergy became a common sight to those at St. Edmund's who tried their best to avoid confrontation. St Gregory's, Douai, and other religious communities in the town were condemned as 'so many nurseries of Aristocracy', and suspicions were inevitably aroused by the English monks' constant refusal to join in the municipal liturgical functions. St. Gregory's chapel, like those in the other two monasteries, was closed to the public by this stage because it belonged to a 'foreign establishment'. Extreme caution was also needed at Dieulouard where the community watched the local nuns being beaten up for refusing to collaborate with the constitutional clergy. Lies were

215

soon spread abroad that the Dieulouard monks had contributed money to help the invading army and a petition was sent to the Department and the constitutional bishop to have the monks turned out for causing 'continual disorder'.[745]

During 1792, the three communities endeavoured to be extremely discreet and to keep a low profile. As always, extracting any pensions from the authorities was a struggle. At Paris, there had been eleven monks receiving a pension in November 1791, but eight months laters, there were only five there. By October 1792, the government stopped paying out capital for pensions from government funds. The few young monks in Paris had by this time fled from the anarchy to seek refuge in the two other houses. At La Celle, Maurus Shaw still struggled along as prior, surviving only because he had taken the new oath of liberty and equality and because he had agreed to hold services in the parish church. In Paris, Prior Parker, bitterly cynical by this time of the motives behind the ecclesiastical reforms, attended meetings of the Convention, taking a guard along as escort.[746] Near the frontier, the other two houses found themselves in the middle of the war which had broken out between France and Austria in April 1792. Like Paris, they were still anxious about their financial state and wondered how long they might hold out against recognising the constitutional church.[747] By this time all correspondence between the President and Priors seems to have ceased.

It was events in 1793 which effectively ended the presence of the Congregation in France. It is doubtful if the monasteries would have survived the policy of 'Dechristianisation' which was to begin in earnest during 1793. Before that got under way, they had been destroyed by the xenophobic legislation and persecution which followed on from the declaration of war against England in February 1793.

The final destruction of the three English monasteries, the revival of those of Douai and Dieulouard in England, and the eventual transfer of the Paris community to the old buildings of St. Gregory's in Douai, has often been told. Seals were affixed in February 1793, to St. Gregory's, Douai, and the property was put under guard. In August, the community was forced to quit, and retired to its farm at Esquerchin nearby. Decrees passed after the beginning of the Terror in September confiscated the properties of all foreigners and ordered their imprisonment. At that point, nine of the Douai community, under Peter Kendall, escaped and made their way to England. The rest were returned under guard to Douai and most were imprisoned with members of the English secular college at Douai in the citadel of Doullens in Picardy. In July 1794, after Thermidor, these monks were freed, and returning to Douai to find their priory dilapidated, they decided to make their way to England in March 1795. They began conventual life once again at the seat of the Smythe family at Acton Burnell in Shropshire, where they were united with Peter Kendall and the first group of refugees.[748]

At Dieulouard, Prior Richard Marsh, despite the presence of guards, had attempted to sell off as much of the land and moveable property as possible in 1793, in order to pre-empt their imminent confiscation by the state. Marsh had been wise enough to secure passports for most of the community, so that he and only a handful remained in the buildings. These were surrounded on the 12th of October 1793 by an armed band determined to confiscate this property belonging to foreigners. Marsh had been warned, and fled, hiding in the undergrowth, and swimming across the Moselle to make good his escape. He reached Trier and met up with other members of the community who had left earlier. These travelled to England and also took up residence at Acton Burnell, at the end of 1793, where they were joined later by the Douai community. The remnant, left behind at Dieulouard, eventually returned to England themselves, although four French lay brothers and choir oblates remained in France, taking the oath of loyalty to the nation and receiving pensions in return.[749] By 1793, there was only a handful of conventuals left at St. Edmund's, Paris. These had already survived massive problems caused by dwindling funds, decrees against foreigners and the threat of being conscripted in the *levée en masse*. During 1793, however, after the decree ordering the arrest of foreigners, they were imprisoned with many other captives in their own monastery. At this time. the 'Dechristianisation' campaign encouraged the gutting of their chapel. Following a year's imprisonment here, the community were then transferred for a further two months' incarceration in the Luxembourg. Freed in December 1794, they too returned to their old monastery, which was to be sequestered by the government in 1799. At that date, we find some of the community, however, still living in the property. After Prior Parker's death in 1817, St. Edmund's was re-erected in 1823 in St. Gregory's old property at Douai.[750] Lambspring was not directly affected by the Revolution in France in the 1790s; its suppression took place later, in 1802.

217

The two communities which had had the good fortune to reach England appeared there just after the passing of the 1791 Relief Act whose benefits they were to enjoy. Their homecoming brought together in close proximity, for the first time since the brief experiment of James II's reign, the two halves of the Congregation, the conventual and the missionary. This union ensured that the Congregation's history in the nineteenth century would be of quite a different character from what it had been under the *ancien régime*.

The Catafalque of King James II in St Edmund's, Paris

NOTES

1   For general surveys of Congregation's history, see D. Lunn, *The English Benedictines, 1540-1688,* London 1980, and his dissertation, 'The Origins and Early Development of the Revived English Benedictine Congregation 1588-1647'(Cambridge, Ph.D. unpublished thesis 1970). B. Green, *The English Benedictine Congregation,* London 1980. *Gallia Christiana,* t. vii, Paris 1744, 1068-89. WM, 6 vols.

2   WM, I, 217-44; II, 483, 523-6; III, 847,936-7,949-52;IV, 3,87, 315-16; V, 314. Lunn, *Benedictines, 174.*

3   Between 1685 and 1688, numbers professed were: 16 (St. Gregory's), 11 (St. Laurence's), 8 (St. Edmund's), 10 (Lambspring). In the communities, the average number resident for this period was: 30 (St. Gregory's), 15 (St. Laurence's), 26 (St. Edmund's), 23 (Lambspring).

4   e.g. A. McInnes, 'The Revolution', 80-95, and J. R. Jones, *The Revolution,* Chap 4.

5   WM, IV, 271-8; V, 255,321. Nancy, H 79, 1687 28 Aug, Loan for Clerkenwell. AH, II, 86 and Appendix, 486; E. E. Estcourt and J. O. Payne, *Non-Jurors,* 359. A. C. F. Beales, *Education,* 427, 258.

6   AH, Appendix, 487. Lunn, *Benedictines, 135-6,* 139. *CSPD,* June 1687-Feb. 1689, 15, 279. Clark, *Wood's Life,* iii, 266.

7   For Ellis, see WM I, 278; IV, 2; V, 491-4; BL Add MSS, 10118, f773; G. A. Ellis, *The Ellis Correspondence,* vols, i, 20, 53, 68, 93, 94, 103, 116, 133, 157, 197, 207, 218, 234, 238-9, 243, 257, 263, 266, 268, 275, 283; ii, 32, 83, 144-5. B. Hemphill, *The Early Vicars Apostolic.* J. Gillow, *A Bibliographical Dictionary,* ii, 161-4; J. A. Williams, 'Bishops Giffard and Ellis,' 218-28. B. Navarra, *Filippo Michele Ellis. For* Corker, see WM, II, 494-515; V, 311-2; AB, 305-15; W. Fuller, *Twenty-Six Depositions,* 6-10. Gillow, *Dictionary,* i, 568-71; Lunn, *Benedictines,* 133-5. T. A. Birrell, 'Catholic Allegiance', 10-12. Clark, *Wood's Life,* iii, 34, 105, 266.

8   For Ellis's conversion work, see *Catholic Record Society, (CRS)* London 1925, xxv, 84. Ellis, *Correspondence,* i, 123; ii, 62. For Corker's, see WM, II 531; V, 494. Aveling, *The Handle,* 233. T. A. Birrell, 'James Maurus Corker'.

9   WM, IV, 1-2. J. S. Clarke, *Life of James II,* ii, 116. Gillow, *Dictionary,* iii, 589. *Catholic Gentleman's Magazine,* August 1818, 707-08. G. Dolan, 'James II', 94-103.

10   AB, 303-05. Gillow, *Dictionary*, ii, 331. Beales, *Education*, 240-1. Lambeth Palace, Gibson 13/941/105. *CSPD* June 1687-Feb. 1689, 797. Clark, *Wood's Life*, iii, 221. J.R.Bloxam (ed.), *Magdalen College and King James II*, Oxford, 1886, 238, 265.

11   Nottingham University, Portland MSS, PwA 2126i.

12   WM, V, 311-12 (quoted). E. Duffy, 'Peter and Jack', 11.

13   For Corker's *Roman-Catholick Principles* see: WM, III, 957-64; V, 311. *Orthodox Journal*, 1814 Jan, 17-20; 1814 Mar, 101-05, 110-15. Gillow, *Dictionary*, i, 193; iii, 402. Birrell, 'Catholic Allegiance'. Lunn, *Benedictines*, 133-5. J. P. Chinnici, *The English Catholic Enlightenment*.

14   Ellis, *Ellis Correspondence*, i, ix-xxiii, 155, 224. Clark, *Wood's Life*, iii, 181, 266, 279.

15   WM, IV, 9-10. Gillow, *Dictionary*, ii, 161-4. Lunn, *Benedictines*, 139, and his 'Origins', 62. F. A. Gasquet, 'Segni', 231-40. G. Scott, 'Fighting Old Battles', 14-15. P. A. Hopkins, 'The Commission', 265-7.

16   WM V, 510. Hopkins, 'Commission', 265-7

17   The Declaration of Indulgence of 1687 allowed owners to keep old monastic lands, and, significantly, came soon after Ellis's sermon, and the same year in which Nathaniel Johnston's *The Assurance of Abby and other Church-lands to the possessors* (London 1687) was published. For Henry Joseph Johnston, see: Chapter on 'Monks and Learning'; J. D. Martin, 'The Antiquarian Collections', 40, 42: G.Scott, 'Benedictine Conspirator'.

18   For Anglo-Gallicanism of Thomas Preston OSB (1567-1647), see D. M. Lunn, 'The Anglo-Gallicanism', Lunn, *Benedictines, Chap.* 2. For monks' appreciation of the Anglican position, especially in regard to Orders, see Lunn, *Benedictines*, 125, and E. C. Messenger, *The Reformation*, ii, 466.

19   See Appendix I for missions.

20   J. Kirk, *Biographies, 234.*

21   G. Dolan, 'James II', with plates of the chapel's interior. J. Miller, *Popery,* 248.

22   Leeds Grammar School, Thoresby Collection. *Gentleman's Magazine*, July 1790, 606-08 (quoted). For York chapel, see J. C. H. Aveling, *Catholic Recusancy in York,* 104-06, and 'Odds and Ends', *Downside Review (DR),* xv, 1896, 97-8.

23   AH, Appendix, 501, 544. J. A. Williams, *Bath and Rome,* 27.

24   Downside MS 825f.231. Gillow, *Dictionary*, iii, 288-9. Estcourt and Payne, *Non-jurors,* 356.

25   AH, Appendix, 554. A. M. C. Forster, 'An Outline History, 14, 15.

26   Stratford-upon-Avon, Shakespeare Trust, Coughton MS 1090. AH, I, 550; AR, 658-9. Gillow, *Dictionary*, iv, 171. Beales, *Education*, 247, 255, 258. Wood, *Athenae*, ii, cols. 905-06, for Reeves as school-master.

27   Kirk, *Biographies*, 234. 'A Forgotten Episode', 259-63. F. O. Blundell, *Lancashire*, ii, 140. J. A. Williams, 'No-Popery Violence', 247, 249, 251-3, 255, 258. Wood, *Athenae*, ii, col.9. CSPD 1691692, 127, 164. E.Cruickshanks (ed.), *By Force or Default? The Revolution of 1688-89*, Edinburgh 1989, 52, 54.

28   See appendices II and IV, and Whelan, *Congregation, passim*. Aveling 'Education', 135-36.

29   WM, IV 52, 270; V 321. Nancy H 48, for Dieulouard statistics.

30   Examples too numerous to cite, but for monks with mercantile backgrounds, see WM, V, 338. 510.

31   See Appendix IVb. For Dieulouard, Almond, *Ampleforth*, 217-18. For Lambspring, Downside MS 205, for full details of novices' origins, financial support and reasons for not persevering.

32   O. Hufton, 'French Church', 20. B. Plongeron, *Réguliers,* for graph of Maurist professions showing decline in 1760s.

33   Lille 35, 1773 28 Dec, 1774 25 Jan.

34   Lille 56, 1777 24 Oct, 1778 10 Jan, 8 April, 8 July, 1779 18 Aug, 1780 20 Feb, 30 May.

35   Paris A. N. G9 66, description of English monasteries. Lille 38, 1778 2 May. Nancy H 47. AR, 219; AH, II, 254.

36   Paris A. N. G9 66 ibid.

37   Lille 37, 1778 15 June, .

38   Paris A. N. EXIX, 1790 14 Mar, Walker's returns to Assembly.

39   Lille 57, 1782 27 Dec, 1785 6 Dec, 1783 20 June, 4 Sept, 25 Oct.

40   Lille 31, 1786 23 Nov, 1787 25 May, 1788 30 April, 12 June, 5 Aug, 3 Sept. Lille 46, 1787 24 Aug, 1791 17 July.

41   Lille 57, 1782 14 Mar, 18 May, 1789 15 Nov.

42   Lille 66, 1787 22 Oct.

43   *CRS,* xxiii, 168n.

44   Woolhampton, vol XXI, 'Statuta 1661', especially chapters 7-19. For early general survey of daily life and observance in the communities, see Lunn, *Benedictines,* 177-82, and for St. Gregory's, Douai, C. Butler, 'Daily Life', 28-49.

45   WM, III, 847 (House Obligations); 923-26 (House Customs and Calendar).

46   WM III, 934-6.

47   WM, III, 926-8.

48   Lille 4.

49   WM, V, 509. Arras (Downside Transcripts), 180-1, 184-6, 188, 190. *DR,* iv, 1885, 32. Lunn, 'Origins', 279-80, 286, 291-2. Lunn, *Benedictines, 179-80.* Butler, 'Daily Life', 31, 39, 40. Cardevacque, *Collège.* 99, 105-06.

50   For organs: Nancy H 74, 1774 registration (Dieulouard). Lille 3, 1773 entry (Paris). Birt, *Downside,* 168; Birt 3/A145 (Douai). 'Lambspring', *DR,* v, 1886, 214; WM, IV, 72 (Lambspring). For music, see Downside MS 445, and Dolan, 'English Benedictine Missions:Berkshire', 226. The composer Faboulier mentioned here was also employed by the English Recollects at Douai, see Woolhampton MS 'Vesperale Minorum Recollectorum Douay 1787'.

51   Arras (Downside transcript), 177, 192-98. Birt, *Downside,* 53-5. 'Among the Archives', *DR, vi,* 52-3. Downside MS 212, 1773-74 entries. Woolhampton, Scott Box 148, 150. Lille 57, 1785 22 Jan, 1786 17 Jan, 7 Mar, 7 April, 20 June, 26 Aug, 1788 3 Jan, 16 Jan, 1789 15 Nov. Lille 62, 1785 10 July.. Lille 47, 1787 15 Dec. Lille 67, 1788 3 Jan, 8 Oct, 1789 4 Jan, 1790 24 Feb. Lille 69, 1788 17 Feb. Lille 28, 1788 1 Mar, 12 Aug, 22 Aug.

52   Cole, *Journal,* 18-19; see also 158, 204. Douai, Bibliothèque Municipale, Robaut Collection, for drawings and plans of St Gregory's Church.

53   Lunn, *Benedictines, 71-72.* 'The Buildings at Dieulouard', 77-85. H. B. Mackey, 'A Pilgrimage', 9-15.

54   Nancy H 48; H 50. AH, II, 73. McCann, *Ampleforth,* 128. G. Clanche, *La Biere,* 20-21.

55   e.g. Oxford, Bodleian, Rawlinson D 1091. Cole, *Journal,* 137-45, 283-6. For new wing in 1750s, Downside MS 206, 1759 entry. The altar-piece is now in the Irish College, Paris.

56   Paris A. N., NIII, Seine 517.

57   WM, IV, 72, 73. Dolan, 'Lambspring Poet', 153.

58   Woolhampton CI R(H) 5. Hull DDEV/60/86 and 56/30 ff.128-29, 149-50 (quoted). DDEV/60/86(b), 1734/35 22 Feb, Potts to Farnworth, and 1735 7 April, 30 May, Potts to Rokeby. AH, II, 220-21. Roebuck, *Constable,* 112.

59   The missioner Lawrence Champney, an ally of President Fenwick, was elected Prior of Dieulouard at the controversial 1717 General Chapter. He continued to oppose the 'orthodox' party under Fenwick's successor, Thomas Southcott, and therefore had to be ejected. He then returned to the mission. See BL Add. MSS 20309/16. RA/SP 56/37; 57/115. AH, II, 113.

60   Hull, Everingham MSS DDEV/60/86(b), 1729 20 Dec, Helme to Potts.

61   e.g. Lille 56, 1780 10 Feb. AB, 459, for an exception: the missioner, Bernard Bradshaw's habits were 'so different from the Conventuals' at Lambspring, that he was not elected abbot.

62   e.g. Lille 27, For letters (1773-75) between Thomas Welch and Bede Bennet.

63   Lille 32, 1789, end of June, 14 Aug.

64   *CRS*, vii, 1909, 88-90. Coughton Court, Folder 44. Roebuck, *Constable*, 7, 35-36, 38-39, 42-43, 46. RA/SP 173/54, 128. Lille 69, 1782 3 Mar, 3 July, 1784 31 Aug, 1786 25 July, 26 July, 16 Nov, 1787 9 Jan, 2 Feb. Lille 26, 1782 20 Aug, 21 Sept, 1789 16 July, 2 Aug, Arundells to Welch. For Dieulouard's position, see J. Mabillon and T. Ruinart, *Opera Posthuma*, iii, 475.

65   Woolhampton, Scott Box, 44-50, 150.

66   Lille 27, 1774 4 Jan. T. Bentley, *Journal*, 70.

67   Lille 27, 1774 9 June.

68   Lille 34, 1783 8 Aug. Lille 36, 1782 9 April, 12 July, Goolde. Lille 66, 1782 1 Aug. Lille 18, 1785 19 Aug, 9 Sept, Garstang.

69   Woolhampton, W. Hewlett, 'Annals', 91-104. WM, V 537-70; VI 571-602, 613. G. Sitwell, 'Crisis', 228-36, 255. AH, II, 32.

70   Lille 38, 1778 28 Nov, Lille 10, 1779 25 Aug. Nancy H 77, 1769 31 Aug, Nuncio to Barrett. Nancy H 77, 1769 6 Feb, Walmesley to Naylor. Nancy H 77, 1769 24 Jan, Bennet to Williams (Naylor). Nancy H 77, 1769 19 June, Heatley to Naylor. AH II, 226; AB 498-99.

71   Lille 32, 1784 10 Nov, 1785 6 Mar. Lille 31, 1785 22 Jan, Catteral.

72   Lille 46, 1787 4 Feb, 18 Oct, 9 Nov, 1788 4 Jan, 23 Jan, 19 Feb, 27 May, 13 June, 1789 10 May. Lille 37, 1788 13 Oc. Lille 45, 1790 10 Sept (quoted), 1 Oct, 17 Nov. Lille 3, 1788 entry. Lille 28, 1790 7 Feb, Bennet to Walker. Lille 46, 1791 4 Oct. B Green, 'The Fall', 81-88.

73   For the Cassinese, see D. Lunn, 'The English Cassinese (1611-50)', 62-69. D. Lunn, *Benedictines, 1-2,* 16-16, 23-33, and Chapters 4 and 8.

74   RActa 73/6; RSOCG 546/6, for Delattre. B. Weldon, *Chronological Notes*, xxii-xxx. WM IV, 75-84, 268-70; V, 494-510, 538-99; AH, II, 32-33. AB, 294-302; Lunn, 'Origins', 159, and *Benedictines,* 90, for Weldon.

75   For dissatisfaction with the observance at St. Edmund's, see WM, III, 835-36; IV 268-70.

76 WM, III, 835-36; IV 62; V 558-59. Ritchie, *Papers from Lambeth,* 145-51. RActa 62/26. WM, V 524, for another Paris monk attracted to La Trappe.

77 Lille 56, 1778 9 Oct, 1779 18 Aug, 28 Aug, 1780 20 Feb, 6 Mar. Lille 31, 1780 13 Jan, 13 Feb. Lille 26, 1779 9 Sept. The lay-brother Anthony Parkinson had also tried unsuccessfully to join La Trappe sometime after 1736; he was thought to be pious and eccentric (AB 470).

78 Lille 57, 1783 23 Mar, 26 Mar, 1788 5 Mar, 1791 28 Oct, 1792 5 May. Lille 26, 1783 23 Mar, Barnes.

79 Lille 57, 1782 14 Mar, 18 May, 18 Nov, 27 Dec, 1783 23 Mar, 1784 31 Jan, 19 June, 8 Sept. Lille 26, 1783 26 Jan, 1784 16 July, 25 Aug, Allam.

80 Lille 57, 1782 18 May, 23 Aug (quoted), 27 Dec, 1783 10 Jan, 21 Jan, 1784 31 Jan, 19 June. Lille 34, 1783 10 Jan, 21 Jan, 3 Mar, Digby.

81 Lille 18 H 10, *passim.*

82 WM, IV, 84-6, 263-5; V 511-13, 537ff.

83 WM, IV 52, 87, 270-1, 291-308. AH, I, 575, 579-82, 595. Agius, 'Council Book'.

84 Lambeth Palace, Gibson 14/942/142. WM, IV, 311-12. B. Whelan, 'A Disputed Election', 274-85.

85 WM, IV, 311-12; V, 318. AB, 279-83.

86 RActa 76/8. WM, V, 523-4. Nancy H 48, 1705 18 Dec, B. Gregson to [?]Watmough; 1706 5 July, Riddell to [?]Gregson; 1706 Aug, Laparre to Watmough. Birt Box 3/A117. AH, II, 17-20.

87 Nancy H 48, 1708 15 July, Gregson to [?]Watmough. AH, II, 20-21. AB, 181.

88 AAW, Ep. Var., vii/70. RA SP 57/115, 1721 (late Aug), Dawney to 'Mr. John'. AH, II, 125-6.

89 Hull, DDEV/60/86(b), 1742 31 July, Potts to Farnworth. AH, II, 220-23.

90 AH, II 203, 215. AR, 211.

91 Nancy H 77, 1770 25 May, Gregson to Naylor, and Hadley to Naylor; 8 July, Eaves to Naylor.

92 Lille 37, 1778 15 June. Lille 31, 1780 17 Aug. AR, 212. AH. II, 156-7, 223-4.

93 Lille 18 H 30, 1782 18 July, 15 Sept, 19 Nov, 21 Dec, 1783 10 Feb, 13 Feb, 1 May, 1784 15 April, 22 April, 19 July, Bolas to Walker. Lille 37, 1783 1 Mar, 1784 6 June, 1785 20 April, 1786 25 May, 14 Aug, 1787 26 April. Lille 66, 1787 22 Oct. Lille 46, 1789 10 May. AR, 240.

94   Lille 37, 1786 21 Oct, 1791 15 Aug (quoted).

95   Lille 37, 1791 15 Aug. Lille 68, 1791 23 Dec. Lille 66, 1792 3 Jan, 1 Aug (quoted). Lille 32, 1792 24 April. Lille 33, 1792 1 May. Lille 28, 1792 31 July.

96   AR, 240. Green, 'Heatley', 87-98.

97   RSOCG 765/9. WM, V, 569; VI, 395-97, 602. Woolhampton, Parker Papers 'up to 1817': Account Book of St. Edmund's, property (c. 1790); I/L/E, 1707 Letters Patent; Hewlett, 'Annals', 105, 108; St. Edmund's Clothing and Profession Book: Declaration not to alienate possessions (benefices) is a common entry from 1714. AB, 437-38.

98   WM, I, 211-44; III 241-4, 813, 936-40; IV 267-8; V 524, 542, 568; VI 584, 600, 603. Downside MS 206. Nancy, H 50. Woolhampton CI/R(H)/5, 5-6. Paris, A. N. S 8926, and Seine et Marne 531 (for plans). Lille 31, 1780 16 Nov, Cowley. Lille 18 H 59, 1779 12 Aug, Simpson. AH, I, 600. Cottineau, *Répertoire*, i, 646.

99   Hewlett, 'Annals', 92, 118, 120-21. Woolhampton, Parker Papers 'up to 1817', c. 1792 Declaration of St. Edmund's Property: 14, 24, 35-37. Paris, A. N. 22 G24, G9 66, 1736 22 Aug, Letters Patent.

100   Hull, DDEV/60/86(b), 1732 17 May, Helme to Potts.

101   For dispute over priory of Layrac, see Birt Box 7, printed *mémoire*. Lille 32, 1780 21 Jan, 1785 8 Aug, 1786 27 May, 1787 18 May, 1788 4 Dec, 17 Dec, 1789 19 Feb, 16 Mar. Lille 69, 1788 15 Aug.

102   Woolhampton, Cab. V R, Foundation Book of St. Edmund's. Nancy H 77, *Status* for 1769. Paris, A. N. H5 3896, St. Edmund's Accounts; S 3656/1. for rents and value of La Celle, see Downside MS 206, and Nancy H 50, 'Rationes Conventus...Cellis'. Beaunier, *Recueil Historique*, 110.

103   Paris A. N. G9 66, *Status* of Congregation for the Commission. Woolhampton, Parker Papers, c. 1792 Declaration of Property of St. Edmund's. Lille 35, 1774 25 Jan. Lille 18 H 3, entries for 1770 16 May, 1771 9 April, 1776 29 Oct. Lille 33, 1777 10 Mar. Lille 32, 1786 10 Sept, 1788 23 Jan, 1789 31 Jan, 9 Feb, 19 Feb. Lille 56, 1779 2 Jan, 12 June, 19 July. Lille 59, 1786 7 Feb, 27 Sept, Simpson. Lille 46, 1787 4 Ja. Lille 59, 1790 10 Feb, Shaw. Lille 53, 1790 25 Aug. Nancy H 77, 1770 22 May, 27 May, Welch to Naylor. Nancy H 77, 1770 26 May, Shaw to Welch. Schmitz, *Histoire*, iv, 74 and footnote. Bugner, *Cadre architectural*, 157, shows that in 1768, the three English houses in France

had a total revenue of 15,114 livres, the second lowest income of all Benedictine Congregations, the Camaldolese having the lowest income.

104 Paris, A. N. G9 66, Letters Patent granting the Congregation benefices. For St. Lawrence's most important benefice, St. Macaire, in Anjou, see Nancy H 48, H 77, H 81, H 94, and Lille 49, 1790 26 May, and WM, VI 461, 599. For Letters Patent, see McCann, 'Gift', 19-26. Lille 31, 1780 23 Feb, 6 Mar, for a proposed Dieulouard benefice. For St. Gregory's, RSRC, Anglia 8, f.561. *Gallia Christiana*, vii, 1073-77.

105 RA SP 57/116; 62/109; 64/33, 38, 171; 66/135, 159, 177; 67/35, 86, 93, 94, 99; 68/138; 69/36, 69; 72/147; 77/97, 132, 176; 116/6, 44, 86, 98; 125/100; 127/93; 139/84, 97. Paris, A. N. V5 1255. Kirk, *Biographies*, 215. W. S. Lewis amd W. H. Smith, *Correspondence of Horace Walpole*, ix, 116. BL Add. MSS 20309/62, 68, 74, 90.

106 Birt Box 6/A347; Ab. Arch. 42. Nancy H 77, Lambspring Accounts; H 77 1769 19 June, Heatley to Naylor;1770 8 July, Eaves to Naylor; 1770 8 Aug, 1771 21 May, Bennet to Naylor. Woolhampton, Scott Box 123. Lille 37, 1778 15 June, 1791 15 Aug. Rees, 'Lambspringe', 308-12. Downside, MS J. Townson, 'Historia Monasterii...Lambspring'. AB 381. AH, II, 221, 224, 262. AR 220.

107 e.g. Woolhampton CI/ L/5, 6; Scott Box 42, 59, 102, 134, 148. Northumberland R. O., RCD 6/4/331. Coughton Court, Box 83. WM V 513-15, 522-24, 601, 603. Birt Box 3/A116, 119, 127, 128; Box 6/A333, 340-41; MS 531 (rents at Shipston for 'Douay House'). RA SP 395/39, 141. Lille 12, 1755 4 Mar. Lille 67, 1779 14 Aug. Nancy H 50, *Status* 1749-51; H 77, 1767 2 April, Gillibrand to Naylor, and 1777 20 Nov, St. Gregory's Council on Anderton Affair. Payne, *Records,* 130-31. J. D. Alsop, 'John Macky's 1707 Account', 340. Dufermont, 'Collèges-Anglais', 53-4.

108 Paris, A. N. G9 66. 1766 1 Nov, Moore on Douai revenues: He speaks of losses due to wars, disturbances and financial crashes as totalling 170,000 livres, a capital sum brought from England. Debts at this time totalled 18,000 livres, with an annual income of 5,463 livres, from foundation funds and investments.

109 Dieulouard Accounts, transactions and Visitation reports in Nancy H 47, 48, 51, 53-57, 60, 62-73, 78, 81, 84-102, which reflect the house's financial difficulties. WM, IV, 3, for *spolia*. Allanson, 'Acts of General Chapter', 446-47. AR, 219.WM, V, 513-15, 522-24. Woolhampton, Scott Box, 131. Paris, A. N. G9 66,

Status E. B. C. Downside MSS 7, 167, 190 *passim,* for money sent from England; MS 206, for St Edmund's as Paris agent. Woolhampton, Cab. IV, for St. Edmund's Accounts, 1773-96. . Lille 18 H 38, 1778 2 May. AH, II, 73, 119, 170, 202. AR, 219. Almond, *Ampleforth,* 207. G. Clanché, La Bière.

110   Lille 57, 1785 6 Dec, 1789 14 Aug. Lille 31, 1786 8 May, Coupe. Lille 35, 1785 10 Jan, 1788 2 Sept, 1789 21 Jan. Lille 32, 1789 31 Jan, 19 June, 28 June, 1790 11 Jan. Lille 46, 1789 26 July, 1792 27 Feb, 12 May. Lille 35, 1790 18 Mar (quoted). Lille 18 H 31, 1790 20 Mar, Coupe. Lille 49, 1790 20 Mar, 7 April, 26 May. AH, II, 315. Clifton 1789-90, 87.

111   WM IV 84-86. AR, 552-55. F. Caraffa, *Monasticon Italiae. I,* 45. Lille 63, 1775 25 Feb.

112   RA SP 201/45, 110. RSOCG, 711/27, and RActa 112/127 ff.186-9. Lille 67, 1778 14 Mar, 1779 20 Jan, 16 April, 12 May, 30 June, 19 Aug, 11 Nov, 1780 19 Jan, 6 Mar, 29 Nov. Woolhampton, Scott Box 134. Nancy H 77, 1766 23 Sept ('Copy of an Account'), 1767 10 Mar, 1768 20 July, 1770 7 Mar,1772 6 Oct, Walker to Naylor. Birt Box 7/368. Woolhampton, Cab. V, St. Edmund's Accounts, 'The President'. 'Among the Archives', *DR,* vi, (1887), 52.

113   Lille 67, 1782 5 Feb, 24 April, 26 June, 1783 19 Mar, 14 April, 17 May, 1789 27 May, 1 July, 21 Oct. Lille 69, 1782 3 Mar.

114   WM, VI, 581. RA SP 56/37.

115   Lille 36, 1777 13 Nov, 1778 19 Jan, 1 April, 2 May, 29 June, 5 July, 12 July, 20 Nov, 31 Nov, 31 Dec, 1779 20 Feb, 1780 19 April, 8 Nov, Grime. Lille 56, 1778 10 Jan, 24 Jan, 8 April, 21 April, 6 July, 9 Oct, 1780 20 Feb, 6 Mar, 13 Mar, 30 April. 29 Aug, 28 Sept. Lille 31, 1779 26 Aug, 1780 23 Feb, Cowley. Lille 37, 1780 21 April, 25 Sept.

116   Lille 31, 1778 20 Sept, 1779 31 June, 9 Oct, 1780 6 Nov, Cowley. Lille 69, 1779 24 April. Lille 52, 1779 24 April. Paris, A. N. OI 405, fol. 12-13. Nancy H 77, 1772 16 Oct, Luton to Moore.

117   e.g. Lille 67, 1778 14 Mar, 8 April, 21 April, 12 May, 30 June, 11 Nov, 1779 20 Jan. Lille 31, 1779 20 May, 12 June, Cowley. Rome, English College, 50/8/2. Woolhampton, Scott Box, 148r. Harris, *Douai College,* 105. Laird, 'English College', 132, 133, 141.

118   Lille 18 H 18, 1784 Oct. AH, II, 188, 222-23, for Lambspring's relationship to its neighbours. Pastoral work was done by Germans engaged as parish priests.

119   WM, IV, 267-8; V, 521; VI, 600, 603. Lille 3, 1770 9 Dec entry. Lille 31, 1777 22 and 19 July, Cowley.

120   McManners, *Death*, 243, 278-9, 311.

121   WM, V 494. Woolhampton, Burial Register of St. Edmund's, Paris: entries for 1751, 1764, 1769, and pasted insertions at back.

122   *DR*, iv, 200-02. AH, II, 109-12. c.f. AAW Ep. Var, vii/12 and Burton (ed.), *Douai College Diaries*, 77.

123   Nancy H 50, *c.* 1728 for procession dispute, and 1751 24 April, Coupe to Catteral. Woolhampton, CIII/L, for list of Dieulouard Mass Obligations.

124   WM, VI, 600. Clifton 1791, 123.

125   Arras, 'Unsorted Papers', (Downside transcripts), 200-03, 205-09. Lille 56, 1778 6 July, 3 Aug, 9 Oct, 1780 10 Feb. Lille 57, 1785 9 April, 1786 13 Mar. AH, II, 248-9. AR,, 218. Lunn, 'Origins', 279-80, 286, 292-93. Lunn, *Benedictines*, 72-3, 182-3. Tyson, *Archives*, iii, 394-99, 401, 404-05. Lille, Série D, fonds de l'Université de Douai, 1780, 2 Mar.

126   This is best seen in reactions to the Commission des Réguliers' recommendation in 1768 that professions be made only at the age of 21 years, a move which threatened the future supply of missioners. The Commission is dealt with elsewhere; the French government's meddling with English Benedictine professions had a long history: see Woolhampton, Abbot's Archive, Clothing and Profession Book of St. Gregory's, Douai 1756-86, for such involvement in 1736, 1762 and 1783.

127   See graph in appendix II, and compare with Aveling, 'Education', 135-36. RActa 134/23 f272 gives 56 missioners in 1764. RSRC, Anglia 5, f42 lists 50 missioners in 1760s. Hemphill, *Vicars Apostolic*, 102, gives 1706 assessment of 40, which is too low. For further discussion, see Bossy, *Community*, 216-18, 226. J. H. Whyte, 'The Vicars Apostolics' Returns', 208-09, 212, 213. T. G. Holt, 'A Note', 3-6; and his 'A Further Note', 160-61; Paris, Arch. Nat. D XIX, 1790 14 Mar, Walker's survey of E.B.C. lists 40 on mission, 53 in monasteries; Lille 13, for 1733 printed list.

128   See appendix II, and Woolhampton: Scott Box 52; Lille 31, 1778 31 Oct.

129   RSOCG 559/15 ff403-04.

130   *Constitutiones Missionis Benedictinorum Congregationis Anglicanae*, Duaci 1689. RSOCG 559/15 ff403-04.

131   RActa 77/15. Potts and his correspondence are discussed in: P. Roebuck(ed.), *Constable of Everingham*,. P. Roebuck, *Yorkshire Baronets*, 186-94. P. Roebuck, 'Four Yorkshire Landowning Families', Chap. 3. R. Cecil Wilton, 'Dom John Bede Potts'

57-68. R. Cecil Wilton, 'Some Annals', 263-79. Hull University Library, DDEV/60/86b, for the correspondence, and transcripts in Northumberland Record Office, Forster MSS 1954.

132   Roebuck, *Constable*,49,63, 66,67,88,98,99. Northumberland Record Office, Forster MSS, Hull III, 105-11,132, 145,149,150,155,158,172,173,175.

133   Lille 3, 1787 entry. AH, II, 252. See also Lille 35, 1774 19 Mar.

134   RSOCG 559/15 ff403-04. AH, II, 301-02. Lille 66, 1782 28 Sept, 1783 27 Aug. Lille 18 67, 1785 13 Sept.

135   Lille 18 66, 1787 22 Oct. Examples of errant missioners in London - *Jerome Digby*: Lille 58, 1782 22 Mar. Lille 34, 1782 8 May, 1783 10 Jan, 21 Jan, 3 Mar, 1784 7 Jan, Digby. Lille 57, 1782 15 Aug, 23 Aug, 27 Aug, 1783 21 Jan, 1784 31 Jan, 19 June, 1785 8 Sept, 29 Oct, 6 Dec, 1786 7 Mar. Lille 30, 1782 19 Nov, 1784 15 April. Lille 66, 1784 19 June, 1786 6 May, 29 June, 1790 30 May. Lille 46, 1785 17 Sept. lille 64, 1786 20 Feb. Lille 28, 1786 24 Feb, 1790 22 Feb. *Dunstan Garstang*: Lille 36, 1785 19 Aug, 9 Sept. Lille 66, 1786 6 May, 29 June, 8 July. *Robert Goolde*: Lille 36, 1782, 9 April, 5 Sept, 1783 17 Jan.Lille 66, 1782 1 Aug, 16 Aug, 28 Sept, 2 Dec, 1783 18 Mar. *Basil Kennedy*: Lille 30, 1783 10 May. Lille 46, 1787 4 Feb, 25 Feb, 13 Mar, 9 Nov. Paris, AN, DXIX 69/447. Lille 45, 1790 10 Sept, 3 Oct, 17 Nov. Lille 53, 1790 23 Sept. Lille 28, 1790 1 Oct. Birt, Box 10, 1790 3 Oct, Parker to Bennet. AB, 485, note 3.

136   Lille 66, 1778 29 May.

137   For an example of an unstable conventual (Benet Cawser), eager to come on the mission, see Lille 3, 1768 Oct entry. Lille 26, 1779 9 Sept, Barnes. Lille 56, 1789 29 Aug. Lille 18 31, 1779 15 Dec,1780 20 Oct, Bulmer.

138   Lille 69, 1786 26 July.

139   WM, V, 537. RSRC, Anglia I f.836.

140   AH, II, 43.

141   Lille 66, 1784 29 June.

142   Lille 66, 1787 6 Feb.

143   Lille 66, 1784 5 Sept, 6 Dec, 1785 29 Ma. Lille 18(10). Lille 32, 1784 15 Dec, 1785 22 Jan. Lille 35, 1785 18 Jan, 1 Mar. Lille 4, 1785 10 Mar. Lille 58, 1785 16 June.

144   e.g. RSRC, Anglia 4, ff39-40. AH, II, 173.

145   e.g. Downside MS 521, Greenwood's annuity.

146   Coughton, Box 83, 1705-12, A. Constable to Sir Robert Throckmorton. Downside MS 206, 118. Downside, North Province Account Book 3. Downside MS 212. Lille 27, 1773 2 July.

147   The large bulk of these two Provincials' accounts demonstrates
        their good housekeeping: Nancy H 77, 1743-70, Presidential
        Accounts (Farnworth and Naylor). 1766-72 Naylor's Accounts.
        1767 c. May, Naylor's Accounts. c. 1770 25 Oct, Eaves to
        Naylor. 1771 27 May, Naylor to Eaves. 1771 16 Dec, Naylor's
        Accounts. 1772 28 Feb, Eaves to Naylor. Downside, Accounts of
        the North Province 1769-1830. Accounts of the South Province,
        Daily Accounts 1738-54. MS 202, South Province Accounts
        1741-1841. MS 168 'M', South Province Accounts 1749-87. MS
        212,South Province Accounts 1751-74. Howard's Accounts with
        the Banker Wright (c. 1730- c. 1750). MS 2013, Naylor's North
        Province Extracts and *Catalogus Benefactorum*. Downside, Ab.
        Arch., 18. Woolhampton, Scott Box, 108, 138. Roebuck, *Constable*, 149.
148   Downside, MS 37, Eaves' Account Book. Box 762, North Province Accounts 1677-1854. MS 424, North Province Records
        1640-1882. MS 186, North Province Accounts, 1769-1830.
        Bastwell's Fund Account Book, 1769-1830. MS 51, South Province Chapter Book, 1681-1781. MS 70, South Province Book of
        Contracts, 1717-1826. MS 68, South Province Cash Book,
        1784-7. MS 52, South Province Accounts 1785-1846. MS 202,
        South Province Accounts, 1741-1841. MS 146,South Province
        Accounts 1782-1800. MS 190, South Province Ledger, 1776-1809.
        MS 168 South Province Accounts 1749-87 (1800). MS 201, South
        Province Day Book, 1769-96. Box 763, South Province Financial
        Statements.
149   *Constitutiones Missionis*, Duaci 1689, Chapter VII. Paris, Arch.
        Nat, LL 1420. Hull, Everingham, DDEV/60/86b, 1736 10 Dec,
        1736/7 9 Jan, 1736/7 18 Jan, 1737 14 April, 27 April, 8 May,
        Potts to Farnworth.
150   Downside, MSS 180, 2013. Northumberland R. O. ZSW 30/2,
        30/4, 44/2, 44/4. 454, 456.Box 23, Memorandum Book of Sir
        John Swinburne. Nancy H 77, 1771 11 May, Eaves to Naylor. A
        detailed analysis of mission funds cannot be attempted here.
151   AH, Appendix, 516. Lille 30, 1778 3 Aug, 1780 26 Ma. Lille 35,
        1778 30 June. Lille 46, 1788 14 Sept, 1791 6 Dec.
152   Williams, *Bath and Rome*, 26-27. Williams, *Post-Reformation
        Catholicism*, lxv, 54-55. R. E. Scantlebury (ed.), *Registers of
        Marnhull*, 165-99. Allanson, 'Acts of General Chapters', 474.
        Woolhampton, South Province Mass Obligations Book, 1,2,60-61,
        and insertion of 19 Aug. 1705.

153   Woolhampton, South Province Mass Obligations Book, 69, 70-78. AH, II, 190-209. Williams, *Post-Reformation Catholicism,* lxv, 56-59, 113-77.

154   Williams, *Post-Reformation Catholicism,* lxv, 62-67, 178-82. AH, Appendix, 504-05.

155   Lille 27, 1774 8 June, 1 July, 24 Aug. Lille 56, 1775 26 Dec. Lille 31, 1777 14 Mar, List of Bath Subscribers. Lille 51, 1778 20 Mar, 14 April, 8 May. Williams, *Post-Reformation Catholicism,* lxv, 66-67, 105-06, 113-77, 178-80.

156   Lille 66, 1778 17 April.. AH, II, 262. Lille 38, 1778 2 May, 22 June. Lille 51, 1778 8 May, 26 Dec, 1779 22 Mar, 14 April, 19 Aug, 5 Nov, 1780 7 Feb. Lille 31, 1778 17 May, 1779, 25 April, Brewer. Lille 28, 1778 12 June, 1780 11 May, 19 May. Lille 35, 1778 30 June. Lille 66, 1778 24 Aug, 12 Sept, 30 Oct, 1779 17 Jan, 15 Feb, 23 April, 7 June, 3 Aug. On subject of certain monasteries having recognised spheres of influence on the mission, see Lille 27, 1774, 1.

157   Lille 66, 1780, 8 July.

158   Lille 31, 1782 9 April, Brewer.. Lille 66, 1782 2 Dec, 1786 6 May, 8 July. Lille 51, 1785 25 Jan, 27 Mar, 1786 16 June. Lille 28, 1786 16 Aug.

159   Lille 28, 1787 9 Jan, 15 Jan, 1 Mar, 12 Aug. Lille 66, 1787 6 Feb, 20 Mar, 5 Oct. Lille 51, 1787 6 Mar, 13 Mar, 17 April, 14 July, 23 July, 5 Oct, 1792 26 Ja. Lille 70, 1787 19 Jun AH, II, 316-17. Clifton 1772-88, 49.

160   A,, II, 276-79. Birt Box 10, A461, 1783 24 Nov, Warmoll to Bennet. Woolhampton, South Province Mass Foundation Book.

161   WM, IV, 62, V, 523-24, VI, 600.

162   e.g. B. Potts, annuity of £10 from family, paid through the Provincial: Estcourt and Payne, *Non-Jurors,* 209-10. Hull University, Everingham DDEV/60/86b, 1733 25 Sept, Potts to his brother George, to Provincial Farnworth, to his nephew Storey. 1733 24 Oct, Potts to Farnworth. 1733 9 Nov, Potts to his brother George. 1734 9 Aug, Potts to his nephew Storey. 1735 22 Feb, Potts to Farnworth.

     B. Steare, annuity of £60 from St. Gregory's, Douai: AH, II, 178. Woolhampton, Scott Box, 79, 109. Downside, North Province Account Book, no. 3.

     G. Greenwood, annuity of £20 from his family: Downside MS 531.

163   e.g. J. C. Wilks: Woolhampton, St Edmund's Mass Obligation Book, 69.

164 Downside, MS 2013, nos. 20 and 38. North Province Account
     Book, no. 3, 7, 8, 18. Northumberland R. O. ZSW 213/12, 456.
     Woolhampton, South Province Obligations Book, 78.
165 Hull University, Everingham DDEV/60/86b, 1740 23 May, Potts
     to Farnworth. Downside, North Province Accounts Book, no. 3
     teare's salary of £20). Downside, MS 531, for Greenwood's
     salary of £25. Clifton I, xxvii (Bennet's salary of £20). Arundel
     Castle MSS (E) 54118.
166 Porter, *English Society*, 13, for conversion tables; 104, 230, 352,
     392 for inflation. For rise in salaries and effects: Woolhampton,
     Parker Papers CI R(A) 219. Downside, MS 2013, nos. 29, 37.
     MS I, A. Caldwell's Accounts. Lille 66, 1783 25 Dec, 1784 29
     June. Lille 30, 1778 3 Aug, 1779 24 July, 1782 26 July, 1784 10
     Nov. Lille 46, 1786 6 June, 1788 19 Feb, 14 Sept, 1789 14 Feb.
     Lille 35, 1774 11 Feb, 1778 30 June, 1785 10 Jan.
     Northumberland R. O., SWZ 29/2, Sir Edward Swinburne's
     Accounts. Downside, North Province Book 3, Aberford Accounts.

167 e.g. of monks' investment and donations to individual missions
     AR, 199. Downside, MS 2013, nos. 26, 49, 50. Woolhampton,
     Scott Box, 135. For Province's control over *peculium*, AH, II,
     167, 174, 210.
168 Lille 3, 1788 entry. Lille 46, 1788 19 Feb, 20 May.
169 e.g. of wealthy monks: A. Geary - Williams, *Bath and Rome*, 29.
     Lille 35, 1785 10 Jan. E. Hadley - Woolhampton, Scott Box,
     35-40. Lille 66, 1783 8 Mar, 25 April, 1784 29 June, 5 Sept. Birt
     Box 10, A496.
170 For Poverty Bills: Hull University, Everingham DDEV/60/86b,
     1733/34 1 Mar, 1735/6 17 Mar, 1736 31 July, Potts to Farnworth.
     Nancy H 77, 1772 2 June, B. Simpson's *Memoriale*.
171 Downside, North Province, Loose Accounts (1721-25).
     Woolhampton, Scott Box, 142b. AH, I, 592, II, 167, 235, 257,
     269-70, 371.
172 For account of Schism: AH, II, 74-82, 106-109. C. Butler, *Notes
     on the Origins,* 37-38, 73. G. Sitwell, 'A Crisis of Authority',
     221-303. Tyson, *Archives*, iii, 395.
173 Howard and at least one of the Scrutators, Gregory Riddell, were
     committed Jacobites. Howard was Prior of St. James's Priory,
     Whitehall in 1685. For his Jacobitism and qualified assent to a
     1716 Oath of Submission, see Gillow, *Dictionary,* iv, 549, E. H.
     Burton and E. Dolan (ed.), *The Douay College Diaries: The
     Seventh Diary 1715-1778,* (CRS xxviii), London 1928, 40-41,
     UCM III, 15-17/vii/1716.

174	RASV, Fondo Albani, tome VI/168 f35. AR, 185-87. AH, II, 66-72. AAW, Main Series XXXVIII/84.
175	AR, 189. Downside, MS 70, S. Province Account Book.
176	Birt Box 3, 146, 151.
177	RActa 90/7; RSRC, Anglia 2, ff183r, 206-09; RSCOG 623/7 ff37-42. Birt Box 3, 146, 147, 149, 153, 154, 155.
178	RASV, Fondo Albani, tome x/145 ff34-5, 37. Birt Box 3, 152.
179	Birt Box 3, 150. AAW, Main Series XXXIX/156, p. 69.
180	Birt Box 3, 156.
181	AAW, Main Series, XXXIX/156.
182	RA/SP 47/40.
183	AR, 190, AH,, II, 80.
184	RA/SP 57/115 (2,3,4). AR, I 195, II 81. Birt Box 3, 183, 184, 205. Bodleian, Carte CLXXX 529, 530, for Fenwick's attempt to perform a clandestine marriage between his brother and Lady Grosvenor, and C.T.Gatty, *Mary Davies and the Manor of Ebury*, London, n.d.,ii, 54-71.
185	AH, II, 86-90.
186	Gillow, *Dictionary*, iv, 549. Hemphill, *Vicars Apostolic*, Chap. VII. E. Duffy, ' "Englishmen in vaine"', 345-66.
187	AAW, Ep. Var. vii/39, 51, 52, 56. RA/SP 63/16.
188	UCM I/145. RA/SP 57/115 (3).
189	AAW, Ep. Var. vii/66.
190	AAW, Ep. Var. vii/70. RA/SP 57/115 (9). AH, II, 91.
191	RSRC, Anglia 2, 370-1. AH, II, 90-105. AR, II, 194. RA/SP 54/112; 55/98, 147; 56/37, 112; 57/64, 115 (9-11); 60/32; 66/155. Sitwell, 'Crisis', 276-82.
192	RASV, Inghilterra, 23 ff19-20. RSRC, Anglia 2, ff238-43, 246, 256, 266-7, 274-5, 309, 311-15, 323-4, 346-7, 352-3, 360-1, 370-1, 396-8; RActa 93/10ff126-7, 93/37ff456-70; RSOCG 639/10ff27-8. RA/SP 54/164. BL. Add. MSS. 20309/51, 66.
193	See appendix III for table of apostates.
194	For Anderton, R. E. Gibson, *Lydiate Hall,* 68-70. Kirk, *Biographies,* 3. Foley, *Records,* v-viii, 74. Estcourt and Payne, *Non-Jurors,* 113, 283, 319, 337-38. BL Add. MSS. 20309/51, 116. For Savage, RSRC, Anglia 2, f83r. Anstruther, *Priests,* iii, 196-7.
195	AH, II, 91, 103. AR, II, 194 (34-35). CRS, 'Lancashire Registers IV', 6-7. Duffy, 'Over the Wall', 12, 20-21. RA/SP 57/115 (9-11, 13-14, 23-26, 29-30); 77/108. AAW Ep. Var. vii/70. For Knowles, RA SP 57/115 ff22, 24, 25; Oxford, Christchurch, Wake, Letters 22/246, 341, 342.

196 William Hudleston, *A Recantation Sermon*, London 1729. *Irresistible Evidence Against Popery*, London 1731. *Divine Truths Vindicated in the Church of England*, London 1731.

197 *Recantation*, 7, 23, 34, 35. *Divine Truths*, 93. *Irresistible Evidence*, 65-66, 140-41. In this last book, Hudleston made much use of the Benedictine seventeenth century 'ecumenist', John Barnes.

198 *Divine Truths*, 94-95.

199 N. Sykes, *William Wake*, i, 261-64, 274-5, 279, 285, 295ff, 316ff, Chapter V.

200 RA/SP 62/136; 56/37; 57/116; 71/38.

201 RA/SP 57/64, 143; 61/25(enclosure); 62/25; 77/97, 129. G. V. Bennett, *The Tory Crisis in Church and State, 1688-1730*, for Atterbury.

202 AAW, Ep. Var. vii/96.

203 RA/SP 118/112; 119/134. BL Add. MSS. 20309/16, 37, 55, 70.

204 RA/SP 57/115. AAW, Ep. Var. vii/51, 52. BL Add. MSS. 20309/60, 70, 100, 106, 107. Woolhampton, Cup1, Shf. 1, Copies 10, 11. Hudleston, *Divine Truths*, 180-210. For involvement of secular clergy and the Vicars Apostolic in Jansenism, see E.Duffy, '"A Rubb-up for Old Soares"', 291-317.

205 BL Add. MSS. 20309/70, 118. RA/ SP 68/138; 74/135; 76/90; 137/54; 167/100; 174/15, 42, 192; 175/18; 168/114.

206 BL Add. MSS. 20309/9, 10, 23, 57, 60. RA/SP 61/48, 73; 62/25, 136; 67/28, 44, 86; 68/138; 74/135; 76/90. AAW, Main Series XXXVIII/119; Ep. Var. vii, 122, 132; viii, 7, 13, 14, 25, 29, 32. Duffy, 'Rubb-up', 304, and Chapter IV for Southcott and Jansenism.

207 BL Add. MSS. 20309/88, 95; 20313, f.175, f185, f189, and 1723 18 Aug, Witham to Gualterio. RA/SP 64/38; 66/177. AAW, Ep. Var. viii, 101.

208 RA/SP 63/83; 64/38; 66/177; 72/43; 77/72, 129. BL Add. MSS. 20309/51, 53, 88, 90, 95, 110, 118, 124; 20313/166, 175. AAW, Ep. Var. viii 25, 29, 32, 36, 41, 46, 101, 117; ix 20, 21, 22, 23, 25, 32, 40, 64, 125. AH, II, 124. Whelan, *Vicars Apostolic*, 37, 43, 120, 122, 126, 143. W. Mazière Brady, *Annals*, 250, 252. G. Anstruther, 'The Appointment of Bishop Williams O. P.', 314-50.

209 For the effects of double land taxation,levies on papists, and forfeiture of estates: J. A. Williams, 'The Problem of the Double Land Tax', 32-36. J. A Williams, 'Sources for Recusant History (1559-1791)', 384-85. Public Records Office, *The Records of the Forfeited Estates Commission*. . W. R. Ward, *The English Land Tax*. M. Rowlands, 'Staffordshire Papists,' 33-38. M. Rowlands,

'The Iron Age of Double Taxes', 30-46. B. Magee, *English Recusants*, 176-81.

210 BL Add. MSS. 20309/14, 18, 37, 55, 57, 62, 64, 66, 68, 74, 86, 88, 96, 144, 118. RA/SP 63/41, 42, 46, 128, 155, 164, 176; 70/86; 105/4.

211 RA/SP 64/33, 38, 64, 73, 127, 144, 171; 66/78, 112, 1214, 135, 159, 177; 67/23, 35, 44, 94, 116, 141; 69/36, 69, 80; 108/49; 118/163; 111/109 (quoted), 154. BL Add. MSS. 20309/20, 21, 23.

212 Birt Papers 317.

213 R. C. Wilton, 'Dom John Bede Potts', 63.

214 Lille 66, 1784 6 Dec.

215 RA/SP 182/166, 167; 183/111.

216 RA/SP 125/100. BL Add. MSS. 20309/90. Woolhampton I/L/E, Confirmation of St. Edmund's Privileges, 1723 16 Mar. For St. Laurence's 'naturality', see J. McCann, 'A Gift from Dieulouard'. For St. Gregory's 'naturality', 'Among the Archives', *DR, v*, July 1886, 284.

217 Hemphill, *Vicars Apostolic*, 3,7,8.

218 RSOCG 559/15 ff403r-04, for procedure observed by missioners *vis-à-vis* the Vicars Apostolic. Brady, *Annals*, 77-103. Bossy, *Community*, 52-56.

219 RASV, Inghilterra, 22/ff1-46; 23/ff1-12. Lunn, *Benedictines*, 110-12, 151-54. M. Lunn, 'Benedictine opposition', 1-20.

220 WM, IV, 4-8. AR, I, 523-24. AH, I, 538ff. Hemphill, *Vicars Apostolic*, 6-7, 10-11. J. Berington, *The Memoirs of Gregory Panzani*. 327-45. J. Miller, *Popery and Politics*, 229-30, 244. C. Dodd, *The Church History*, iii, 466-67, 528.

221 WM, IV 1-6. For Ellis, G. A. Ellis, *The Ellis Correspondence*. J. A. Williams, 'Bishops Giffard and Ellis', 218-28. Hemphill, *Vicars Apostolic*, 20-21. J. C. H. Aveling, *The Handle*, 236.

222 *Historical Manuscripts Commission*, Stuart I, 81. Berington, *Panzani*, 381. Edinburgh: Scottish Catholic Archives, W. Lesley Papers. Ellis, Letter 11.

223 AAW Main Series XXXVI/39. *CRS*, 1964, lvi, 'Papers from Lambeth Palace Library', 126-28. Berington, *Panzani*, 378-80, 386. Scott, 'The Privileges', for subsequent dispute.

224 WM I, 'To the Religious Reader'; I, 1-3, 161; IV, 88-230. for the Benedictine context of the dispute, A. D. Wright, 'Catholic History', 126-27.

225 Bodleian: Carte MSS, 181 f162v; 204 f44; 208 ff27-29,37-38,41-42; 209 ff33-35. AAW, Main Series XXXV/49. *Historical Manuscripts Commission*, Stuart I, 89-91, 94-95, 101.

235

226 AAW, Main Series XXXVI/52,54,55, 57,185. WM, IV, 230. *Historical Manuscripts Commission,* Stuart I, 91.
227 AAW, Main Series XXXVI/63.
228 WM, IV, 230-31.
229 RActa 67/20. *Historical Manuscripts Commission,* Stuart I, 96-97. AAW, Main Series XXXVI/62.
230 Edinburgh: Scottish Catholic Archives, Lesley Papers, Ellis 3. AAW, Main Series XXXV/118; XXXVI/60, 62, and pp 195-96. WM' IV, 232-35.
231 WM IV, 232-33, 235. Bossy, *Community,* 64-65. 60-9, for Blacklo and Sergeant.
232 RCP, ff2r-107r. WM, IV, 235, 236,237-38,239,242-52. AAW Main Series XXXVI/68,69,74,77.
233 AAW Main Series XXXVI/78,79, 81,86. For Stuart nomination of Vicars Apostolic until 1765, Ward, *Dawn,* i, 218.
234 CRS, 'Old Brotherhood Archives', 31, for the secular clergy and the Oath.
235 WM, III, 788-95, for the list of Benedictine privileges, and Birt Box 6/A309, for a 1731 list of faculties granted to a missioner by his Provincial, who reserved matrimonial dispensations to himself. Also, WM, IV, 243-46. London, Forest Gate JC.2. RASV, Inghilterra 22 ff74-8. AAW, Main Series XXXVI/74; XXXVII/34. AH, I, 564.
236 WM, IV 239-41. AAW, Main Series, XXXV/93; XXXVI/84, pp379-80.
237 WM IV 259-60. AAW, Main Series XXXVI, pp 365-67. Dodd, *Church History,* iii, 528-29. CRS, lvi, 119-21, 123.
238 AAW, Main Series XXXVI/92. WM,, IV, 262.
239 AAW, Main Series XXXVI/87. WM, IV 260-62.
240 AAW, Main Series XXXVI/88,93. The numbers here were deliberately inflated.
241 WM, VI, 931. AAW, Main Series XXXVI/91 and p 389.
242 WM IV, 236-37. AAW, Main Series XXXVI, 99-100.
243 AAW, Main Series XXXVI/99.
244 RASV, Fondo Albani, tome i, 163 ff263-74, 285. AAW, Main Series XXXVI/98.
245 AAW, Main Series XXXVI/113.
246 *Bullarium Romanum,* Rome 1734, ix, 440-41. AAW, Main Series XXXVI/111, 115.
247 RSRC, Anglia 2, ff81-83r; RCP 32 f4. AAW Main Series XXXVI/195; XXXVIII/23. WM, V 522-24; VI, Appendix: 1701 General Chapter address to Pope and Cardinals.

248 WM, V 337, 531,533-36; VI, Addenda 17. AAW XXXVIII/29, 121. Ep. Var. i/2,3,27,35; ii/3; v, 1715 30 May, Ingleton to Mayes. Hemphill, *Vicars Apostolic,* 31,32, 34-38. J. A. Williams, 'Bishops Giffard and Ellis', 223-36. B. Navarra, *Ellis.*

249 BL Add MSS 20209/24, 60, 76, 100, 102, 106, 107, 110, 118, 166. AAW, Ep. Var. viii/7,13,14,25,29,32. AAW, Main Series XXXVIII/125.

250 RCP 85/61r, 172r, 176r, 193r, 200r-01, 220v. RA/SP 64/38; 66/177. AAW, Ep. Var. viii/41,46. BL Add MSS 20313 f175. 20309/53,88, 122.

251 AAW, Ep. Var. viii/36, 1723 23 Aug, Ingleton to Mayes.

252 RCP, 85ff200-01; RSRC, Anglia 2, ff477-8. BL Add MSS 20309/90,94,95,124. RA/SP 74/135; 76/90, 168. AAW, Ep. Var. viii/101, 117. AH, II, 124. AR' II, 196. G. Anstruther, 'Appointment', 316,317,321,323,339,340.

253 RSRC, Anglia 2, 548-9. AAW, Ep. Var. ix/20,21,22,23,25, 32,40,64,125.

254 RA/SP 182/167.

255 RSRC, Anglia 2, ff548-9. RA/SP 182/166; 207/70.

256 RActa 110/16; RSOCG 703/23, 706/16, 798/9; RSRC, Anglia 4, ff22, 31-4. 38. RA/SP 222/13, 95, 152. Box I/158. AAW, Main Series XL/33.

257 AH, II, 163.

258 RA/SP 246/177, 188; 249/69; 250/183; 252/13; 253/184; 255/144. For Walmesley *DNB,* 1922, xx, 615.

259 AAW, Main Series XL/50. Birt Box 6/A328. RSRC, Anglia 4, ff87, 89, 93, 108. AH, II, 194-97. Burton, *Challoner,* i, Chaps. XVI, XIX; ii, Appendix D.

260 RA/SP 293/3, 97. AAw, Main Series XL/67. AR, 201,204,205,206. UCM II/71. Woolhampton CI/R/9 *Copia Authentica Bullae..quae incipit Plantata,* 1748.

261 Woolhampton, *Lettre d'un Seigneur Anglois à un Ami,* (dated 14th June 1749). London, Forest Gate, D. 4 BF. LX and D. 48F. LX. AR 207,208. Ampleforth, Box 261, 1749 19 Mar, Naylor to Fisher.

262 AAW, Ep. Var xiii, 1752 14 Aug, Holden to Stonor. 1753 14 Mar, Green to Stonor. 1753 26 Mar, Holden to Stonor. 1753 4 May, Petre to Stonor.

263 *Regulae observandae in Anglicanis Missionibus,* Rome 1753. RCP 116/ff3v-303. AAW, Main Series XL/52. AH, II 199-208. Burton, *Challoner,* i, Chap. XIX. G. Holt, 'Bishop Challoner', 138-41. Clifton 1791, 120.

264 AAW, Ep. Var. xiii, 1753 23 July, 6 Aug, 20 Aug, 5 Nov, Holden to Stonor. Main Series XL/97. Woolhampton, 'Epistolae' of Provincials Naylor and Wyburne to the Vicars Apostolic (Nov. 1753), and the latter's replies. Woolhampton, President Howard to a Benedictine Cardinal (late 1753). London: Farm Street, Letters of Bishops and Cardinals 17533-1853, I, 1753 1 Jan, York to Carteret. Birmingham Archdiocesan Archives, C.572, 578, 579. RSRC, Anglia 2, ff693-6, Anglia 4, ff466-79, 209-22, 224-31, 340, 365-6.

265 RA/SP 350/193; 353/63. AR, 225. Clifton 1792, 77.

266 AAW, Bishop Challoner's letter-book: entry for Oct. 1755, 'To Card. Spinelli'. RA/SP 362/96; 363/101,115; 365/59,153; 367/164. UCM II/90. RActa 126/9ff101-07, 133/9, 10; RSRC, Anglia 4 ff431-2. Lille 18, 1756, Sept and 1756 Autumn. Lille 60, 1756 July. London: Farm Street, Letters of Bishops and Cardinals, 1753-1853, I/32. AH, II, 211-14.

267 AAW, Ep. Var. xiv, 1758 31 Oct, 1759 4 May, Fisher (Challoner) to Stonor. UCM III/141. AR, 214, pp 168-69.

268 e.g.Anselm Bolton of Gilling: Lille 30, 1778 15 May, 8 July, 3 Aug, 31 Oct, 19 No. Lille 46, 1778 29 Oct.

269 Lille 24, 1762 5 June.

270 AAW, Ep. Var. xiv, 1761 23 Nov, Petre to Stonor. Main Series XLI/22, 23,26. AR, 214. Burton, *Challoner,* ii, 6, 32-33; Chap. XXVII.

271 AAW, Ep. Var. xiv, 1763 9 Jan, Hornyold to Stonor, 1765 31 May, c. Dec, Fisher (Challoner) to Stonor. Letter-book of Bp. Challoner, 18 May 1765 entry. Main Series XLI/36,55. Birmingham, C.675, A.105. RActa 134/23; RSRC, Anglia 4, ff433-7. Burton, *Challoner,* ii, 78-85.

272 Downside, Ab. Arch. 34. MS 70, *passim,* for monks carrying out Rome's orders. AAw, Main Series XLI/102,116,134. Lille 35, 1773 9 No.

273 UCM II/13. Lille 33, 1777 10 Mar. Lille 31, 1777 15 July, Cowley.. Lille 67, 1778 3 June, 1779 8 Dec. Nancy, Meurthe H 77, 1770 7 Mar, 4 April, 21 May, Walker to Naylor. 1771 18 Jan, 24 May, Bennet to Naylor.

274 Nancy, Meurthe H 77 1770 2 May, Walmesley to Naylor.1770 21 May, Walker to Naylor. Lille 63, 1773 15 Dec (quoted). Clifton I, vii-ix, xi-xiv.

275 Lille 67, 1779 20 Jan, 16 April, 12 May, 9 June. Lille 64, 1779 7 April.

276 Lille 18 H 67, 1779 7 July, 24 Aug, 1779 22 Sept. Lille 31, 1779 8 July, 7 Oct, 9 Oct, 20 Nov,26 Dec, 1780 19 Jan, 6

Mar(quoted), Cowley. Lille 64, 1779 14 Oct, 1780 30 April. Lille 69, 1779 7 Nov, 1780 29 Mar. Lille 27, 1779 17 Dec. Lille 37, 1780 2 Jan. Lille 31, 1780 16 Feb, Castelli. Lille 56, 1780 30 May. Rome, English College, 50/9/6, 1779 21 Oct, Walmesley to Corsini.

277 Lille 67, 1782 2 Feb, 26 June, 1783 1 Jan,19 Mar, 2 April, 1 July, 21 Oct, 1790 24 Feb,21 April. Lille 66, 1783 25 April, 1790 30 May. Lille 28, 1790 7 April, 30 April. UCM IV/285b. RActa 164/3; RSRC, Anglia 5 ff1-2. AR, 115 (d), 232.

278 Lille 66, 1787 22 Feb, 10 July, 22 Oct, 1788 18 Jan. Lille 67, 1787 4 July, 28 Nov, 1788 3 Jan. Lille 32, 1787 10 Sep. Lille 57, 1787 26 Oct, 1788 3 Jan. Lille 28, 1787 4 Dec, 1788 1 Mar. Lille 64, 1788 15 Jan. Lille 56, 1788 9 Feb. AH, II, 318-333. Ward, Dawn, Chap. VI. E. Duffy, 'Ecclesiastical Democracy Detected, II, 309-31. Clifton 1772-88, 69; 1789-90, 29, 49.

279 Lille 57, 1790 9 Jan. Lille 28, 1790 7 Feb, 26 April, 30 April. Lille 67, 1790 3 Mar. Lille 64, 1790 22 May. Lille 66, 1790 30 May. Clifton 1772-88, 90, 98, 118, 136, 141.

280 Northumberland R. O., RCD 1/1/13; 1/1/17; 1/1/42. For Widdrington, Lunn Benedictines, 38-56. Clifton 1789-90, 119; 1791, 20.

281 Northumberland R. O. RCD 1/1/12,19,20. Lille 33, 1791 3 Mar. Lille 57, 1791 5 Mar. Clifton 1791, 21, 25, 27, 37, 117.

282 Lille 28, 1791, 5 July. Lille 46, 1791 17 July. Lille 67, 1791 10 Aug. Lille 66, 1791 27 Aug. Clifton 1789-90, 88; 1791, 53, 109, 120, 123.

283 Birt Box 6, 9/B15. Lille 64, 1791 14 Nov. Lille 62, 1791 17 Nov. Clifton 1791, 141, 142, 143, 146, 147,150, 152, 159, 161, 165, 166, 170, 171, 173, 175, 176, 177, 180, 181, 182, 184, 185, 188, 190, 192, 193, 194, 197, 200, 202, 203, 208, 215, 214, 209, 210, 212; 1792 9 Jan.

284 Lille 46, 1792 28 Jan, 27 Feb. Clifton 1792 5 Jan.; 1792 vol. 4, 16, 17, 22, 30, 36, 37, 43, 49, 53, 56, 139.

285 Lille 53, 1792 25 April. Lille 33, 1792 1 May. Lille 57, 1792 5 May. Lille 66, 1792 11 May, 8 July. Lille 46, 1792 12 May. Clifton 1792 vol. 62, 73, 77, 83.

286 AH II, 332-33. Ward, Dawn, ii, 66,143,145,147, 157-59,236-39.

287 See appendices I and II for missions and monks. For chaplaincies in general, see Bossy, Community, Chap. 7 and Duffy, 'Peter and Jack', 6-12.For chapel destruction, WM,, IV, 84-86;CRS, xxiii, 1922, 125-26; Kirk, Biographies, 234; Aveling, Handle, 241; 'A Forgotten Episode', 259-63. CSPD 1689 Feb.-April 1690, 146.

288   e.g. A.M.C. Forster, 'An Outline History', 13; AH, Appendix 534; Birt, *Obit Book,* 71.

289   WM, VI, 66. AH, I, 497, 558.

290   RSRC, Anglia 2, f435. WM IV, 1,5, 51, 61-62; V, 321;494. BL Add MSS 10118, 298v. AH, I, 486. *CRS,* xxxviii, 77. Coughton Court, Box 83, 1705 15 Sept, 6 Oct, Constable to Throckmorton. *CRS,* lvi, 152.

291   WM, V, 318. AH II, 53-54.

292   For statistics: AAW Main series xxxviii/2, and J. A. Williams, 'The Distribution of Catholic Chaplaincies', 42-48. Hemphill, *Vicars,* 102. Bossy, *Community,* 216-19. Duffy, 'Peter and Jack', 12-13, for riding missions in general.

293   Williams, *Bath and Rome,* 27. AH, Appendix 520.

294   RActa 116/10 f178r, 8 monks in London District in 1746. Duffy, *Challoner,* 15.

295   BL Add MSS 28,237. AH, Appendix, 501-02. A. McInnes, *The English Town,* 6. Williams, *Bath and Rome,* 25, 90. Williams, *Post-Reformation Catholicism,* lxv, 49, 52.

296   WM, I, 481. Aveling, *West Riding,* 157. Aveling, 'Catholic Recusancy', 391-92. Bossy, *Community,* 221-22. R. E. Scantlebury,(ed.), *Hampshire Registers I,* 5(note). G. Dolan, 'Benedictine Hampshire', 112-18.

297   Birt Box 3/A139. AH, Appendix 540.

298   *CRS,* xxv, London 1925, 110-15. *CRS,* xxxii, London 1932, 204-88.

299   Northumberland R. O., RCD 6/2/109. J. P. Smith (ed.), *Lancashire Registers III,* (CRS xx), 9. J. P. Smith (ed.), *Lancashire Registers IV: Brindle and Samlesbury,* 23(note).

300   e.g. common suffrages: RA SP 57/115, 1721 10 July, Dawney to Hardcastle. Hull, Everingham, DDEV/60/86b, *passim,* (Potts). Gillow, *Dictionary,* iv, 458-9 (Mannock). RA SP 57/115 and J. A. Williams, 'Benedictine Missions in Wiltshire', 253-73, (Bath, Fonthill and Sutton Mandeville).

301   Bossy, *Community,* Chap. 11, for comparison of Benedictine Mission and English Mission in general. *CRS,* xxxii, 202-07. *CRS,* xxvi, 133. W. Nicholson, *St. Mary's Church, Hexham,* 38.

302   RA SP 57/115, 1721 Sept, Dawney to Lady Southcott.

303   Downside MS 255 (Everingham). *CRS,* xxiii (Brindle). Downside, North Province Cash Book 1806-09 (transcript)(Hengrave). Preston, Lancs. R.O. for Ormskirk transcript.

304   Woolhampton J XXVIII (Ormskirk). AH, Appendix, 521. J. C. Almond, 'Religious Parsimony at Brindle', 129-39.

305   Woolhampton, C I C (Hardcastle's Register).

306   Woolhampton, Sefton/Netherton Register. Downside, North
        Province Account Book 3, for Parlington Register.
307   See Appendix I for mission list of surviving registers. AH, II,
        142-3. Bossy, *Community*, 135.
308   AH, Appendix, 512; AB, 439. Downside MS 2013,
        'Catalogus',no. 17 (Bedale). Aveling, *East Yorkshire*, 48,55.
        Longley, *Heir*, 5-6. Downside, Ab. Arch. 43 (Wilitoft). AH,
        Appendix, 519. Downside MS 2013, p 13; North Province, Loose
        Accounts, 3A. Hull, Everingham DDEV/60/86b, 1742 2 May,
        Potts to Naylor (Whenby). Woolhampton, S. Province Mass
        Foundation Book, 78; Scott Box 75 Norfolk R. O. Box/Dis 9.
        CRS, xxvii, London 1927, 'Miscellanea', 9 (Oxburgh). AH,,
        Appendix 491 (Hengrave and Bury). *CRS*, xxiii, 116. Gillow,
        Dictionary, iii, 330 (Park Hall). *CRS*, xxviii, 153. Gillow, *Dic-
        tionary*, i, 50-51. AH, Appendix 483 (Thorndon). Berks R.O.
        D/EZ 14 F1. AAW Main series XL/34. Gillow, *Dictionary*, v,
        91-92 (Fawley).
309   e.g. Northumberland R. O. ZSW 213/11, 12. ZSW 456, 1753 31
        May entry.
310   Payne, *Missions*, xx, 89. *CRS*, ii, London 1906, 'Miscellanea'.
        AH, Appendix 488 (Cheam). Aveling, *West Riding*, 265.
        Downside MS 2013 no. 58 (Knaresborough). T. G. Ward and L.
        Warren, *The Manor Mission*, 19. Downside MS 2013, no. 19
        (Lindal). AH, Appendix, 535 (Tanfield). AH, 'Appendix', 518.
        Williams, *Bath and Rome*, 29 (Easton Grey). Wiiliams, 'Benedic-
        tine Missions', 271-73. A. Warne, *Church and Society*, 87. G.
        Dolan, 'English Benedictine Missions: Dorset, Devon, Cornwall',
        275 (Marlborough and Kirkham House). Longley, *Heir*, 5
        (Holme). Gillow, *Dictionary*, iv, 458, v, 433 (Kelvedon). Lille
        51, 1754 5 Oct, (Birtley).
311   e.g. AH, Appendix, 517. Estcourt and Payne, *Non-jurors*, 332.
        Woolhampton, Scott Box 91. Downside MS 2013 nos. 25,43,50
        (Lawkland). AH, II, 174; Appendix 522. Woolhampton, Scott Box
        135. Downside MS 2013 nos. 26,30,32, 34,36,40,41,pp 13,14
        (Cuerdon and Brindle). AH, Appendix 534. J.H.H., 'An Old
        Northern Mission', 28-35. E. Walsh and A. Forster, 'The
        Recusancy of the Brandlings', 52-55. A. Onslow, 'The Felling
        Mass Vestment', 26-28 (Birtley).
312   RA SP 222/13, 95.
313   See graph in Appendix II. RSRC, Anglia 5, ff50-53. Bossy,
        Community, 408-09, 422. J-A. Lesourd, *Les Catholiques dans la
        Société Anglaise 1765-1865*, i, 42-110. J. H. Whyte, 'The Vicars
        Apostolics' Returns of 1773', 205-14 (44 monks on mission). T.

G. Holt, 'A Note on Some Eighteenth-Century Statistics', 3-10, and his 'A Further Note', 160-61 (monks just under 10 of 11 missioners in 1773).

314 Woolhampton, Scott Box 52. Lille 30, 1778 31 Oct. Nancy H 77, 1771 28 Nov, Bennet to Naylor (quoted).

315 Lille 27, 1774 25 Mar, 1775 28 April. Lille 3, entry for 1775 6 Sept. Lille 35, 1774 15 Mar. T. G. Holt, 'Some Further Notes on the 18th Century Jesuit Priests in Essex': *Essex Recusant*, iv, 3, Dec.1967, 112 (for Witham Place).

316 Lille 35, 1773 26 Nov.

317 Lille 3, 1781 entry. Lille 66, 1780, 2 Oct, 17 Nov.

318 AH, II, 252. Lille 35, 1774 19 Mar.

319 Lille 30, 1780 26 Mar, 7 April, 26 May, 9 June, 6 July, 4 Aug, 1784 30 Jan (quoted). Lille 31, 1780 17 Aug, 16 Dec, Cowley.

320 Lille 66, 1779, 7 June.

321 Lille 27, 1775 30 June. Lille 3, 1776 Sept entry. Lille 33, 1777 10 Mar. Lille 54, 1778 24 Aug, 1779 23 Mar. AH, II, 249. Kirk, *Biographies*, 151.

322 Kirk, *Biographies*, 116. Lille 3, 1780 entry. Duffy, 'Over the Wall', 18.

323 Lille 35, 1778 30 June, 1785 10 Jan, 1 Mar, 1786 12 June, 22 July. Lille 30, 1782 26 July, 1785 22 Apri. Lille 46, 1789 10 May. Lille 63, 1785 5 Sept, 'The flock of Mr Gregson' (quoted). Birmingham Archdiocesan Archives, A 262, 258, Longley, *Heir*, 12. Bossy, *Community*, 258-60. W. Price, 'Three Jesuits', 165. Clifton 1792, 22.

324 AH, Appendix, 533 (Alderley), 508 (Leighland). Woolhampton, Scott Box, 47, 48 (Brise Norton). For families on the move: Lille 57, 1785 29 Oct, 1786 15 Feb, 26 Mar, (Selbys). Lille 67, 1788 17 Dec, 1789 4 Jan, (Standish). Lille 57, 1783 20 June; Lille 69 1782 10 June, 20 Dec, 23 Dec, 1783 18 Mar, (Arundells). Lille 35, 1783 12 July, (Constables). Lille 35, 1783 12 July, 1785 1 Mar, (Langdales and Butlers). Lille 30, 1784 19 July; 69, 1783 30 Dec; Lille 62, 1782 19 May, Swinburne. Lille 46, 1789 14 Feb, 10 May, (Howard of Corby). Lille 66, 1784 29 June (Canning). Lille 46, 1791 17 July, 16 Oct, 1792 27 Feb. Lille 66, 1792 3 Jan, (Lacon).

325 AH, Appendix, 522 (Gillmoss). Lille 67, 1779, 7 Dec.. Lille 31, 1780 1 Nov, Cowley. Dolan, *Lancashire*, 30. Robinson, *Dukes of Norfolk*, 174. Aveling, *West Riding*, 260-61. AH, Appendix, 511, AB, 469. Bossy, *Community*, 68-69 (Parlington). Clifton 1772-88, 79 (Parlington), 1792, 83.

326 e.g. AH, Appendix, 533 (Alderley).

327   Lille 30, 1779 27 Mar, 17 April.
328   Lille 35, 1773 9 Nov (quoted), 26 Nov, 28 Dec, 1774 25 Jan, 11 Feb.
329   Nancy H 77, 1770, 23 Mar, Bulmer to Naylor.
330   Lille 27, 1773 23 Aug (quoted), 20 Sept, 1774 8 June, 16 June. Lille 30, 1780 7 April. Lille 46, 1788 19 Feb, 1789 14 Feb, 1790 19 Jan, 2 May, 11 Sept, 17 Nov, 1791 4 Oct, 16 Oct, 17 Nov. Lille 47, 1790 5 Mar, Langdale (quoted). Lille 62, 1785 7 July, Turner (quoted). Lille 66, 1783 25 Dec.
331   Lille 3, 1769 entry. Lille 27, 1774 20 Sept, 1775 28 April, 1775 26 May, 1779 2 Feb (quoted). Lille 66, 1778 17 April. Bossy, *Community,* 152-60, for importance of women in the English Catholic community.
332   Lille 27, 1773 14 Dec, 1775 12 May, 16 May, 20 May, 25 Aug.
333   Lille 35, 1773 31 Oct. Lille 66, 1782 16 Aug, 2 Dec, 1783 8 Mar, 25 April, 1784 29 June, 5 Sept. Lille 55, 1786 14 Sept. Lille 46, 1787 18 July, 1788 4 Jan, 1789 14 Feb. Lille 30 1784 19 July. Woolhampton, Scott Box, 36-38, 40. Birt Box 10/A496. B. Charlton, *The Recollections,* 124, 127-28.
334   Nancy H 77, 1772 16 Sept, Fisher to Naylor. Lille 30, 1778 15 May, 8 July, 3 Aug, 31 Oct, 19 Nov, 1779 27 Mar, 24 July, 24 Sept, 1780 26 Mar, 26 May, 1783 3 June, 8 Aug, 1779 3 Dec. Lille 46, 1778 29 Oct, 1785 17 Sept, 1786 20 Mar (quoted), 15 April, 24 May, 1789 8 Sept, 17 Nov, 1791 18 Jan. Lille 31, 1786 27 June, Bolton. H. Aveling, 'The Catholic Recusancy of the Yorkshire Fairfaxes, III', 42-45. Aveling, *Northern Catholics,* 376,378,385. *Ampleforth Journal,* 'The King Against Father Bolton', 212-28. J. McCann, 'The Bolton Manuscript, (Part I)', 117-24. H. Willson, 'The Fairfaxes', 138-40. Upholland, Banister, Box II, 1786 1 Jan, 23 April. Clifton 1772-88, 69. Green, 'Bolton'.
335   Lille 35, 1777 17 Oct.
336   Lille 31, 1779 26 Aug, Cowley.. Lille 37, 1786 17 Aug.
337   e.g. AH, Appendix, 489-91 (Flixton); 517 (Lawkland). *Gentleman's Magazine,* June 1787, 545. Lille 46, 1787, 18 July, 1788 27 May, 13 June, 14 Aug, 2 Dec, (Beaufront).
338   Lille 30, 1779 27 Mar, 17 April. Lille 34, 1779 7 April, Daniel.
339   Lille 35, 1777 17 Oct (quoted). LIlle 30, 1778 8 July, 31 Oct, 19 Nov, 1779 27 Mar, 17 April, 24 July, 26 Aug, 24 Sept. K. Stewart, *A Short History.* W. J. Nicholson, 'Catholics in Morpeth', 11-21.
340   Lille 46, 1790 19 Jan, 20 April, 1791 16 Oct. AH, Appendix, 531, 539-40. B. Plumb, *The Warrington Mission,* 6-7.

341   UCM III/212.

342   Lille 30, 1778 3 Aug, 1780 26 May (quoted). Lille 35, 1778 11 Feb. UCM III/267. AH, Appendix, 516. Clifton 1772-88, 79.

343   1767 Returns in: J-A. Lesourd, *Les Catholiques dans la Société Anglaise, 1765-1865*, i, 70-208. E. S. Worrall (ed.), *Returns of Papists*, i-ii. A. M. Forster, 'Catholicism in the Diocese of Durham in 1767', 68-92. K. M. Macgrath, 'Catholicism in Devon & Cornwall, 1767', 136-66. 1780 Returns in Lesourd, i, Chap. VI.

344   See Appendix I for date of registers. Allanson, 'History', II, 219-20. *CRS*, iv, London 1907, 282. Bossy, 'Four Catholic Congregations', for Benedictine chaplaincies of Hesleyside and Biddlestone.

345   Birmingham Archdiocesan Archives: Salford entries in Coughton Register. Lille 31, 1779 20 Nov (quoted), Cowley. Lille 30, 1779 11 Nov, 24 Nov, 28 Dec, 1779 3 Dec, 1780 17 Sept.

346   J. Whyte, 'Returns', 210. Nancy H 77, 1770 25 May, Hadley to Naylor.

347   Lille 46, 1788 4 Jan, 1789 14 Feb, 1790 2 May. Lille 54, 1789 29 May. Lille 66, 1782, 28 Sept, 1783 8 Mar. AH, Appendix, 513, 514, 524. Gillow, *Dictionary*, i, 268, iv 469-70. Horney, *Sefton*, 118. Clifton 1792, 83; 1793, 11.

348   Lille 30, 1782 26 July, 1783 21 Oct, 2 Nov, 17 Nov, 1784 19 July, 1785 22 April. Lille 34, 1784 21 Feb. Lille 31, 1783 2 Dec, Catterall. Lille 46, 1786 6 June, 4 Nov, 1787 14 Jan, 18 July, 9 Nov, 1788 4 Jan. Northumberland R.O. ZSW 529/4, 530/1. Upholland, Banister, Box II, 1786 9 June. Clifton 1772-88, 79.

349   Lille 66, 1782 28 Sept (quoted). AH, II, 301-02.

350   Lille 66, 1783 27 Aug, 1784 5 Sept, 1787 22 Oct (quoted). Lille 67, 1785 13 Sept. Lille 28 1784 9 April. Lille 57, 1783 20 June, 1787 19 Oct. Clifton 1793, 11.

351   Lille 58, 1782 22 Mar. Lille 34, 1782 8 May, 1783 10 Jan, 21 Jan, 3 Mar, 1784 7 Jan, Digby. Lille 57, 1782 15 Aug, 23 Aug, 27 Aug, 1783 21 Jan, 1784 31 Jan, 19 June, 1785 8 Sept, 29 Oct, 6 Dec, 1786 7 Mar. Lille 30, 1782 19 Nov, 1784 15 April. Lille 66, 1784 29 June, 1786 6 May, 29 June, 1790 30 May. Lille 46, 1785 17 Sept. Lille 64, 1786 20 Feb. Lille 28, 1786 24 Feb, 1790 22 Jan. Clifton 1792, 83, 128.

352   Lille 66, 1784 29 Mar, 29 June, 1790 30 May. Lille 46, 1790 8 June, 29 Oct, 1792 27 Feb.

353   Lille 36, 1782 9 April, 12 July, Goolde. Lille 66, 1782 1 Aug.

354   Lille 30, 1783 10 May. Lille 46, 1787 4 Feb, 25 Feb, 9 Nov. Lille 45, 1790 10 Sept, 1 Oct, 17 Nov, Kennedy. Lille 53, 1790

23 Sept. Lille 28, 1790 1 Oct. Paris, Arch. Nat. DXIX 69/447.
Birt Box 10, 1790 30 Oct, Parker to Bennet. AB, 485 (note 3).

355 Lille 3, 1788 entry. J. Bossy, 'Catholic Lancashire', 54-69, for Lancs. expansion.

356 Lille 66, 1782 2 Dec, 1783 27 Aug. Lille 64, 1788 15 Jan. Lille 28, 1788 11 Nov, 1789 17 Mar, 1790 22 Jan. Lille 46, 1787 9 Nov, 1789 14 Feb, 1790 2 May. UCM IV/285b.

357 UCM III/129, for 1783 statistics. Lille 63, 1785 5 Sept, gives 203 for Sefton congregation. Lille 30, 1784 10 Nov. G. P. Connolly, 'The Secular Missioner of the North', 12.

358 Lille 3 1783 entry. Lille 46, 1790 2 May. Gillow, *Dictionary*, iii, 392-95. AH, II, 279-87. Bossy, 'Catholic Lancashire', 63-4. Bossy, *Community*, 338-39, 342-44. J. A. Hilton, The Case of Wigan', 1-7 (for a comparison with nearby Wigan). Blundell, *Lancashire*, i, 60-62. Burke, *Liverpool*, 12, 16-24. Clifton 1772-88, 43. Edwards. *Jesuits*, 135-6.

359 Lille 30, 1783 13 Feb, 27 Feb, 10 Mar, 21 Mar, 1 May, 10 May, 3 June, 8 Aug, 16 Aug, 23 Aug, 21 Oct (quoted). Lille 69, 1783 22 Aug. Lille 66, 1783 27 Aug.

360 Lille 30, 1783 2 Nov, 17 Nov, 1784 15 April, 25 May, 1785 22 April. Lille 46, 1785 17 Sept, 1786 20 Mar, 15 April, 26 May, 6 June, 12 June, 22 July, 4 Nov, 1787 4 Jan, 25 Feb, 13 Mar, 5 June, 18 July, 1788 19 Feb, 20 May, 24 Aug, 14 Sept, 1790 29 Oct. Lille 18 H 32, 1786 15 July, Propaganda to Gibson. Farm Street, College of St. Aloysius, 1787 14 April, Sewall to Meynell. UCM III/267. Clifton 1772-88, lxxxvi, 5, 30, 44, 69, 71.

361 Lille 30, 1784 30 Jan, 15 April (quoted), 22 April, 25 May, 19 July, 10 Nov, 1785 10 Jan. Lille 66, 1784 29 June, 5 Sept. Birmingham Archdiocesan Archives, C. 702 (a).AH, II, 305.

362 Lille 46, 1781 4 Jan, 19 Feb, 1787 24 Aug, 10 Oct, 1788 8 Oct, 2 Dec, 1789 10 May, 1790 19 Jan, 8 June, 11 Sept, 16 Dec. Lille 59, 1790 23 Aug, Simpson. Downside, Ab. Arch. 49. Birmingham Archdiocesan Archives, C. 984, for Berington. AH, II, 287, 527. *Orthodox Journal*, 1834 11 Jan, 145-46. *A Century and a Half*, 3. Blundell, *Lancashire*, i, 64.

363 J. A. Williams, *Post-Reformation Catholicism in Bath*, lxvi, Introduction, 120. Clifton 1791, 100; 1792, 62.

364 Lille 66, 1781 7 Mar, 2 Dec, 1783 25 April, 27 Aug, 1784 29 June, 5 Sept, 6 Dec. Lille 58, 1782 4 Jan, 6 Dec, 1785 5 May, 1786 20 Feb. Lille 51, 1785 28 Jan. Lille 65, 1786 8 Feb. Lille 28, 1786 24 Fe. Lille 57, 1786 7 Mar. Lille 67, 1786 19 April. Gillow, *Dictionary*, i, 292. AH, II, 264, Appendix, 505-06.

365   Lille 66, 1786 6 May, 29 June, 1787 22 Feb(quoted), 22
       Oct(quoted). Lille 65, 1786 12 Dec, 1787 21 Dec. Lille 70, 1787
       19 June. Clifton 1772-88, 24. Wilks, *A discourse*. 1791, 27, 37;
       1792, 124.
366   Lille 33, 1789 10 Aug, 14 Aug, 20 Oct, 11 Nov. Lille 35, 1790
       16 Sept. Williams, *Post-Reformation Catholicism*, lxvi, 61. Clifton
       1792, 37.
367   Lille 66, 1791 17 Mar, 27 Aug, 13 Oct, 1792 5 April(quoted), 5
       May, 8 July, 15 Aug(quoted). Lille 53, 1791 29 Mar. Clifton
       1791, 188, 190, 208; 1792, 7; 1793, 11.
368   Hanley, *Ormskirk*, 11-12.
369   Lille 66, 1784 25 Feb, 25 Mar.
370   The spiritual direction given by Benedictine missioners is dis-
       cussed in the chapter on Spirituality. For Benedictine vocations
       from the mission, see the chapter on the Monasteries, and for
       nuns, J. Gillow and R. Trappes-Lomax (ed.), *The 'Blue Nuns' of
       Paris*, 176. Lille 69, 1788 17 Feb, 16 April, 15 Aug. Lille 26 (3),
       1788 19 Feb, Ann.
371   Hull University, DDEV/60/86(b), 1735 14 May, Potts to Con-
       stable, 1739 17 June, Potts to Montgomery, 1742 18 April,
       Langdale to Potts, 1742/43, 2 Mar, Potts to Naylor.
372   *CRS*, xxvii, 271. Woolhampton, M. Bulmer's Mass Obligations
       Book. Lille 66, 1783 27 Aug. Lille 59, 1790 23 Aug, Simpson.
373   Coughton MSS 46/10, 14.
374   Scott, 'A Berkshire Benedictine Mission', 22,24.
375   *CRS*, iv (Holme Register). *CRS*, ii (Cheam Register). Bossy,
       'Four Catholic Congregations', for general statistics.
376   Lille 35, 1773 26 Nov. AB, 463.
377   *CRS*, xxii, 221. Aveling, *West Riding*, 257.
378   Lille 62, 1780 13 May, Throckmorton.
379   Lille 48, 1777 31 Jan. Lille 3, 1768 Oct. entry. Lille 26, 1779 9
       Sept, Barnes. Lille 56, 1780 29 Aug. Lille 31, 1779, 15 Dec,
       1780 20 Oct, Bulmer.
380   Potts and Bolton are treated elsewhere. For Farnworth,
       Northumberland R. O. ZSW, 454, entries for 1734 28 July, 1737
       10 Nov, 1739/40 4 Feb, 1741 29 May. ZSW 212/2,3,15,18;
       213/7. Bossy, *Community*, 258-60, for domestic chaplains being
       given useful tasks by patrons.
381   For Bath as centre, J.A. Williams, *Post-Reformation Catholicism*,
       i, Introduction, especially 63-6; Woolhampton, Scott Box 134. For
       Scarborough and Harrogate, Downside MS 255, and E.S. Worrall,
       Returns, 85.

382   Lille 27, 1775 28 April. M. B. Pembridge, *The Whole Duty of a Christian*, 1775, Part III. Clifton 1778-88, lxii.

383   Lille 31, 1778 5 July, 1779 25 April, Brewer.

384   Nancy H 77, for Mrs. Throckmorton's correspondence.

385   Nancy H 77, 1775 25 May, Fisher to Naylor. Nancy H 77 also contains Hadley's correspondence. Westminster City Archives, 344/174/159.

386   Lille 31, 1782 9 April, Brewer. Compare this with Bp. Walmesley's instructions to a missioner, in Williams, *Bath and Rome*, 52-3.

387   Woolhampton, M. Bulmer's Mass Obligations' Book. Lille 46, 1788 14 Sept, 1792 27 Feb. Lille 30, 1783 8 Aug, 16 Aug, 23 Aug. Lille 34, 1783, 8 Aug. Lille 49, 1784 19 Oct. Lille 62, 1784 22 Oct, Trafford.

388   Hull University, DDEV/60/84(g), 1726 5 Dec, Potts to Constable. 60/86(b), 1733 25 Sept, Potts to Farnworth. BL Add MSS 6401 f. 169, 1765 11 Oct, Simpson to Cole. Cole, *Journal*, 200-1. Almond, 'Religious Parsimony', 36. Ollard and Walker, 'Visitation Returns 1743', lxxi, page x; lxxii, 72. Lotherton Hall, West Riding, has a painting of late 18c of an Anglican vicar and Benedictine chaplain caught poaching by the latter's patron. Tablets at Linley (Bede Anderton) and Weston Underwood (Gregory Gregson).

389   For Corker, T.A. Birrell, 'James Maurus Corker', 466-7. Lunn, *Benedictines*, 133-5. Corker, *Queries*, 3-6.

390   RA SP 57/115, Dawney to Lady Cottington, Lady Barlow and C. Shaftoe and Lady Southcott. For gentry opposition to proselytism, see Bossy, *Community*, 276-7, and 'Lancashire', 57-9.

391   Bodleian, Rawlinson D 1348/12.

392   (A.M. Ramsay), *The Life of François de Salignac de la Motte Fenelon*, London 1723, 24-5. For Southcott's proselytism, RA SP 56/37, 57/116, 71/38.

393   AAW, Ep. Var. viii/7, 13. *CRS*, xxxii, 1932, 244, 381-88. Hull University DDEV/60/86, 1733 25 Sept, 10 Oct, 1735, 22 Aug, Potts to Constable; 1733 24 Oct, 1735 9 Aug, 14 Nov, Potts to Farnworth; 1733 20 Oct, Potts to 'Most Honoured Primate'; 1729 20 Dec, Helme to Potts. *HMC*, Carlisle MSS, 60. H. Willson, 'The Fairfaxes of Gilling', 2, 1931, 132-4. Aveling, *Northern Catholics*, 379.

394   Northumberland R.O., ZSW 213/11, ZSW 456, 1753 31 Dec, entry.

395   Williams, *Post-Reformation Catholicism*, lxv, 59-62.

396   *CRS*, ii, Cheam register, especially 324,335.

397   Birmingham Archdiocesan Archives, Coughton register.
398   *CRS*, xxiii, Brindle register. Lesourd, *Catholiques*, i, 312. Bossy, *Community*, 171-3, 178, 180-1, and 'Lancashire', 58, for household conversions. Duffy, 'Poor Protestant Flies', for evidence of the changing social class of converts.
399   AH, II, 306-10.
400   Woollett, *A Hundred Years*, 20-37. Durrant, *Memorials*, 9. Lille 27, 1774 23 Aug. Downside MS 212, 1763 Nov entry, for Barnes.
401   Williams, 'A Wiltshire Recusant Family', 147. AB, 339. Unwin, Charity Schools, 6, 14, 19.
402   *CRS*, iv, 267,273.
403   Nancy H 77, 1771 9 July, Bennet to Naylor (quoted), 28 Nov. Aveling, 'Catholic Recusancy of the Yorkshire Fairfaxes. Pt.IV', 102.
404   RA SP 57/115. AH, II, 158.
405   Lille 35, 1777 17 Oct. Bossy, 'Four Catholic Congregations', 94, 100-5, *Community*, 176.
406   Nancy H 77, 1770 25 May, Hadley to Naylor. For persecution in Shropshire against 'a noted preacher', see AB, 459.
407   Nancy H 77, 1770 21 April, Bulmer to Naylor; 1775 25 May, Fisher to Naylor.
408   J.P. Smith (ed.), *Lancashire Registers IV*, 125-6. Gillow, *Dictionary*, iii, 288. for mission architecture of the period in general, see R. O'Donnell, 'The Architectural Setting of Challoner's Episcopate'.
409   Aveling, 'Catholic Recusancy of the Yorkshire Fairfaxes, Pt. III', 33. G.Sitwell, 'The Brandsby Mission', 114.
410   Northumberland R.O., ZSW 212/5, and also ZSW 212/8, and *CRS*, xiv, 238.
411   Roebuck, *Constable of Everingham*, frontispiece, 20. Aveling, *East Yorkshire*,53. R.C. Wilton, 'Early Eighteenth-Century Catholics', 383-4.
412   A. Garnnons Williams, 'The Formation of a Yorkshire Estate', 29. J. Lomax (ed.), *Church Art from Catholic Yorkshire*. Westminster City Archives 344/93/138 for Stockeld's 1784 altar furnishings.
413   K.M. Longley, *Heir of Two Traditions*, 7-9. Little, *Catholic Churches*, 31.
414   Wigan R.O., D/DSt C4/4 10. Blundell, *Lancashire*, iii, 150 (Standish Chapel).
415   Information from Fr. W. Nicholson.

416 Lille 34, 1777 25 Aug (quoted), 1 July, Errington. *CRS,* xxvi, 225. Arundel Castle, MS A.1932.
417 AH, Appendix, 521, and other examples, 516, 529, and Lille 34, 1779 7 April, Daniel. Blundell, *Lancashire,* i, 137, 139, 141.
418 Whittle, 'St Alban's, Warrington', 147-56. *The Work of the Benedictines in West Cumbria,* 11. Plumb, *The Warrington Mission,* 7-8. For Ormskirk, see Blundell, *Lancashire,* iii, 99, and Woolhampton, J XXVIII. For Gillmoss, Blundell, *Lancashire,* i, 69, 72-3. For Netherton, Little, *Catholic Churches,* 44 and plate facing 48. For Brownedge, see Bolton, *Salford,* 80.
419 Preston, Lancs. R.O., RCH i/6. Little, *Catholic Churches,* 42-3. Blundell, *Lancashire,* ii, 68-70. Clifton 1792, 83.
420 *CRS,* xxiii, 8. Lille 3, 1788 entry. Westminster City Archives 344/93/138; 344/174/29-30, 175, 320-1, 331; 344/98/1562, 1575f. Clifton 1793, 30.
421 Downside, Ab. Archives, 49. *Orthodox Journal,* 1834 11 Jan, 145-6. AH, Appendix, 527. *A Century and A Half: St. Peter's, Seel Street,* 3,4.
422 Birmingham Archdiocesan Archives C. 984. Burke, *Liverpool,* 25-6, for chapel and its impressive music.
423 *CRS,* xxxiii, p xxiv, 170-2. Lille 28, 1779 2 Feb.
424 RA SP 222/13, 95. AH, Appendix 501-2. Williams, *Post-Reformation Catholicism,* lxv, 61.
425 Lille 31, 1778 17 May, July, Brewer. Lille 35, 1778 30 June. Lille 66, 1779 15 Sept. Lille 56, 1780 1 May. Williams, op. cit., 66.
426 Lille 66, 1778 12 Sept.
427 Lille 18 H 66, 1783 25 April, 27 Aug, 1784 29 June, 5 Sept, 6 Dec, Warmoll to Walker. Lille 64, 1784 4 Jan, 6 Dec. Lille 31, 1782 9 April, Brewer. Lille 51, 1785 28 Jan, Naylor to Pembridge. Williams, *Post-Reformation Catholicism,* lxv, 70.
428 Lille 66, 1778 17 April, 24 Aug, 12 Sept. For singing in embassy chapels in the 1770s of which Brewer would know, see E. E. Reynolds, 'Some Catholic Musicians of the 18th Century', 149-56.

429 W. Hudleston, *A Recantation Sermon,* London 1729, 34-5.
430 Lille 3, 1787 entry. AH, II, 304.
431 Lille 28, 1789 17 Mar. Lille 31, 1784, Burgess. R. O'Donnell, 'The Architectural Setting' 56, 60-1, for Wardour. Blundell, *Lancashire,* i, Appendix I, for Fernyhalgh.
432 For Baker and his teaching: CRS *xxii.* P. J. McCann and R. H. Connolly(ed.), 'Father Augustine Baker and English Benedictine Records'. Lunn, *The English Benedictines,* Chap. 8. Spearritt,

'The Survival of Medieval Spirituality'. McCann, 'Father Baker's Dame Gertrude', 163-64.

433   Examples of converts: E. A. Llewellyn: WM I 476-80, IV 2, II 530. M. P. Ellis: WM I, 278. J. M. Corker: Birrell, 'James Maurus Corker', 463,465-66. Lunn,*Benedictines*, 133. R. W. Reeve: CRS,xxxiii, 156, 157, 275, 276, 278, 280, 282, 285-87, 291, 293. WM III 1041f,II 391. R. B. Weldon:WM I 278 -II 399, M. Norman,'Dame Gertrude More', 202.

434   Spearritt, 'Survival', 293. Benedictines of Stanbrook, *In a Great Tradition*, 22. Lille 20 H 10 ff. 341-412, 479-80, 510, 539-552, 20 H 13 k, l, o, q (See Jones, 'Calendar'. Wood, *Athenae*, ii, col.531.

435   WM IV, 70.

436   e.g. A. Whitfield (ob. 1688), CRS, xxxiii, 276. N. Birt,*Obit Book*,(H. Connolly's annotated copy at Downside Abbey, p58). M. Corker (ob. 1715), *CRS*,xxxiii, 282. WM, IV 68, 70. B. Nelson (ob. 1699): Aveling, 'Benedictines', 167.

437   CRS xxxiii, 282,286. This monk was Dunstan Hutchinson; for examples of his spiritual poetry, see Dolan, 'A Lambspring Poet'. Lunn, *Benedictines*, 133-35. Birt Box 3/A97.

438   Birt Box 3/A139. WM V, 533-36. Birrell, *Catholic Allegiance*, 10-12, and his 'James Maurus Corker', 465-67. Corker, *Queries*, 1-3.

439   RA SP, 56/37, 57/116, 71/38

440   Lille 18 H 18.

441   Spearritt, 'Survival', 299-301, 303.

442   A. M. Ramsay, *The Life of François de Salignac de la Motte Fénelon*, London 1723, trans. by Nathaniel Hooke, 'a warm disciple of Fénelon'. For Ramsay and Fénelon, see G. D. Henderson, *Chevalier Ramsay*, 25-28, 46-47, and Chapter VII, and Chevallier, *Franc-Maçonnerie Française*, i, 16, 17.

443   RA SP 62/36.

444   For British interest in contemporary Catholic spirituality, and in Fénelon, Norman, 'Gertrude More',196, B. Lenman, *The Jacobite Risings*, 129-131. Pourat, *La Spiritualité Chrétienne*, IV, Chaps VII and X. Spearritt, 'Survival', 308, compares the seventeenth-century Anglican Little Gidding's spirituality to that of Baker. Ramsay, *Fénelon*, 216, 241,274,307. *DNB*, ix, 1922, 1176, Hooke's translation of Fénelon dedicated to the Earl of Oxford. .sp2 445) Lille 16.

446   See A. Cherel, *Fénelon au XVIIIe siècle en France*.

447   *CRS* xxxiii, 284,287. Spearritt, 'Survival', 303, 305. Aveling, 'Benedictines', 167.

448	Nancy, H 48
449	Lille 4. Lille 58, 1782 22 Mar. WM I 229-31, 239-40, II 505-06, III 923.
450	WM II, 524. Lille 4, 1774 11 Feb., Fisher.
451	Lunn, 'Origins', 279-80, 291-92, 286. WM V, 509. Arras, H (Downside Transcripts 180-86). Butler, 'Daily Life', 39-40.
452	For La Trappe, WM I, 227, 430-33, IV, 4, V, 524, 550. 558. WM III, 813-14, for hermits. AH, II, 115, for Weldon with the Camaldolese. Gillow, *Dictionary*, I, 42-43. *CRS*,lvi,145-51.
453	Lille 26, 1779 9 Sept, Barnes. Lille 31, 1780 13 Feb, Cowley. Lille 57, 1783 23 Mar (quoted).
454	WM, V 562, 555, quoting Denis Amelote's 'biographie psychologique' of Condren, (1643). Bremond, *Histoire Litteraire*, iii, 209, 341-58, 395. Orcibal, *Bérulle*. Hufton, 'The French Church', 18. P. Chaunu, 'Jansenisme', 46-55. Judge, 'The Congregation of the Oratory', 46-55. Paris, Bib. Nat. fonds francais 17774 f.26.
455	WM, VI, 593. AH, I, 588. Woolhampton MS XIII, 38.
456	WM, V 563, 570- VI 571- 72. For Jansenism around Dieulouard, see Taveneaux, *Le Jansenisme en Lorraine*, especially Book I, Book II: Chap. VI, Book III: Chap. II, Book IV: Chap. II.
457	The idea that Southcott helped the notorious Jansenist Dr. Richard Short to translate part of Quesnel's *Réflexions morales* is found in Clarke, *Strangers*, 164-70, Gillow, *Dictionary*, v, 515-16, Duffy, 'Rubb-up', 304, and is suggested in RSRC, Anglia 2, ff13-14, 34v, 35r, 54v; ff33r-45r makes it clear that Southcott did, in fact, translate Quesnel on John, but can be exonerated from the accusation of Jansenism because he translated it *before* the publication of *Unigenitus*. But BL Add MSS 20309/70 and 20309/110 has Southcott (to Cardinal Gualterio, 1723 3 Aug and 1723 8 Oct) condemning this rumour as emanating from the secular clergy, whom he blamed for distributing Jansenist works, with the connivance of the Vicars Apostolic. See also BL Add MSS 20309/57, 62, 110,118.
458	RA SP 62/136.
459	AAW, Ep. Var. xiii, 1753 5 Nov, J. Holden to C. Stonor.
460	Lille 15, T. Welch's appointment as censor(1769, 1773) by C. de Beaumont, on his full submission to *Unigenitus*. AR II, 214, Public acceptance of *Unigenitus* by the Congregation in 1745.
461	Downside MS 456. J. D. Crichton, 'Jansenism', 16-24. Paris, Bibliothèque Mazarine, MS 4057, St Edmund's Library Catalogue.

462 WM, VI 587. AH II, 188, 222-3. Nancy, H 72, permission to read forbidden books, save for Molinos and astrological works. AB, 386-9, for the apostate J. Peyton.

463 Lunn, *Benedictines*, 129. Davies, *Worship and Theology*, 463, 487-8. WM, I 387, 418, V 312, III 795, 799-802, 1041ff. Gillow, *Dictionary*, v, 463-65. Anstruther, 'Cardinal Howard', 321.

464 Ampleforth MS 169. Birt, A 206, MS, 'Modus Recitandi Rosarium', as recited at the Sodality of St. Gregory's, Douai in 1722. Editions of the same manuscript were published later at Douai and include additions of further Marian devotions. Scott, 'Confraternity', 152-4, for EBC Confraternity in 18th century.

465 *CRS*,xiv, 217-223. RSRC, 1708-27, Anglia f208. Woolhampton, Sefton/Netherton register contains a Rosary List, 1745-53.

466 *Congregationis Missionis*, Duaci 1689. *CRS*, xxxviii, 77. AH II, 72, 1717 Registration of patrons receiving the Benedictine scapular.

467 Lunn, *Benedictines*, 133,206.

468 J. Porter, *The Flowers of the Most Renowned Saints*, Doway 1632. V. Sadler, *Lives of the Saints*, 1677. WM, II, 482. W. Reeve, 'Athanasius Anglicus, or the Life of St Wilfrid', 1676. Gillow, *Dictionary*, V, 404.

469 WM, I, 229-40, III, 923-6, 936-41. For Gallican liturgical differences, see Johnson, *Guéranger*, Chap. III.

470 WM, II, 514-15. Gillow, *Dictionary*, I, 570. 'Among the Archives',DR, v, 1886, 39-40. UCM, IV, 290. Clifton 1791, 136.

471 Scott, 'Sacredness'.

472 AB, 355 n.1 (1725), 365-6 (1733).

473 Downside MS 576. Burton, *Challoner*, i, Chap xiv. Duffy, *Challoner*, 21, and R. Luckett, 'Bishop Challoner', 81,86. *Calendarium Congregationis Anglo-Benedictinae*, Duaci 1755. AH, II, 185.

474 Nancy, H 77, 1770, 21 April, Bulmer to Naylor. 1775 25 May, J. Fisher to Naylor. *E.B.C. Bullarium*, 56. Bossy, *Community*, 120-21. Lille 64, 1784 4 Jan. AH, II, 249. Lille 67, 1782 11 Dec, 1783 1 Jan, 19 Mar, 2 April, 14 April, 7 May, 24 June, 10 Dec, 1784 Dec, 1785 16 Feb, 16 May, 30 Sept. Lille 69, 1782 11 Dec, 1783 21 Nov, 30 Dec. Lille 28, 1783 11 April, 28 Oct, 1786 18 Aug. Lille 57, 1783 25 Oct, 1787 19 April. Lille 58, 1785 7 Jan, 1787 19 April, 1790 4 June. Lille 64, 1784 4 Jan. RActa 153/13 ff187-9. 154/15. RSOCG 862/13; 867/15.

475   Power, St. Cuthbert, part 2', 28. Hull, DDEV/60/86b, 1737 30
May, Potts to Farnworth. Lunn, *Benedictines,* 133, and footnote
61. Scott, 'Some Notes'.

476   Lille 64, 1791 22 Aug. UCM IV, 290. Clifton 1791, 136.

477   Although the *Constitutiones Missionis* 1689 (8:21) had ordered the
recitation of the monastic breviary on the mission if possible, there
is much evidence for the use of the Roman breviary here rather
than the monastic continental breviaries (e.g. Downside MS 531
f164). The houses in France seem, on the other hand, to have
preferred the Maurist office books, and Lambspring, those of the
Bursfeld Congregation and Einsiedeln.

478   *Constitutiones Missionis,* 8:17-21.

479   For sermons, see Wilton, 'Annals', 277, and Downside, Ab.
Arch. 13. For Bordley, see UCM III, 279c. Clifton, Misc.Items,
54.

480   Duffy, 'Richard Challoner 1691-1781: A Memoir', 2, 16-17.
Luckett, 'Bishop Challoner', 80-82. Duffy, 'Richard Challoner
and the English Salesian Tradition', 449-455. Duffy, 'The English
Secular Clergy', 214-230. McManners, *Death,* 198. 18th-century
Benedictine mission libraries of Netherton, Lancs. and Wooton
Wawen, Warwicks., now at Woolhampton, include examples of
many of these spiritual works owned by monks. I am grateful to
Mr John Aveling for a list of provenances of books belonging to
missionary monks, now at Ampleforth.

481   AH, I, 614. AR, 189, 214. Clifton 1772-88, 8.

482   Townson, *Enchiridion,* 31-32. For confessional manuals in the
eighteenth century, McManners, *Death,* 245. T. Deutscher,
'Seminaries', 306-07.

483   Downside MS 678, read by Gregory Riddell, the Benedictine
censor, at Lambspring. J. W. O.S.B., *The Creed Expounded,*
1735. AB, 394. Northumberland R. O., ZSW 454, 1735 25 June
entry. Downside MS 531, 1735 22 Nov entry.. For catechism in
18th century, see Delumeau, *Catholicism,* Introduction, Part II,
Chap. 4.

484   Gillow, *Dictionary,* iii, 46-47. Downside MS 595, Greenwood's
'Catechistical Instructions', 1717. Downside MS 532,
Greenwood's 'Catechistical Instructions, or A Short Method of
Catechising Children', 1721. Downside MS 533, Greenwood's
'Catechistical Instructions.. originally in French by..(the) Bp. of
Montpellier', 1736. Downside MS 635, T. A. Constable, 'An
Abridgement of Christian and Catholic Doctrine', 1703.

485   Downside MS 596, F. Bruning, 'Compendium totius sacrae
Scripturae', 1732. Downside MS 532, F. Bruning, 'Epistles and

Gospels for Lent', 1734. A revision of the work of Gregory
Mallet (ob. 1681) by adding to it Gother's *Reflections*, (1686).
Downside MS 534, F Bruning, 'Reflections on the Epistles and
Gospels', 1731. RA SP 57/115. Hull DDEV/60/86b, 1733/4 i
Mar, Potts to Farnworth.

486 Downside MS 566.

487 R. Porter, *English Society*, 296-97, O. Chadwick, *The Popes*,
7-11, Doyle, *Order*, 153, Malcomson, *Life*, 89-92, for decline of
witchcraft.

488 J. M. Blom, *English Primer*, 159 and Chapter VI. RA SP 57/115,
entry for mid-April 1721.

489 Schmitz, *Histoire*, vi, 311. Gillow, *Dictionary*, i, 218, iv, 458-9.
Kirk, *Biographies*, 158. AB, II, 441.

490 Downside, Box 783, Sermons and instructions of Oswald Smithers
O.S.B. (ob. 1725). Downside MS 596, F.Bruning (ob. 1747),
'Compendium totius sacrae scripturae'.

491 Woolhampton, MS C/111/R, Section 7, 'For a Right Understanding of the Mass'. Downside, North Province Account Book 3,
40-46, 1761-66, purchase of catechisms. Bossy, *Community*,
272-5.

492 For the structure of eighteenth-century catechisms: Burton,
Challoner, ii, 159-62. S. Marron, 'Bishop Challoner', 111-20. B.
Pickering, 'Bishop Challoner', 6-15.

493 Lille 54, 1778 24 Mar. Lille 66, 1778 20 Oct, 1779 15 Feb.
Clifton 1789-90, 173.

494 (A. B. Macdonald), *The Lay-Mans Afternoon Devotion*, Preston
1778, 1793. Rev. Mr. McDonald, *A Companion to the Altar*,
Liverpool 1792. Blom, *Primer*, 161. Aveling, 'Benedictines', 166.
Gillow, *Dictionary*, iv. 369-72.

495 Downside MS 212.

496 Gillow, *Dictionary*, iv, 370. Aveling, *Handle*, 332. Lille 36,
1791, 16 Jan, 3 July, Gregson. Northumberland R. O., RCD
1/1/15. Birt 10/H95. Clifton 1791, 6, 8, 17, 20; 1792, 32, 33.

497 e.g. Vernet, 'Spiritualité', 647-9.

498 Vovelle, *Piété*, 266-76.

499 Aveling, 'Benedictines', 166-7.

500 For this crusade, see Viguerie, 'Quelques aspects'.

501 Lille 69, 1779 30 April, 1782 3 Mar, 1786 17 Aug, 5 Oct, 29
Nov. Daniel-Rops, *Church*, 66.

502 Lille 69, 1783 18 Mar, 15 April (quoted). For disasters' effect on
society, see Plongeron, *Théologie*, 19-29.

503 For Pastorini, see Chapter V, and Scott, 'The Times', and my
forthcoming article in *JEH* (1985).

504   For Labre, see *DR*, 'Among the Archives', vi, July 1887, 131, Plongeron, *Théologie*, 27, Chadwick, *Popes*, 23-4, and Daniel-Rops, *Church*, 169-72. Clifton 1778-88, lxxxvii.

505   Woolhampton, Cab/I/RJ, 1771, A Collection of Sermons by B. C. Paris.

506   AH II, 39, 58; RASV, Fondo Albani, Tome X, 145/f37, for Professors of Philosophy, and Theology. Lunn, *Benedictines*, 182 for decline of Douai.

507   WM, I, 481,522, IV, 51. For Thomist theses: T. Southcott's *Conclusiones theologicae...ad Summam Theologiae S. Thomae Aquinatis..una cum annexis additionalibus ad duos priores libros Decretalium Gregorii Noni*, Duaci 1695. Nancy H 83 and Lille 16, and DR, vi, 'Bibliographia Gregoriana', 137, for G. Riddell presiding over J.Stourton's disputation, *Theses Theologica ex Secunda Secundae D. Thomae Aquinatis*, Duaci 1700. Burton and Nolan (ed.), 'The Douay College Diaries:The Seventh Diary', 59. For later theses, and diplomas from the Sorbonne, Birt 6/A349,A357,A358. For Brewer's and Wilks's theses: Lille 3, , 1770 July 21 entry.. Gillow, *Dictionary*, III, 371-72. J. B. Brewer, *Theses theologico-Hebraicae de Prophetia, in Sorbona propugnanda*, Paris 1766. J. C. Wilks, *Theologico-Hebraicae Chaldaicae et Graecae Theses*, Paris 1766. BN MS Latin 9154-61, 15440, for list of English Benedictine Parisian graduates.

508   WM, IV, 52-56, 79-80, 270; VI, 509, 585.

509   WM, I 25, 144-45;IV 267-68;V 553,576,587-90. Scott, 'The Collector'.

510   Woolhampton, Weldon, 'The Memorials', 5 vols, 1707-12. Woolhampton and Downside, 'Chronological Notes', 1709, 1711. B. Weldon, *Chronological Notes*, Worcester 1881 (1709 ed.). B.L. Add. MSS 10118, 'Collections for a Life of James II'. For Weldon, E. Bishop, 'The Beginning of Douay Convent', 21-30.

511   Douglas, *English Scholars*, 319.

512   Lunn, *Benedictines*, 108-10, 131-3. D. Farmer, 'Historical Influences', 5-16. The convert monk Richard Reeve was also in this tradition, see Clark, *Wood's Life*, ii, 264, 268-70, 273, 275-6, 280, 401; iii, 253, 295, 320, 350.

513   WM, I, 2, 14.

514   J. D. Martin, 'The Antiquarian Collections', 188-89. WM, IV, 74, 81, 82. Scott, 'Conspirator'.

515   Lambeth Palace MS 1770 ff. 58v, 71-3v. Gillow, *Dictionary*, iii, 642-46. F. Cabrol, 'Bossuet', 551, 558.

516   Johnston, *A Vindication*, 112.

517   Bossuet, *An Exposition*, (trans. and preface by H. J. Johnston), 4,7,8,20.

518   *Assurance*, 5,6,41,202. Martin, 'Antiquarian Collections', 40,42.

519   Douglas, *Scholars*, 330-53.

520   Hearne, *Collections*, ii, 19. *Remains*, 417.

521   Linker, 'Catholics', 154, for Hearne and Throckmortons. Hearne's 1715 ed. of John Leland's 'Collectanea' was a gift of Charles Eyston to Dieulouard in 1725, and is now at Woolhampton.

522   Hearne, *Collections*, vi, 329, 333.

523   Oxford, Bodleian, Rawlinson: Letters VII, 133,137.

524   Oxford, Bodleian Library, Rawlinson: Letters VII, 134,135. Aveling, *Northern Catholics*, 386.

525   Oxford, Christchurch, Wake Letters 22/152, 153, 246, 339, 341, 342; 30/181, 241, 253. Hearne, *Collections*, viii, 36,93-94,104,106-07. Oxford, Bodleian Library, Rawlinson VII, 136.

526   BL Sloane 4047 f.312-13. Aveling, *Northern Catholics*, 385. Woolhampton possesses the Sefton/Netherton libraries, and much of the South Provincial's. For individuals' libraries: Nancy H 77 (W. P. Naylor's), and Birt 10/A495 (M. B. Pembridge's), and Lille 58, 1788 9 Feb (G. Sharrock's), and Downside A/C Bk. I (W. A. Caldwell's).

527   The Guisborough Breviary, for instance, belonged to T. A. Constable (ob. 1712). See Egbert, *The Tickhill Psalter*, 109-11, 205-08. For suggestion of Benedictine chaplain's involvement in collection of books from Durham Priory, see Doyle, 'Library', 89-91. Ker, *Medieval Manuscripts*, xiii-xiv, 24, 381-3, 412-19, 419-77 for medieval manuscripts still in the possession of the monasteries.

528   For St. Gregory's, H. R. Duthilloeul, *Catalogue des Manuscrits*, and Dehaisnes, *Catalogue*, nos.341, 491, 545, 788, 852, 921, 929. For St. Edmund's, Paris, Bibliothèque Mazarine, MS 4057 (Appendix describes three illuminated MSS). A. Franklin, *Les anciennes bibliothèques*, ii, 369-71. For St. Lawrence's, Nancy H 83. For Lambspring, D. Rees, 'Lamspringe', 313-15, and Zarnecki, *English Romanesque Art*, 93, for Lambspring's possession of the St. Alban's Codex. For medieval manuscripts held at present in the three oldest communities, see Ker, *Medieval Manuscripts*, ii.

529   At Woolhampton, Franklin, *Bibliothèques*, ii, 369-71.

530   WM, IV, 263, for rules. AH, II, 73. J. McCann, Ampleforth, 128. (A. Calmet et A. Fange), *Documents inédits sur correspon-*

dence de Dom Calmet et Dom Fange, Nancy 1875, 28, and Bodleian, Carte 222/62, for Dieulouard fire.

531 WM, IV, 4, 49.
532 WM, IV,323;V, 321. Woolhampton, Hewlett, 'Annals', 81.
533 RA SP 147/64.
534 e.g. WM, VI, Addenda, 1-14, For son of King of Tartary's acquaintance with the monks in Paris and with Bossuet.
535 For the crucial role of Jacobitism, see Chapter VII and Chaussinand-Nogaret, 'Une Elite insulaire', Lenman, 'From Despair to Integration', 7-10, Cruickshanks (ed.), *Ideology and Conspiracy,* 10-11.
536 AB, 415. O'Leary, 'The Last of the Southcotes', 22-29. Sherburn (ed.), *The Correspondence of Alexander Pope,* i, 122, 151-2, 155, 233,236; ii, 294; iii, 6, 18. A. Pope, *Epistolae,* IV, 16. RA SP 57/116; 64/33,38,171; 66/135,159,177: 67/35,86,93,94,99; 68/138; 69/36,69; 72/147; 77/97,132,176; 125/100; 127/93; 139/84,97. Paris, A. N. V5 1255. Kirk, *Biographies,* 215. Scott, 'Sacredness'. W. S. Lewis and W. H. Smith (ed.), *The Correspondence,* ix, 116. Mack, *Pope,* 155.
537 Oxford, Christchurch, Wake Letters 22/339 (quoted). For Ramsay, see Henderson, *Chevalier Ramsay,* Neveu, 'A Contribution', 142, and Gregg, 'The Jacobite Career', 191. Lautel, 'André Michel Ramsay'.
538 Paris, A. N. M865/24. Henderson, *Ramsay,* 109. Palmer, *Catholics,* 80, 97. Hazard, *European Thought,* 94 (for Houtteville). Bodleian, Carte 226/350.
539 For Ramsay, Freemasonry and Jacobitism: Henderson, *Ramsay,* 167-68. Chevallier, *Franc-Maçonnerie,* i, 16-24, 75-82. Nordmann, 'Les Jacobites écossais', 94-96. Chaussinand-Nogaret, 'Elite', 116.
540 Woolhampton, Cab. S/r, 'Memoirs of the Society of St. Edmund'. Woolhampton, Cab 3/K, Catalogue of the library of the Society of St. Edmund. Woolhampton, Parker Papers: Declaration of the property of St. Edmund's, Paris (describes the Society's library *c.* 1791). Cunningham, 'Society'.
541 'Memoirs', G. A. Walker, 1749 1 July, 'Parallel between the effects of thunder and lightning, and those of Electricity etc'. 1749 15 Nov., 'Of the Rising of Vapours'. 1749 2 Dec., 'Some Observations on the Flames of Candles'.
542 Palmer, *Catholics,* 109-12, on contemporary interest in inhabited planetary systems and the possibility of infinite numbers of Saviours.

543	'Memoirs', J. P. Naylor, 'Antient Coins'. T. Welch, 'An Essay on the Computation of time of the Ancients... according to the Principles of Sir Isaac Newton, to which will be added some tables'.
544	'Memoirs', T. Welch, 'A Dissertation upon the Origine, Nature, Doctrine and Extinction of the Druids'.
545	'Memoirs', B. Catterall, 'Dissertatio de variis scripturas sensibus, et Regulis ad eam intelligendam observandis'.
546	'Memoirs', C. Walmesley, 'A Dissertation upon the Principle of Action in Beasts'. Palmer, *Catholics,* Chap. VI, for discussion of the 'âme des bêtes' controversy. K. Thomas, 'No Compassion', 6. McManners, *Death,* 156, 163.
547	'Memoirs', T. Welch, 'Vindication of the ancient Benedictin Monks from Slanderous aspersions cast upon them by Wm. Guthrie in his history of England'.
548	'Memoirs', A. Walker, 'On HRH Charles Prince of Wales'. P. Naylor, 'An English Monarch of right against one in fact only'.
549	There are some thirty pieces of verse by John Barnes, written between 1751 and 1756. Identical pieces also found in his own MS anthology at Woolhampton (CIII L).
550	Clifton 1789-90, 89. For Walmesley's scientific background see Scott, 'The Times' and RSOCG 765/9.
551	Downside, MS 531, 113.
552	Scott, 'A Monk's View', 3-12. Clavering, 'Catholics', 15-24.
553	'Memoirs', 'Extract of a letter from Philip Howard Esq. For Howard, Gillow, *Dictionary,* iii, 439. Kirk, *Biographies,* 131.
554	McManners, *Death,,* 28-29 and Chadwick, *Popes,* 157-8, for the priest as medical expert.
555	WM, I, 223. BL Add. MSS 28,228 f329, for Augustine Southcott's interests here. For Joseph Whittell's interests: Woolhampton, Cub 3s.lL, 'A Collection of Receipts in Physick, Surgery, Cookery &c., London Feb. 17th 1753'. Berkshire R. O., D/EBt F26, Bryan Barrett's Note Book, 1752-53, with 'receipts' from monks in Paris, some of which are identical to those in preceding 'Collection'.
556	Lille 27, 1774 16 June, 1 July, Bennet.
557	Kirk, *Biographies,* 107. J. King and C. Ryskamp (ed.), *The Letters,* ii 353, 561, iii 393, 396, iv, 77, 79, 88, 292, 382, 400, 453. Nancy H 77, 1771 3 Jan. Gregson to Simpson.
558	Paris Bib. Mazarine, MS 4057. Woolhampton for Paris Catalogue of 1786. Woolhampton MS XIII, 124-29.
559	Gwynn, 'Theologian', 259-68, Palmer, *Catholics,* 41, 51, 65-75. Hazard, *European Thought,* 119-20.

560   Dolan, 'English Benedictine Missions: Bedfordshire, 61-70. King,
        Letters, ii 615, 620-21, iii 156-7, 371, 374.
561   BL Add. MSS 6401 f169. Cole, *A Journal,* 18-24, 137-45,
        283-86. Linker, 'English Roman Catholics', 154.
562   Russell, 'Dr. Johnson', 139-48. Tyson and Guppy (ed.), *The
        French Journals,* 60-61, 97, 110, 153-4, 171, 219, 222-27.
        Osborn, *Dr. Johnson,* 1-18. Hilles (ed.), *New Light,* 297ff.
563   Lille 67, 1778 8 April, 1780 6 Mar. Farm St, Thorpe, f.221v.
564   Lille 50, 1778 24 Mar. Lille 67, 1778 14 Mar, 8 April, 19 Aug,
        11 Nov, 29 Nov, 1779 16 April, 12 May, 9 June, 30 June, 11
        Nov, 7 Dec, 1780 19 Jan, 6 Mar, 29 Nov. Lille 69, 1779 8 Aug.
        Lille 34, 1782 7 Feb, Fermor. Gibbon, *Memoirs,* 142. Craddock,
        Young Edward Gibbon, 223, 227, shows Byres as the young
        Gibbon's cicerone. *Critical Review,* vi.
565   Lille 27, 1774 22 Feb. Lille 63, 1775 25 Feb. BL Add. MSS
        331000 f69 and 35520 f47, f131. Lille 67, 1778 5 April, 12 May,
        9 Aug, 11 Nov, 7 Dec. 1779 12 May, 8 Dec.1780 6 Mar, 19
        Nov. Rope, 'Notes', 87-91. Swinburne, *Travels,* The Preface.
566   Belsey, 'Cameos', 48-49. Friedman, 'Sir Thomas Gascoigne',
        17-23. Waters's artist friends also included Christopher Norton,
        Robert Strange, Thomas Jenkins, and William Parry. See Denvir,
        Art, Design and Society, 8, 101-03, 104, 106, 110, 111, 112,
        148-49, 162-63, 171-72, 194, 252-53. Wildenstein & Co., *Sou-
        venirs,* 9, 12, 13. All the above works are recent. There are
        extensive bibliographies for each of the artists mentioned. Lille 67,
        1782 14 April, 26 June, 11 Dec. 1783 1 Jan, 14 April, 24 June,
        10 Dec. 1784 28 Jan, 5 May, 4 Aug. 1785 16 Feb, 12 May. 1786
        19 April. 1787 28 Mar, 16 May, 4 July, 28 Nov. 1788 3 Jan, 25
        June, 8 Oct. 1789 4 Jan, 27 May, 9 Dec. 1790 24 Feb, 8 April,
        21 April, 19 May. 1791 4 Jan, 17 Aug.
567   Dennistoun, *Memoirs,* ii, 18, 116-18. L. Lesley, *Connoisseurs,*
        11, 144, 153-69, 226. Hodgkinson, 'Christopher Hewetson',
        42-54. Ford, 'James Byres', 446-61. Clifton, 1789-90, 152.
568   Lille 18 H 50, 1778 14 Mar, Mylne to Walker. Lille 18 H 67,
        1778 14 Mar, 8 April, 12 May,11 Nov. 1779 20 Jan. 1780 6 Mar,
        29 Nov. 1788 17 Dec. 1789 4 Jan, Waters to Walker. BL, MSS
        41, 189f.80.
569   Lille 67, 1791, 17 Aug.
570   McManners, Death, 337. Gillow, *Dictionary,* iv, 371. A.
        McDonald, *Some of Ossian's Lesser Poems, rendered into verse,*
        Liverpool 1805. A. McDonald, *Fingal, an Epic poem, by Ossian,*
        Liverpool 1808.
571   For Hooke, Palmer, *Catholics,* 40-41, 51, 117-26.

572   Birt 6, 349, 357, 358: Naylor's certificates. For Brewer and
        Hooke: Lille 27, 1773 3 Dec. 1774 4 Jan, 22 Feb, 25 Mar. Lille
        8. Nancy H 77, 1772 25 Sept, Brewer's books at Paris. Bromley,
        Sacramentis, for Brewer presiding over defence of thesis.
573   Lille 3, 1770 21 July entry. Woolhampton CIR (H), 18. C. Wilks,
        Theses. For Asseline, Chinnici, *Enlightenment*, 103.
574   Green, *Congregation*, 30. Lille 67, 1779 16 June, 7 July, 24 Aug.
        For Muratori, see Chadwick, *Popes*, 30, 395-402. Welch was
        used by enlightened French theologians to carry heterodox books
        back with him from England, see A.Jobert *Un théologien au siécle
        des lumières: Bergier*, Lyon, 1987, 120.
575   Lille 24, 1762 5 June. See also, Lille 67, 1783 10 Dec.
576   Lille 66, 1784 29 June.
577   Lille 66, 1789 17 Mar. Northumberland R. O., RCD/1/1/55.
578   Lille 69, 1777 7 Dec. 1778 24 Sept. Lille 3, 1774 28 Aug entry.
        Lille 31, 1778 7 Dec, 17 Dec. 1780 2 Oct, 1 Nov. 1781 22 May.
        1782 18 Mar, Compton. Lille 31, 1779 19 July, 26 Aug, 20 Nov.
        1780 7 July, 17 Aug, 9 Oct, Cowley. Lille 56, 1780 2 Aug. Lille
        28, 1782 21 June. Lille 67, 1782 26 Jun
579   Lille 69 1782 1 July.
580   Lille 28, 1783 6 May. Lille 66, 1782 1 Aug, 16 Aug, 28 Sept.
        1783 27 Aug. Lille 30, 1782 1 July. Lille 69, 1782 11 July, 27
        Oct. 1783 18 Mar, 15 April. A lage number of monks who
        apostatised ended up, like Compton, as Anglican clergymen. Since
        their Orders were recognised by the Church of England, this was
        an obvious step to make, and it is seen most vividly in the career
        of Benedict Mordaunt who apostatised in 1709: see Oxford,
        Christchurch, Wake Letters 10/175, 176; 23/68.
581   AB, 471. Gillow, *Dictionary*, i, 190-92. Kirk, *Biographies*, 116.
        Duffy, 'Ecclesiastical Democracy I', 201-07. Duffy, 'Over the
        Wall', 17-19. Woolhampton,Cab. IV, 1773-93, St. Edmund's
        Account Book, for books bought by Hawkins. Lille 3, 1780 entry.
        Lille 31, 1780 16 Dec, Cowley. Lille 66, 1778 17 April. 1779 3
        Aug. 1780 17 Nov.1783 25 Dec. Lille 67, 1779 24 Aug. Lille 69,
        1782 3 Mar. Lille 64, 1782 27 Mar. Lille 57, 1787 17 Jan.
        Clifton I, xxi.
582   Aveling, 'The Education', 135-52. AR, 213. Woolhampton
        C/III/R,
        'A Method of Studies...adapted by R. Rev. C. Walmesley O. S.
        B.'. For Walmesley's interest in studies, see AH' II, 211, and
        Lille 64, 1779 14 Oct. Aveling, *Northern Catholics*, 385-6, *West
        Riding*, 267, *The Handle*, 311, and 'Benedictines', 167-68. Lunn,

Benedictines, 186. Woolhampton MS XIII, 65, 69, 82, 91, 103, 111, 118, 123, 129.

583   Lille 56, 1777 10 July. 1778 9 Oct. 1780 6 Mar. Clifton I, xxi. BL. MSS 4320f.93. Newton's teachings remained acceptable up until the Revolution, see the Newtonian philosophy theses of April 1789 from Dieulouard, in Paris, Bibliothèque Nationale, Z Senne 2725 (11).

584   Birt, *Downside,* 60-67. Almond, *Ampleforth,* 207-10. Lille 56, 1777 19 July. 1778 8 April, 21 April, 6 July, 8 July, 9 Oct, 30 Nov. 1779 2 Jan, 16 May, 13 July, 18 Aug, 28 Aug. 1780 20 Feb, 6 Mar, 1 May, 30 May, 29 Au. Lille 31, 1778 20 Sept. 1779 20 May, 12 June, 17 June, 23 July, 13 Aug, 26 Aug, 20 Nov, 26 Dec. 1780 13 Jan, 17 Aug, Cowley. Lille 63, 1778. Lille 38, 1778 31 Oct. Lille 66, 1779 7 June. Lille 67, 1779 9 June. Lille 64, 1779 14 Aug. Lille 69, 1780 1 April. Nancy H 79 (Downside transcripts 829), 1780 28 Aug, Welch to Walker.

585   Lille 10, 1781. Lille 66, 1784 25 Feb. 1789 17 Mar.

586   Lille 3, 1784 entry. Lille 57, 1782 18 May, 23 Aug. Lille 69, 1782 11 July. Lille 65, 1783 20 Aug. Lille 33, 1786 17 April. Lille 31, 1786 6 May, 15 Sept, 23 Nov, 16 Dec. 1787 10 Sept, Cowley.. Lille 31, 1787 15 Mar.1788 5 Aug, 3 Sept, Coupe.

587   Lille 10(6), 1787. Lille 67, 1789 27 May. Lille 48, 1792 5 Aug, Mann.

588   Lille 18 H 10.

589   Lille 10, speech to 1781 General Chapter. Lille 10(4), 1784. Lille 20 H 14 c, d, h, i. 20 H 4 b.

590   Lille 10(7), 1788.

591   Lille 69, 1784 31 Oct. Lille 64, 1784 6 Dec.

592   Scott, '"The Times"'. Picot, *Mémoires pour servir,* iv, 570-1. Plongeron, *Théologie,* 19-27. Doyle, *Order,* 155. Becker, *City,* 41, 137. Clifton I, xxxvi; 1791, 217. Picot, *Memoires...*

593   Walmesley's copy of Hamilton at Woolhampton. Woolhampton, St. Edmund's Account Book, entry for 1781 24 April, 10 copies of the *General History* from Walmesley to Frisi. Lille 64, 1784 6 Dec. Clifton I, 1772-88, 8 Jan (printed enclosure), xxi, lxii, 2, 6, 73; 1789-90, 2, 119; 1791, 37; 1792, 42; 1793, 113.

594   For earlier history, Lunn, *Benedictines,* 176-77, 186-193.

595   e.g. Hull DDEV/60/86(b), 1734 7,27 June, 9 Aug., Potts to Stourton. 1736/37 12 Feb., Potts to Farnworth. 1737 12 Dec. Potts to Reynoldson. Roebuck, *Constable,* 103, 160 (footnote). AAW, Ep. Var. iii, 71. AR II, 198. Downside MS 205.

596   WM, IV, 87, Appendix.

597   *CRS,* xl, 152, 181, 186-7, 189.

598   London, Forest Gate: Antony Parkinson,'The State of the Prov-
        ince 1716', for Osmotherley. AH II, 123.
599   Examples of bursaries in: Woolhampton, 'St. Edmund's Mass
        Obligation Book', 61-69. Birt 3/A96, A97, 141, and MS 205
        passim. WM IV, 271-72. AR II, 182, 191, 198; AH, II I59, 139,
        148.
600   RSOCG 676/21 ff414r-16r. Hull DDEV/60/86(b), 1733 2 Mar,
        Potts to Constable, 1733 17 Oct, Potts to Rogers. AH II, 140.
        Woolhampton, 'Mass Obligation Book', 65-66. UCM III/78. RA
        SP 178/176.
601   AR 178'. Birt 6/A310, 332, 607. Woolhampton, Scott Box 2 a-e,
        for a wholly lay fund. AR II 199, (61-62), 200 (63-64).
        Woolhampton, 'Mass Obligations Book', 63-64.
602   WM, II, 420, 423, 483. Beales, *Education,* 247, 255, 258.
        Aveling, *Catholic Recusancy in York,* 104-6. AH, I, 550, AR,
        658-59. Nancy H 79, (Downside transcript).
603   RSOCG 676/21 ff414r-16r, 678/16 ff271-2; RSRC, Anglia 3,
        ff560-61; RActa 103 21/ff397-9, 104 16/ff98-102. G. V. C., *List.*
        Birt, *Downside School,* 33, 36, 39, 40. RA SP 178/176. Nancy H
        50. WM, VI, 601, 603. Berington, *State,* 176, gives 30 students at
        St. Gregory's in 1780.
604   Nancy H 48. Aveling, 'Pensioners', 35-39. WM, VI, 589-90. AH,
        II, 273.
605   Downside MS 205.
606   Beales, *Education,* 239. Lunn, *Benedictines,* 190-1. WM, II, 391.
607   Woolhampton, 'Mass Obligations Book', 61-9, and CI R(H)5.
        AH, II, 179, 214. Woolhampton, Hewlett, 'Annals', 117-18.
        Downside MS 206. Nancy H 50 gives twelve 'adolescentes' at La
        Celle in 1750s.
608   Lille 20 H 14 e, f. Langley, *Life.* H. van Zeller, *Downside,*
        13-14. Birt, *Downside School,* 41-8. *DR,* xix, 1900, 117-34.
        Langley's appreciative comments about his education at St
        Gregory's should be compared with those of Lord Palmerston who
        in the early nineteenth century felt his friend and ex-St Gregory's
        pupil, Francis Cholmeley,to be 'not very well educated'; see
        K.Bourne, *Palmerston,* London 1982, 16.
609   Woolhampton, Cab S/r, 'Memoirs of the Society of St. Edmund',
        G. Walker, 'Poplina'; J. Barnes, 'Ad R. D. C. Walmesley, De
        Adventu ad Cellas Gratulatio', 'An Elegy on leaving La Celle', 'A
        Dialogue Poem to Cuthbert Simpson'.
610   e.g. Hull DDEV/60/86(b), 1737 10 Sept, Potts to Champney, for
        the training of a girl to serve Mass. London, Forest Gate JC.2.
        (Faculty 9) indicates that it was a Benedictine privilege to employ

a female in serving mass if a male could not be found. G. Bradley, *Yorkshire Catholics*, 17, for female altar-server training in the 17th century.

611 Williams, 'Benedictine Missions', 253, 263-75. Lille 33, 1790, 2 Dec. Almond, *Ampleforth*, 252-53. Lille 31, 1779 8 July, Cowley. Lille 38, 1778 2 May. Malone, *Peter Newby*, 68-69. E. S. Worrall (ed.), *Returns, 3.* Clifton 1789-90, 152; 1791, 39, 41.

612 Lille 35, 1778, 30 June.

613 Lille 30, 1778, 8 July. For growth of education for commercial classes, Berington, *State*, 169, Rowlands, 'Education', 73. Porter, *English Society*, 176, 180.

614 Lille 30, 1778 31 Oct, 19 Nov, 1779 2 Mar. Lille 35, 1779 14 Mar.

615 Lille 57, 1782 14 Mar. Lille 58, 1782 22 Mar. Lille 31, 1782 9 April, Brewer. Clifton 1772-88, 37, 48; 1791, 120. Nancy H 77 contains letters from Eaves and Gregson (1768-70)to Naylor regarding school fees. Downside MS 205, shows numbers of students sent to Lambspring by Naylor.

616 Lille 30, 1782 22 Aug. Downside, Bastwell's Fund Account Book, 1786-1813. Lille 46, 1789 Sept. Woolhampton JXXVIII. Clifton 1772-88, 47, 50, 53, 72: 1789-90, 49; 1791, 120; 1792, 55.

617 Lille 46, 1787 5 June, 14 Aug, 9 Nov, 1788 27 May, 2 Dec, 1789 8 Sept. Lille 66, 1787 10 July, 22 Oct. Lille 28, 1788 1 Mar. Lille 33, 1789 10 Aug, 14 Aug, 1790 2 Dec. Almond, *Ampleforth*, 252-53. Clifton 1772-88, 69.

618 Lille 66, 1778 29 May, 12 Sept. Williams (ed), *Post-Reformation Catholicism*, i, 57, for earlier day school in Bath. Lille 46, 1791 12 April.

619 Nancy H 77, The Memorial was drawn up by Charles Howard of Corby, later 10th Duke of Norfolk. AR, 224, for a similar scheme.

620 Paris, Arch. Nat. G9 66, 1766 1 Nov, Moore's report. Woolhampton, Parker Papers, 1768 (after March), Petition of St. Gregory's. Paris, Arch. Nat., G9 66, 1768 (after March), Description of monasteries for the Commission.

621 'Among the Archives', *DR,* vi, 1887, 52-3. Arras (Downside transcript), 192-98. Downside MS 212, North Province Account Book 3. Woolhampton, Scott Box, 148, 150. Birt, *Downside,* 53-61. Lille, Série D, fonds de l'Université de Douai, 1770 10 Feb. Cardevacque, *Collège,* 122.

622 Lille 35, 1773 26 Nov, 1774 20 April, 21 April. Lille 27, 1774 27 Sept, 1775 16 May, 26 May, 30 June, 25 Aug. Lille 56, 1777

10 July. Woolhampton, Scott Box, 148, 150. Lille 35, 1773 31
Oct. Ampleforth, Box 261/11.

623   Lille 56, 1778 8 and 21 April.

624   Lille 27, 1774 8 June, 22 July, 17 Sept, 27 Sept, 27 Dec, 1775
16 May. Lille 35, 1774 24 Jan. Lille 40, 1774 29 June. Lille 18 c.
1774, 'concerning the Benedictines'. Lille 56, 1777 10 July, 1778
10 Jan. Woolhampton, Scott Box, 59, for an example of a Flemish
student educated in late 1750s at St. Gregory's. Nancy H 77, 1769
7 Dec, A plea for the abolition of the 'toga talaris', as an 'old but
unnecessary custom'. Bishop, 'A Gossip', 238-57, for life in St
Gregory's school in the 1770s. Harris (ed.). *Douai College,* 355,
359 for interchange of students between St Gregory's and English
College, Douai in 1773 and 1774. Upholland, Banister, Box 1,
1784 1 July. Dufermont, 'Colleges', 25, 28.

625   Lille 56, 1778 8 April.

626   Downside MS 205.

627   Birt Box 7.

628   Nancy H 77, 1770 25 May, Hadley to Naylor.

629   Lille 56, 1777 19 July, 1778 8 April, 21 April, 6 July, 8 July, 9
Oct, 30 Nov, 1779 2 Jan. Lille 31, 1778 20 Sept, Cowley. 63,
1778 3 Oct. Lille 38, 1778 31 Oct, 28 Nov. Clifton I, 1778 13
April, 22 May.

630   Lille 66, 1779 15 Feb, April. Lille 56, 1779 20 Feb. Lille 28,
1779 9 Mar. Lille 35, 1779 14 Mar. Lille 69, 1779 April and 30
April.

631   Lille 56, 1779 16 May, 13 July, 18 Aug, 28 Aug, 1780 20 Feb,
2 Aug. Lille 31, 1779 20 May, 12 June, 23 June, 8 July, 13 Aug,
26 Aug, 20 Nov, 26 Dec, 1780 13 Jan, 7 July, 19 Dec, Cowley.
Lille 66, 1779 7 June. Lille 64, 1779 14 Oct. Lille 28, 1780 11
May. Lille 31, 1780 2 Oct, 1 Nov, Compton. Lille 32, 1780 21
Jan. Lille 24, 1787 23 Sept, Walker's directive regarding
Dieulouard. Nancy H 93, 97, 98, 99, show increase of pensioners
at Dieulouard.

632   Lille 18 H 56, 1780 6 Mar.

633   Lille 33, 1786 16 Dec, Coupe. Clifton 1772-88, 10, 13, 39; 1789-
90, 179.

634   Lille 57, 1782 14 Mar, 1786 16 Aug. Lille 33, 1787 15 Mar, 25
May, 1788 30 April, Coupe.. AR, 229. Woolhampton, Parker
Papers, St. Edmund's Accounts, *c.* 1792, show St Edmund's had
5 pensioners at Dieulouard in 1791.

635   Lille 64, 1784 4 Jan. Lille 53, 1784 11 July, 1786 11 April. Lille
57, 1785 29 Oct, 1786 7 Mar, 26 Aug, 10 Nov, 1787 22 Jan,
1790 11 April,1791 1 Feb, 16 Sept, 31 Dec. Lille 46, 1791 16

Oct. Birt, 'An Old Douai Account Book', 18-35. Birt, 'An Old Account Book', 140-46.

636   Lille 57, 1791 13 Dec. Lille 50, 1790 5 Oct, Courtrai magistrates.

637   Coughton Court MSS, Folder 44/41. WM, V, 565.

638   Stratford-upon-Avon, Shakespeare Trust, Cought MS 1090 (Fenwick). Coughton Court MSS, Folder 44/1-3, 5-39. The Throckmorton tutor here, William Phillips is almost certainly the monk William Philips alias Pestel. WM, II, 530 (Stourton). *HMC, Finch* III, 362 (Tempest). Coughton Court MSS, Folder 2/2, for licences to travel abroad.

639   Coughton Court MSS, Folder 44/41.

640   Forster, 'An Outline History', 13. Charlton, *The Recollections,* 154-57. UCM I/140.

641   Woolhampton, 3 S:L, (1712) W. Champney, 'His Collections & Remarks in travells from 1706 to 1712'.

642   Coughton Court MSS, Folder 44/4, 6,8,17-19,21,23,24,34,35. *CRS,* vii, 'Thomas Marwood's Diary', 88-90. Roebuck, 'An English Catholic Tour', 156-59. Joyce, 'The Haggerstons', 180. Northumberland Record Office ZSW, Box 23, Memo. Book of Sir John Swinburne.

643   Gillow, *Dictionary,* v, 157-60, 554-55. Northumberland R. O. ZSW 518, 1754-59 entries. Downside MS 206.

644   Lille 27, 1774, 1 Mar.

645   Lille 40, 1774 29 June. Lille 27, 1774 20 Sept, 27 Dec, 1775 25 Aug, 1778 12 June. Lille 63, 1775 25 Feb. Lille 28, 1777 27 Aug. Lille 43, 1777 4 Nov. Lille 62, 1780 13 May. Lille 66, 1778 20 Oct.

646   Northumberland R. O., ZSW 521/9. Lille 55, 1787 3 Feb, 2 April, 18 April, 24 May, 15 Sept, 25 Sept, 11 Dec. Lille 9, 1787 19 Jan-25 April, Walker's receipts for Salvin. Lille 18, 1787 1 Nov, Salvin. Lille 28, 1787 4 Dec. Durham Record Office D/Sa/C 86 1-3.

647   Lille 27, 1774 22 Feb, 17 Dec, 1775 17 Jan, 31 Jan, 10 Feb, 28 April, (9) Sept.. Lille 3, 1775 22 Feb. entry. Lille 69, 1779 16 April. Farm St.,Thorpe, f.126v.

648   Lille 68, 1777, 17 Oct. Lille 69, 1777 7 Dec, 1778 24 Sept, 10 Oct, 1779 30 April, 9 June, 8 Aug. Lille 63, 1778 3 Oct.

649   Lille 31, 1779 20 Nov, Cowley.. Northumberland R. O., ZSW, 464, 1780-3, payment of pensions to Cowley.

650   RA SP 79/12. Clifton I, vii, xiii.

651   Woolhampton, Scott Box, 34e. Lille 63, 1775 25 Feb. Lille 35, 1777 17 Oct. Lille 43, 1777 4 Nov. Lille 56, 1778 24 Jan. Lille

67, 1778 14 Mar, 19 Aug, 11 Nov, 1779 20 Jan, 16 April, 12 May, 16 June, 24 Aug, 22 Sept, 7 Dec, 8 Dec, 1780 19 Jan, 6 Mar, 29 Nov. London, Farm St., Thorpe MSS ff.33, 34v, 136v, 154, 257, 284v.

652   Lille 28, 1783 11 April, 6 May. Lille 67, 1783 7 May, 24 June. Lille 35, 1783 12 July. Lille 36, 1783 25 July, Geary. Lille 54, 1783 15 Aug, Riddell. Clifton 1772-88, lxxxvii, 2.

653   Lille 67, 1783 10 Dec, 1784 17 Mar, 16 June, Dec. Lille 54, 1784 17 Mar, 19 May, 28 Oct, 10 Nov, Riddell.

654   Lille 35, 1785 10 Jan. Lille 67, 1785 16 Feb, 12 May, 13 Sept, 1786 19 April, 16 Aug, 30 Sept, 6 Dec, 1787 28 Mar. Lille 54, 1785 1 Mar, Riddell. Lille 62, 1785 7 July, Turner. Clifton 1772-88, 13.

655   Lille 67, 1790 8 April.

656   Of all the English Catholic Regulars, the Benedictines seem to have been most enthusiastic for the Jacobite cause; see Paris, Bibliothèque Nationale, Nouvelles acquisitions françaises 7488 f.37, 1698 2 Jan, Abbé Renaudot's memorials of English affairs (I am grateful to Dr. P. A. Hopkins for this reference).

657   For Weldon, see Chapter V,and for his Jacobitism and his attack on Anglican jurors, see BL Add. MSS 10118, ff. 217, 217b, 232b, 287b, 331b, 406b-407b, 479-490, his 'Course and Rough first draught of ye History of England's late Most Holy and most glorious Royal Confessor and Defender of the True Faith, James II' (composed 1706). G. Scott, 'Sacredness', 2-8.

658   WM, IV, 84-86, 266-67.

659   WM, II, 391; 'James II', 311, 432, 450, 529, 769; 'Chronological Notes', 218-19. Dolan, 'Lambspring Poet', 154-5. But the friendship of the Jacobite Dean of Durham, Denis Granville, with the monks should be noted: see E.T.Corp & J.Sanson, *Le Cour des Stuarts à Saint-Germain-en-Laye au temps de Louis XIV,* Paris 1992, 200, no.260.

660   Williams, 'Sources', 339, 340, 348, 350, for summary of anti-Jacobite legislation.

661   A. G. Petti (ed.), *Recusant Documents,* 284-89, 296, 300, for example of Throckmorton. G. A. Ryan and L. J. Redstone, *Timperley,* 82, 83, and Aveling, *Northern Catholics,* 350, for examples of monks concealing themselves in England after the Revolution.

662   W. Beaumont (ed.), 'The Jacobite Trials'. *H. M. C.,* 'Stuart', i, 96-7. Garrett, *Triumph, ,* 52-3. P. A. Hopkins, 'The Commission for Superstitious Lands', 269-75, and his 'Sham Plots', 95, 96, 106n.

266

663   J. Garrett, *Triumph, passim*. P. Burger, 'Spymaster', 136. For
       Johnston: see Chapter V, and WM, V, 320-1; Howell, *State
       Trials*, xii, 1301, 1321-22, 1348-54, xiii, 19, 294-5; Lambeth
       Palace MS 933/84, 1697 15 Nov, Johnson's 'apologia', which
       shows Congregation *officially* anti-conspiratorial (reference kindly
       given by Dr. P. A. Hopkins); *H. M. C.*, 'Finch', IV, London
       1965, 113; *Calendar of State Papers Domestic, 1696*, 96, 254,
       340; Sitwell, 'Crisis', 274; W. Beaumont 'Jacobite Trials', xxvii,
       li, lii, shows Johnston's involvement in Lancashire Plot. For
       Knightley: Weldon, 'James II', 363b, 441. It is also possible that
       the conspirator Robert Lowick (Garrett, *Triumph*, 118) was a
       relation of the Paris monk and Jacobite Henry Bernard Lowick
       (1612-1720). G.Scott, 'Benedictine Conspirator', and T.Goyet,
       'Le traducteur anglais de Bossuet était-il un conspirateur?', *Les
       Amis de Bossuet*, 19, 1990, 24-29.
664   Scott, 'Sacredness', 8-9. Bodleian, Carte 210/374-7.
665   For the '15, see Dixon, 'Notes', 93-112, especially 105. Jarvis,
       Collected Papers, ii, 317. Lenman, *Jacobite Risings*, 117, 118,
       122, 157. On missioners persecuted, see Northumberland R. O.,
       RCD 6/4/335. Gillow, *Dictionary*, iii, 262.
666   Hopkins, 'Commission', 269, 270, 277. Purcell, 'The Jacobite
       Rising', 418-32, especially 423, 431. Public Records Office,
       Forfeited Estates, especially 12, 20, 21, 46, 55. Estcourt and
       Payne, *Nonjurors*, especially 58, 209, and Appendix II. Payne,
       Records, 126 especially. Lenman, *Risings*, 171-3. Williams,
       'Sources', 362-3, 384-7, 392. Dolan, *Lancashire*, 40.
667   Jarvis, *Papers*, ii, 317 (Basil Warwick, prof. 1698). Blundell,
       Lancashire, ii, 94-5 (Edward Chorley, prof. 1698). *H. M. C.*,
       'Stuart', i, 107, 108: vii, 400; Woolhampton, Parker papers 'up to
       1817', 'Table of Revenues of St. Edmund's, Paris; WM, V, 524
       (Lawrence Delattre, prof. 1699). *CRS*, xiv, 102n (Benedict
       Shaftoe, prof. 1715).
668   WM, V, 515-21; VI, 594, 602-03. BL Add MSS 38851 ff127,
       154, 185, 190. *H. M. C.*, 'Stuart', vii, 699. Oxford: Bodleian,
       Rawlinson D 1091, ff1r, 15v, 61. Woolhampton, Burial Register
       of St. Edmund's, Paris. Hearne, *Collections*, vi, 330-1. Bodleian,
       Carte 180/6-7, 14-17, 18-29, 76, 77. BL . Scott, 'Sacredness'.
       MSS 29, 477f. 27v.
669   See Chapter V for Southcott and Pope. AB, 415. Hartham,
       'Benedictines', 36. Gillow, *Dictionary*, V, 515-16. *H. M. C.*,
       'Stuart', i, 155. J. Gillow and R. Trappes-Lomax, (ed.), *Diary*,
       243-4. Holt, *Letter Book*, 119. O'Leary, 'Last of the Southcotes',
       22-9.

670   *H. M. C.*, 'Stuart', i, 428-9; ii, 59, 62-3, 75, 95, 117, 130, 139, 182, 185, 188-9, 205-08, 235-6, 245-6, 271, 324, 360, 380, 393, 455, 477-81, 486, 536; iii, 27, 42, 160, 175, 178-82, 202, 232, 234-5, 143-4, 262-3, 277-8, 289, 401, 416, 444; iv, 97, 134, 137, 150, 180, 283, 364, 398-9, 416, 493, 562; v, 104, 426; vi, 120, 295-7, 354-5, 483. Bennett, *The Tory Crisis,* 209. Jones, *The Main Stream,* 107, 126-7.

671   BL Add MSS, 20309/9-10. RA SP, 47/40; 51/156; 53/134; 54/112; 55/16, 98, 147; 56/35, 37, 112; 57/64, 21, 116; 58/29, 53, 146; 60/32, 71, 77, 89, 91, 115; 63/1; 67/86; 98/130; 113/19; 125/151; 140/198. RSRC, Anglia 2, ff370-1, 379.

672   RA SP 60/125, 155, 162; 61/24, 48; 62/25, 152; 63/83, 106, 128, 164.

673   RA SP 63/16, 41, 42, 46; 69/36, 69, 80; 72/43; 76/90; 103/119; 104/4, 30, 126; 105/4, 44, 82; 106/125; 107/3; 108/49, 69, 101; 109/78; 110/64; 115/7; 111/109, 154, 192; 116/44; 118/112, 163; 119/134; 120/65, 98; 121/56; 122/130; 125/100, 166; 126/7; 127/93; 129/163; 137/54, 190; 139/84, 97; 162/109, 130; 174/15, 42; 175/18; 201/10; Box 1/68; Box 2/566; Box 5/89, 111. AAW, Ep. Var, ix/74. RSRC, Anglia 3 ff5, 6. BL Add MSS, 20309 *passim,* is Southcott's correspondence with the Cardinal Protector, Gualterio, dealing with the same concerns as found also in his letters to the Stuart Court.

674   For its European influence, see Chaussinand-Nogaret, 'Une élite insulaire'. For Jacobite exiles and long-term visitors, see RA SP 118/112 (Stafford); 119/134, 120/65 (Throckmorton).

675   RA SP 68/138; 69/13; 72/14, 43, 72, 82, 129, 135,139; 73/87; 76/90, 133, 168; 77/72, 108, 132, 176, 179; 78/31, 57, 164, 165; 79/12, 29, 120; 80/103; 83/104; 84/120; 103/119;116/6, 44, 98; 118/112, 141; 119/134; 121/56; 147/64; 149/64; 125/129; 150/2, 142; 156/5, 144; 159/146; 167/32, 100; 168/114; 173, 54, 128; 178/19, 176. AAW, Ep Var, ix/72.

676   RA SP 62/41; 63/83; 68/138; 69/13; 72/43, 112; 75/63; 76/90, 133, 168; 77/ 72, 108, 129, 176; 78/31, 164; 79/12, 29; 131/54, 130; 183/111; 200/45; 207/70. BL ADD MSS, 20309, ff90, 95. Anstruther, 'Williams', 316.

677   RA SP 240/10; 249/69; 287/175; 195/59. Hull, Everingham DDEV/60/86(b), 1738/9 6 Mar, Potts to Farnworth. Birt 6/A329.

678   RA SP 235/117, 119; 236/196, 198.

679   RA SP 220/4; 221, 33.

680   RA SP 222/13, 95, 152; 235/115; 246/177, 188; 249/69; 252/13; 253/184; 289/104.

681 RSRC, Anglia 4, ff76-7. E. Cruickshanks, *Political Untouchables,* Appendix I, for list of country gentry, many of whom were Benedictine patrons, expected to support a Stuart restoration in 1743. J. A. Williams, 'Change or Decay?', 43, and his 'No Ordinary Residence', 217-19. Dolan, *Lancashire,* 36, and R. C. Davis, *Collected Papers,* ii, 319, for Ormskirk Chapel.

682 Northumberland R. O., ZSW 456 (Swinburne). Roebuck, *Constable,* 20; Wilton, 'Some Annals', 267 (Constable). Aveling, *West Riding,* 262, for Sir Edward Gascoigne's comment on the rebels as 'a rabble of naked disturbers of order'. Collyer, 'Yorkshire', 83-4.

683 RA SP 273/4.

684 The best examples are Ranald (Anselm) Macdonald, and Archibald (Benedict) Macdonald: see Prebble, *Culloden,* 199-201, and Wigan R. O., RO D/D WRC 4/8 Dem. 14.

685 RA SP 342/64, 149; 345/19; 380/134; 400/ 112; 401/5, 18, 134; 402/141; 406/95; 419/114 (quoted).

686 Woolhampton, Cab. s/r, 'Memoirs of the Society of St. Edmund', 1750 3 Mar, 15 Dec.

687 RA SP 484/180, 192, 193; 479/188; 485/1, 6, 9, 11, 19, 29, 40, 56, 64, 69, 79, 128, 140, 141, 152, 153, 161; 485/ 64, 96, 100, 162, 171, 174; 486/30, 31, 40, 45, 56, 57, 77, 86, 147; 487/4, 18, 21, 37, 38, 55, 72, 82, 95, 102, 117; 489/36, 45, 88; 494/94, 164; 495/2, 16, 31, 41, 71; 496/96, 51; 497/67, 37, 79, 85, 112, 122, 191, 232; 498/11, 16, 24, 60, 65, 77, 132, 146, 160, 187; 499/3, 17, 69, 85, 131, 150; 501/15, 182, 189, 191, 113; 503/2, 6, 9, 13, 25, 28, 35, 39, 46, 54, 62, 64, 70, 82, 96, 100, 110, 112, 113, 117, 125, 133, 147, 155, 170; 504/1, 5, 26, 34, 46, 59, 99, 114, 121, 130, 143, 149, 160; 505/1, 9, 14, 17, 27, 35, 52, 57, 60, 98, 103, 111. Woolhampton, IL/D/Stuart 2-5; IL/D/Stuart, ix. Tayler, *Prince Charlie's Daughter,* 86, 97, 106. Dennistoun, *Memoirs,* ii, 213-15.

688 Lille 66, 1784 5 Sept. Clifton 1789-90, 149, 152.

689 The artists' circle in Rome and Walker's friendship with Lumisden is dealt with in Chapter V. RA SP 446/18, 42, 43, 50, 79, 142; 448/8, 161; 450/117; 453/57; 454/66; 459/74, 164; 473/154; 480/67, 115, 158; Box 1/557. Lille 61, 1775, 2 June. Lille 24, 1763-66, Account of King's death.

690 Nancy H 77, 1767 32 Aug, 1770 7 Mar, 4 April, 31 May, Walker to Naylor. McLynn, *Charles,* 342.

691 Woolhampton IL/D/7. Lille 67, 1783, Dec, 10 Dec, 1786 19 April, 9 Aug, 30 Sept, 6 Dec, 1787 9 Jan, 16 May, 28 Mar (quoted), 1788 21 Mar, 17 Dec, 1789 4 Jan. Lille 50, 1784 4

June, Morrison. Lille 66, 1786 16 Nov. Edinburgh, National Library of Scotland, MS 8291. Forbes MSS 1792, 2 Dec. Clifton 1772-88, 30, 36. Tayler, *Daughter,* 98, 101, 105, 119, 120, 131, 133.

692   Lille 67, 1786 30 Sept, 1788 2 Feb, 13 Feb, 21 Mar, 11 June, 13 Aug. Lille 26, 1788 5 Mar, 30 April, Duchess of Albany. Lille 70, 1788 9 Mar, Cardinal York. Lille 69, 1788 30 Mar.

693   Lille 67, 1788 17 Dec, 1789 4 Jan, 22 April, 21 Oct, 9 Dec, 1790 Jan, 24 Feb; Lille 70, 1790 20 Jan, Waters. Clifton 1789-90, 89, 185.

694   Lille 67, 1790 8 April, 21 April, 19 May, 1791 4 Jan, 21 July. Lille 36, 1790 6 Mar, 26 April, Fitzjames de Chimay. Lille 53, 1790 8 Nov, 6 Dec, Parker to Walker. Paris, A. N., DXIX 50 no. 95; DXIX 30/472, piece 2. Birmingham Archdiocesan Archives, C974.

695   Woolhampton, Parker Papers, for correspondence relating to Waters, 1805-10. For Waters and the Stuart MSS, see *H. M. C.,* 'Stuart', i, London 1902, Introduction. Clarke, *James II,* i, xiii-xviii. M. F. Gain, 'The Stuart Papers'. Toynbee, 'Dom Placid Waters', 10*-13*. BL MSS 33, 380. and 34, 637f.448.

696   Clifton I, vi. AHII, 263. Burton, *Challoner,* ii, 292-4. Lesourd, *Catholiques,* i, 318-21. Williams, 'Sources', 416.

697   Lille 66, 1778 29 May, 1779 15 Feb. Lille 28, 1778 11 June, 7 July. Lille 67, 1778 30 June. Lille 31, 1778 5 July, Brewer. Lille 56, 1778 8 July.

698   Clifton I xv, xxxiii, xxxiv, xxxviii. Lille 56, 1779 16 May, 1780 29 Aug, 28 Sept. Lille 67, 1780 19 Jan. Lille 66, 1780 8 July, 2 Oct (quoted), 1781 7 Mar. RA SP 499/3. AH II, 264; Appendix, 505. Gillow, *Dictionary,* 1, 292. Burton, *Challoner,* ii, xxxii, xxxiii. Rudé, *Paris* and *London,* 289-90. Williams, *Post-Reformation Catholicism,* i, 68-70; 'Sources', 394-5.

699   For the Committee, see: Ward, *Dawn,* Chap. V. Duffy, 'Ecclesiastical Democracy Detected: I', 193-209. Chinnici, *Enlightenment,* Introduction. J. C. Throckmorton and J. C. Eustace had been educated at St. Gregory's, Douai, amongst others. For Eustace, see Lille 57, 1782 14 Mar, 18 May. Lille 69, 1782 12 May. Woolhampton, St. Edmund's Clothing Book. Gillow, *Dictionary,* ii, 182-85. Chinnici, *Enlightenment,* 37, 120. For views in monasteries about English Catholic liberals like J. Berington, see Lille 69, 1782 3 Mar. Lille 57, 1788 3 Jan.

700   Clifton 1772-88, 69, 71, 72. See Chapter V for attitudes to William Gregory Gregson's 'liberal' prayer-book, and to Augustine Hawkins's apostasy.

701   For continental suspicion of liberalism, see Lille 67, 1787 4 July.
702   Lille 66, 1786 29 June. For his interest in a vernacular liturgy and in the aims of the Catholic Committee, Wilks should be compared with his contemporary, Alexander Geddes, see R.C.Fuller, *Geddes*.
703   The complex dispute between the Catholic Committee and the Vicars Apostolic, which centred on formulating an acceptable Relief Bill and Oath, but which incorporated questions about jurisdiction and theology, is found in: RSRC, Anglia 5, *passim*. AAW, Main Series, XLII, *passim*. Ward, Dawn, Chap. VII. Lesourd, *Catholiques*, 338-402. Duffy, 'Ecclesiastical Democracy Detected I', 193-209, and his 'Ecclesiastical Democracy Detected: II', 309-31. Clifton 1778-88, 62, 105; 1789-90, 23.
704   Lille 67, 1789 22 April, 27 May, 21 Oct, 1790 24 Feb, 3 Mar, 8 April, 19 May. Lille 54, 1789 29 May, Pembridge. Lille 69, 1789 15 June. Lille 28, 1789 3 Nov, 1790 29 Jan, 7 Feb, 26 April, 30 April. Lille 46, 1789 17 Nov, 1790 8 April. Lille 57, 1790 9 Jan. Lille 64, 1790 22 May. Lille 66, 1790 30 May. Birt 10, 1789 13, Nov, Story to Bolton. Woolhampton, C. Walmesley transcripts, 1789 10 Oct, 22 Nov, 5 Dec, 17 Dec, 1790 3 Jan, 11 Jan, 14 Jan, 22 Jan, Jan, 9 Feb, 2 Mar, Walmesley to Weld. Birmingham, Archd. Archives, C. 1037. Ward, *Dawn*, Chap. XXXI, and pp. 218-25. Clifton 1772-88, 84, 88, 91, 98; 1989-90, 22, 119, 133, 151; 1791, 6, 8, 17, 20.
705   Lille 46, 1790 29 Oct. Clifton 1789-90, 179; 1791, 6, 100, 114, 115.
706   Lille 53, 1791, 15 Mar, 29 Mar. Birt 9, B2.
707   For registrations, see Lesourd, *Catholiques*, i, 369-79. Clifton 1791, 122, 125.
708   e.g. Lille 66, 1792, 5 April.
709   For the Commission, see Lecestre, *Liste générale*. Lemaire, *La Commission*. Schmitz, *Histoire*, iv, 68-75. Pastor, *Popes*, xxxvii, 381-91. Chevallier, *Loménie de Brienne et l'ordre monastique*, Book I, Chap. iv; Book IV, Chap i, for Benedictines. McManners, *French Ecclesiastical Society*, 77-78. Delumeau, *Catholicism*, Part II, Chap. 5.
710   Lille 69, 1782 3 Mar, 12 May, 1784 1 Mar, 1786 25 July. Lille 67, 1782 5 Feb, 26 June 1784 5 May, 1786 6 Dec, 1787 4 July, 1788 25 June. Lille 32, 1782 11 Mar, Cowley. Chadwick, *The Popes*, 420-28. Clifton 1772-88, 36.
711   Taunton, *Black Monks*, ii, 183-84. Almond, *Ampleforth*, 207-08.
712   Nancy, H 77, 1770 2 May, C. Walmesley to Naylor. Nancy H 77, 1769, Naylor's speech to General Chapter. Paris, Arch. Nat.

G9 66, Reports on the English Benedictines for the Commission. Birt 7, 365(a). Nancy H 77 (Downside transcript 280-81), H 82 (transcript 282-83). Bugner, *Cadre architectural,* Annexe 4, shows of 11 Benedictine Congregations in France, the English was the smallest, with 3 houses, and the second poorest, with 15,114 *livres* in yearly revenue; statistics taken from reports to the 1768 Commission.

713   Woolhampton, Parker Papers, 'Observations presentées...à la Cour du Parlement de Flandre', and a 'Petition' to the Flemish Parlement. Paris, A. N. G9 66, 'Mémoire pour la Congregation des Bénédictins'. (Undated) description of the English monasteries. 1768 July, Petition of British Religious for Exemption. 1768 20 Dec, Choiseul to Archbishop of Rheims. 1769 3 Feb, Moore and Sharrock to Choiseul. Nancy H 77, 2 Petitions of St. Gregory's, Douai, to the King. Nancy H 77, 1770 31 May, Moore to Naylor. Nancy H 77, 1768 Dec, Copy of letter from Procureur-General of Parlement of Flanders . Nancy H 77, 1769, 4 April, Bennet to Naylor.

714   Lille 27, 1773, 12 Nov, 14 Dec, 1779 9 Mar. Lille 35, 1777 17 Oct, 1779 14 Mar, 1778 30 June. Lille 56, 1777 24 Oct, 1778, 30 Nov.

715   Lille 57, 1783 20 June, 4 Sept, 25 Oct. AH, II, 247-8, 251.

716   Chevallier, *Loménie de Brienne, passim,* indicates the degree of reforming zeal within the French monasteries.

717   B.L. Add MSS, 35,190. Ampleforth, Box 261, 1772, Welch's Preface to new Constitutions, and 1773 17 Sept, Fisher to Welch. Lille 15, 1773 14 Aug, Procurators deputed. Lille 35, 1773 26 Nov, 28 Nov, 1774 25 Jan. AR, 223, 204-42; AH, II, 288-98. Aveling, 'Benedictines', 164-65.. Schmitz, Histoire, 70-71.

718   Lille 35, 1774, 11 Feb, 15 Mar, 19 Mar, 20 April, 21 April, 23 April. Lille 27, 1774 1 July, 22 July, 18 Nov, 1775 26 May, 30 June, 9 Dec. Lille 3, 1774 entry. Ampleforth, Box 261, 8 and 12. AR, 223.

719   Lille 69, 1775 2 Jan, Kellet to Welch. Lille 43, 1775 16 Oct, 10 Dec, 15 Dec, 1775 (undated), 1777 18 Aug. Lille 56, 1775 10 July, 2 Dec, 11 Dec, 23 Dec, 26 Dec, 1776 11 Jan, (undated ?1776), 1778 10 Jan, 21 April, 1780 1 May. Lille 28, 1775 30 June, 25 Aug. Lille 31, 1777 8 July, 16 Dec, Cowley. Lille 3, 1777 entry. Lille 35, 1777 17 Oct. Lille 69, 1777 7 Dec, 1779 21 April (quoted). AR, 223. Clifton I, xlvii.

720   Lille 69, 1779 25 April, 1780 1 April (quoted), 21 April (quoted). Lille 43, 1779 8 May. Lille 31, 1779 17 June, 20H 4 b. 1780 13 Feb, Cowley. Lille 66, 1780 8 July, Lille 32, 1784 10 Nov, 1

Dec, 15 Dec, 1785 22 Jan, 6 Mar, Cowley. Lille 10, 1781 (July),
1784, Walker to General Chapter. Lille 58, 1782, 22 Mar, 1785 7
Jan. Lille 64, 1782 27 Mar, 1785 6 Dec. AH, II, 295-96.
Constitutiones Congregationis Anglicanae Ordinis Sancti Benedicti,
Paris 1784, with *Formularium* and *Ritualis Compendium.*

721   Lille 69, 1782 1 June. Yeo, *Structure,* 281, shows how the profession formula was changed to suit this prevailing centralising
mentality.

722   Lille 32, 1785 6 Mar, Cowley. Lille 66, 1787 6 Feb. Lille 28,
1784 6 Aug. Lille 65, 1784 16 Aug. AR, 239.

723   Lille 18 H 66, 1786 29 June, Warmoll to Walker. Lille 18 H 67,
1788 11 June, 25 June, 13 Aug, 8 Oct, Waters to Walker.

724   Paris, A. N., G9 66, *Status* of the Congregation, for St.
Edmund's demand for control of benefices. Woolhampton, Cab
IR/9/10, 1772 14 Aug, Letters patent. Parker Papers, *c.* 1792
Declaration of St. Edmund's property, 53-57. St. Edmund's
Obligation Book, 1772 31 Mar entry. Lille 35, 1774 25 Jan. Lille
31, 1779 13 Aug. 16 Nov, 1780 23 Feb, 6 Mar, Cowley. Lille 3,
1776 29 Oct entry. Lille 33, 1777 10 Mar. Lille 56, 1779 2 Jan,
12 June, 19 July.

725   Lille 3, entries for 1770 16 May, 1771 April. Lille 33, 10 Mar.
Schmitz, *Histoire,* iv, 74 and footnote.

726   Lille 3, 1768 24 Oct entry (quoted). Lille 59, 1779 12 Aug,
Simpson to Walker; 1778 16 Oct, Shaw to Walker (quoted).
Nancy H 77, 1770 22 May, 27 May, Welch to Naylor; *c.* 26
May, Shaw to Welch.

727   Lille 3, 1789 entry. Lille 32, 1787 10 Sept, 1789 18 Feb, 25 Feb,
6 Mar, 15 Mar, 6 April 13 June, 1791 28 May, Cowley. Lille 31,
1790 20 Mar, Coupe. Lille 53 1790 14 Oct. AB, 493: 'On the
breaking out of the French Revolution, he was carried away with
the cries of liberty and joined the Republican army in which he
acted as a Drummer, and appears to have come to an untimely
end'.

728   Lille 57, 1782 27 Dec, 1785 6 Dec, 1787 20 Feb, 1788 5 Mar, 12
Sept. Lille 32, 1785 8 Aug, 1787 20 July, 25 Aug, 10 Sept, 1789
end of June, 14 Aug, Cowley. Lille 3, 1788 entry. Lille 66, 1787
9 Oct. Lille 59, 1789 23 July, 15 Aug, 20 Aug, 7 Sept, 14 Sept,
Shaw. Lille 69, 1789 27 Aug. Lille 28, 1789 8 Sept. 20 H 14 d.
Ampleforth, Box 261, 9, 11, and 1773 1 Oct, Fisher to Moore.

729   Lille 10 (3), 1789, Walker's speech to General Chapter. Scott,
'"The Times"'.

730   Lille 53, 1789 23 Oct (quoted), 1790 15 Aug, 16 Aug, 13 Nov.
Lille 46, 1789 17 Nov, 1790 2 May, 1792 8 Aug. Lille 57, 1791

5 Jan, 1792 5 May. Lille 31, 1790 20 Mar, Coupe. Lille 33, 1791 28 May. Lille 31, Cawser. Lille 49, 1792 13 Aug, 17 Aug, P. Marsh. Birt Box 9, B2; Box 10, A501, A506, 507. Clifton 1789-90, 87.

731   Birt 9, B2,

732   Lille 69, 1779 16 April, 30 April, 1780 18 Nov. AB', 470, for an earlier example of such patriotism.

733   Lille 57, 1783 25 Oct. Clifton 1772-88, 91.

734   Plongeron, *Réguliers de Paris,* 63, for list of Paris regulars at beginning of 1791: 16 remained at St. Edmund's, 2 had left.At St. Germain-des-Prés and St. Martin-des-Champs, the respective figures were 34 and 10, 14 and 9.

735   Lille 69, 1786 16 Nov (quoted), 29 Nov. Lille 66, 1783 25 Oct, 1787 22 Oct. Lille 57, 1787 18 April. Lille 32, 1787 25 Aug, 10 Sept, 1788 4 Dec, 17 Dec. RA SP 504/160.

736   Lille 32, 1789 9 Feb (i.e. Mar), 15 Mar, 3 June, 19 June, 28 June, Cowley. Lille 69, 1789 8 May, 15 June. Paris, A. N. H5 3896, 1769 St. Edmund's disbursements. McManners, *French Ecclesiastical Society,* 222, for limited involvement of monks in electoral assemblies, and p. 239 for grain riots which instigated anti-clericalism. Doyle, *Origins,* 150-51.

737   Lille 57, 1789 14 Aug. Lille 69, 1789 27 Aug. Lille 49, 1789 5 Sept, R. Marsh. Lille 28, 1789 8 Sept, 15 Sept. Lille 53, 1789 14 Sept. Lille 43, 1789 29 Sept. McManners, *French Ecclesiastical Society,* 235-6, for dedication of National Guard's banners.

738   Lille 33, 1789 10 Oct, 11 Nov. Lille 57, 1789 15 Nov. Lille 18, n.d., A Missioner to a Definitor. Clifton 1789-90, 158.

739   Cambrai, Archives communales, GG Liasse, 241, 1790 9 Jan, Parker to a nun. Lille 69, 1789 Dec, 28 Dec. Lille 49, 1789 16 Dec, 30 Dec, R. Marsh. Woolhampton, Scott Box 53. Allanson, 'History', II, 335. Doyle, *Origins,* 178. Clifton 1789-90, 108.

740   Lille 57, 1790 9 Jan. Lille 32, 1790 11 Jan, Cowley. Lille 46, 1790 19 Jan. Lille 67, 1790 20 Jan. Lille 49, 1790 16 Jan. Clifton 1789-90, 145.

741   Lille 57, 1790 17 Feb, 3 May, Prior and Religious of Douai to Walker, 1790 11 April, 3 May. Lille 58, 1790 4 June. Lille 49, 1790 26 May. Lille 46, 1790 6 June. Lille 67, 1790 24 Feb, 3 Mar, 8 April. Lille 59, 1790 10 Mar, 24 April. Lille 69, 1790 25 Mar. Paris, A.N., DXIX 10, doss. 145, 1790 14 Mar, List. D XIX 30, doss. 472, no 8, 1790 Petition for English Benedictine exemption. D XIX 50, no. 95, 1790 27 Mar, and D XIX 430, no. 4, 1790, St. Edmund's exemption.S 4619, 1790 24 Feb, St. Edmund's Revenues. Nancy Q 195, St. Laurence's inventory.

Woolhampton, Parker Papers, for St. Edmund's inventories. Daumet, *Etablissements Britanniques*, 206-18. Plongeron, *Réguliers*, Appendix II, and p. 443. McManners, *French Revolution*, 31-35. Schmitz, *Histoire*, iv, 76-78. Dechristé, *Douai*, 239, for St. Gregory's inventory. Clifton 1789-90, 118, 141.

742 Lille 49, 1790 26 May, 22 July, 20 Sept. Lille 53, 1790 15 Aug, 16 Aug, 25 Aug, 29 Aug. Lille 57, 1790 15 Sept. Lille 35, 1790 16 Sept. Nancy L. 2039, 1790 24 Aug, Order to continue brewing. Birt 10, A501, A503. Paris, A. N. Q2, 117, 1790 *Status* of St. Edmund's. Plongeron, *Réguliers*, 63, 147, 306, 362, 382. Clifton 1789-90, 143, 145, 152; 175, 185.

743 Birt Box 9. B3. Box 10, A503, A504, A505, A506, A507. Lille 49, 1790 20 Sept, 1791 11 Mar, Marsh to Walker. Lille 53, 1790 23 Sept, 6 Oct, 14 Oct, 30 Oct, 8 Nov, 6 Dec, 1791 5 Jan, 10 May, 15 May, 10 June. Lille 47, 1790 4 Oct, 5 Oct, 9 Oct. Lille 57, 1790 1 May, 5 May, 18 Oct, 2 Nov, 21 Dec, 1791 5 Jan, 1 April. Lille 46, 1790 29 Oct, 16 Dec, 1791 18 Jan. Lille 50, 1790 5 Oct, Magistrates of Coutrai to Walker. Lille 33, 1790 1 May, 2 Dec, 1791, 2 Feb, 3 Mar, 28 May. Lille 66, 1790 12 Dec, 1791 19 Jan. Lille 67, 1791 4 Jan. Lille 65, 1790 29 April, C. Walmesley. Paris, A. N. D XIX, 89/ 729, 1791, Demand for pensions; S 3696-7, 1791 4 Nov,pensions. Northumberland R. O., RCD/I/I/47. AH, II, 335-6. Daumet, *Etablissements*, 218-27. Almond, *Ampleforth*, 226-7. Birt, *Downside*, 101. Schmitz, *Histoire*, iv, 79-80. McManners, *French Revolution*, 54-5, 61. Clifton 1789-90, 175, 179; 1791, 7, 47, 53; 1792, 22.

744 Lille 57, 1791 28 Jan, 5 Mar, 1 April, 9 April, 20 April, 23 April, 1 May, 18 June. Lille 53, 1791 15 Feb, 15 Mar, 29 Mar. Lille 49, 1791 11 Mar. Lille 28, 1791 4 July. Lille 67, 1791 20 July, 10 Aug. Paris, A. N., D XIX/81, no. 628; LL 1420, 1791 20 Feb, certification for St. Edmund's. Birt 9, B2. AR, 228. McManners, *French Revolution*, 49. Douai, Archives Municipales, Serie P, Section I, no.21; Clifton 1791, 39, 100, 119, 122.

745 Lille 28, 1791 4 July. Lille 67, 1791 20 July, 10 Aug. Lille 53, 1791 14 July, 17 Sept, 7 or 8 Oct, 31 Sept. Lille 43, 1791 8 Aug. Lille 31, 1791 8 Aug, Cawser. Lille 57, 1791 17 July, 30 July, 31 Aug, 7 Sept, 16 Sept, 26 Nov. Lille 18 H 18, 1791 31 Dec, J. Sharrock.. Lille 49, 1791 23 July, 15 Sept, 6 Nov, 20 Nov. Woolhampton, EX 11/ll, 49, 62. Paris, A. N. D XIX/30. no. 472; S 3696, 1791 17 Sept, Decision regarding St. Edmund's; H5 3896. Birt Box 9, B11, B12, B16. AR, 228; AH, II, 336. Daumet, *Etablissments*, 219-20. Ward, *Dawn*, ii, 74. McCann,

Ampleforth, 201. Almond, *Ampleforth,* 227-9. Dechristé, *Douai,* 266-75, 278. Clifton 1791, 200, 207; 1792, 17.

746   Birt Box 9, B18, B21, B25, B29. Lille 53, 1792 10 Jan, 7 Feb, 13 Mar, 25 April, 7 July. Lille 49, 1792 13 Aug, 17 Aug, P. Marsh. Lille 49, 1792 20 Aug. Lille 57, 1792 5 May, 3 June. Woolhampton, E11/27; Parker Papers, 1792 6 Mar, Kellet's inventory. Paris, A. N., H5 3896, St Edmund's Accounts, 1792 Mar entry. AH, II, 336. Plongeron, *Réguliers,* 362.

747   Lille 57, 1792 27 April, 5 May, 3 June, 9 Sept. Lille 47, 1792 9 Sept. Lille 49, 1792 9 June, 22 June. Lille 33, 1792 12 April. Lille 32, 1792 24 April, Cowley and Definitors. Birt Box 9, B27, 29. AH, II 368. Clifton 1792, 124.

748   AH, II, 338-45. AB, II, 97-101. A. P. Wilson, 'A Fugitive', 42-8. Birt, *Downside,* Chap. 4. Guilday, *Refugees,* 229-30. Ward, *Dawn,* ii, 76-80. H. Chadwick, 'Seizure', 147-57. Dechristé, *Douai,* 340-2, 344, 366-70. Dolan, 'English Benedictine Missions: London', 284-85. Douai, Archives Municipales Série P, Section I, no.21. Clifton 1793, 8,9,12,17,28,33,34,133,138,139,141.

749   Nancy, L 2039, Q 695, Q 38/210. AH, II, 346-50. R. Marsh, 'Account of his escape', 61-74, 229. McCann, *Ampleforth,* 202-06. Almond, *Ampleforth,* 231-44. Clifton 1793, 31, 135, 158.

750   Woolhampton, St. Edmund's Accounts, Procurator Kellet's Accounts 1790-96. Birt Box 9, B47, B78, B82. AH, II, 351-52. F. C. Doyle (ed.), *Tercentenary,* 28-30. Guilday, *Refugees,* 236. Daumet, *Etablissements,* 221-28. S. Marron, 'St. Edmund's: A Prison', 20-29, and 'Paris to Douai', 173-80. Wilson, 'The will'.

NOTE ON DATES AND SPELLING

The New Year is always taken as starting on 1st January. Until 1752, England followed the Julian Calendar *(Old Style),* whilst most of the Continent conformed to the Gregorian Calendar *(New Style).* In the early Eighteenth Century, therefore, monks in England used the former while their counterparts on the Continent used the latter.

Direct quotations are generally reproduced with their original spelling, but punctuation has been modernized.

LIST OF ILLUSTRATIONS

APPENDIX

ENGLISH BENEDICTINE MISSIONS 1685-1794.

South Province:

Cornwall.
Lanherne 1762-96 Register 1710-1855.

Devon.
Kirkham House [Newton St. Cyres] 1752-55; Ugbrooke 1765-67.

Dorset.
Marnhull 1772-1786 Register 1772-1786.

Hampshire.
Brambridge 1764-1815 Register 1766-1840; (near)Winchester 1717-1769.

Sussex.
Burton Park 1775-1780 Register 1720-1844; West Grinstead 1682-1686.

Kent.
Hawkwell Place 1698-1704.

Somerset.
Bath 1685-1932 Register (c.1685)1781 onwards; Leighland 1624-1767.

Wiltshire.
Bonham 1714-1719, 1785-1850 Register 1785; Easton Grey 1738-c.1755; Fonthill 1710-1721; Marlborough 1754-1794; Merevale c.1721; Stourton 1652-1714; Sutton Mandeville c.1721.

Berkshire.
Fawley 1670-1748.

Surrey.
Cheam 1753-1785 Register 1757-1780; Dorking 1786-1792; Reigate 1761-1762; Woburn Park c.1700.

London/Middlesex.
Alfarthing c.1739; Clerkenwell 1687-1718; Portuguese Embassy Chapel 1692-1814 Register 1684-1814; Provincial's residence

1693-1721,1737-69,1774-77; St James's Palace 1685-1689; Sardinian
Embassy Chapel c.1723; Somerset House 1689-1698.

Buckinghamshire.
Weston Underwood 1715-1837 Register 1710-1785.

Oxfordshire.
Brize Norton 1702-1768; Heythrop 1794-1796; Kiddington c.1685-1745;
Tusmore 1777-78; Waterperry 1772-1774 Register 1700 onwards.

Gloucestershire.
Bourton-on-the-Water 1711-1744; Farmcote 1700-1725; Hartpury Court
1767-1778; Horton 1772-77 Register 1772-87.

Herefordshire.
Holme Lacy 1771-1781; Rotherwas 1776-1780.

Monmouthshire.
Clytha Hall 1769-1772.

Essex.
Great Bromley Hall 1735-1738; Kelvedon Hall 1759-1783; Ockenden Hall
1770-1773; Thorndon Hall 1732-1760; Witham Place 1726-1774.

Hertfordshire.
Standon Lordship 1705-1733.

Warwickshire.
Abbots Salford 1727-1774 Register 1763 onwards; Brailes 1704-1720;
Coughton 1613 onwards Register 1744 onwards; Foxcote 1709-1848
Register 1765 onwards; Wootton Wawen 1733, c.1753, 1789.

Worcestershire.
Hanley Castle 1736-1741; Little Malvern 1760-1787 Register 1783-1875;
Redmarley 1730-1740; Spetchley Park 1730-1764 Register 1750-1856;
Woollas Hall 1745-1806.

Suffolk.
Colley Wood 1715-1717; Coldham Hall 1717-1737; Flixton 1657-1856;
Hengrave Hall/Bury St Edmunds 1732-1755 Register 1734-1751.

Norfolk.

Barningham 1701-1716; Colkirk 1711-26; Oxburgh Hall 1715-1759; Shelton Hall 1771.

Staffordshire.
Swynnerton Park 1782-1787; Tixall c.1703, 1792-1798.

Shropshire.
Acton Burnell 1712-1923 Register 1769-1837; Buttington Hall 1792-1793; Linley 1772-1837; Plowden 1794-1802.

North Province:

Leicestershire.
Clifton c.1719.

Cheshire.
Alderley 1739-1778.

Yorkshire (East Riding).
Everingham 1717-1743, 1751-1761, 1771-1813 Register 1771-1840; Holme Hall 1743-1762 Register 1744-1840; Houghton Hall 1766-1770, 1788-1805 Register 1787 onwards; Willitoft c.1753; Wyton 1740-1743.

Yorkshire (West Riding)
Aberford 1780-1983 Register 1780 onwards; Broughton Hall c.1703; Follifoot 1762-1797; Frickley c.1725-c.1735; Hazelwood 1713-1737; Huddlestone Hall 1748-1755; Kirby Overblow c.1735; Lawkland 1744-1850 Register 1745 onwards; Lotherton c.1728; Middleton Lodge 1645-1865; Parlington 1721-1780 Register 1757-1780; Plumpton 1693-1762; Saxton c.1728; Stockeld Park 1650-1793; Stourton House 1785-1803; Towton 1688; Wetherby c.172l.

Yorkshire (North Riding)
Angram 1770-1774, 1793-1794; Bedale 1691-1743; Brandsby 1761-1794; Craike 1794-1827; Danby Hall 1761-1794; Easingwold 1743-1764; Gilling 1660-1793; Helmesley c.1735; Kilvington 1633-1731; Newburgh Hall 1710-1719; Richmond 1794-1814; Stay House 1710-1717; Whenby 1666-1743; York 1693-1728.

Lancashire.
Aigburth Hall 1714-1717; Brindle 1680 onwards Register 1721-1834; Brownedge 1780 onwards Register 1764-1845; Childwall 1733-1765; Cowley Hill 1785-1786; Crosby Hall 1786-1860; Croxteth Hall 1756-1768; Cuerdon 171? -1780; Farnworth c.1716; Fishwick 1695-1695; Gillmoss 1768-1773 Register 1757-1860; Leigh c.1687; Lindell 1741-1742; Little Mosna (Hanbridge) c.1720-1780; Liverpool, Edmund St. 1783 onwards; Liverpool, Seel St. 1788 onwards Register 1788-1837; Low Hall c.1650-1765; Lytham Hall 1794-1804; Netherton 1793 onwards Register 1793 onwards; Ormskirk 1732 onwards Register 1736 onwards; Park Hall 1720-1751; Sefton Hall 1618-1717, 1742-1792 Register 1742-1792; Standish Hall 1741-1882 Register 1742-1764; Strangeways Hall 1758-1789 Register 1758-1830; Warrington 1774 onwards Register 1771-1834; Westby Hall 1791-1820; Woolston 1677-1831 Register 1771 onwards; Woolton 1720-1928 Register 1756-1856.

Westmorland.
Kendal c.1730.

Cumberland.
Castleheads c.1716; Corby Castle 1726-1776; Lanercost 1713, 1721; Warwick Bridge 1774 onwards Register 1765 onwards; Warwick Hall 1715-1774; Whitehaven 1706 onwards Register 1764 onwards; Workington c.1716.

County Durham.
Birtley 1746-1977 Register 1745-1826; Chester-le-Street 1696-1746; Gateshead c.1685; Lintz 1685; Stella 1688-1731; Tanfield 1750-1753.

Northumberland.
Beaufront 1668-1796; Biddlestone 1760-1823 Register 1764-1837; Capheaton 1727-1787 Register 1769-1839; Chesters 1785-1791; Dilston Castle c.1722-1736; Etal 1783-1785; Felton Park 1792-1883; Fenham c.1695; Hesleyside 1747-1759, 1761-1781, 1793-1797 Register 1775-1837; Morpeth 1780-1970; Netherwitton c.1728; Newbiggin Hall c.1724; Newcastle-upon-Tyne 1685-1689; Swinburne Castle 1696-1832; Thirlwall c.1724; Tone Hall 1785-1787.

BIBLIOGRAPHY

ABBREVIATIONS

AB	Ampleforth Abbey, Allanson MS, 'Biographies'.
AH	Ampleforth Abbey, Allanson MS, 'History'.
AR	Ampleforth Abbey, Allanson MS, 'Records'.
AAW	London, Archives of the Archbishop of Westminster.
Birt	Downside Abbey, Birt Papers.
CRS	*Catholic Record Society* volumes.
DR	*Downside Review.*
EBC	English Benedictine Congregation.
HMC	*Historical Manuscripts Commission* volumes.
JEH	*Journal of Ecclesiastical History.*
Lille	Archives du Nord, 18 H.
Nancy	Nancy, Archives Meurthe-et-Moselle.
Paris AN	Paris, Archives Nationales.
RActa	Rome, Propaganda Fide, Acta.
RA SP	Windsor, Royal Archives, Stuart Papers.
RASV	Rome, Archivio Segreto Vaticano.
RCP	Rome, Prop.Fid., Congregazioni Particulari.
RH	*Recusant History.*
RSOCG	Rome, Propaganda Fide, Scritture Originali referite nelle Congregazioni Generali.
UCM	Ushaw College, Durham, Manuscripts.
WM	Woolhampton, Weldon MS, 'Memorials'.

BIBLIOGRAPHY A

ARCHIVES

Ampleforth Abbey, York.
Peter Athanasius Allanson's Manuscripts:
Box 261. MSS 169, 284.

Arras (Downside Transcripts).
Archives départementales du Pas de Calais, Série H.

Berkshire Record Office.
Barrett Papers. D/EZ 14.

Birmingham: Archives of the Archdiocese.
A. 19, 105, 258, 262. C.520(b), 572, 578, 579, 580, 657, 859, 974, 984, 1037. Coughton Mission Register. Foxcote Mission Register.

British Library.
Add. MSS 4320 f.93, 6401 f.169, 10118, 20309, 20311, 20313, 28228 f. 329, 28237, 29477, 33100 f.69, 33380, 34637 f.448, 35190, 35520 ff.47 131, 37661. 38851 ff.127 154 185 190, 41199 f.80. Sloane 4047 f.312.

Cambrai.
Archives communales, GG Liasse 241.

Clifton Diocesan Archives.
Bound vols: II, II, III, IV, 1789 ff. Misc. Items, 54.

Coughton Court.
Box 83. Folders 2/2, 44, 46.

Douai, Archives Municipales.
Série P.

Douai, Bibliothèque Municipale.
MS 548. Robaut Collection.

Douai Abbey, Woolhampton.
Abbot's Archives: B.Weldon, 'Memorials', 5 vols., and his Chronological Notes. Eighteenth-century uncatalogued MSS collection, MSS Cab IR/9/10. Cab III/L. Cab. IV (St. Edmund's Accounts). C I R (H) 5.

I/L/D Stuart. I/L/E. MSS XII, XIII, XV, EX11/11, 27, 49, 62. W. Hewlett, 'Annals'. Kellet's Accounts, 1790-96. Mackey Transcripts, 'Memoirs of the Society of St. Edmund, 1749-56', 5 vols. Library Catalogue of the Society of St. Edmund. St. Edmund's, Paris: Clothing and Profession Book 1671-1781. St. Edmund's, Paris: Mass Obligations Book. St. Edmund's, Paris: Library Catalogue, c. 1791. Scott Box, 35-40, 44-50, 47, 48, 52, 53, 59, 79, 91, 102, 108, 109, 123, 131, 134, 135, 138, 140, 142b, 148, 150. South Province Mass Obligations Book. Burial Register of St. Edmund's, Paris. C. Walmesley: transcripts.

Downside Abbey, Bath
Abbot's Archives: Arras Transcripts. Bastwell Fund's Account Book. Birt Papers: Boxes 3, 6, 7, 9, 10. Boxes 762, 763, 783. Howard/Wright Account Book. MSS: 37, 51, 52, 58H, 68, 70, 146, 168, 180, 186, 190, 201, 202, 205, 206, 212, 255, 424, 425, 445, 456, 531, 532, 533, 534, 566, 576, 590, 595, 596, 635, 677, 678, 2013. Nancy Transcripts. North Province Account Book, 3, North Province Accounts 1769-1830. North Province, Loose Accounts. South Province Daily Accounts 1738-1754. South Province Accounts 1717-1826. MS J. Townson, 'Historia Monasterii...Lambspring'. MS B. Weldon, 'Chronological Notes'.

Durham Record Office.
Birtley Mission Register (transcript).

Edinburgh: National Library of Scotland.
MS 8291. Forbes MSS.

Edinburgh: Scottish Catholic Archives.
William Lesley MSS: Ellis Letters, 1-11.

Hull University Library.
Everingham Estate Correspondence, DDEV/60/84, 86. Arundel Castle MSS (E) 54118.

Lanherne: Carmelite Monastery.
Lanherne Mission Register.

Leeds Diocesan Archives.
Confirmation Returns.

Leeds: Grammar School.
Thoresby Collection.

Lille.
Archives du Nord: 18 H, 20 H, Série D.

Little Malvern Catholic Church.
Malvern Mission Register.

London (Farm Street): Archives of the English Province S.J.
College of St. Aloysius, Correspondence. Letters of Bishops and Cardinals, 1753-1853 I. Thorpe, Misc. Letters.

London (Forest Gate): Archives of the English Province O.F.M.
Parkinson MSS, D. 48F. LX; D. 4BF. LX; BF. XLIV; JC. 2.

London (Kensington) see Westminster.

London: Lambeth Palace.
MSS 932, 933, 1029, 1770. Gibson 13/941/105; 14/942/142.

London: Somerset House.
Lawkland Mission Register.

Nancy.
Meurthe-et-Moselle, Séries H 47-102; L 2039; Q 38, 195, 695.

Northumberland Record Office.
Forster, Transcripts. Swinburne of Capheaton Papers (ZSW).

Norwich: Norfolk Record Office.
Box Dis/9.

Nottingham: University Library.
Portland MSS PwA 2126a-i.

Oxford: Bodleian Library.
Carte 180, 181, 204, 208, 209, 210, 222, 226, 281. Rawlinson: Letters VII, D 1091, 1348.

Oxford: Christchurch.
Wake MSS: Letters 10/175, 176. 22/152, 153, 246, 339, 341, 342. 23/68. 30/181, 241, 253.

Paris: Archives Nationales.
Série D XIX, Comité ecclésiastique. Série E 1946, 2079 ff.207-12,

Conseil du Roi. Série F 19, 6283. G9 66, Commission des Réguliers. Série H5 3896, Etablissements Religieux: Bénédictins Anglais. Série LL 1420, Registres: Bénédictins Anglais. Série K 1303, nos. 26-57, 106-07, Monuments Historiques:Histoire Etrangère; Angleterre. Série M 865, Mélanges et Manuscrits et papiers diverses; Série M 797, Mélanges. Série NII 53, Seine-et-Marne. Série N III 307, 517, Seine. Série O1, 24, 28, 30, 405, Maison du Roi: Registres des depêches ministerielles. Série Q2 117. Série S 1925, Baux de propriété. Série S 3656, 3657, Biens des Etablissements Religieux Supprimés: Paris, Bénédictins anglais; Série S 4619, Bénédictines anglaises. Série S* 6926, 6959, Biens des Etablissements Religieux Supprimés: La Celle. Série V5 1250, 1253, 1255, 1258, Grand Conseil. Série X1A 8679 f.456, Parlement du Paris: Registres. Série Z1F 609 ff.96-8, Bureau des Finances. Série 22 G 24, Fonds de...Meaux.

Paris: Bibliothèque Mazarine.
MS 4057.

Paris: Bibliothèque Nationale.
Nouvelles acquisitions françaises, 7488 f.37. Manuscrits français 21612 ff.13-14. Fonds Français 17774 f.26. Z Senne 2725 (II). MS Latin 9154-61, 15440.

Preston: Lancashire Record Office.
Mission Registers: Brownedge; Gillmoss; Hindley; Liverpool, Seel Street; Ormskirk; Standish; Walton-le-Dale/Brownedge; Warrington; Woolton. RCHi/6.

Rome: English College.
MS 50. Scritture, 71:1.

Rome: Propaganda Fide.
Acta: 37; 62/26; 67/20; 73/6; 76/8; 77/15; 90/7; 93/10; 103/21;104/16; 110/23; 111/16; 112/127; 116/10; 126/9; 133/9, 10, 14; 134/23; 149/3; 153/13; 154/15; 164/3. CP: 32; 85; 116. SOCG: 546/6; 556/6; 559/15; 623/7; 639/10; 641/37; 676/21; 678/16; 703/23; 706/16; 711/27; 765/9; 798/9; 852/3; 862/13; 867/15. SC: dal 1627 al 1707: Anglia 1: CP dall'Anno 1708 atto. il 1727: Anglia 2: CP dal 1728 al 1740: Anglia 3: 1741-1760: Anglia 4.

Rome: Archivio Segreto Vaticano.
Fondo Albani: Tome II: VI/168. Tome I: I/163 X/145,37. Segretaria di Stato: Nunziatura di Inghilterra: 22; 23; 24; 25.

Stratford-upon-Avon: Shakespeare Trust.
Coughton MS 1090.

Upholland.
Banister MSS.

Ushaw College, Durham.
Ushaw College MSS (UCM), I-V.

Warwick Bridge Catholic Church.
Warwick Mission Register.

Westminster, Archives of the Archbishop of Westminster.
Main Series volumes: XXXV, XXXVI, XXXVII, XXXVIII, XXXIX, XL, XLI, XLII. Epistolae Variorum, vii, viii, ix, xiii, xiv. Bishop Challoner's Letter-Book. Ware Series, 12.

Westminster City Archives.
Gillow MSS.

Whitehaven Catholic Church.
Whitehaven Mission Register.

Wigan Record Office.
D/DSt/ C4/4 10. D/D STC 4/4 and 7. D/D WRC 418. D/D WRC 4/8Dem.14.

Windsor Castle: Royal Archives.
Stuart Papers.

Woolhampton: see Douai Abbey.

Worcester: St. George's Church.
Spetchley Park Mission Register.

York: Bar Centre.
Everingham MSS.

BIBLIOGRAPHY B

PRINTED CONTEMPORARY BOOKS AND ARTICLES

J. Berington, *The Memoirs of Gregory Panzani*, Birmingham 1793 (repr. 1970).

J. Berington, *The State and Behaviour of English Catholics*, London 1780.

J. B. Brewer, *Theses Theologico-Hebraicae de Prophetia*, Paris 1766.

A. Bromley, De Novae Legis Sacramentis, *Nancy 1771*

Calendarium a Congregationis Anglicanae Ordinis S. Benedicti Monachis Observandum, Paris 1784.

Calendarium Congregationis Anglo Benedictinae, Duaci 1755.

R. Challoner, *Britannia Sancta*, London 1745 2 vols.

Constitutiones Congregationis Anglicanae Ordinis Sancti Benedicti; Formularium E.B.C. Ritualis Compendium E.B.C., Paris 1784.

Constitutiones Missionis Benedictinorum Congr. Anglicanae. Duaci 1689

(J. M. Corker), *Meditations on the Passion*, London 1694.

(J. M. Corker), *A Rational Account given by a Young Gentleman to his Uncle of the Motives and Reason why he became a Roman Catholick* (n.d.) (by M.B.)

(J. M. Corker), *Queries to Dr Sacheverell from North-Britain*, ?1710.

(J. M. Corker), *A Sermon on the Blessed Eucharist*, London 1695.

C. Cosin, *The Names of the Roman Catholics, Nonjurors and others who refus'd to take the Oaths to..King George*, London 1746.

(A. A. Crowther and T. V. Sadler), *A dayly exercise of the devout christian*, 1685, and London 1688.

C. Dodd (H. Tootell), *The Church History of England from...1500,... to...1688*, Brussels (Wolverhampton), 1739-42.

P. Ellis, *The first sermon*, (London) 1686.

P. Ellis, *The fourth sermon*, (London) 1686.

P. Ellis, *A sermon preach'd..November the 13, 1686*, (London) 1686.

P. Ellis, *A sermon preach'd..the fifth of December, 1686*, (London) 1686.

P. Ellis, *The sixth sermon*, (London) 1686.

P. Ellis, *The third sermon*, (London) 1686.

P. Ellis, *Two sermons*, (London) 1686.

P. Ellis, *A sermon preached before the Queen Dowager,...St. Stephen's day*, (London) 1687.

A Select Collection of Catholic Sermons, Preach'd before their Majesties, London 1741, 2 vols.

W. Fuller, *Twenty-Six Depositions of Persons of Quality...Proving the whole management of the suppositious birth of the pretended Prince of Wales*, 1702.

Gallia Christiana in provincias ecclesiasticas distributa...Opera et studio Monachorum Congregationis Sancti Mauri, tom. VII, Paris 1744.

P. G(ilmore), *A pious monitor of the Divine Presence*, London 1746, 1756, 1773.

J. Hawkins, *A general defence of the principles of the Reformation, in a letter to the Rev. J. Berington*, 1788.

M. Heatley, *Chronologia Sacra*, Hildesheim 1788.

Histoire du rétablissement de la Congrégation Bénédictine anglaise, Paris 1748.

L. J. Hooke, *Religionis naturalis et revelatae principia*, Paris 1774 (ed. J. B. Brewer).

R. Hudleston, *A Short and plain way to the Faith and Church*, (ed. John Hudleston), (London) 1688, (Edinburgh), (Dublin).

W. Hudleston, *A Recantation Sermon*, London 1729.

W. Hudleston, *Divine Truths Vindicated in the Church of England*, London 1733.

W. Hudleston, *Irresistible Evidence Against Popery*, London 1731.

H. J. Johnston, *A Vindication of the Bp. of Condom's Exposition of the Doctrine of the Catholic Church*, London 1686.

H. J. Johnston, *A Reply to the Defence of the Exposition of the Doctrine of the Church of England*, London 1686 and 1687.

H. J. Johnston, *A repy to the defence of the doctrine*, London 1687.

H. J. Johnston, *A Full Answer to the Second Defence of the Exposition of the Church of England*, London 1687.

H. J. Johnston, *A Letter from the Vindicator of the Bishop of Condom*, London 1687.

N. Johnston, *The Assurance of Abby and other Church-lands to the possessors*, London 1687.

G. Knowles, *Materia Medica Botanica*, London 1723.

G. Langley, *The Life and adventures of G.Langley*, London 1740.

Lettre d'un Seigneur Anglais à un Ami, (1749).

Lettres des Provinciaux Bénédictins, et Responses de Messieurs les Vicaires Apostoliques, (1753).

J. Mabillon and T. Ruinart, *Opera Posthuma*, Paris 1724 (repr. Farnborough 1967), 3 vols.

Rev. Mr. McDonald (A. B. Macdonald), *A Companion to the Altar*, Liverpool, 1792, 2nd ed.

A. McDonald, *Fingal, an Epic Poem, by Ossian*, Liverpool 1808.

(A. B. Macdonald), *The Lay-Man's Afternoon Devotion*, Preston 1778, 1793, 1820(*'as used at Brown-edge, Ormskirk, and Warrington Catholic Chapels. ').*

A. B. M(a)cDonald, *Moral Essays*, Liverpool 1796, 2 vols.

A. B. M(a)Donald, *Select Discourses on the Gospels*, Liverpool 1801, 3 vols.

A. McDonald, *Some of Ossian's Lesser Poems rendered into verse*, Liverpool 1805.

J. Macky, *A Journey through the Austrian Netherlands*, London 1732.

(J. A. Mannock), *The Christian Sacrifice*, London 1726.

(J. A. Mannock), *The Poor Man's Catechism*, London 1752,1762,1770, York 1806,Derby 1843.

J. Mannock, *The Poor Man's Controversy*, 1769.

W. M(arshall), *A Sermon Preach'd before the King and Queen...October 24, 1686*, London 1687.

E. Martène and U. Durand, *Voyage littéraire de deux religieux bénédictins*, Paris 1717-20.

Method of saying the rosary...in the English Benedictine college of St. Gregories at Douay, Douai 1684, 1686 (by N. T.), 1687.

Modus Recitandi Rosarium sicut recitatur in Sodalitate Collegii anglo-Benedictini S. Gregorii. Duaci, n.d.

M. P. (Michael Pembridge), *A Manual of Daily Prayers and Duties of a Christian, with Historical Lessons from the Old and New Testaments, very useful for Children*, London 1785.

(M. B. Pembridge), *The Family Manual of Morning and Evening Prayers*, Hereford 1777.

M. B. Pembridge, *The Roman Catholic Church and religion vindicated*, Bath 1806.

M. P. (Michael Pembridge), *The Whole Duty of a Christian,,* 1775.

J. Porter, *The Life of St. Edward, King and Confessor.* 1710

A. M. Ramsay, *The Travels of Cyrus, to which is annexed A Discourse upon the Theology and Mythology of the Pagans*, Berwick-upon-Tweed 1765, 2 vols.

A. M. Ramsay, *The Life of François de la Motte Fénelon, London* 1723.

Regulae observandae in Anglicanis Missionibus, Rome 1753.

Sig. Pastorini (Charles Walmesley), *Ezechiel's Vision Explained*, London, 1778.

Sig. Pastorini (Charles Walmesley), *The General History of the Christian Church from her birth to her final triumphant state in Heaven, chiefly deduced from the Apocalypse of St. John the Apostle,* 1771, Wigan 1782, Dublin 1790, London 1798, and many subsequent Irish, American and European editions.

Sacrae Congregationis Episcoporum et Regularium, *Facti et Iuris...
Memoriale...Summarium... Card. Tanara Ponente Anglo-Benedictina
praetensae Nullitatis Electionis pro Rmo. Laurentio Fenuick contra
Nonnullos P(atres)*, (Romae) 1720.

T. V. Sadler, *A Daily Exercise of the Devout Christian*, Dublin 1743.

T. Southcott, *Conclusiones theologicae ad universam Summam Theologiae
S. Thomae Aquinatis, juxta ejusdem principia, una cum annexis
additionalibus ad duos priores libros Decretalium Gregorii Noni*, Duaci
1695.

J. Stourton, *Thesis Theologicae ex Secunda Secundae D. Thomae
Aquinatis*, Duaci 1700.

*Summarium...Restrict. Facti et Juris..Benedicto XIV una cum Congregatio
Particulari per S.S. Deputata..Anglicana pro Superioribus Missionum, ac
earum Missionariis*, Rome (1750).

H. Swinburne, *Travels in the Two Sicilies in the years 1777, 1778, 1779
and 1780*, London 1783.

(G. A. Touchet), *Historical collections*, London 1686.

J. Townson, *Brevis Explicatio Missae*, Hildesheim 1703.

J. Townson, *Enchiridion Confessariorum*, Hildesheim 1705.

C. Walmesley, *Analyse des Mesures, des Rapports, et des Angles*, Paris
1749, 1754.

C. Walmesley, *Catechism for First Communicants*, London 1781, 1829.

C. Walmesley, *De Inaequitalitatibus Motuum Lunarium*, Florence 1758.

C. Walmesley, *Exhortations to be used in the Administration of the Sacraments...in the Western District*, 1769.

C. Walmesley, *Instructions, Regulations and Prayers for the Indulgences in
the Western District*, 1764.

C. Walmesley, 'On the Irregularities in the Motion of a Satellite', *Philosophical Transactions, 1758.*

C. Walmesley, 'On the Irregularities in the Planetary Motions', *Philosophical Transactions, 1761.*

C. Walmesley, *Theorie du Mouvement des Apsides*, Paris 1749.

C. Walmesley, *The Theory of the Motion of the Apsides in General, and of
the Apsides of the Moon's Orbit in particular*, London 1754.

J. C. Wilks, *A discourse (at Bath) pronounced during the Illness of his
Majesty in 1788*, Birmingham 1801.

J. C. Wilks, *Theses Theologico-Hebraicae Chaldaicae et Graecae*, Paris
1770.

J. Wilson (trans.), *Histoire générale de l'Eglise chrétienne..traduit de
l'anglais de Mgr. Pastorini, par un religieux bénédictin de la Congregation
de S. Maur*, Rouen 1777.

J. W. O.S.B. (J. Wythie), *The Creed Expounded*, 1735.

A. Wood, *Athenae Oxoniensis*, London 1721.

BIBLIOGRAPHY C

PRINTED BOOKS AND ARTICLES.

D. Agius, 'The Lambspring Council Book, 1715-1802', *DR, 355, April 1986, 156-61*.

C. Almond, *The History of Ampleforth Abbey*, London 1903.

J. C. Almond, 'An Old Catholic Controversy', *Ampleforth Journal*, xv, 1, July 1909, 67-82.

J. C. Almond, 'Religious Parsimony at Brindle', *Ampleforth Journal*, xx, 2, Jan. 1915, 129-39.

J. D. Alsop, 'John Macky's 1717 Account of the English Seminaries in Flanders', *RH, xv*, 5, May 1981, 537-41.

'The King against Father Bolton', *Ampleforth Journal*, xxv, 3, May 1920, 212-28.

G. Anstruther, 'The Appointment of Bishop Williams O. P.', *Archivuum Fratrum Praedicatorum*, xxx, 1960, 314-50.

G. Anstruther, 'Cardinal Howard and the English Court 1658-947', *Archivuum Fratrum Praedicatorum*, xxviii, 1958, 315-61.

G. Anstruther, *The Seminary Priests. vol. 3: 1660-1715*, Great Wakering, 1976.

G. Anstruther, *The Seminary Priest. vol. 4: 1715-1800*, Great Wakering, 1977.

H. Aveling, *The Catholic Recusants of the West Riding of Yorkshire, 1558-1790*, (Proceedings of Leeds Philosophical and Literary Society, x, 6, Sept. 1963).

H. Aveling, 'The Catholic Recusancy of the Yorkshire Fairfaxes, Part III', *RH*, vi, 1, Jan. 1961, 12-54.

H. Aveling, 'The Catholic Recusancy of the Yorkshire Fairfaxes, Part IV', *RH*, vi, 2, 1961, 95-111.

H. Aveling, 'An Early Laurentian (Sir Edward Gascoigne)', *Ampleforth Journal*, lxi, 1, Feb. 1956, 39-40.

H. Aveling, 'The Education of Eighteenth-Century English Monks', *DR*,lxxix, 255, Spring 1961, 135-152.

H. Aveling, *Northern Catholics*, London 1966.

H. Aveling, 'Pensioners at the Benedictine College at Dieulouard (1619-1756)', *RH, v*, 1, Jan. 1959, 35-39.

H. Aveling, *Post-Reformation Catholicism in East Yorkshire, 1558-1790*. (East Yorks. Local History Society) 1960.

H. Aveling, 'Some Aspects of Yorkshire Catholic History', in *Studies in Church History*, ed. G. J. Cuming, iv, Leiden 1967, 98-121.

J. C. H. Aveling, *Catholic Recusancy in York 1589-1791*, (CRS monograph 2), 1970.

J. C. H. Aveling, 'The Eighteenth-Century English Benedictines', in E. Duffy, *Challoner and His Church*, London 1981, 152-73.

J. C. H. Aveling, *The Handle and the Axe*, London 1976.

B. Bassett, 'The Arundells of Wardour', *The Month*, clxxxii, 954, Nov-Dec 1946, 422-9.

A. C. F. Beales, *Education under Penalty*, London 1963.

W. Beamont (ed.), 'The Jacobite Trials at Manchester in 1694', *Chetham Society*, xviii, Old Series, 1853.

Dom Beaunier, *Recueil Historique des Archévêchés, Evêchés, Abbayes, et Prieurés de France*, Paris ed. 1905, 1906, 2 vols.

C. L. Becker, *The Heavenly City of The Eighteenth-Century Philosophers*, New Haven 1959.

D. A. Bellenger, *English and Welsh Priests,1558-1800*, Bath, 1984.

Benedictines of Stanbrook, *In a Great Tradition*, London 1956.

G. V. Bennett, *The Tory Crisis in Church and State, 1685-1730*, Oxford 1975.

T. Bentley, *Journal of a Visit to Paris, 1776*, Univ. of Sussex 1977.

T. A. Birrell, *Catholic Allegiance and the Popish Plot*, Nijmegen 1950, and *DR*, lxviii, 214, Oct. 1950, 439-61.

T. A. Birrell, 'James Maurus Corker and Dryden's Conversion', *English Studies*, liv, 5 Oct. 1973, 461-70.

H. N. Birt, 'A Batch of Letters throwing light on the History of St. Gregory's', *DR*, xviii, Dec. 1899, 260-77.

H. N. Birt, *History of Downside School*, London 1902.

H. N. Birt, 'List of Students at St. Gregory's School, Douai, from the year 1781 to 1793', *DR*, xviii, July 1899, 147-59.

H. N. Birt, *Obit Book of the English Benedictines from 1600 to 1912*, Edinburgh 1913, reprinted Farnborough 1970.

H. N. Birt, 'An Old Douai Account Book', *DR*, xviii, Mar. 1899, 18-35.

H. N. Birt, 'An Old Account Book', *DR*, xviii, July 1899, 140-46.

G. Birtill, *In the Footsteps of the Faithful: St. Joseph's, Brindle, 1677-1977*, p. p. 1977.

H. H. Bisbee, 'John Tatham, alias Gray', *The Pennsylvania Magazine of History and Biography*, lxxxiii, 3 July, 1959, 253-64.

Bishop Richard Challoner, 1691-1781: A Bicentennial Exhibition, London 1981.

E. Bishop, 'The Beginning of Douay Convent', *DR*, xvi, March 1897, 21-35.

E. Bishop, 'A Gossip over some Old Account books', *DR*, xv, Dec. 1896, 238-57.

E. Bishop, 'The First Prior of St. Gregory's, *DR*, vi(xxv), 1, Easter 1906, 52-66.

J. M. Blom, *The Post-Tridentine English Primer*, (CRS monograph 3), 1982.

F. O. Blundell, *Old Catholic Lancashire*, London 1925, 1938, 1941, 3 vols.

J. Bossy, 'Catholic Lancashire in the Eighteenth Century', in *Essays Presented to Michael Roberts*, ed. J. Bossy and P. Jupp, Belfast 1976, 54-69.

J. Bossy, *The English Catholic Community, 1570-1850*, London 1975.

J. Bossy, 'Four Catholic Congregations in Rural Northumberland, 1780-1850', *RH, ix, 2*, April 1967, 88-119.

G. Bradley, *Yorkshire Catholics*, Leeds, 1985.

W. Mazière Brady, *Annals of the Catholic Hierarchy in England 1585-1786*, London 1877.

H. Bremond, *Histoire littéraire du sentiment religieux en France*, Paris, 1923-32, 9 vols.

M. Bugner, *Cadre architectural et vie monastique des bénédictins de la congrégaion de Saint-Maur*, Nogent-le-Roi 1984.

M. Bruchet, *Répertoire Numérique des Archives Départmentales du Nord.* Série H, Lille 1928.

'The Buildings at Dieulouard', *Ampleforth Journal*, i, July 1895, 77-85.

T. Burke, *The Catholic History of Liverpool*, Liverpool 1910.

E. H. Burton, *The Life and Times of Bishop Challoner*, London 1909, 2 vols.

E. H. Burton and E. Nolan (ed.), *The Douay College Diaries: The Seventh Diary 1715-1778*, (CRS xxviii), London 1928.

Charles Butler, *Historical Memoirs respecting the English, Irish and Scottish Catholics*, London 1819-21, 4 vols.

Cuthbert Butler, 'Daily Life at Old St. Gregory's', *DR*, xi, 1892, 28-49.

Cuthbert Butler, *Notes on the Origin and Development of the Restored E.B.C., 1600-1660*, p.p. 1887.

Calendar of State Papers, Domestic, 1696, London 1913.

Calendar of State Papers, Domestic, June 1687-February 1689, 1691-1692, 1696.

W. J. Callahan and D. Higgs (ed.), *Church* and *Society in Catholic Europe of the Eighteenth Century*, Cambridge 1979.

R. F. Campbell, 'The English Benedictines', *The Month*, xv, 268, Oct 1886, 228-38.

F. Caraffa, *Monasticon Italiae. I, Roma e Lazio*, Rome 1981.

A. de Cardevacque, 'Le Collège de Saint-Vaast', *Mémoires de la Société d'Agriculture de Sciences & d'Arts séant à Douai*, Douai, xv, 1882.

A Carmelite, 'Lanherne', *South Western Catholic History*, ii, 1984, 44-46.

G. V. C., (G.V. Cavanagh and D.Dewar) *List of Boys at St. Gregory's,* Downside Abbey, Bath 1972.

Catholic Record Society, London 1905, i, 'Miscellanea I'.

CRS, London 1906, ii, 'Miscellanea II'.

CRS, London 1906, iii, 'Miscellanea III'.

CRS, London 1907, iv, 'Miscellanea IV'.

CRS, London 1909, vi, 'Miscellanea V'.

CRS, London 1909, vii, 'Miscellanea VI'.

CRS, London 1910, viii, 'The "Blue Nuns" of Paris'.

CRS, London 1911, ix, 'Miscellanea VII'.

CRS, London 1913, xii, 'Obituaries'.

CRS, London 1913, xiii, 'Miscellanea VIII'.

CRS, London 1914, xiv, 'Miscelleanea IX'.

CRS, London 1914, xv, 'Lancashire Registers I: The Fylde I'.

CRS, London 1915, xvi, 'Lancashire Registers II: The Fylde II'.

CRS, London 1915, xvii, 'Miscellanea X'.

CRS, London 1916, xx, 'Lancashire Registers III: Northern Part'.

CRS, London 1917, xix, 'Miscellanea XI'.

CRS, London 1921, xxii, 'Miscellanea XII'.

CRS, London 1922, xxiii, 'Lancashire Registers: Brindle and Samlesbury'.

CRS, London 1925, xxv, 'English Dominican Papers'.

CRS, London 1926, xxvi, 'Miscellanea XIII'.

CRS, London 1927, xxvii, 'Miscellanea'.

CRS, London 1931, xxxi, 'Lancashire Registers V'.

CRS, 1932, xxxii, 'Miscellanea'.

CRS, 1941, xxxviii, 'Registers of the Catholic Chapels Royal and of the Portuguese Embassy Chapel 1662-1829, I, Marriages'.

CRS, 1943, xl, 'Liber Ruber of the English College, Rome'.

CRS, London 1968, lx, 'Documents from the Ellesmere Manuscripts'.

CRS, 'The Old Brotherhood of the English Secular Clergy: Catalogue of Part of the Archives', London 1968.

A Century and a Half: St. Peter's, Seel Street, 1788-1938, p.p. 1938.

H. Chadwick, 'The Seizure of the English College, Douai, and the imprisonment at Doullens, 1793-94', *RH,* viii, 3, Oct 1965, 147-57.

O. Chadwick, *The Popes and European Revolution,* Oxford 1981.

B. Charlton, *The Recollections of a Northumbrian Lady, 1815-1866',* London 1949.

E. Charlton, *Memorials of North Tyndale,* Newcastle 1871.

P. Chaunu, *La civilisation de l'Europe des lumières,* Paris 1971.

P. Chaunu, 'Jansenisme et frontière de catholicité(xviie et xviiie siecles). A propos du Jansenisme Lorrain', *Revue Historique,* ccxxvii, 1962, 46-55.

G. Chaussinand-Nogaret, 'Une Elite insulaire au service de l'Europe les Jacobites au xviiie siècle', *Annales, Economies, Societés, Civilisations*, 28, 1973, 1097-1122.

Y. Chaussy, *Les Benedictins Anglais Refugiés en France au XVIIe siècle, 1611-1669*, Paris 1967.

A. Cherel, *Fénelon au xviiie siècle en France (1715-1820). Son prestige, son influence*, Paris 1917.

P. Chevallier, *Histoire de la Franc-Maconnerie Française*, Paris 1974, 3 vols.

P. Chevallier, *Loménie de Brienne et l'ordre monastique 1768-1789*, Paris 1959, 1960, 2 vols.

J. P. Chinnici, *The English Catholic Enlightenment*, Shepherdstown 1980.

G. Clanché, *La Bière des Bénédictins Anglais de Dieulouard*, Nancy 1933.

T. H. Clancy, *English Catholic Books, 1640-1700*, Chicago 1974.

A. Clark (ed.), *Wood's Life and Times*, Oxford 1892-94, ii, iii.

R. Clark, *Strangers and Sojourners at Port Royal*, Cambridge 1932.

J. S. Clarke, *The Life of James II*, London 1816, 2 vols.

E. Clavering, 'Catholics and the Rise of the Durham Coal Trade', *Northern Catholic History*, xvi, Autumn 1982, 15-24.

W. Cole, *A Journal of my Journey to Paris in the Year 1765*, ed. by H. Waddell, London 1931.

G. P. Connolly, 'Shifting Congregations: Catholic rural migration in late eighteenth-century Lancashire', in *Catholic Englishmen*, ed. J. A. Hilton, Wigan 1984.

G. P. Connolly, 'The Secular Missioner of the North in the Evangelical Age of the English Mission', *North West Catholic History*, x, 1983, 8-31.

L. H. Cottineau, *Répertoire topo-bibliographique des abbayes et prieurés*, Macon 1939, 1970, 3 vols.

M. N. L. Couve de Murville, *Catholic Cambridge*, London 1983.

G. R. Cragg, *The Church and the Age of Reason*, Harmondsworth 1970.

A. Cramer, 'St. John's Easingwold', *Ampleforth Journal*, lxxxix, 1, Spring 1984, 21-28.

J. D. Crichton, 'Jansenism and the English Recusants', *Worcestershire Recusant*, 41, June 1983, 16-24.

J. D. Crichton, 'The Laity and the Liturgy c. 1600 to 1900', *Worcestershire Recusant*, 43, June 1984, 1-14.

F. A. Crisp, *The Catholic Registers of Weston Underwood*, p.p. 1887.

Critical Review, London 1758, vi.

E. Cruickshanks (ed.), *Ideology and Conspiracy: Aspects of Jacobitism 1689-1759*, Edinburgh 1982.

E. Cruickshanks, *Political Untouchables: The Tories and the '45*, London 1979.

Cumbria Archives Department, 'Sources on Roman Catholic History in the Cumbria Record Office, The Castle, Carlisle', *North West Catholic History'*, vii, 1980, 20-25.

J. I. Cummins, 'Newburgh Priory and the Fauconbergs: Part II', *Ampleforth Journal*, xx, 3, May 1915, 236-44.

J. I. Cummins, 'St. Cuthbert's Relics', *Ampleforth Journal*, xxx, 1, Autumn 1924,1-6; xxx 2, Spring 1925, 102-03; xxxi, 2, Autumn 1925, 37.

J. I. Cummins, 'A Yorkshire Hermitage: Easingwold', *Ampleforth Journal*, xxiv, 3, May 1919, 182-88.

P. Cunningham, 'The Rt. Rev. Charles Walmesley', *Douai Magazine*, xvi, 4, Autumn 1951, 181-7.

P. Cunningham, 'The "Society of St. Edmund", Paris, 1749-1756', *Douai Magazine*, Spring 1956, 3-10.

H. Daniel-Rops, *The Church in the Eighteenth Century*, London 1964.

L. Dancoisne, *Histoire des établissements Religieux Britanniques fondés à Douai avant la révolution française*, Douai 1880.

G. Daumet, *Notice sur les Etablissements religieux anglais, écossais et Irlandais*, (in Memoires de la Societé de l'histoire de Paris et de l'Isle-de-France, Paris 1912, xxix, 1-224).

H. Davies, *Worship and Theology in England from Andrewes to Baxter and Fox, 1603-1690*, Princton 1975.

L. Dechristé, *Douai Pendant La Révolution*, Paris 1880.

L. Dechristé, *Les Tableaux, vases sacrées...appartenant aux Eglises Abbatiales, Collègiales et Paroissales de Douai...au moment de la Révolution*, Douai 1877.

C. Deshaisnes, *Les archives départementales du Nord pendant la Revolution*, Lille 1873.

C. Dehaisnes, *Catalogue de Bibliothèque, Douai*, Paris 1878.

C. Dehaisnes, *Notice sur les archives communales de Douai*, Lille 18 68.

C. Dehaisnes, *Notice sur la bibliothèque publique de Douai*, Douai 1868.

J. Delumeau, *Catholicism from Luther to Voltaire*, London 1977.

W. S. Dempsey, *The Story of the Catholic Church in the Isle of Man*, Billinge 1958.

J. Dennistoun, *Memoirs of Sir Robert Strange, Knt.,...and of his Brother-in-Law Andrew Lumisden*, London 1855, 2 vols.

B. Denvir, *The Eighteenth Century: Art, Design and Society 1689-1789*, London 1983.

J. P. Dewis, *A Brief History of the Catholic Church in Wooton Wawen from the Reformation to the Present Day*, p.p., 1983.

J. G. Dolan, 'English Benedictine Missions: the Diocese of Shrewsbury', *DR, xxvi(New* series vii), 78, Dec. 1907, 254-63.

J. G. Dolan, 'English Benedictine Missions: Monmouthshire and South Wales', *DR,* iv(xxiv), 3, Christmas 1904, 292-304.

J. G. Dolan, 'English Benedictine Missions: Oxfordshire', *DR*, v(xxiv), 1, Easter 1905, 85-104.

J. G. Dolan, 'English Benedictine Missions: Staffordshire', *DR*, xxvi(New Series vii), 76, March 1907, 52-57.

J. G. Dolan, 'English Benedictine Missions, Warwickshire', *DR*, vi(xxv), 2, July 1906, 204-91.

J. G. Dolan, 'English Benedictine Missions: Worcestershire', *DR*, v,(xxiv), 3, Christmas 1905, 307-26.

G. Dolan, 'After the Revolution, Perseverance under Difficulties', *DR*, xviii, July 1899, 165-77.

G. Dolan, 'The Carylls of West Grinstead', *DR*, xiii, Dec. 1894, 264-72.

G. Dolan, 'English Benedictine Missions: Bedfordshire, Buckinghamshire, and Northamptonshire', *DR*, xvi, March 1897, 61-70.

G. Dolan, 'English Benedictine Missions: Berkshire and its Benedictine Associations', *DR*, xix, July 1900, 221-27.

G. Dolan, 'English Benedictine Missions: Bonham, Bath etc.', *DR*, iii(xxii), 3, Dec. 1903, 293-304.

G. Dolan, 'English Benedictine Missions: Dorset, Devon, Cornwall', *DR*, 1 (new series), Dec. 1901, 264-77.

G. Dolan, 'English Benedictine Missions: Gloucestershire', *DR*, ii(xxii), 3, Dec. 1902, 266-85.

G. Dolan, 'English Benedictine Missions: Hampshire', *DR*, 1 (new series), July 1901, 104-18.

G. Dolan, 'English Benedictine Missions: Kent and Sussex', *DR*, xix, July 1900, 164-71.

G. Dolan, 'English Benedictine Missions: London, south of the Thames', *DR*, xviii, Dec. 1899, 278-86.

G. Dolan, 'English Benedictine Missions: Norfolk', *DR*, xv, July 1896, 162-71.

G. Dolan, 'English Benedictine Missions: Somerset', *DR*, iii(xxii), 2 July 1903, 187-99.

G. Dolan, 'English Benedictine Missions: Suffolk', *DR*, xv, Dec. 1896, 258-70.

G. Dolan, 'English Benedictine Missions: Wiltshire', *DR*, ii (xxi), April 1902, 89-100.

G. Dolan, 'Gleanings in Italy', *DR*, xix, Mar 1900, 90-6.

G. Dolan, 'James II and the Benedictines in London', *DR*, xviii, Mar. 1899, 94-103.

G. Dolan, 'A Lambspring Poet', *DR*, ii (xxi), July 1902, 146-56.

G. Dolan, *Lancashire and the Benedictines, p.p.* 1898, and *Trans. of the Historic Society of Lancashire and Cheshire*, xlix (new series xiii), 1898.

G. Dolan, 'An Old Somerset Mission: Leighland', *DR*, xii, Dec. 1893, 239-48.

Douai (Archives Municipales), *L'Université de Douai, 1560-1790*, Douai 1960.

Douai Abbey and School, p.p. 1936, 1937.

D. C. Douglas, *English Scholars*, London 1943.

Downside, A Monk of (A.F.Flemming), *The Mission and Church of St. Edmund, King and Martyr*, Bungay 1900.

F. C. Doyle, 'St. Edmund's, Paris, I', *DR*, xxxii, 95, 1913, 125-47. F. C Doyle, 'St. Edmund's, Paris, II', *DR*, xxxiii, 96, 250-75.

F. C. Doyle (ed.), *Tercentenary of St.Edmund's Monastery*, London 1917.

J. C. Dufermont, 'Les Colleges-Anglais, Ecossais, Irlandais, à Lille et à Douai, de l'Avenement de Jacques II à la Mort de Louis XVI (1685-1793)', *University of Lille, 1967*.

E. Duffy (ed.), *Challoner and his Church*, London 1981.

E. Duffy, 'Ecclesiastical Democracy Detected: I (1769-1787)', *RH*, x, 4, Jan. 1970, 193-209.

E. Duffy, 'Ecclesiastical Democracy Detected: II (1787-1790)', *RH*, x, 6, Oct. 1970, 309-31.

E. Duffy, ' "Englishmen in vaine": Roman Catholic allegiance to George I', in *Studies in Church History*, ed. S. Mews, xviii, Oxford 1982.

E. Duffy, 'The English Secular Clergy and the Counter-Reformation', *JEH*, xxxiv, 2, April 1983, 214-30.

E. Duffy, 'Over the Wall: Converts from Popery in Eighteenth Century England', *DR*, xciv, 314, Jan. 1976, 1-25.

E. Duffy, 'Peter and Jack: Roman Catholics and Dissent in Eighteenth Century England', *Dr. Williams's Trust*, 36th Lecture, London 1982.

E. Duffy, ' "Poor Protestant Flies": Conversions to Catholicism in Early Eighteenth-Century England', in *Studies in Church History*, ed. D. Baker, xv, Oxford 1978, 289-304.

E. Duffy, 'Richard Challoner 1691-1781: A Memoir', in his *Challoner and his Church*, London 1981, 1-26.

E. Duffy, 'Richard Challoner and the English Salesian Tradition', *Clergy Review*, lvi, 12, Dec. 1981, 449-55.

E. Duffy, 'A Rubb-Up for Old Soares: Jesuits, Jansenists and the English Secular Clergy', *JEH*, xxviii, 3, July 1977, 291-317.

D. B. S. Durrant, *Memorials of the Sidneys & Woolletts*, Liverpool 1911.

H. R. Duthilloeul, *Catalogue des Manuscrits de la Bibliothéque de Douai*, Douai 1846.

H. R. Duthilloeul, *Histoire Ecclesiastique et Monastique de Douai*, Douai 1861.

E.B.C. Bullarium, Fort Augustus 1912.

E. Edwards, 'Salford Hall, or 'The Nunnery', *Worcestershire Recusant*, 27, June 1976, 2-14.

F. Edwards, *The Jesuits in England from 1850 to the Present Day*, Tunbridge Wells 1985.

D. D. Egbert, *The Tickhill Psalter and Related Manuscripts*, New York/Princeton 1940.

G. A. Ellis, *The Ellis Correspondence*, London 1829, 2 vols.

E. E. Estcourt and J. O Payne, *English Catholic Non-Jurors of 1715*, Farnborough 1969 (reprint).

J. Evans, *Monastic Architecture in France, from the Renaissance to the Revolution*, Cambridge 1964.

J. Evans, *Monastic Iconography in France, from the Renaissance to the Revolution*, London 1968.

Extract from the proceedings of the Board of Administration of the District of Douai, 14th December,1791, realative to the five English, Scotch and Irish houses in that City, London 1792.

D. Farmer, 'Historical Influences on the Early Development of the E.B.C.', *E.B.C. History Symposium Papers*, i, 1, 1981, 5-16.

A. F. Fleming, *A Brief Account of the Benedictine Mission in Bath*, p.p., 1888.

H. Foley, *Records of the English Province of the Society of Jesus*, v-vii, London 1879-83.

B. Ford, 'James Byres, Principal Antiquarian for the English Visitors in Rome', *Apollo*, cxix, June 1974, 446-61.

'A Forgotten Episode in Benedictine History', *DR*, xiii, Dec. 1894, 259-63.

A. M. C. Forster, 'Catholicism in the Diocese of Durham in 1767', *Ushaw Magazine*, lxx, 215, July 1962, 68-92.

A. M. C. Forster, 'An Outline History of the Catholic Church in North East England. V. Northumberland 1688-1720', *Northern Catholic History*, Autumn 1979, 10-16.

B.Fothergill, *The Cardinal King*, 1958.

J. C. Fowler, *The Benedictines in Bath during a Thousand Years*, Yeovil 1985.

R. S. France (ed.), *The Registers of Estates of Lancashire Papists 1717-88. iii, 1717*, (Record Society of Lancashire and Cheshire, xcviii, cviii, cxvii), 1945, 1960, 1977.

A. Franklin, *Les anciennes bibliothèques de Paris*, Paris 1873, 2 vols.

Fra Paolo, *Common Sense versus Pastorini*, Dublin 125.

T. F. Friedman 'Sir Thomas Gascoigne and His Friends in Italy' *Leeds Arts Calendar*, Leeds 1976, 16-23.

R. C. Fuller, *Alexander Geddes, 1737-1802. A Pioneer of Biblical Criticism*, Sheffield 1984.

M. F. Gain, 'The Stuart Papers at Windsor', *Royal Stuart Papers*, xvii, 1981. J. Garrett, *The Triumph of Providence*, Cambridge 1980.

A. Gasquet, 'Segni', *DR*, xvi, Dec 1897, 231-40.

J. P. Gavin, 'An Englishman in Exile: A Recent Work in Recusant History', *RH, xv*, 1, May 1979, 11-14.

T. E. Gibson, *Lydiate Hall and its Associations*, 1876.

J. Gillow, *A Biographical Dictionary of the English Catholics*, London 1885, 5 vols.

J. Gillow, 'Lancashire Catholicism', *Trans. of the Historic Society of Lancashire and Cheshire*, liv (new series xviii), 1902, 212-22.

J. Gillow and R. Trappes-Lomax (ed.), *The Diary of the 'Blue Nuns' of Paris 1658-1810*, (CRS viii), London 1910.

B. Green, 'Anselm Bolton O.S.B.', *Ampleforth Journal*, lxxxxi, ii, Winter 1985, 27-32.

B. Green, 'Bede Brewer, the Founder of Modern Ampleforth', *Ampleforth Journal*, lxxxiv, 2, Autumn 1979, 134-38.

B. Green, *The English Benedictine Congregation*, London 1980.

B. Green, 'The Fall of Abbot Heatley', *DR*, cvii, 327, April 1979, 81-98.

B. Green, 'Prior Richard Marsh', *Ampleforth Journal*, cx, i, Spring 1985, 9-11.

P. Guilday, *The English Catholic Refugees on the Continent, 1558-1795*, London 1914.

A. Gwynn, 'A Forgotten Irish Theologian', *Studies*, Autumn 1974, 259-68.

D. Gwynn, *Bishop Challoner*, London 1946.

D. Gwynn, *The Struggle for Catholic Emancipation 1750-1829*, London 1928.

J. H. H., 'An Old Northern Mission', *Douai Magazine*, March 1903, 28-35.

E. E. Y. Hales, *Revolution and Papacy, 1769-1846*, London 1969.

L. Hanley, *A History of St. Anne's, Ormskirk*, Ormskirk 1982.

P. R. Harris (ed.), *Douai College Documents*, (CRS lxiii), 1972.

M. J. Hartharn, 'The Benedictines in Post-Reformation Essex', *Essex Recusant*, ii, 1, April 1960, 32-7.

J. H. Harting, *London Catholic Missions*, London 1903.

P. Hazard, *European Thought in the Eighteenth Century*, Harmondsworth 1965.

T. Hearne, *Collections*, (Oxford Historical Society), 1885-1918, 11 vols.

T. Hearne, *The Remains*, London 1966.

B. Hemphill, *The Early Vicars Apostolic in England*, London 1954.

G. D. Henderson, *Chevalier Ramsay*, Edinburgh 1952.

G. D. Henderson (ed.), *Mystics of the North-East*, Aberdeen 1954.

M. Henderson and L. Lascelles, *Catholic Registers of Little Malvern*, p.p.1975.

F. W. Hilles (ed.), *New Light on Dr. Johnson*, New Haven 1959.

J. A. Hilton, 'The Case of Wigan: Catholic Congregationalism in the Age of Revolution', *North West Catholic History*, x, 1983, 1-7.

J. A. Hilton, 'The Cumbrian Catholics', *Northern History*, xvi, 1980, 40-58.

Historical Manuscripts Commission, Carlisle MSS, London 1897.

Historical Manuscripts Commission, 'Finch MSS III, IV', London 1957, 1965.

Historical Manuscripts Commission, 'Stuart Papers', London 1902-23, 7 vols.

B. Hoban, 'The Philosophical Tradition of Douay', *Ushaw Magazine*, 189, Dec. 1953, 145-59.

T. Hodgkinson, 'Christopher Hewetson, an Irish Sculptor in Rome', *Walpole Society*, xxxiv, 1958, 42-54.

A. M. Hodgson, 'History of Malvern Court VI', *Worcestershire Recusant*, 43, June 1984, 32-45.

G. Holt, *The English Jesuits 1650-1829*, (CRS vol lxx), 1984.

G. Holt (ed.), *The Letter Book of Lewis Sabran S.J.*, (CRS lxii), 1971.

G. Holt, *St. Omers and Bruges Colleges, 1593-1773*, (CRS vol lxix), 1979.

T. G. Holt, 'A Further Note on Some Eighteenth-Century Statistics', *RH*, xi, 3, Oct. 1971, 160-61.

T. G. Holt, 'A Note on some Eighteenth-Century Statistics', *RH*, x, 1, Jan. 1969, 3-10.

P. A. Hopkins, 'The Commission for Superstitious Lands of the 1690s', *RH*, xv, 4, Oct 1980, 265-82.

P. A. Hopkins, 'Sham Plots and Real Plots in the 1690s', in *Ideology and Conspiracy: Aspects of Jacobitism, 1689-1759*, ed. E. Cruickshanks, Edinburgh 1982, 89-110.

E. Horney, *Sefton: A Descriptive and Historical Account*, London 1893.

G. Huelin, 'Some Early Eighteenth-Century Roman Catholic Recusants', *JEH*, vii, 1, April 1956, 61-68.

O. Hufton, 'The French Church', in W. J. Callahan and D. Briggs (ed.), *Church and Society in Catholic Europe of the Eighteenth Century*, Cambridge 1979, 13-33.

P. Hughes, *The Catholic Question 1688-1829*, London 1929.

G. A. M. Janssens and F. G. A. M. Aarts (ed.), *Studies in Seventeenth-Century English Literature, History and Biography*, Amsterdam 1984.

R. C. Jarvis, *Collected Papers on the Jacobite Risings*, Manchester 1971, 2 vols.

J. C. Jeaffreson, *Middlesex County Records*, iii, London 1888.

P. Jebb, 'The Archives of the English Benedictine Congregation kept at St. Gregory's, Downside', *DR*, xciii, 312, July 1975, 208-25.

P. Jenkins, 'A Welsh Lancashire? Monmouthshire Catholics in the 18th century', *RH*, xv, 3, May 1980, 176-88.

C. Johnson, *Prosper Guéranger, (1805-1875): A Liturgical Theologian*, Rome 1984.

G. H. Jones, *The Main Stream of Jacobitism*, Harvard 1954.

J. R. Jones, *The Revolution of 1688 in England*, London 1972.

R. Jones (ed.), 'Calendar of Lille, Archives du Nord 20 H', in *E.B.C. History Symposium Papers, p.p. 1987, 49-89*.

M. B. Joyce, 'The Haggerstons: The Education of a Northumbrian Family', *RH*, xiv, 3, May 1978, 175-92.

H. G. Judge, 'The Congregation of the Oratory in France in the late Seventeenth Century', *JEH*, xii, 1, April 1961, 46-55.

H. A. L. Jukes (ed), 'The Visitation (Returns) of Bishop Thomas Secker, 1738', *Oxfordshire Record Society*, xxxviii, 1957.

B. W. Kelly, *Historical Notes on English Catholic Missions*, London 1907.

N. R. Ker, *Medieval Manuscripts in British Libraries*, Oxford 1977, ii.

J. King and C. Ryskamp (ed.), *The Letters and Prose Writings of William Cowper*, Oxford 1979-84, 4 vols.

J. Kirk, *Biographies of English Catholics*, London 1909.

N. Kowalsky and J. Metzler, *Inventory of the Historical Archives of the Sacred Congregation for the Evangelization of the Peoples or 'De Propaganda Fide'*, Rome 1983.

A. Laird, 'The English College, Rome, under Italian Secular Administration, 1773-1798', *RH*, xiv, 2, Oct. 1977. 127-47.

'Lambspring', *DR*, v, 1886, 209-18.

H. Lane-Fox, *Chronicles of a Wharfedale Parish*, Fort Augustus 1909.

A. Lautel, 'André Michel Ramsay', in *Dictionnaire de Spiritualité*, ed. M.Viller, xiii, Paris 1987, cols. 72-81.

L. Lecestre, *Abbayes, prieurés et couvents d'hommes en France. Liste générale d'apres les papiers de la Commission des Réguliers en 1768*, Paris 1902.

Leeds City Art Gallery, *Church Art from Catholic Yorkshire*, Leeds 1979.

J. Lees-Milne, *The Last Stuarts*, London 1983.

A. Le Glay, *Notice sur Charles Walmesley*, Lille 1858.

S. Lemaire, *La Commission des Reguliers 1766-1780*, Paris 1926.

B.Lenman, *The Jacobite Risings in Britain, 1689-1746*, London 1980.

J-A. Lesourd, *Les Catholiques dans la Societé Anglaise 1765-1865*, Lille/Paris 1978, 2 vols.

L. Lewis, *Connoisseurs and Secret Agents in Eighteenth-Century Rome*, London 1961.

W. S. Lewis and W. H. Smith (ed.), *The Correspondence of Horace Walpole*, ix, Yale 1941.

M. D. R. Leys, *Catholics in England 1559-1829*, London 1961.

W. S. Lilly and J. E. P. Wallis, *A Manual of Law Specially Affecting Catholics*, London 1893.

R. W. Linker, 'The English Roman Catholics and Emancipation: The Politics of Persuasion', *JEH*, xxvii, 2, April 1976, 151-80.

B. Little, *Catholic Churches since 1623*, London 1966.

K. M. Longley, *Heir of Two Traditions: the Catholic Church of St. John the Baptist, Holme-on-Spalding-Moor, 1766-1966*, p.p. 1969.

R. Luckett, 'Bishop Challoner: The Devotionary Writer', in *Challoner and His Church*, ed. E. Duffy, London 1981, 71-89.

D. Lunn, *The English Benedictines*, London 1980.

D. M. Lunn, 'The Anglo-Gallicanism of Dom Thomas Preston', in *Studies in Church History*, ed. D. Baker, ix, Cambridge 1972, 239-46.

D. M. Lunn, 'The Origins and Early Development of the Revived English Benedictine Congregation, 1588-1647', Cambridge Ph. D. thesis, 1970.

M. Lunn, 'Benedictine Opposition to Bishop Richard Smith (1625-1629)', *RH*, xi, 1, Jan. 1971, 1-20.

K. M. Macgrath, 'Catholicism in Devon & Cornwall', *Buckfast Abbey Chronicle*, 1960, 136-66.

M. Mack, *Alexander Pope: A Life*. Yale 1985.

H. B. Mackey, 'From Rome to England, June 1904', *Douai Magazine*, ix, 30, Oct. 1904, 151-62.

H. B. Mackey, 'A Pilgrimage to Dieulouard', *Douai Magazine*, v, 17, Aug. 1899, 9-15.

J. McCann, 'The Bolton Manuscript (Part I), *Ampleforth Journal*, l, 3, Sept. 1945, 117-34.

J. McCann, *English Benedictine Missions*, Oxford 1940.

J. McCann, 'A Gift From Dieulouard', *Ampleforth Journal*, xxxii, 1, Autumn 1926, 19-26.

J. McCann and H. Connolly (Ed.), *The Life of Father Augustine Baker O.S.B. (1575-1641)*, London, n.d.

J. McCann, 'Ten More Baker Manuscripts', *Ampleforth Journal*, lxiii, 2, June 1958, 77-83.

J. McCann and H. Connolly, (ed.), *Memorials of Fr. Augustine Baker*, (CRS xxiii), 1933.

A. McInnes, *The English Town 1660-1760*, London 1980.

A. McInnes, 'The Revolution and the People', in *Britain after the Glorious Revolution, 1689-1714*, ed. G. Holmes, London 1980.

F. McLynn, *Charles Edward Stuart*, London 1988.

J. McManners, *Death and the Enlightenment*, Oxford 1981.

J. McManners, *French Ecclesiastical Society under the Ancien Régime*, Manchester 1968.

B. Magee, 'England's Catholic Population in Penal Times', *Dublin Review,* Oct 1935, 253-68, and Jan 1936, 66-83.

B. Magee, *The English Recusants,* London 1938.

L. Mahieu, 'La philosophie a l'université de Douai au xviiie siecle', *Mélanges de science religieuse,* xiv, 1957, 71-82.

M. Marion, *Dictionnaire des Institutions de la France aux XIIe et XVIIIe siècles,* Paris 1979 repr.

S. Marron, 'Bishop Challoner and his Catechism', *Douai Magazine,* ix, 2, Autumn 1936, 111-20.

S. Marron, 'Paris to Douai: A Chapter of our History', *Douai Magazine,* i,3, Jan 1923, 173-81.

S. Marron, 'St Edmund's: A Prison in the Reign of Terror', *Douai Magazine,* i, 3, Jan 1920, 20-29.

S. Marron, 'Weldon and his Critics', *Douai Magazine,* ii, 2, 1922, 7-19.

V. Marron, 'Some Sources for English Benedictine History', *DR,* lxxxi, 262, Jan. 1963, 50-60.

R. Marsh, 'Dr. Marsh's Account of his Escape from Dieulouard', *Ampleforth Journal,* vi, Dec. 1900, 174-92, vi, April 1901, 307-25, vii, July 1901, 61-74.

J. D. Martin, 'The Antiquarian Collections of Nathaniel Johnston (1629-1705)', Oxford B. Litt. thesis, 1956.

D. Mathew, *Catholicism in England,* London 1938.

J. Miller, *Popery and Politics in England 1660-1688,* Cambridge 1966.

P. Miller, *James II,* London 1971.

J. Milner, *Supplementary Memoirs of English Catholics addressed to Charles Butler,* London 1820.

A. J. Mitchinson, 'The Return of the Papists for the Diocese of Chester, 1705', *North-Western Catholic History,*1956.

Lord Mowbray, Segrave and Stourton (ed.), *The History of the Noble House of Stourton,* London 1899, 2 vols.

T. Murphy, *The Position of the Catholic Church in England and Wales during the Last Two Centuries,* London 1892.

N. Mutton, 'Shropshire Recusants in 1706, 1767 and 1780', *Worcestershire Recusant,* 24, Dec. 1974, 18-31.

B. Navarra, *Filippo Michele Ellis,* Rome 1973.

M. Nédoncelle, *Trois Aspects du Problème Anglo-Catholique au xviie siècle,* Strasbourg 1951.

B. Neveu, 'A Contribution to an Inventory of Jacobite Sources' in *Ideology and Conspiracy: Aspects of Jacobitism 1689-1759,* ed. E. Cruickshanks, Edinburgh 1982, 138-58.

W. Nicholson, *St. Mary's Church, Hexham,* p.p. 1980.

W. J. Nicholson, 'Catholics in Morpeth in the Eighteenth Century', *Northern Catholic History,* viii, Autumn 1978, 11-21.

E. R. Norman, *Church and Society in England 1770-1970*, Oxford 1976.

C. Nordman, 'Les Jacobits écossais en France au xviiie siècle', in *Regards sur l'Ecosse au XVIIIe siècle, ed.* M. S. Plaisant, Univ. of Lille III, 1977.

E. R. Norman, *Roman Catholicism in England from the Elizabethan Settlement to the Second Vatican Council*, Oxford 1985.

M. Norman, 'Dame Gertrude More and the English Mystical Tradition', *RH*, xiii, 3, April 1976, 196-211.

R. O'Donnell, 'The Architectural Setting of Challoner's Episcopate', in *Challoner and His Church*, ed. E. Duffy, London 1981, 55-70.

J. G. O'Leary, 'The Last of the Southcotes of Witham', *Essex Recusant*, ii, 1, 1969, 22-29.

G. Oliver, *Collections illustrating the History of the Catholic Religion in Cornwall, Devon, Dorset, Somerset, Wilts., Gloucester*, London 1857.

S. L. Ollard and P. C. Walker, 'Archbishop Herring's Visitation Returns 1743', i-iv, *Yorks Archaeological Society*, lxxi, lxxii, lxxv, lxxvii, 1928, 1929, 1930.

P. A. O'Neill, 'Alma Mater: St. Gregory's and the Revolution', *Douai Magazine*, vii, Dec. 1895, 3-21.

A. Onslow, 'The Felling Mass Vestment', *Northern Catholic History*, viii, Autumn 1978, 26-28.

J. Orcibal, *Le Cardinal de Bérulle. Evolution d'une spiritualité*, Paris 1965.

J. M. Osborn, *Dr. Johnson and the Contrary Converts*, Yale 1954.

R. R. Palmer, *Catholics and Unbelievers in Eighteenth Century France*, Princeton 1939.

J. O. Payne, *Old English Catholic Missions*, London 1900.

J. O. Payne, *Records of the English Catholics of 1715*, London 1889. J. Peter and C. Poulet, *Histoire Religieuse du Departement du Nord Pendant la Revolution, (1789-1802)*, Lille 1930, 2 vols.

A. G. Petti (ed.), *Recusant Documents from the Ellesmere Manuscripts*, (CRS lx), 1968.

B. Pickering, 'Bishop Challoner and his Catechism', *Clergy Review*, lxv, 1, Jan. 1980, 6-14.

M. Picot, *Mémoires pour servir à l'Histoire Ecclésiastique Pendant le Dix-Huitième Siècle*, Paris 1853-57, 7 vols.

B. Plongeron, *Les Réguliers de Paris devant le Serment Constitutionnel*, Paris 1964.

B. Plongeron, *Théologie et politique au siècle des lumières 1770-1820*, Geneva 1973.

B. Plongeron, *La Vie quotidienne du clergé français au XVIIIe siècle*, Paris 1974.

B. Plumb, *The Warrington Mission: A Bi-Centenary*, p. p., n.d.

R. Porter, *English Society in the 18th Century*, Harmondsworth 1982.

P. Pourat, *La Spiritualité Chrétienne*, Paris, 1930, iv.

J. Prebble, *Culloden*, Harmondsworth 1979.

W. Price, 'Three Jesuits at Plowden Hall in Shropshire in the 18th Century', RH, x, 3, Oct 1965, 165-75.

Public Records Office, *The Records of the Forfeited Estates Commission*, London 1968.

P. Purcell, 'The Jacobite Rising of 1715 and the English Catholics', *EHR*, xliv, July 1929, 418-32.

D. Rees, 'Lamspringe' and 'Englische Benediktiner in Niedersachsen' in *Germania Benedictina*, Band vi, Norddeutschland, ed. U. Faust, Munich 1979, 299-320, 525-49.

C. I. A. Ritchie (ed.), *Papers from Lambeth College Library*, (CRS lvi), 1964, 23-32.

J. M. Robinson, *The Dukes of Norfolk*, Oxford 1982.

P. Roebuck(ed,) , 'Constable of Everingham Estate Correspondence 1726-43, *(Yorks. Archaeological Soc. Records Series, cxxxvi)*, 1976.

P. Roebuck, 'An English Catholic Tour in Europe 1701-03', *RH*, xi, 3, Oct. 1971, 156-59.

P. Roebuck, 'Four Yorkshire Landowning Families 1640-1760', Hull, PhD. dissertation 1969.

P. Roebuck, *Yorkshire Baronets 1640-1760*, Oxford 1980.

H. E. G. Rope, 'Notes on Some Members of the Swinburne Family', *Biographical Studies*, ii, 1953, 87-91.

J. Rowe, *The Story of Catholic Bury St Edmunds, Coldham and the Surrounding District*, p.p. 1980.

M. Rowlands, 'The Iron Age of Double Taxes', *Staffordshire Catholic History*, iii, Spring 1963, 30-46.

M. Rowlands, 'Staffordshire Papists and the Levy of 1723', *Staffordshire Catholic History*, ii, Spring 1962, 32-38.

G. Rudé, *Paris and London in the Eighteenth Century*, New York 1970.

C. Russell, 'Dr. Johnson and the Catholic Church', in *Johnson Club Papers*, ed. by G. W. and J. S., London 1920, 139-58.

G. A. Ryan and L. J. Redstone, *Timperley of Hintlesham*, London 1931.

St. Peter's Seel Street: Centenary Commemoration, p.p. 1938.

B. Sandeman, 'An Interim List of Archives Kept at Ampleforth Abbey, York', *E.B.C. History Symposium Papers*, 1982, 28-33.

R. E. Scantlebury (ed.), *Isle of Wight Registers*, (CRS lix), 1967.

R. E. Scantlebury (ed.), *Registers of Marnhull, Dorset, 1772-1826*, (CRS lvi), 1964, 165-99.

R. E. Scantlebury (ed.), *Hampshire Registers I*, (CRS xlii), London 1948.

P. Schmitz, *Histoire de l'Ordre de S. Benôit*, Maredsous 1942-49, 6 vols.

G. Scott, 'Benedictines and Jacobites', *E.B.C. Symposium Papers*, i, 1, 1981, 17-35.

G. Scott, 'A Benedictine Conspirator: Henry Joseph Johnston (*c.*1656-1723), *Recusant History*, 20, i, May 1990, 58-75.

G. Scott, 'The Collector: a look at Benedictine Archives through the eyes of Bro. Benet Weldon, 1674-1713', *Catholic Archives*, 6, 1986, 25-43.

G. Scott, 'The English Benedictine Confraternity', *DR*, 359, April 1987, 143-63.

G. Scott, 'English Benedictine Missions in Seventeenth and Eighteenth Century Gloucestershire', *Worcestershire Recusant*, 50, Dec 1987, 1-21.

G. Scott, 'A Berkshire Benedictine Mission in the Eighteenth Century', *South Western Catholic History*, 1, 1983, 19-28.

G. Scott, 'Fighting Old Battles: The English Benedictine Mission 1689-1715', *DR*, xcviii, 330, Jan. 1980, 9-24.

G. Scott, 'A Monk's View of the Durham Coal Industry in 1750', *Northern Catholic History*, xv, Spring 1982, 3-12.

G. Scott, '"The Privileges of Trading in that Country": the controversy between the Vicars Apostolic and the Benedictines in the late seventeenth century', in D.A.Bellenger (ed.), *Opening the Scrolls: Essays in honour of Godfrey Anstruther,* Bath 1987, 84-99.

G. Scott, 'Sacredness of Majesty: The English Benedictines and the Cult of King James II', *Royal Stuart Society Papers* XXIII, 1984.

G. Scott, 'Some notes on the Benedictine Secret regarding St Cuthbert's Body in the eighteenth century', *Northern Catholic History*, xxv, Spring 1987, 14-17.

G. Scott, '"The Times are Fast Approaching": Bishop Charles Walmesley O.S.B. (1722-1797) as Prophet', *JEH*, 36, 4, Oct 1985, 590-604.

G. Scott, 'The School of St.Laurence's in the Eighteenth Century', *E.B.C. History Symposium Papers*, p.p. 1991, 30-42.

M. Sharratt, 'Excellent Professors and an Exact Discipline', in *Challoner and His Church,* E. Duffy (ed.), London 1981, 112-25.

G.Sherburn (ed.), *The Correspondence of Alexander Pope,* Oxford 1956, 5 vols.

G. Sitwell, 'The Brandsby Mission', *Ampleforth Journal,* xliv, 2, Spring 1939, 102-13.

G. Sitwell, 'A Crisis of Authority in English Benedictine History', *RH,* xvi, 3, May 1983, 221-303.

G. Sitwell, 'The Foundation and Recruitment of the English Benedictine Congregation', *DR,* ci, 346, Spring 1984, 48-59.

C. Smith, 'The Husseys of Marnhull', *South Western Catholic History*, 2, 1984, 32-43.

J. P. Smith (ed.), *Lancashire Registers IV: Brindle and Samlesbury,* (CRS xxiii), London 1922.

J. P. Smith (ed.), *Lancashire Registers III: Northern Part,* (CRS xx), London 1916.

R. J. Smith, *The Gothic Bequest*, Cambridge 1987.

W. V. Smith, *Catholic Tyneside*, p.p., n.d.

W. V. Smith, 'Durham Recusants' Estates, 1717-1778', *Ushaw Magazine*, lxxiii, 218, July 1963, 89-100.

W. V. Smith, '18th-Century Education in Co. Durham', *Ushaw Magazine*, lxxiii, Mar 1963, 217, 20-27.

T. B. Snow, *Necrology of the English Benedictine Congregation, from 1600 to 1883*, London 1883.

P. Spearritt, 'The Survival of Medieval Spirituality among Exiled English Black Monks', *American Benedictine Review*, xxv, 3, Sept. 1974, 287-316.

B. Stapleton, *A History of the Post-Reformation Catholic Missions in Oxfordshire*, London 1906.

K. Stewart, *A Short History of St. Robert's Church, Morpeth*, p.p. 1969.

R. J. Stonor, *Liverpool's Hidden Story*, Billinge 1957.

'The Register of the Estates of Roman Catholics in Northumberland', *Surtees Society* cxxxi, 1918.

'Durham Recusants' Estates 1717-1778' (ed. C. Roy Hudleston), *Surtees Society* clxxiii, 1962.

N. Sykes, *William Wake*, Cambridge 1957, 2 vols.

T. Tackett, *Priest and Parish in Eighteenth-Century France*, Princeton 1977.

R. Taveneaux, *Le Jansenisme en Lorraine 1640-1789*, Paris 1960.

E. L. Taunton, *The English Black Monks of St. Benedict*, London 1897, 2 vols.

A. and H. Tayler, *The Stuart Papers at Windsor*, London 1929.

H. Tayler, *Prince Charlie's Daughter*, London 1950.

M. R. Toynbee, 'Dom James Placid Waters (1740-1808): A Suggested Portrait', *DR*, lxix, 217, July 1951, 10*-13*.

T. Trappes-Lomax, 'Mr. Brian Magee and the English Recusants', *Ampleforth Journal*, xliv, 3, Summer 1939, 201-17.

Abbot Turner, 'The Story of the Abbey Lands, Part I', *Ampleforth Journal*, xlvi, 1, Jan. 1941, 1-11.

J. M. Tweedy, *Popish Elvet: Part I*, p.p. 1981.

E. Tyrer (ed.), *The Great Diurnal of Nicholas Blundell*, (Record Soc of Lancashire and Cheshire, cx, cxii, cxiv), 1968, 1970, 1972.

G. Tyson (ed.), *Inventaire Sommaire des Archives Départmentales Pas de Calais Archives Ecclésiastiques* - Série H, iii, Arras 1906.

M. Tyson and H. Guppy (ed.), *The French Journals of Mrs. Thrale and Doctor Johnson*, Manchester 1932.

R. W. Unwin, *Charity Schools and the defence of Anglicanism: James Talbot, Rector of Spofforth, 1700-08*, York 1984.

D. Van Kley, *The Jansenists and the Expulsion of the Jesuits from France 1757-1765*, New Haven and London 1975.

H. van Zeller, *Downside By and Large*, London 1954.

F. Vernet, 'Spiritualite Anglaise' in *Dictionnaire de Spiritualite*, ed. M Viller, Paris 1937, i, 625-59.

J. de Viguerie, 'Quelques aspects du Catholicisme des Français au xviiie siècle', *Revue Historique*, cclxv, 1981, 335-70.

M. Vovelle, *Piété baroque et déchristianisation en Provence au XVIIIe siècle*, Paris 1978.

E. Walsh and A. Forster, 'The Recusancy of the Brandlings', *RH*, x, 1, Jan. 1969, 35-64.

B. Ward, *The Dawn of Catholic Revival in England 1781-1803*, London 1909, 2 vols.

F. D. Ward, 'The Education of Youth at St. Edmund's, Paris', *Douai Magazine*, xx, 3, Spring 1959, 161-8.

T. G. Ward and L. Warren, *The Manor Mission of Low Furness*, p.p. 1975.

W. R. Ward, *The English Land Tax in the Eighteenth Century*, London 1953.

W. R. Ward, *Religion and Society in England 1790-1850*, London 1972.

A. Warne, *Church and Society in Eighteenth-Century Devon*, Newton Abbott 1969.

C. Webster, 'Richard Towneley and the Towneley Group', *Trans. of the Hist. Society of Lancashire and Cheshire*, cxviii, 1976.

R. Webster, 'The Will of Mrs. Prudence Pointz of Leighland', *DR*, xxxvi, 106, 71-76.

B. Weldon, *Chronological Notes*, Stanbrook 1881.

B. Whelan, 'The Appointment of English Bishops in the Penal Times', *Clergy Review*, xl, 12, Dec 1956, 727-34.

B. Whelan, 'A Disputed Election at Lambspring', *DR*, lxxviii, 253, Autumn 1960, 274-85.

B. Whelan (ed.), *A Series of Lists Relating to the English Benedictine Congregation*, Worcester 1933.

P. J. Whittle, 'St. Alban's, Warrington', *Ampleforth Journal*, xv, 2, Dec. 1909, 147-56.

J. H. Whyte, 'The Vicars Apostolics' Returns of 1773, ' *RH*, ix, 4, Jan. 1968, 205-14.

A. Garnnons Williams, 'The Formation and Development of a Yorkshire Estate: Stockeld Park', Univ. of Leeds dissertation, 1978.

J. A. Williams, *Bath and Rome*, Bath 1963.

J. A. Williams, 'Benedictine Missions in Wiltshire in the Seventeenth and Eighteenth Centuries', *DR*, lxxviii, 253, Autumn 1960, 263-73.

J. A. Williams, 'Bishops Giffard and Ellis, and the Western Vicariate, 1688-1715', *JEH*, xv, 2, Oct. 1964, 218-28.

J. A. Williams, *Catholic Recusancy in Wiltshire 1660-1791*, (CRS monograph 1), 1968.
J. A. Williams, 'Change or Decay? The Provincial Laity 1691-1781', in *Challoner and his Church*, ed. E. Duffy, London 1981, 27-54.
J. A. Williams, 'The Distribution of Catholic Chaplaincies in the early Eighteenth Century', *RH*, xii, 1, Jan. 1973, 42-48.
J. A. Williams, 'No Ordinary Residence: Bishop York and the 'Forty Five', *RH*, xvi, 2, Oct 1982, 217-19.
J. A. Williams, 'No-Popery Violence in 1688: Revolt in the Provinces', in *Studies in Seventeenth-Century English Literature, History and Biography*, ed. G. A. M. Janssens and F. G. A. M. Aarts, Amsterdam 1984.
J. A. Williams, *Post-Reformation Catholicism in Bath*, (CRS lxv, lxvi), 1975, 1976.
J. A. Williams, 'Sources for Recusant History (1559-1791) in English Official Archives', *RH*, xvi, 4, Oct. 1983, 331-451.
J. A. Williams, 'An Unexamined Aspect of the Penal Laws: The Problem of the Double Land Tax', *Dublin Review*, 479, Spring 1959, 32-36.
J. A. Williams, 'A Wiltshire Recusant Family', *Dublin Review*, 488, Summer 1961, 146-148.
M. E. Williams, *The English College, Rome*, London 1979.
H. Willson, 'The Fairfaxes of Gilling', *Ampleforth Journal*, xxxvi, 1, Autumn 1930, 1-24.
H. Willson, 'The Fairfaxes of Gilling', *Ampleforth Journal*, xxxvi, 2, Spring 1931, 129-46.
A. P. Wilson, 'A Fugitive in 1793', *Ampleforth Journal*, vi, July 1900, 42-48.
K. Wilson, 'The Will and Inventory of James II', *The Historian*, 7, Summer 1985.
R. C. Wilton, 'Dom John Bede Potts', *DR*, xxxv, 103, 57-68.
R. C. Wilton, 'Early Eighteenth-Century Catholics in England', *The Catholic Historical Review*, iv, 3, Oct. 1924, 367-88.
R. C. Wilton, 'Some Annals of Everingham', *Dublin Review*, clxi, Oct. 1917, 263-79.
H. Woollett, *A Hundred Years Ago*, London n.d..
Workington, Our Lady and St. Michael, 1876-1976, p.p. 1976.
The Work of the Benedictines in West Cumbria, p.p. 1980.
E. S. Worrall (ed.), *Returns of Papists, 1767, Diocese of Chester*, (CRS Occasional Pubn. 1), 1980.
E. S. Worrall (ed.), *Returns of Papists, 1767, Vol 2*, CRS 1989.
R. Yeo, *The Structure and Content of Monastic Profession*, Rome 1982.

311

INDEX